TESORO BOOKS

Ambassador's Journal: A Personal Account of the Kennedy Years
John Kenneth Galbraith

Here to Stay
John Hersey

The Road Back to Paris
A. J. Liebling

On Becoming American
Ted Morgan

On Becoming American

On Becoming American

TED MORGAN

PARAGON HOUSE PUBLISHERS
New York

First paperback edition, 1988

Published in the United States by

Paragon House Publishers
90 Fifth Avenue
New York, NY 10011

Library of Congress Cataloging-in-Publication Data

Morgan, Ted, 1932-
On becoming American.

(Tesoro books)
Reprint: Originally published: Boston :
Houghton Mifflin, 1978.
1. Immigrants—United States—History.   2. Minorities
—United States—History.   3. United States—
Emigration and immigration.   4. Morgan, Ted, 1932-
5. French Americans—Biography.   I. Title.
[E184.A1M676   1988]   973'.0441024   87-29128
ISBN 1-55778-070-6 (pbk)

THIS BOOK IS DEDICATED
TO THE MORGANS

I would like to acknowledge
my debt to my agent, Carl Brandt,
whose idea this book was,
and to my editor, Robert Cowley,
whose contribution to its final form
is the opposite of negligible.

CONTENTS

PART ONE

ON DISCOVERING AMERICA

Joe the Super

Joe the super is sitting in McDonald's, breakfasting on coffee, a quarter-pounder, and a jelly donut. His navy blue yachting cap is set at a jaunty angle, and he is wearing his Confederate Flag T-shirt. Joe is reading the Racing Form, picking winners with a pencil. Yesterday, he tells me, he should have won the daily double. Should always gets in the way. His 750 cc. Yamaha with torque induction is parked outside, and soon Joe will be off to Belmont. During the building workers' strike he spent an uninterrupted week there. In the evening, back from the track, he moonlights as an elevator man in another building. In his absence, his wife vacuums the lobby and takes the garbage out. Joe is five years removed from the mountains of Yugoslavia. Each year, he gets his wife "with child," as they say in the old country, and, after six months, the baby is sent home to his or her parents. This is called having the best of both worlds — warehouse your children in the old while gaining a foothold in the new.

Joe is learning to be American. He is exercising his freedoms — the freedom to be a junk-food junkie, to moonlight, to play the horses and otherwise demonstrate his fiscal irresponsibility, the freedom to play both ends against the middle, the freedom to make mistakes. If he had stayed in Yugoslavia, he would be eating yogurt for breakfast and the only horse in his life would be the one pulling the plough on the state farm.

I like Joe, even though I silently curse him on mornings when there's no hot water. I feel that he is a kindred spirit. One of the reasons I came back to this country in 1973 is that this is where the mistakes are being made. I came back with my wife and two children, and we brought nothing with us except our luggage allowance on Icelandic Airlines. We left the children with my brother in New Jersey while we hunted for an apartment. We were like immigrants just off the boat, starting a new life. We bought furniture at the Salvation Army. One can live very well here on what other people throw away. I went one step further than Joe, who has an unpronounceable Serbian name. I changed my name from Sanche de Gramont to Ted Morgan. A lot of people told me that was the wrong thing to do, because it was a fine old name, and one that I had written seven books under, but to me, it was part of becoming American.

Americans Are the True Existentialists

When I was at the Sorbonne in the fifties, there was a fad for Jean-Paul Sartre and existentialism. This was basically a philosophy of self-reliance. There were no props or crutches. Man was not the result of divine intelligence. He was not the product of genes or environment. He was a being who existed before he could be defined by a concept. Man was self-defining. He was what he willed himself to be. There were no excuses, such as a fixed and given human nature. Man was condemned to freedom; he was nothing else than the sum of his decisions and his works.

Years later, it dawned on me that Americans are the true existentialists. An American is the sum of his undertakings. He chooses his values and his appliances, his religion and his make of car, his lifestyle and his burial plot. He makes himself and is responsible for himself. He can't blame bloodlines or bad breaks. Americans are given enough elbow room to succeed or go bust. They are left on their own, to triumph or to cultivate their self-disgust. Our casualties are not due to regimentation. They are the casualties of freedom, the people who have O.D.'d on choices. Anybody can try anything — after all, it's his funeral. Every American is given by birthright enough rope to hang himself.

Two things that set the American experiment apart are the opportunity quotient and the anxiety quotient. Americans are people who made the big jump. They deliberately planted themselves in a wilderness populated by unpredictable natives. The anxieties that greeted them were worse than those they had fled. There was in this enterprise a desire for distinctness that bordered on arrogance. It is no sinecure to be a "new man." Take the earliest settlers at Jamestown. In the first ten years, hundreds of them died, as much from loneliness and alienation as from disease and climate. They died because they had attempted too much.

In New England, God was the armor against despair, but the best of the Puritans were in doubt about their state of grace, while the others had to be brought into line with jeremiads. One could write a history of America through the various stages of its anxieties. This is the dark side of the natural paradise. The greatest success story the world has known was anguish-ridden. Those generations freed from the wilderness anxiety had a fresh set of worries. In Europe, each man had his station, competition was muted, careers were based on class assignments. In classless America, competition determined rank. In America, it is illegal not to compete — industrial collusion is a crime.

Where there are winners, there have to be losers. When John Adams traveled through New England before the War of Independence, riding circuit with the royal judges, time and again he saw Harvard classmates who had fallen on evil days. It took his son John Quincy, our sixth President (1825 to 1829), years of effort before he could earn a living. His letters to his father are eloquent with self-doubt. His brothers Thomas and Charles were failures. One lived off his parents and the other died a drunkard. And these were the sons of a President, connected by marriage to influential New England families. Scratch an American hero, and you will find a troubled human being. Lincoln was an enormously complicated man, estranged from his father, and afraid that he was sexually inadequate with women. He is presented in textbooks as a wise and equable statesman, but he cursed, flew into rages, shook his fist, and stamped his feet, much like some of our recent Presidents. He was, like James Madison, subject to fits of morbid melancholia.

Or take that classic American hero, Meriwether Lewis, who, with William Clark, made the first successful overland trip to the Pacific Ocean, reaching the Great Divide in 1805 after traveling 4000 miles. Lewis, an aristocratic Virginian who had served as Thomas Jefferson's private secretary, was made governor of part of the Louisiana Territory, in 1807. Two years later he died in a seedy tavern, probably a suicide. A high incidence of breakdown among men and women in public life seems always to have been the case. The arrest of sixty-six-year-old Major General Edwin A. Walker, the right-wing activist, in a Dallas men's room, on a charge of public lewdness, in June 1976, is one recent example. Pat Nixon's stress-related stroke in July 1976 is another. The 1976 arrest of the former federal judge G. Harrold Carswell, a one-time aspirant to the Supreme Court, in Tallahassee, on a charge of "attempting to commit an unnatural and lascivious act," is a third.

In general, there is something anxiety-making about being American, so much so that ours is the only society which has, in certain professions, institutionalized anxiety. Air traffic controllers suffering from anxiety can retire on 75 percent of their salary in workmen's disability compensation. This is called "punching out." An outside physician or psychiatrist can certify that the stress of their job disabled them. Anxiety becomes a loophole thanks to which a large number of air traffic controllers are enjoying early retirement. But anxiety is always with us, and I would imagine that those who feigned anxiety may eventually wind up with an ulcer anyway, from the fear of having it discovered that they have taken another job, or from general self-disgust. Anxiety is the price that must be paid for boundless opportunity, including the opportunity to cheat the system, and not everyone can handle it.

The Immigrant as Homo Americanus

Who is the Homo Americanus? The big-game hunters who walked across the Bering Strait when it was a land bridge and wiped out the giant sloths on their march to California? Archeologists are now telling us that the two-legged upright model misleadingly called *sapiens* arrived in America first. Diggers in La Jolla are finding bones 40,000 years old, dated by a new technique called amino-acid racemization. They think that long before the first Cro-Magnon man set up house in a Carpathian cave, the Homo Americanus had settled on the West Coast and was already polluting the environment and endangering species of prehistoric animal life. The California Man! Older than Cro-Magnon. California, where it all began . . . the whole ball of wax.

Now skip about 40,000 years, until we come to historical time, and a land populated by Indians. The Indians are a good example of the way we atone for our sins through the myth-making process. The first

thing the pilgrims did when they reached Plymouth Rock was fall on
their knees, and the second thing they did was fall on the Indians,
so successfully that Hitler modeled the Final Solution on their extinc-
tion. Today, the Indians are held up as the custodians of native
American values. In fact, the Indians were no more the first Americans than the aborigines were the first Australians. They did not see
themselves as Americans but as Sioux, or Iroquois, or Blackfeet. Left
to themselves, they would still be carrying firewood across the Missouri in willow baskets (not that what we have today is necessarily an
improvement). In the making of America, the Indians were typecast
as progress-impeding savages. They could not have cared less about
the Declaration of Independence, or the three branches of government, or the flag with the stars representing the number of states, or
a country named after a fifteenth-century Italian navigator.

As for the native sons, they were American as a result of place of
birth. They had no say in the matter. They grew up American, as
naturally as a horse grows up hoofed. It was an effortlessly achieved
and unquestioned component of their lives. It is in native-born
Americans that one most often finds a nostalgia for Europe. I am
thinking of those members of old New England families who are
appalled by American vulgarity, and who long for Gothic cathedrals,
cobblestoned villages, and millenary traditions. The unself-conscious
energy of their own country dismays them. Henry James and T. S.
Eliot felt this way, and took out English citizenship, and the phenomenon persists.

The true American, in the existential sense of the man who makes
himself, is the immigrant, for he is American by choice. His nationality was not handed to him with his birth certificate. It came as the
result of a deliberate effort. He *wanted* to *become* American. He
gave up another life, and often another language, to be American. He
made the leap of faith, from the web of Old-World associations to a
new infancy. The true American is the one just off the boat, with a
tag pinned to his coat (as in the Ellis Island days) announcing his
destination, which he mispronounces. The actor Karl Malden's father, Petar Sekulovich, came from Serbia in 1906 with a tag pinned
to his coat that said San Francisco. But there wasn't much left of San
Francisco that year, and the immigration inspectors sent him to
Gary, Indiana, instead. *"Subdina,"* Petar Sekulovich said in Serbian,
"that's fate."

Every American began this way. In every story of ancestry, there
comes a point where a boat enters the picture. Genealogy becomes

a matter of ships' arrivals, and that is a minor matter. There is no difference in kind between the Puritans, who left England to be free to impose on others the religious restrictions that had been placed on them, and a Bolivian immigrant who arrived last week and hopes one day to run a Spanish-language methadone program in the South Bronx. They are both informed by a desire to improve their lot under the banner of laissez-faire.

I Am What I Am

I know something about old families, having been born into one that traces its origins back to the morning hours of Western civilization. That's why I've never given a damn about what was in or not in, and I've never had much interest in people or places that trade on being fashionable. Once the film director Frank Perry gave a party for one of my books. He was obsessed with celebrity to the point of having become one himself. When someone asked him for an autograph, his chubby frame shook with little tremors of satisfaction. When he went to Elaine's and was given a good table, he seemed to be treading water in puddles of contentment. Frank was a celebrity junkie. If he didn't have his daily fix, whether it was being mentioned in a column or being recognized by a doorman, he fell into melancholia. At the party, he took me aside and said in a loud stage whisper: "There are a lot of heavyweights in there." I told him I wasn't impressed by people who, in Daniel Boorstin's phrase, were well-known for being well-known.

The first Gramont lived in the first half of the eleventh century. He was the son of the viscount of Dax, a powerful family descended from the dukes of Gascony, who was given some property in the Pyrenees mountains called Gramont, and adopted the name. The family motto is *"Gratia Dei, sum id quod sum"* (thanks to God, I am what I am). The family coat of arms shows a lion in the first quarter, a greyhound in the third quarter, and three downward-pointed gold arrows in the two other quarters.

In 1974, my brother Pat got a letter from Nancy L. Halbert in Bath, Ohio, informing him that "the family name Degramont (sic) now has an exclusive and particularly beautiful coat of arms. This may surprise you, since Degramont (sic) is an extremely rare name. Of the

60 million households in the United States, fewer than 49 carry the Degramont (sic) name. We discovered this while doing some research on the family name. We've had one of our specially-trained heraldic artists interpret and create the Degramont (sic) Coat of Arms exactly as the heralds of medieval times did it for the knights and noblemen. This drawing, along with other information about the name, has been printed up into an attractive one-page report, which you may want to have."

My brother, a thrifty soul, did not want to shell out $4.50 for the report, but I sent Nancy L. Halbert a check and I received in the mail the same mass-produced coat of arms that thousands of gullible fools astray in the forest of family trees must have received. A capital *D* had been inked in (already a mistake, since the *de* is in small letters and the capital should be *G*) on a printed coat of arms showing wings in two quarters and two bars in the third. Small print at the bottom of the page informed me that "no genealogical representation is intended or implied by this report, and it does not represent individual lineage or your family tree." I wrote Nancy L. Halbert to congratulate her for having so successfully cashed in on the curious American yearning for heraldry, and to point out that the coat of arms she had sent did not remotely resemble mine, but that it had been worth $4.50 to gauge the extent of national credulity. It seems that every American's secret wish is to trace his origins back to a Saxon cave. Genealogical libraries are mobbed. But to me, being American means starting my own family tree, and the subtitle of this book should be "Rootless." I also wrote the Postmaster General that the Halbert operation struck me as a clear case of using the mails with intent to defraud.

Antoine II de Gramont was made a hereditary duke and peer in 1643, by Louis XIV, who was then five years old. The Gramonts became a ducal family, and still are. Even though France is a republic, titles are still in use, and will continue to be, as long as the French remain the pluperfect snobs they are. By my count, the present duke is the thirteenth Antoine, and his title is inscribed in his passport. This is one of the small courtesies the Fifth Republic extends to its relics.

The duke is the head of the Gramont family, all of whose other male members are given the title of count. There is also a free-floating title, Prince de Bidache, which comes from the name of the area where the Gramont castle used to stand before it was burned down in 1796 by a Jacobin custodian who had embezzled the funds for its upkeep. Anyone in the family can call himself Prince de Bidache, although no one does. I seriously considered it at one time. With a modest capital investment — the price of engraved calling cards from Tiffany's and a copy of the *Gotha* to prove my bona fide — I could have gone to Palm Springs and put my title up at the widows' auction. I could then have commissioned from Nancy Halbert's heraldic experts a brand new coat of arms, with a golden goose in all four quarters. What rich and elderly Palm Springs hostess could resist becoming Princesse de Bidache, which would make her a strong contender to chair the Bob Hope Desert Classic ball and the backgammon tournament at the Racquet Club?

The Georgian prince Mdivani had landed Barbara Hutton, even though, as she was warned by a friend, "anyone in Georgia who's got six sheep and a brick shit-house is a prince." The Prince de Bidache would have his pick of the crop. Eventually, I decided against it. My reason was best stated by Boni de Castellane, the turn-of-the-century man-about-town who married Jay Gould's daughter and built an impressive palace of pink marble on the Avenue Foch. He was showing it to a friend one day, and when he got to the bedroom, he said: "And here is the chapel of expiation."

My Last Duchess

I mention this tiresome family history only as a way of situating myself. My grandfather Agénor was duc de Gramont. He married three times. His first wife was a young French woman of good family who died in childbirth. Several years later, he married the daughter of a Frankfurt Rothschild, resigned his army commission, and devoted the rest of his life to spending his wife's money. He bought a mansion on the Champs-Elysées, with stables and horses, which he furnished with Italian masters and Gobelin tapestries. He bought 4000 acres of woods and ponds 25 miles north of Paris, and built a castle called Vallière, a copy of one of the Loire castles. Here was an authentic duke who lived in a fake sixteenth-century castle, like Hearst at San Simeon, giving off the scent of new money. His Rothschild wife gave him three children and died in 1905. Two years later, when he was fifty-four, he married a nineteen-year-old Italian girl named Maria Ruspoli. He wrote his children by former marriages, all of whom were older than his bride: "I'm marrying dona Maria Ruspoli. Consult the *Gotha,* page so and so." On their wedding night in the seaside resort of Dieppe, Agénor took a suite in the best hotel, with separate rooms. Food was brought up by a battery of servants, and after a copious meal, Agénor said good night to his young bride and retired. The next day Maria's mother called and asked how everything had gone. Maria wept and asked if she could come home. "You didn't like the convent either," her mother said, "but you got used to it."

Maria did get used to it, and gave my grandfather two sons in the first two years of their marriage, my father Gabriel and my uncle Gratien. Breast-feeding would have interfered with the duke's social life, and they were turned over to wet nurses. Activities at Vallière revolved around hunting and eating. Every morning the chef in his starched hat presented Maria with the day's menu. As a concession to her origins, there was a second chef in charge of pasta. Agénor had a third chef brought from England to supervise breakfast. "The French don't know how to make muffins," he explained.

When they were not at Vallière, they lived in Agénor's house on the Champs-Elysées, which was still an avenue of private homes with stables that were converted into garages when the motorcar came into use. Agénor had a passion for old masters, but never wanted to pay top dollar. He had a Rembrandt, but it was a *dubious* Rembrandt; he had a Turner, but it was more like a *school* of Turner; he had a Tintoretto of checkered provenance. When he died, they were bought back by the dealers at a premium. The dealers could now say that the paintings had been in the collection of the duc de Gramont, implying that they had been there for centuries, perhaps commissioned by an ancestor. This was known among Paris dealers as putting old masters of doubtful authenticity "in nursery."

With a charge account at Cartier's and invitations to all the dressmakers' collections, Maria was one of the beautiful people of her day. Augustus John painted her portrait. Man Ray photographed her. Proust wrote her ten-page thank-you notes. She visited America, and was met at the dock by William Randolph Hearst, who offered her his private railroad car to see the country. She was diligent at being beautiful. Around 1920, she heard that a young American woman had set up shop in Paris, and gave treatments that did wonders for the skin. She hopped into her Hispano-Suiza, navy blue with white ducal crowns on the doors, and told the chauffeur to take her to 255 Faubourg Saint-Honoré. On the fourth floor, a bouncy little lady named Elizabeth Arden rubbed her face with orange skin food and wrapped her in bandages like an Egyptian mummy. Maria began visiting Miss Arden's tacky little salon twice a week. She and Miss Arden became friends. It was a hands-across-the-water friendship of the Old World and the New. Maria, titled, poised, and indolent, had never had to work for anything. Miss Arden, self-made, told Maria that her motto was "think, fight, and work."

The Old World could teach the New a few things about taste and manners. The New World could come to the rescue of the Old. In 1939, Maria was in New York when the war was declared, and decided to remain in America. She was wondering what to do next when one day, at 2 A.M., her phone rang. It was Miss Arden, who said: "I hear you're going to be here indefinitely. Would you like to work for me?" And so the glamorous duchess who had helped discover Elizabeth Arden became her employee. Maria, now in her fifties, was gainfully employed for the first time in her life, as a buyer. Miss Arden, whose one true god was efficiency, despaired at Maria's scatterbrained approach to business matters, but kept her on, as a sounding board, a companion, a Mediterranean buffer zone. She took Maria to Main Chance, her fancy fat farm, and to her stud farm at Belmont, where she rubbed her "magic" Eight Hours Cream into her horses' fetlocks, as her trainer tried to keep a straight face. Miss Arden was single-minded and peremptory, and Maria acted as her mediator. Once Miss Arden was wearing her latest scent, "It's You." They were driving to Belmont, and the driver said, "Something smells good." "It's You," said Miss Arden. "No, ma'am," the driver said. "Yes, It's You," Miss Arden insisted. Maria broke up this Abbott and Costello routine.

After the war, Maria kept working for Miss Arden in Europe as a scout and buyer. The "Arden tone," the get-it-done-or-else tone of one of the most successful griffins America has produced, is caught in this letter sent to Maria in 1951:

"How could you send that silver lace dress from Chaumont, costing $1100, and not get the identical fabric for a duplicate? We sold the dress immediately to a woman (who is very difficult to sell) for a wedding, with the promise it would be ready within three weeks. Then we cabled you to rush the material, only to discover it is unobtainable! Now the client is furious — and so am I.

"This is too shocking, Maria, and I am just about at the end of my patience. Repeatedly, I have begged you not to select models if you cannot duplicate the fabric. What sense is there in buying a model if it cannot be copied? Women are the same the world over —

show them an expensive custom-made dress in a particular fabric and they want *that* fabric and no other. We must get sufficient yardage for duplicates. There is no possible excuse for such carelessness, especially since I have stressed the importance of this point again and again and again.

"This letter may sound harsh, but that is my feeling at the moment. I am about ready to throw up the sponge! Perhaps your enthusiasm for Dior is affecting your work with me? Nothing could be more of a failure than he was in New York. His models are not the least bit exclusive — they are copied right down the line into $14.98 dresses. Dior apparently thinks the world owes him a living. Time and again I have requested reports on exactly what Paris is doing from a fashion viewpoint, yet invariably the reports arrive after I've read the news in the fashion magazines. I want news on the spot! The color trends are very important to me when I am making new lipsticks. Fortunately I'm smart enough to instinctively sense what color is right and will be a success. None of you in Paris are any help — including my sister. I have always done it myself and I might as well continue."

The New World dictating to the Old. The impatience of know-how with the lackadaisical attitudes of ancient civilizations. Maria was a woman who conquered with charm. She was accustomed to being told how marvelous she was. Only one person, that manic overachiever Elizabeth Arden, was ever able to browbeat her. Not even her husband the duke could do that.

The duke had died in 1925, a disappointed man. His greatest ambition, never realized, had been to shoot more than a thousand pheasants in a single day. He was furious when he heard that the Rothschilds had shot thirteen hundred in their neighboring property of Armainvilliers. Agénor was the last of the do-nothing dukes. He truly believed that his title set him above other mortals. Although he had long left the army, he continued ordering everyone about as if they were soldiers. He was overbearing by divine right. He did not have to accomplish anything to prove his worth — he only had to be. He was the duc de Gramont, and that was quite enough. He probably never in his life experienced a single moment of doubt. He was steeped in certainty. His function was to embody the values of his title and his class. He would willingly have died to defend his country, while holding 98 percent of its citizens in open contempt.

As a descendant of my grandfather's third marriage, I inherited none of the Rothschild blood or the Rothschild money. When Agénor died, his estate went to his Rothschild children, the eldest of whom became duke. My grandmother made a cash settlement with the new duke, forfeiting all claims to the estate, but keeping the title of dowager duchess. She threw away her rights to a huge fortune because she was no more interested in money than the driver of a car is interested in engine oil. For her, money was lubrication, it made the engine of her needs turn, and was taken for granted until the engine started coughing.

The settlement just about covered her debts, which were staggering, and she continued to spend as if there were no tomorrows. She took her sons to the zoo and gave them live trout ordered from Fouquet's restaurant to feed the seals. She bought a lapis lazuli bracelet at Bulgari's encrusted with diamonds arranged to read *"Dio ti proteggia,"* as if that glimmering message was a talisman to ward off insolvency. As my uncle Gratien put it: "She always traveled first class, without a ticket." She died in August 1976, at the age of eighty-eight, and was buried in a Saint-Laurent dress, wearing the Bulgari bracelet, on the one occasion where it might do her some good.

Man Dies and Leaves a Name
The Tiger Dies and Leaves a Skin
(Indian Proverb)

My father grew up as a poor relation of his Rothschild half-brothers. He had been brought up at Vallière, where he was now invited as a guest. He had no land or stock portfolios to look after. When he finished his studies, he had to look for a job, which in his day was still an unusual thing for a young man of noble birth to do. It was as a result of my father's job-hunting that I was born in Switzerland. While preparing his foreign service exams, he was hired by the Italian automobile maker Bugatti to sell his cars in Geneva. It was not a very demanding job, since Bugatti produced about twenty cars a year, and only a few of those reached Geneva. After a year in Geneva, during which he sold three cars, my father returned to Paris, passed his exams, and was sent to Washington as third secretary.

I am glad that I was born in Switzerland, which is less a country than a state of mind evoking multilingual neutrality, and which has a tradition of kindness toward displaced persons, from James Joyce to Lenin to Timothy Leary. Being born in Switzerland is like being born aboard an ocean liner: one has no feeling of commitment to one's place of birth. It seemed fitting that I should be born outside France, since I did not inherit my grandfather's certainty about his place in society. I did not entirely feel that I belonged to the Gramont family. I had the name, the title, and the family history. But my life was not rooted in property or class convention. I did not even have that much French blood, since my grandmother was Italian and my father had married a Greek woman whose family, the Negropontes, was of Venetian origin.

The other Gramonts were fair and blue-eyed, decidedly northern in appearance, while my Mediterranean blood lines made me look like a native of Palermo, Corinth, or Marseilles (I have always thought of the Mediterranean as a nation rather than a sea, whose inhabitants resemble one another more than they do the other inhabitants of their respective countries. A Neapolitan waiter and an Algiers longshoreman are closer to each other in appearance than the Neapolitan is to a Milanese or than the Algérois is to a Bedouin).

As a child, dark and curly-haired, I was nicknamed Le Négus, after Haile Selassie. My given name was Sanche, chosen from the limited fund of family names, most of them forbidding, like Agénor, Gratien, and Corisande. But Sanche seemed to me the most forbidding of all, a name that I constantly had to spell, and explain, and tell people how to pronounce. It was actually a shortened version of Saint Charles, and a Gallicized version of Sancho, hearkening back to the Gramont family's origins in a Franco-Spanish border region. But in French schools it all too easily became *singe* (monkey), and once I came to the United States it became less a name than a cross I had to bear. I answered to Cinch, Sanchee (rhymes with banshee), and Saunch (rhymes with paunch). Every time I heard my name called I was reminded of my foreignness. One summer I was working on a surveying team on the New York State Thruway, and my coworkers informed me that they had no intention of trying to cope with a tongue-twister like that and would call me Jake. It was then that I first felt the pleasure of having a name that was truly common. Later, when I was working on the *Herald Tribune,* which had just been bought by Jock Whitney, and got my first by-lines, the rumor spread that Sanche de Gramont was Whitney's pen name. This would have been quite a feat, since Whitney at the time was American ambassador to the court of St. James's, while I was writing New York local stories. The *Trib,* however, was the kind of place where the crazier a rumor was, the longer it persisted, and the curious came from other floors to confirm that I existed, as the curious come from distant lands to the Barcelona zoo to see the only white ape in captivity.

No, Virginia, Jock Whitney was not commuting to New York to write stories under a bizarre pen name. He just paid the bills, at least until 1966, when he folded his tent and silently stole away. But in those early days on night rewrite, I felt as if I was on "To Tell the Truth": Will the real Sanche de Gramont please stand up? Some years later, while promoting a book I wrote about the French, I did go on "To Tell the Truth."They taped about six shows a day in a Broadway theater, and there was a lot of waiting around. When my turn came, I was seated between the headwaiter of a French restaurant on Ninth Avenue and a teacher at Berlitz. As the only one who spoke English without an accent I was the least convincing of the three. All the panelists voted for the headwaiter, who won a pen and pencil set. When I heard the words, "Will the real Sanche de Gramont please stand up," I hesitated. How could I be sure it was me since not even Kitty Carlisle thought so? I probably should have taken lessons, like Charles Boyer in Hollywood, to keep up my accent. On my next television appearance, the late-night Joe Franklin show, I faked the accent and told risqué anecdotes. I was a huge success. I could see myself condemned to playing the stock Frenchman, like that wonderful actor Marcel Dalio (Jean Gabin's sidekick in *La Grande Illusion*) who came to Hollywood during World War II and was type-cast as an excitable headwaiter in Betty Grable movies, swelling the ranks of ethnic character actors like S. Z. ("Cuddles") Sakall, Cesar Romero, and Barry Fitzgerald. I did not want to become an ethnic character actor.

A Cultural Hybrid

I had a problem. I was a cultural hybrid, as in the dictionary definition: derived or bred from heterogeneous sources. I was born French, but I had come to the United States in 1937, at the age of five, when my father was posted there. We lived near the French embassy in Washington, and I went to Mrs. Cook's school on Massachusetts Avenue. Mrs. Cook was a large woman with white hair piled on top of her head like cotton puffs and a penchant for lace bodices, and each morning at assembly she sat at the piano and led the school in singing "America the Beautiful." On my first day at Mrs. Cook's, my mother dressed me up in a sailor suit from Le Petit Navire, the chic Paris shop for children's clothes. The other boys wore dungarees. It was Little Lord Fauntleroy meets the Dead End Kids. I came home bruised and bleeding, the one advantage being that my sailor suit was too shredded for further use.

In addition to having the Frenchness pounded out of me, I had the English language drummed into me. It took, indelibly, like a tattoo. The English teacher, a formidable lady with a helmet of gray hair, told us: "Cuddle the dictionary. I'm going to be tough but it's for your own good. If you put i's where your y's should be you'll grow up to be a reject." I have been cuddling the dictionary ever since. It is my Georgia plantation, my offshore oil well, my Florida condominium. The language is the only natural resource that can be mined without depletion.

The high point of my first year in Washington was an invitation to the White House. Harry Hopkins' daughter Diana was my classmate, and I was invited to her sixth birthday party, arranged by Eleanor Roosevelt. I was glad to meet Mrs. Roosevelt. There was a large photograph of her over my bed. I was a thumb-sucker, and my mother put the photograph up and told me: "If you don't stop sucking your thumb you're going to look like her." I shook Mrs. Roosevelt's hand and stared at her teeth. Shortly after, I switched to nail-biting. There was ice cream shaped like animals at the White House birthday party, and a white cake on a large oval table, and firecrackers with party favors in them, and those things that uncurl when you blow into them. Wherever you are, Diana, it was a terrific party. My life since has been a slow decline. I was never asked to the White House again.

Going to War

We left Washington in 1939, going in the opposite direction from the thousands of refugees who were fleeing Europe. My father was a strange man. He thought that France was going to win the war. From the moment we arrived in Washington, he started taking flying lessons so that he could join the air force when the day came. Saint-

Quentin, the French ambassador under whom he served, called him a combination of Joan of Arc and Don Quixote.

We were back in France in time for the opening of hostilities, and my father was assigned to an escadrille near Caen, but for some reason the planes never left the ground, and in June 1940 the armistice was signed. Then de Gaulle made his famous broadcast from London ("France has lost a battle but France has not lost the war"), and my father found a fishing boat to take him across the Channel. That was the last time I saw him. He was sent to flight school in South Africa and on the way back to England his ship was torpedoed off the coast of Africa. He reached shore in a lifeboat and got back to England in time to pilot eight bombing missions over Germany before he was killed in a training flight in 1943.

When he joined de Gaulle, my father decided that we should go back to America. He was afraid of reprisals against the families of Gaullists. As it turned out, we could have sat out the war quite peacefully in the unoccupied zone. As a result of my father's unfounded fears, the circumstantial pattern of my Americanization continued. He managed to get us American visas by stamping our passports himself while the consul was called out of his office. Then he left for London and we left for a Basque village in the Pyrenees called Ustaritz.

One late afternoon in June, we heard the sound of tramping boots, went to the window, and saw a German infantry regiment goose-stepping down the cobblestoned street. My four-year-old brother George had been so traumatized by the language changes from France to America and back again that he refused to speak. He must have thought that if we were going to move around so much, the only sensible solution was silence. On that June afternoon, as we watched the columns of men in gray-green uniforms march down the street, George suddenly uttered his first words: *"Sales Boches!"* Passion had made him articulate. My mother clasped her hand over his mouth. The sound of the boots drowned out his cry.

Then Marshal Pétain set up his government in Vichy, half of France became an unoccupied zone, and one day there were no more German soldiers in Ustaritz. Obeying my father's instructions, my mother took us across Spain and Portugal, where we waited for weeks for a boat, and in 1941 I was back in Mrs. Cook's school, with stories to tell my friends. My mother was active in the Free French movement. She raised money and knitted socks. She went to Free French functions and saw Free French friends. There was quite a little Free French enclave in Washington. One of her friends was Jean Davidson, the son of the American sculptor Jo Davidson, who had become a French citizen and was a Washington correspondent for the Agence France Presse. She took me to his apartment once, and hanging from the ceiling of his living room was a weird assemblage of painted metal and wire shaped to represent several Crosses of Lorraine. It was an early Calder mobile, made as a propaganda effort for the Free French. This cross, swaying gently in Jean Davidson's living room, was the one that Churchill called "the heaviest cross I ever had to bear."

I was a fervent Gaullist. The general could do no wrong in my eyes. World War II was the last war in which it was easy to choose sides. It was a war of angels against devils. Hitler and Tojo were the embodiment of absolute evil. My father had done the right thing. He was on the side of the angels. I thought of the children of traitors, the children of Gestapo men, the children of guards in concentration camps, and how they must feel. I later met the daughter of an SS sergeant. She had been raped by four Russian soldiers in Nuremberg in 1945. She felt that she had done her bit in the atonement department.

De Gaulle came to Washington in 1945, and my mother and I were invited to a reception in his honor at the French embassy. We stood in a long line of admirers, many of them recent, and inched closer to the human flagpole in a two-star general's uniform. He stood in a doorway with an aide who explained who each person was. My turn came and I looked up into a pair of surprisingly spaniel-like brown eyes and said: *"Mes respects, mon général." "J'ai connu votre père,"* de Gaulle said. *"C'était un homme d'honneur."* (I knew your father. He was a man of honor). I moved away quickly, because tears stung my eyes.

My fervor for de Gaulle abated. He was no longer merely a hero. He was like all politicians, a user of men. From a distance, the pedestal he stood on looked like stone, but on closer examination it was made from the corpses of his followers. He had placed himself in a position where personal glory and the destiny of France were one. My father had died for a cause, but also for the advancement of an ambitious man. My distrust of office-seekers goes back to that day, when I measured the distance between de Gaulle's kind words (a moment, a phrase) and what had been asked of my father. "No, I distrust great men," E. M. Forster wrote in *What I Believe.* "They produce a desert of uniformity around them and often a pool of blood, too, and I always feel a little man's pleasure when they come a cropper."

In general, it's a mistake to meet people one admires. They can only disappoint you in the flesh. Once there was a girl whose idol was Mick Jagger. She became a rock groupie. Every time she made it with a musician, he would ask her how it was. "It was fine," she said, "but it wasn't Mick Jagger." Finally she spent the night with Mick Jagger. He asked her how it was. "It was fine," she said, "but it wasn't Mick Jagger."

I felt guilty about having sat out the war in Washington. I had fantasies about being a courier for the resistance. I saw myself carrying important messages in the lining of my beret, as I rode across Paris on my bicycle. One day I was stopped at a checkpoint. I swallowed the message I was carrying before it was found. I was tortured but I didn't talk. I survived and was awarded the Legion of Honor. Later, when I was back in France, I saw one of my cousins, who was about my age, and who *had* been a courier during the war — not for the resistance, for the black market. He rode his bicycle from a farm in the Bresse into Paris, laden with eggs and cheese and chickens and bacon. He was brave and took risks, and he was never caught. He had ways of getting in and out of Paris that not even the resistance knew about. After the war, he had enough money to buy himself an apartment in Montparnasse.

One of the key differences between Europe and America is that America has never been occupied. Territorially, America is a virgin. Occupation is an interesting opportunity for self-discovery. All sorts of things come out, most of them nasty, like rats in an earthquake. The hoarding instinct, for instance. The "I've got mine" mentality. The black-market mentality, which teaches you to be surreptitious. A historian once told me that it was impossible to understand the French national character without explaining how the black-market mentality had rubbed off on people. The black-market mentality was a way of saying: My country is occupied, but my chief concern is making life as comfortable as possible for myself. As long as I have butter to put on my bread, the situation is tolerable. The black market was a subtle form of collaboration. People's energies were diverted from resisting the occupier to finding bacon and eggs.

The occupation opened up all sorts of possibilities. You could make a fortune on the black market or join de Gaulle in London. You could get a good job with the Gestapo or take to the hills. You could sabotage trains or turn in your neighbor. Or, not being drawn to extremes, as most people are not, you could try to get by, making only the necessary compromises. The point I'm making is that a nation can never know ahead of time how it's going to behave under occupation. Americans cannot predict what will happen if America is occupied by the Russians. Would armies of partisans take to the mountains and the swamps? Would urban guerrillas ambush Russian soldiers in the street? Would there be massive uprisings against the occupier? Or would the population be too numbed to resist? Would the good life have softened people to the point of acceptance? Would a quisling government in control of the media tell people that to get along, you have to go along? Would the *New York Times* publish in Cyrillic? Would McDonald's feature borscht? Would General Motors be turned over to the workers? Would Alaska become a detention camp? We won't know until it happens.

Because America has never been occupied, the line "home of the brave" in "The Star-Spangled Banner" is pure speculation. How does anyone know? America has led a sheltered life. The vast majority of its people has never had a chance to discover whether it is brave or not. Only a tiny percentage of Americans has had to fight its country's battles. We have never had mass conscription, but only selective service. The first draft goes back to the Minutemen, who, contrary to popular opinion, were reluctant to volunteer. The poet John Berryman once told his colleague James Dickey that what bothered him more than anything else in this country was that a man could live all his life without finding out whether he was a coward or not. Not to mention women, who are socially conditioned to be chicken-hearted. In 1972, my American wife and I crossed the Sahara in a Land-Rover. The Algerian authorities do not let inexperienced travelers cross the desert alone, since they have to look for them when something goes wrong, and we started out in a convoy of three cars. We took turns in the lead and followed the tracks of the trans-Saharan trucks that carry sheep north and dates south. On the third day a sandstorm covered the truck tracks. I was in the lead and abruptly there were no more tracks. There was nothing but sand, even and noncommittal. I kept going until I stalled. Another advantage of following the truck tracks was that they were hard. The two cars behind me did not catch up. I began to think that I had somehow gone off the track, and that the other cars had continued in a different direction. Nancy asked me what was going on. "I think we're lost," I said. Her eyes welled with tears. She saw her bones in an unmarked desert grave. Nothing like this had ever happened to her. She was in her mid-thirties, and no moment of her life, unless one counts the risks that attend childbirth, had ever involved the clear and present danger of her own death. She had grown up in New Jersey, gone to college, been married and divorced, raised children, written poetry, and lived a full American woman's life, always sidestepping the void. And now, halfway around the world, far from all that was familiar, she was keeping her Appointment in Samarra. Or so she saw it, for someone who has never been in a tight spot tends to overdramatize. A moment later, the other cars came into view. They had stopped to pick up a Bedouin, who, for a price, would show us the way. After that, we had several other troublesome incidents, but I never again saw on Nancy's face that expression of undiluted hopelessness. She had discovered, not that she was a coward, because she wasn't, but that the earth is not a secure place. She had to leave America to find that out, because, compared to other lands, America is a warm cocoon, an overprotective mother, a nation of 220 million, all wearing their seat belts. An American woman's duty in times of crisis is to weep. Remember the Nixon speech: "I saw a gentle Quaker mother, with a passionate concern for peace, quietly weeping when he went to war, but understood why he had to go . . ." According to Nixon, the weeping mothers were giving the Viet Nam war their emotional support.

Women in fact have pockets of courage that men know nothing about. Nancy had a father who wanted to be a surgeon, but he lost the tip of one of his fingers, and, there not being much demand for nine-fingered surgeons, he joined his father's advertising agency. This compromise with life soured him, and he retired to Coral Gables, Florida, at the age of fifty to mull over his disappointment with the world. Nancy had a stepmother who went around the house compulsively cleaning ashtrays. Nancy married an Ivy League senior when she was seventeen to escape this zombie couple. Six months later she told her father she was getting a divorce. "Does he beat you?" her father asked. Nancy said he did not. "Is he unfaithful?" her father asked. Nancy said he was not. Her father could not conceive of any other grounds for divorce. "If I stay married another six months," Nancy said, *"I'll* be unfaithful to *him."* Unaccustomed as he was to candor, her father called her unpleasant names and threw her out. What Nancy did took courage. Hemingway's celebrated definition of "grace under pressure" in fact rarely applies. Most often, courage is a failure of the imagination. If you could imagine what you were getting yourself into, you wouldn't. In rare cases, courage is clarity of vision. Nancy saw what she had to do, rather than wait for circumstances to take their course.

To get back to World War II, I fantasized about being a courier for the resistance, and I was also an active supporter of the war's longest and most bitterly fought campaign — the Warner Brothers-R.K.O. campaign. I was with John Garfield when he shook his shell-shocked buddy by the shoulders, looked into his glazed eyes, and asked: "What's your name, soldier?" I was with Richard Conte when he wiped out a nest of Japanese snipers. I was with Gregory Peck when he was unable to climb aboard his bomber for his final mission. I was with Dana Andrews when his platoon got lost behind German lines. I was with Dane Clark when he looked through the periscope of his submarine and saw the Japanese fleet in Tokyo harbor. I was with John Wayne when he led his squad up Mount Suribachi to plant the flag.

Among the conventions of those war movies, such as the gallery of hometown types and the unsuspected native heroism, there was one that I found captivating. It had to do with a German passing for an American, or an American passing for a European. Alan Ladd, a shot-down airman whom Michele Morgan was helping to escape in *Joan of Paris,* was betrayed by his table manners. Sitting in an outdoor restaurant, he cut his meat with his knife in his right hand, put it down, and picked up his fork. Observing this American way of eating, two Gestapo men arrested him. When German agents were sent behind American lines, posing as GIs, they were usually caught because of their unfamiliarity with current standings in the National and American leagues. It was unthinkable that you could be a GI and not follow baseball.

The German behind the lines had not been dreamed up by a Hollywood screenwriter. Hitler's commando chief Otto Skorzeny had started a "school for Americans" where his men learned slang and custom. In the Battle of the Bulge, seven jeeploads of Skorzeny's men managed to get behind the lines and mingle with American troops, spreading confusion, changing signposts, and cutting telephone wires. Worse, they made the real Americans suspicious of each other. Your password and your dogtag were no longer bona fide. You had to know the capital of Delaware, the identity of "Pruneface," and how many homers Babe Ruth had hit.

Years later, when I was living in Morocco, I picked up a young hitchhiker on the road between Tangier and Fez. He told me he was American, which I didn't question, even though he spoke with a

German accent. I asked him where he was from. The Middle West, he said. He had tripped up, like the Nazi agents in the World War II movies. Someone from the Middle West doesn't say he's from the Middle West, he says he's from the Midwest. I asked him about his favorite baseball team. He knew even less about baseball than I did. I never learned what obscure benefits he was hoping to derive by pretending to be American. But I did learn that being American supposes that one has absorbed large amounts of irrelevant information. An American doesn't have to recite the Presidents or the states by alphabetical order, but he does have to know who Joe Namath is. If you can't stand inside the Frame of Reference, you don't belong.

It's funny the things that give you away. I think of myself as American, but sometimes I betray my origins. Sometimes I use Gallicisms, modes of speech peculiar to the French. I was telling a friend about visiting the sculptor Calder in France. "He lives on the Loire, doesn't he," my friend asked? "No," I said, "he lives on the Indre, an affluent of the Loire." "An American wouldn't say 'affluent,' " my friend said, "he'd say 'branch.' " I am working on saying branch instead of affluent. Another thing that gives me away is shaking hands. "You still shake hands like a Frenchman," my friend said, "you pump." He was right. Americans don't really shake hands, they clasp hands. The French really shake, with an up-and-down motion. I am working on keeping my arm still when I shake hands.

Postwar Wandering

My mother was being courted by a Belgian diplomat, Jacques de Thier, who was in his early forties but had never married. The embodiment of diplomatic detachment, he lived by the procedural rules of his calling. He was comfortable in those situations where the rules were defined. He could have posed for Prudence in the group statue of the Virtues. I think my mother saw him as a role model for us. Jacques was sent to Spain sometime in 1945, but the courtship went on by correspondence. All the letters were opened by the same Spanish censor, identified by number. He took an avuncular interest in the people whom he got to know through reading their mail, and when Jacques proposed and my mother accepted, he wrote *"felicidades"* on the back of Jacques's next letter.

At that time, having been raised a Catholic, I was attending Georgetown Prep, a Jesuit-run establishment in Bethesda, Maryland. The Jevvies carried wooden paddles conveniently strapped to the belts of their cassocks as part of their teaching equipment. I did not take to their blend of religious observance and corporal punishment. We went to mass daily, and after mass we said prayers "for the conversion of Russia." I learned that if you touched the communion wafer with your teeth it didn't count, that masturbation led to insanity, and that the only unforgivable sin was suicide, because there was no possibility of absolution. In the month of May, we recited long and turgid litanies to the Virgin Mary. It was at Georgetown that I was first called a "frog" by student and teacher alike. This apparent reference to a gastronomic custom seemed less offensive than some of the other ethnic nicknames that the Irish-American Jesuits, themselves only a generation removed from the peat bog, were fond of, such as dago and wop and spic and kike (surprisingly, there were several Jewish students at Georgetown). Being called a frog was nothing I felt I had to fight over to defend my honor. I had never eaten frog's legs in my life.

I did get into a fight one day after football practice, when a ninth-grader (I was an eighth-grader) said: "Hey frog, carry my helmet." As I say, I didn't mind the frog part, but I declined to carry the helmet. I had the frogness pounded out of me. My days on the football team were short-lived. I was big, and the coach thought he could make a fullback out of me. He tried me out in a play where I was supposed to go through the line, off the center. "Go through the middle with your head down and your knees high," he said. The center snapped the ball back, I tucked it under my arm, but my legs would not follow my brain's command, and I scampered around left end and was tackled. It was my nature to make lateral moves at the line of scrimmage. The coach was so disgusted he wouldn't talk to me. It strikes me in retrospect that, in many ways, I have always been an end runner. My dream is a field with no bounds and a limitless end around which to run. Years later, when I was writing for the *Saturday Evening Post,* I went to the Congo to do a piece on the Tshombe government. I was in and out of there in two weeks, hating every minute of it. The editor, Bill Emerson, who wrote a sort of backstage page, congratulated me for my "run around right end." I had met him only once, but I felt that he understood me.

In 1946 I was paroled from Georgetown before my term was up so that my mother could take us to live in Spain. Liners were in short supply, and we left aboard a freighter. Again, the process of my Americanization had been interrupted. I seemed destined to cross the Atlantic every few years, to slip into a new climate, a new language, a new school. For both my brothers and myself, these changes of scene were confusing.

The Belgian embassy in Madrid was a mansion heavily populated with servants. I learned to appreciate the little things that make life bearable. Each morning I was awakened by the sound of curtains rustling, as a maid in a blue and white uniform drew them. The light streamed into the room, a breakfast tray was placed on my bed, and the maid said, "Buenos días, señor Sancho." Never since has waking up been so pleasantly ceremonious. We belonged to the American embassy club, which showed American movies. One evening I brought a Spanish classmate to the club and we were turned away. Official Americans have a way of isolating themselves abroad. The club was not for host-country nationals.

After a year in Spain, Jacques was called back to Brussels, and I entered yet another French *lycée*. I may have been dropped another grade, I'm not sure. All this moving around was making me increasingly moronic. The same went for my brothers. They had been bounced around so much that a psychologist friend later told them that they were like people who have been institutionalized in childhood, in that they remembered almost nothing about their early years. Jacques waited two years in Brussels for a foreign assignment, and was eventually named consul general in New York. Again, it was not the pull of the magnet that brought me back to America, it was the throw of the dice.

My Nationality Is the Language I Write in

I went to the French *lycée* in New York and passed my first baccalaureate in 1950. By that time, I had lived a total of eight years in America, and I could feel the Frenchness leaking out of me. I had a natural affinity for English. I *preferred* American English to French. Each language seemed a reflection of its society. American English was an open language, a language of unlimited horizons, with a high tolerance for absorbing new arrivals. French was a closed language, defending itself against impurities, a language for diplomats and lawyers (Stendhal read the Napoleonic code as a model of style). A French friend of mine, who had come to New York to teach at Berlitz, was having trouble with English and said: "How can one learn a language that uses the same word to mean two completely opposite things?" The word was "cleave," which means to adhere, to stick, as well as to divide by force, to split or rive. I told him that the language, like the society, was full of contradictions, but that at least it was alive. French was so fossilized that it seemed in danger of joining Latin as a dead language. I felt when I had to speak it that I was wearing a wing collar. Speaking American English was more comfortable, like wearing a wool turtleneck, and so was writing it. One of the problems I had when I started to write professionally was that I had a French name and a French passport, and yet I wrote in American English.

I once came across a phrase of Joseph Conrad's that suited me perfectly. Conrad, born a Pole, had not learned a word of English until he was twenty. "My nationality," he wrote, "is the language I write in." The interesting thing is that Conrad, who was born Joséf Teodor Konrad Korzeniowski, left Poland when he was seventeen and went to France. He was fluent in French. But he did not have the same affinity for French that he had for English. One can develop an affinity for a language, as for a person. It is a matter of temperament, of mental chemistry. As a seaman in Marseilles, Conrad heard his first words of English when he was helping a French harbor pilot board a British freighter. A sailor on the freighter said, "Look out there," as he threw down a rope. Here was, Conrad later wrote, "the speech of my secret choice, of my future, of long friendships, of the deepest affections . . . of thoughts pursued, or remembered emotions — of my very dreams." At the same time, Conrad felt that adopting a new language implied a betrayal of his mother tongue, just as by leaving Poland he felt he had betrayed his family and his country, which was under Russian and Austrian occupation. To a Polish friend, he gave a misleading explanation of the reason he wrote in English. "I hold our beautiful Polish literature in too high esteem," he wrote, "to introduce to it my poor writing. But for the English my abilities are sufficient and secure my daily bread."

According to his friend and collaborator Ford Maddox Ford, it was the "blurred quality" of English that attracted Conrad, making it the perfect language for his oblique narrative style. "Oaken in French means made of oak wood — nothing more," Ford wrote. "Oaken in

English connotes innumerable moral attributes; it will connote sto-
lidity, resolution, honesty, blond features, relative unbreakableness,
absolute unbendableness—also made of oak . . . The consequence is
that no English word has clean edges; a reader is always, for a fraction
of a second, uncertain as to which meaning of the word the writer
intends. Thus, all English prose is blurred."

Perhaps a writer with an adopted language labors under a permanent sense of insecurity. Conrad disparaged his work, referring to it
as "dullest trash" and "the most rotten twaddle." But Ford reminds
us that "what is miraculous is that he took English, as it were by the
throat, and wrestling till the dawn, made it obedient to him as it has
been obedient to few other men."

I love the image of Jósef Korzeniowski wrestling the language,
sweat beading his brow, his muscles straining, his feet pushing for
leverage, maneuvering it into a hammerlock, and finally pinning it
to the mat. My own struggle with the language has been a long but
inconclusive arm-wrestle, with no winner yet in sight.

Portrait of the Writer as a Young Count

In accordance with my mother's plan, I went back to France in 1951
to pass my second *bachot* and live with a French family, which was
picked by the present duc de Gramont, Antoine, who had been
appointed my legal guardian. Antoine was a shy, fussy man who hid
his erudition behind an air of vagueness. He was a gifted painter, but
he felt there was something vulgar in original work, and that it was
more dignified to copy the masters. In his concern for small matters
of propriety, and in his devotion to the obligations of his class and
title, he was like a character out of Proust. His father Armand was
said to have been one of the models for Proust's Saint-Loup. Armand
had befriended Proust long before he was taken seriously as a writer,
at a time when he was contributing articles to newspapers under the
pseudonym Horatio. When Proust was famous, Armand introduced
him to his father (my grandfather) Agénor at Vallière. After lunch,
Agénor handed him the guest book, and, with the total disdain of the
nobleman for the artist, said: "Just your name, Mr. Proust. No
thoughts."

Antoine's was one of those minds that belong to an earlier period of history. Whenever I saw him, I felt I was in the presence of an eighteenth-century cardinal. There was something ecclesiastic about the way he folded his hands and the way he spoke, in a hushed voice, as if in a confessional. "You will be staying with the Lastours," he explained. "They are members of the provincial nobility. A good family, although not the top of the basket. The son is about your age, and I am sure you will get along. The father is a retired colonel and a member of the Jockey Club. The mother is quite amusing, I believe, knows Molière by heart, that sort of thing. They have had a financial embarrassment, which is why they take paying guests. You have the son's room, and the son has been moved to a sixth-floor maid's room. I'm very pleased that I've found a family of your own *milieu.* I'm sure they will keep you on the right track. I have enrolled you in the *lycée* Janson. It's a short walk from where you will be staying. Of course, you will meet young men from all walks of life there, but that is not necessarily a bad thing. I made some discreet inquiries about your teachers. Some of them lean to the left, but that is unavoidable these days. I have ordered some engraved calling cards made for you. They will be necessary to answer invitations. Don't forget to bend the upper right-hand corner. And on the envelope, always put *madame* twice, one under the other; it's considered a mark of special consideration. Because of your name, which as you probably know is one of the oldest in France, although not quite so old as La Trémoïlle, you will be asked to all the coming-out parties as a matter of course, and you will meet the young ladies of your *milieu.* It's a good way to avoid misalliances. You know what a misalliance is, don't you? Three months of happiness and thirty years below the salt."

I felt that a time machine had landed me in a Versailles drawing room where I was being briefed on how to behave at court. In a way, I admired the strength of a class which had managed to maintain its prestige despite its loss of power. It had resisted homogenization, and continued to insist on ceremony in an unceremonious age. Despite the French Revolution and four republics, it had been able to keep alive the social importance of titles. There was in this a continuity that I had to applaud. Antoine's brother Charles attended the Bestegui ball in Venice in an eighteenth-century costume that he did not have to rent — it was in the family.

French snobbery had a touching simplicity, obsessed as it was with kinship in its most anthropological form: who married whom. This was the exact same thing that Margaret Mead was studying among the natives of Manus, in New Guinea. Since I was new on the scene, every time I met someone, I was asked, *"Mais qu'est-ce que vous êtes par rapport à. . ."* (how are you related to such and such?), mentioning the name of another Gramont, and I would have to go into a laborious account of my grandfather's three marriages to establish the structure of kinship, and my membership in the tribe.

It all seemed slightly unreal. At the same time, I liked being asked to parties by rich and titled persons with castles in the country and marriageable daughters, who more often than not showed signs of genetic fatigue from generations of inbreeding. I liked receiving the stiff cards with the engraved invitations, which I arranged along the edges of the mirror over the fireplace in my room. I had learned from Antoine the proper way of replying to these convocations, always in the third person, and I covered the calling cards he had given me with the correct phrases, such as "infinitely grateful" and "most honored to attend." I liked arriving at these sumptuous residences and giving my name to the uniformed usher at the door known as an *aboyeur* (literally, a barker), which he repeated in a loud and sonorous voice, drawing out every syllable: "Le comte Sanche de Gramont." I always wondered where the *aboyeurs* were recruited, and what they did the rest of the time. Perhaps they were spear-carriers at the Opéra. I liked being in the *Bottin Mondain,* the French *Social Register,* a dictionary of the well-born and the parvenus, which included among the descriptive symbols that followed one's name, like the crossed knives and forks in the Michelin restaurant guide, a tiny castle. If I played my cards right, I could one day have a tiny castle next to mine. My name was my capital, and marriage was the logical outcome of the round of parties I attended. One of my cousins, who had been engaged several times, made a point of researching the net worth of his future in-laws. He said it was a necessary precaution, since there were families that went into debt in order to give an impressive coming-out party for their daughters.

I was also asked for weekends in the country and on one occasion I went to the Sologne property of an elderly lady named the princesse de Faucigny-Lucinge. The weekend was memorable for two reasons. Gladwyn Jebb, then English ambassador to France, and later Lord Jebb, was there. Someone suggested after-dinner charades, and I can still see Jebb prancing across the living room, riding and whipping an imaginary horse, his other hand veiling the lower half of his face, as he tried to make us guess that he was Lawrence of Arabia. The second reason was that several days after I had sent the princesse de Faucigny-Lucinge a thank-you note, I received a call from an alarmed Antoine. "What have you done?" he asked. It was a rhetorical question. "The salutation in your thank-you note to the princesse de Faucigny-Lucinge was *sentiments distingués,*" he said. "*Sentiments distingués* is what you write to your plumber or your grocer. You should have said *dévouements très respectueux* or *respectueux hommages.* She thinks you did it on purpose. I explained that as a result of your years in America you had something of Rousseau's good savage but that you meant well. You will have to write a note of apology. Of course, you may be sure that this will get all over Paris." Judging by Antoine's tone of voice, this was a matter of the highest importance, and I took pen in hand to explain that I had been tripped up by the language, and to avoid getting a reputation as a *mufle* (an extremely rude person).

I had a lot to learn, although on the whole I was accepted, like a returning émigré after the Bourbon Restoration of 1815. A place could have been made for me in the upstairs-downstairs world of the Gramonts. But what seemed pleasant enough for a year or two would have been stultifying for a lifetime. This small and self-absorbed group was as cut off from the present as Margaret Mead's New Guinea natives. Their concern with the minutiae of social observance, their insistence on judging people according to their birth, their indifference to the events of their own time, all these things had nothing to do with me. They were dedicated to preserving a system of values I had no sympathy with. I had returned to the Bourbon Restoration and discovered that I was still an émigré.

Having passed my second *bachot* without incident, I enrolled in the Sorbonne, which was overcrowded and undernourished. Students were encouraged to pick up mimeographed copies of lectures rather than attend them. If you wanted a book out of the library, it might take all day. Talking to a teacher after class was unheard of. I made the attempt once, and the teacher said: "I have three hundred students in this class. What if they all wanted to talk to me?"

The high point of my year at the Sorbonne was Faulkner's talk. He and several other American writers had been invited to France by the Congress of Cultural Freedom. During his stay in Paris, he was to share the platform at the Sorbonne with André Malraux. When he arrived in mid-May of 1952, he was blind stinking drunk. His talk was the next day, and he was taken to his hotel and given buckets of hot tea to boil him out. Faulkner was incoherent. The next morning he was not much better. He could barely stand up. He was practically carried to the Sorbonne and dumped at a table on a stage. The auditorium was packed. The Communists were there in force, hoping to turn the talk into an anti-American demonstration. As Faulkner was given a flowery introduction by Malraux, his head sagged until it almost touched the table.

It was Faulkner's turn to speak. He lifted his head and said, in a slurred Southern voice: "Europeans will never understand America because in America we are still adding stars to the flag." Then he said: "The French and the British have the brains, and the Americans have the muscle." The other members of the American delegation, Glenway Wescott, Allen Tate, and Katherine Anne Porter, instinctively reached for their biceps. Faulkner's head drooped again, this time for good. Everyone in the audience started shouting and throwing leaflets, and the talk turned into a free-for-all. Faulkner was carried off before any further damage could be done. It turned out that he had been drinking to ease the pain of a broken back, the result of a riding injury. The riot police were summoned, and several dozen students were arrested.

I began to wonder what I was doing in this madhouse posing as a university. I also began to question the idea of being a diplomat just because my father had been one. It used to be that when I saw a Rolls-Royce with a chauffeur I thought it must belong to an ambassador. Today when I see one I think it must belong to a rock star. We live in a world of shifting meritocracies. An ambassador's duties consisted of dispensing a daily ration of inconsequential civilities. It was enough to make the most gregarious man a misanthrope. The only time I ever saw my stepfather lose his temper was when he was ambassador to London. Prince Albert, the king of Belgium's brother, and Princess Paola, she of the pretty pout, were arriving for a state visit. I was staying in the room they would occupy. It was furnished with two eighteenth-century single beds with cane footboards. While stretching in my sleep in one of these beds made for stunted eighteenth-century men, my feet went through the caning. When my stepfather saw the hole he blew his stack. There was no time to repair the damage. Albert and Paola would have to be lodged in another, less impressive room, as indeed they were. If they were given a room with a mutilated bed they would report it back to the king. Careers had been ruined for less. I was declared persona non grata at the embassy. I had to move to a hotel.

On top of not wanting to be a diplomat, I did not really want to be a de Gramont. I was like an actor who knows his lines but feels miscast. I was occupying the place I had been assigned by birth, but it was not my natural place. I was ill at ease. I did not have a sense of affinity with the community, a sense of wanting to contribute to its future. I had to ask myself who I was and where I belonged. My trial run as a de Gramont had not provided the answer. The young man who wore tails on Sunday at Longchamps in the section reserved for the Jockey Club and who wrote flowery thank-you notes was not me. The young man who was addressed by servants as *monsieur le comte* was not me. The young man who was invited to the British embassy to dance with Princess Margaret because he knew how to waltz was not me. The young man who was expected to marry well and fortify the bastions of his class against the outside world was not me.

Once, Antoine took me to a garden party where I met his grandmother, the celebrated comtesse Greffulh, grandest of all the *grandes dames*. She was ancient but still glamorous, dressed in a long gown of the same green that Boldini had painted her in. Around her neck was a river of diamonds, atop her head a forest of egret feathers. "Look at her bone structure," Antoine said. "There won't be any more like her. They have broken the mold." While I told her how honored I was to meet her, I reflected that here was a relic no less wonderful than the ivory bas-reliefs of the early French church, and that all the Gramonts were relics, and that I was in training to become a relic.

Days of Ivy

I decided to go back to America. Instead of taking my assigned place, I would see what kind of place I could make for myself. Instead of living in a country where everyone had an assigned place, I would move to a country which recklessly chose to guarantee the fullest development of each of its members. Perhaps that was a myth too, but it was an improvement over the myth of birth. Previously, I had gone to America as the result of circumstance. For the first time, I was going there by choice. I was doing what Thoreau advised: living deliberately.

I got into Yale as a transfer student. I liked it there so much that

I wished I could have stayed longer than two years. It was a vast and convenient department store of learning. You could select from a wide assortment your courses and your activities, your friends and your social life, and you could shop when you wanted to. Teachers were not remote figures of authority, but friendly floorwalkers. They encouraged browsing, and did not pressure you to buy. I was astonished by the efforts they made to mingle with the students. Thomas Mendenhall, the master of Berkeley, my residential college, made it a practice to put up the dates of half a dozen students in his home every weekend, which struck me as valorous beyond the call of duty. The small things that were a struggle at the Sorbonne, like finding a book, were a pleasure at Yale.

I was part of an undergraduate body that became known as the silent generation. We wore J. Press sports jackets, button-down shirts, ties with regimental stripes, and white buckskin shoes. The thing to be was "shoe," which meant diffidence in all matters. To be "shoe," you had to show a casual interest in sports, get good grades without being a grind, and go away on weekends. Anything that smacked of obvious effort or strenuous commitment was "un-shoe." Enthusiasm had to be understated. The best example of this that I can remember came not from Yale but from super-shoe Princeton, in an issue of its alumni magazine, where, among the class notes, there was this item: "We hear that Adlai Stevenson is running for President. Good luck, Ad."

Mine were the days when the on-campus CIA recruiters competed for seniors with the Dow Chemical Company recruiters. The CIA recruiters touched base at 400 campuses. I did not question the use of the university as a training ground in political conformity. After the chaos of the Sorbonne, I was grateful for a place that worked. I knew of course that there was an inner core of money and power to which I could not belong. However objectionable, the system of selection was not as closed as a hereditary aristocracy, as I learned at the end of my first year, when I was tapped by a secret society. I had often wondered what they were up to, those seniors who on Thursday nights made their way in single file, in dark flannel suits with black knit ties, toward their windowless Greek revival temples. What went on inside those tombs? A Yale *Daily News* reporter had gone to the New Haven Department of Buildings, studied the building plans, and come up with the information that the Skull and Bones tomb had an Olympic-sized swimming pool. Why all the fuss just to go swimming? Actually, the secret societies were precursors of the human potential movement of the seventies. They were America's first encounter groups, instinctively employing some of Fritz Perl's "gestalt" therapy techniques, such as the "hot seat." Everyone would zero in on one member and tell him what was wrong with him. He didn't use deodorant, he was a hog for the butter, his roommates were kept awake at night by the thumping of his bedsprings. He was a social disgrace, a Neanderthal, and a weenie. Football captains, it was rumored, were reduced to tears. The secret society doctrine, like that of today's fulfillment seminars, was that you have to break down the personality to build it up again. It would arise, like a phoenix from the ashes, with an increased wingspread.

I was tapped by a recent, upstart society, which had none of the cachet or New Haven real estate of Skull and Bones and Scroll and Key. It was called Manuscript, it shunned self-improvement methods, and it was intended to attract undergraduates of a literary bent. Founded by a Colgate heir, the first of his dynasty to be ignored by "Bones," Manuscript began in a cold-water flat over a tobacconist's, and has since prospered and moved to a fine house near the campus.

It was also at Yale that I discovered an activity which led to my first piece of published writing. I had two scholarly friends who felt that they needed physical risk to round out the life of the mind. One was a Russian scholar who eventually joined the CIA. The other was an authority on James Joyce who later wrote a guide to *Finnegans Wake.* From Oxford, they had transplanted the sport of night-climbing. This consisted in climbing Yale's Gothic towers while the rest of the university slept. Satisfaction was derived from the climb itself, from the care they took not to damage the buildings, and from the total stealth of the enterprise. The beauty of it was that no one knew it was being done. Night-climbing was the exact opposite of a Yale team sport, which was conducted during the day, in front of numerous spectators, and in which the object was to win. Night-climbing was done in the dark, with no spectators and no winners. It was an act of defiance to the values of team spirit and competitiveness (Bulldog, Bulldog, Bow Wow Wow) that Yale stood for. Drawn to this surreptitious activity, I started cutting morning classes because I had been out most of the night in sneakers climbing Dwight Hall or Calhoun College. After exhausting the towers of Yale, we extended our activities to New York, and climbed the George Washington Bridge, starting at the river, crawling up the steel cross-beams to the top, and walking down the cable to the middle of the bridge, which sounds frightening but was really pretty easy. St. John the Divine

Cathedral was by contrast very scary, a veritable Everest of night-climbing, with long chimneys (parallel walls that one has to climb with the back against one wall and the feet against the other), and awkward overhangs. We worried about being spotted by the police, but night-climbing taught us that people on the ground never look up. Our greatest coup was the library of New York's Union Theological Seminary on Claremont Avenue. There was a lovely Gothic tower about 25 feet high that could only be reached through the library stacks. We hid in the stacks until the library closed, and then we pried loose from the inside one of the tiny glass panes of the tower window, which was encased in soft lead. With the window open, we had access to the tower, which turned out to be a bitch of a climb. The trick is never to look down, and to concentrate on your next hold. You forget that you're twenty stories up without ropes or pitons. Night-climbing made me realize that I was not a total physical coward. I never made the football team, but I felt that I had earned my letter. Once I graduated, I wrote about the experience, and we went back to some of our climbs to take pictures. I showed the story and the pictures to *Collier's*, which turned them down because it was afraid it would be sued by the university. *Mademoiselle*, a magazine aimed at college girls, had no such qualms, ran the piece in 1955, and paid me $350, the first money I ever made writing.

I went back to Yale in the fall of 1976 to watch the Yale-Princeton football game, on November 6. After lunch in Cox's Cage, a vast hangar near the Yale Bowl, where the old grads were grouped around their class-year banners like Napoleon's Old Guard around its tattered flag, we went to the stadium. I thought the girl cheerleaders were an improvement over the male undergraduates of my day, all in white with voice amplifiers. But where was the Yale mascot, the growling bulldog, Handsome Dan? Was he a casualty of the women's movement? I expected at any moment to see him replaced by a French poodle bitch with a pink ribbon in her tail, called Pretty Donna. As part of the half-time festivities, along with the bands forming letters and the prancing Princeton tiger, a speaker for Yale announced that "Dr. Renée Richards, Yale fifty-five, the well-known sex-change tennis player, has been appointed athletic director of Yale College. As her first move, Dr. Richards has decided to cut her staff." There was general laughter on both sides of the stadium. Looking puzzled, a pretty undergraduate sitting beside me said: "What are they laughing about? It's just a personnel decision."

Sediments of Frenchness

In my unqualified passion for Yale, in my conviction that its campus was the repository of an ideal way of life, I was like the refugee who thinks everything in the new country is wonderful because he goes to bed at night with a full stomach. I had what Saul Bellow called a "kiss-the-ground-at-Ellis-Island" attitude. On the other hand I continued to play the Frenchman when it served my purpose. I was in love with a girl who admired the poetry of Ezra Pound, and I made arrangements to take her to meet him in St. Elizabeth's Hospital, where he had been committed as insane in 1945 rather than face treason charges for having talked on the Italian radio during World War II. I wrote Pound a letter in French and used my title, hoping that he would be impressed. In case that was not enough, I said that I had come from France especially to see him. Within days I received a letter in his sprawling hand urging me to come on the following Sunday. We spent the afternoon with him in the federal lunatic asylum outside Washington. His room was in Chipmunk Hall, and he was allowed to receive visitors in a window alcove of the hallway.

Pound was in his late sixties, with an unruly mane of frizzy gray hair, a pointed gray beard, bushy brows, and the animated blue eyes of a young man. He wore sneakers, khaki shorts, and a sweatshirt, and insisted on making tea. This was before the days of speed, but he was high like someone on speed, talking nonstop in great bursts of free association, and pacing the hallways as catatonic patients wandered by. The only crazy thing about him was his manic enthusiasm amid depressing surroundings. He was kept busy writing to his dozens of correspondents, enlisting support for his release, and keeping track of the publication of his works in many languages. When he was not working, he held court. St. Elizabeth's had never been put to more civilized use. Pound asked me about my family and said that as a young man he had walked around the Languedoc region of France like a medieval troubadour.

He was proud of his pioneer heritage. His family, he said, had come to America aboard the *Lion,* one of the first ships to dock after the *Mayflower.* His grandfather Thaddeus had been born in a log cabin in Pennsylvania, and had moved to Wisconsin, where he started a lumber business and went into politics. He became lieutenant governor and was elected to Congress for three terms. His father, Homer, had worked for the Federal Land Office and been sent to Hailey, Idaho, to process mining claims. It was there that Ezra was born, in 1885, five years before Idaho became a state. The last thing one would have expected such a rough-and-tumble upbringing in a Western territory to produce was a poet. Pound was a new species to me, a combination of artist and frontiersman.

At six, an attendant came to get him for the evening meal. I saw him go into a large dining hall and sit on a wooden bench next to two inmates who were using their spoons as catapults to throw peas at each other. Pound sat there with his head bent, staring at his plate. He had made the mistake of not flying over the cuckoo's nest. It was unsettling to see this man, who with Eliot and Frost was one of the three major American poets of the first half of the twentieth century, among the lunatics. His supporters held that his contribution to literature had nothing to do with his politics. In 1948, he had won the Bollingen Prize in poetry for the *The Pisan Cantos.* And in 1954, the year I went to see him, when Hemingway won the Nobel Prize, Pound was one of the other writers who had been considered. In his remarks to the Swedish academy, Hemingway said: "This would be a good year to release poets." Four years later, the indictment against Pound was dismissed, and he was allowed to return to Italy. I felt that he should have been released much earlier. He had some crazy ideas, and he spoke on the Italian radio, but I wonder whether a single witness could have been produced by a prosecutor in a treason trial to testify under oath that he had been influenced by Pound's diatribes. He was no Axis Sally, he was a poet who was wrong-headed when it came to politics. He had probably done less damage than a war profiteer who sold defective snowshoes to the infantry and got off with a fine. He made the mistake of believing that First Amendment rights should not be suspended in wartime.

The summer that followed my first year at Yale, I used my Frenchness to get a job at the Falmouth Playhouse on Cape Cod. A large shaggy man named Leonard Rosenfeld had taken over the restaurant at the summer playhouse and was recruiting waiters. He thought it would give the place class to hire students from various Ivy League colleges and national origins. Once again, I played the ethnic character actor, and was hired. I arrived at the Playhouse in mid-June and was given a room in the basement and a uniform consisting of black slacks, a cummerbund, and a red jacket. I thought of my guardian, Antoine, telling me it was important for me to keep to people of my own background. I thought of my cousin, the one who checked into his fiancées' net worth, who had finally married a young lady with a suitable dowry. His in-laws, who had a house of cut stone on the Bois de Boulogne with a *vue imprenable* (a view that could not be built on), had offered the newlyweds the top floor. Twice a week my cousin had lunch with his in-laws, and on weekends he joined them at their country estate in Normandy. A life more trammeled and duty-bound I could not imagine. I preferred my Falmouth basement.

We worked the pre-theater buffet and the after-the-theater night-club. During the day, we hung out with the casts of the touring companies, and sometimes we had small parts in the productions. I was a cockney in the Covent Garden scene in *Pygmalion*, starring Carol Channing as Eliza and Branwell Fletcher as Henry Higgins. I played tennis with Edward Everett Horton, who was touring in *Springtime for Henry.* He was so old that he stood in the center of the court like the king of Sweden, and you had to hit the ball to him. When he missed it, he did one of his famous double takes. I took Ella Raines to the beach. Her lips moved as she read movie magazines. Her husband, a jet pilot, flew up from his base in North Carolina to attend her performance in *I Am a Camera*. As Sally Bowles, she may have had the syrup, but it didn't pour. The high point of the season was Marlon Brando in Shaw's *Arms and the Man.* Brando had just scored a personal triumph in *Streetcar,* but chose to spend the summer in stock. He had formed a company on the strength of his name to keep his actor friends employed. He was taking Equity, $150 a week, and playing the second lead, his first comic role. He came on in the second act, and every night, as the curtain rose, you could hear a buzz go through the audience: "Where's Brando?" Brando was not into saving the Indians yet; he was just nice to his friends.

Brando had arranged to be at Falmouth at the same time as his close friend Wally Cox, who was starring in *Three Men on a Horse.* Brando's company rehearsed the week that Cox was on. Cox spent the day on the pond behind the Playhouse, paddling a rubber boat with his feet, memorizing his lines. He *was* Mr. Peepers, a mild and modest man whose weapon was subtlety. There was no pretentiousness among the actors. No one played the star. They didn't pull rank or patronize the apprentices. I got to know them all. Except for Brando and a few others, the actors shared a common problem: full employment. I remember Walter Matthau, who was in *Three Men on a Horse,* saying one night at the actors' lodge, as if challenging the others to believe him: "I've worked every week this year."

If anything, the actors got too friendly. One of the gamblers in *Three Men on a Horse* was Teddy Hart, the younger brother of Lorenz, who wrote the words to Richard Rodgers' best songs. He was type-cast, and, as soon as the performance was over, he and his cronies repaired to the basement for an all-night crap game. I had gone drinking with Teddy Hart a couple of times, and on the basis of our new friendship, he shook me awake one night and insisted that only I could save him. His real gift was not acting but coaxing money out of people. By the end of the week he was into me for over $100, having already lost his entire summer's salary. He was entertaining, but expensive, and I was relieved when the Wally Cox–Walter Matthau–Teddy Hart floating crap game moved on.

Being a waiter was not that bad. You served the guests drinks and appetizers. Then they helped themselves at the buffet. Behind the buffet stood a large black Jamaican wearing a chef's hat, who sharpened knives and saw to things. When the stews and vegetables in the chafing dishes were low, he mixed them together. Once a dignified white-haired lady came through the line and asked him, pointing to the dish of leftovers: "I beg your pardon, could you tell me what that is?" "Why yes, madam," the chef replied, "that is Indian corn pone." "It looks very good," said the lady. After three weeks, the Jamaican chef was fired for going after François, the headwaiter, with one of his carefully sharpened knives.

François's real name was Frank. He was an English sailor who had jumped ship in Hoboken and found a job at Claridge's in Atlantic City, working his way up to headwaiter. A frustrated actor, he put all his repressed theatrical mannerisms into seating people at tables, waving his arms and jutting out his chin and snapping his fingers and otherwise hamming it up. I learned how to hustle tips from Perry Silverman, a veteran of seven Cape Cod seasons who looked like a young W. C. Fields and who snapped his fingers in parody of François. He would stroll among the waiting guests and say: "Ask for Perry Silverman for the best tables." When their turn came to be seated, he would shout: "Request, François, request."

One night I had the starlet Gloria De Haven at one of my tables. She had come in about half an hour before the 8 P.M. curtain, and was wearing a backless halter. I said: "You don't have much time. May I suggest that you go to the buffet while I get your appetizers?" She gave me a scathing look and said: "I didn't come here to talk to the waiters." I had a short fuse in those days and when I brought her tomato juice I spilled it down her tanned back. She shrieked and called for the manager and said I had done it on purpose, as I dabbed her damp clavicle with a napkin. François twittered like a sparrow in heat and told me I was fired. But when I turned in my uniform Lennie Rosenfeld hired me back, and told me to stay out of François's way. I obeyed his instructions scrupulously, which resulted in my being fired and rehired again. During the rush hour one evening, I pushed the kitchen IN door and saw François holding a burning caldron and screaming "Help, somebody grab this." Ignoring him, I went out the OUT door. He had bandages on his hands for a week, which made him look pretty foolish when he stuck one out for a tip.

I don't want this to be a series of anecdotes about a summer on the Cape. I want to show what it taught me about America. When Perry Silverman walked in one morning, navigating his beer belly between the tables, the first thing he said was: "I'm Perry Silverman and my keys are in my car." I thought that was a magnificent thing to say. It proved that Americans are the only ones who understand the automobile. A car is just an appliance, a way of getting from one place to the other. It's no big deal, and there's always one available, Perry Silverman's or somebody else's. To Perry Silverman, a car wasn't even personal property, it was something anybody could use, as long as they put in a quart of oil with every tank of gas. Try to borrow a man's car in France, where the car is a sacred object. He'd rather lend you his wife. I once heard a French philosopher at the Sorbonne lecture on the "Ontological Aspects of the Automobile." The kernel of his talk was that the car incorporates both the masculine and the feminine principles, since it is both a projectile and a womb. Instead of worrying about the gender of the automobile, Americans buy them and discard them as easily as shoes.

Every other year, some eager David in search of a Goliath writes a book about the coming demise of the automobile, and worries about the pollution, the landscape blighted by highways, and the urban desolation of parking lots. This is nothing new. There are always Guelphs and die-hards to tell you that the cookie-cutter won't cut. When Woodrow Wilson was President of the country, he saw the car as a menace to the American way of life. "Nothing has spread Socialist feelings in this country more than the automobile," he said. "It offers us a picture of the arrogance of wealth." Current Guelph arguments are just as specious. Highways are often nicely wedded to the landscape. Crossing the flat Kansas wheat country on Route 6 and seeing the great purple wall of the Rockies loom into view is worth the trip. And there are freeway interchanges in Southern

California that should win the sculpture prize at the Venice Bien-
nale. Parking lots can be built underground as they are in
Paris, and emission standards can be controlled to lower the pollution rate.

But the Guelphs want us to regress to one of those Indian societies
in Central America where they could not find any use for the wheel.
The fact is, no country is better suited to the car than America, with
its long distances and unencumbered highways. Try spending the
day behind a diesel truck on a two-lane Spanish coastal road in the
middle of August if you think that driving is hell. Cars are necessary
to America's vision of itself as a society on the move. As Stephen
Vincent Benet said, "Americans are always moving on" — in Fords,
Chryslers, and Chevrolets. One of my favorite sights on the highway
is the couple close together on the front seat, leaving three quarters
of it unoccupied. Seen through the rear window, their heads look like
tenpins. The car is as important to love and courtship as the rope
ladder was to troubadours.

I don't go along with people who lavish more care and attention
on their car than they ever give a human being, and whose memories
of their first car make their eyes mist over. The national love affair
with cars tends to get out of hand. As a corrective we have Perry
Silverman, for whom a car was never more than wheels. At the end
of my Falmouth summer, I had saved $300 to buy my first car, a
spinach-green 1940 Cadillac, as big as a hearse, with leather-trimmed
upholstery, and a back seat like a double bed. I did not become an
amateur mechanic, sensitive to its every heartbeat, and I did not
spend my weekends waxing it. I left it alone until it broke down a
year later, and then I abandoned it, without a quiver of remorse. I
believe in the "discardo" culture. America is great for what it dis-
cards.

It was also at Falmouth that I learned the meaning of equality. It
meant the opportunity to make something of oneself, like a young
apprentice named Tammy Grimes, who knew all the show tunes by
heart. Tammy claimed that Brando had made a big play for her. He
had asked her to come to the star cottage, and when she did, the first
thing he told her was to take off her clothes, which she declined to
do. It was Branwell Fletcher who spotted Tammy as the most promising of the apprentices, and who helped her out when she started
auditioning on Broadway. She was in her second year of stock that
summer, after which she could qualify for an Actors' Equity card.

But for all those who could not qualify, equality meant the chance to hustle, for in America two societies co-exist: the people who believe in the old verities — that honesty is rewarded, and that if you work hard you will succeed — and the hustlers.

At the Falmouth Playhouse, hustling was so general it became the norm. The dusky nightclub singer was hustling cocaine. The head of the apprentices was using the little leverage he had to hustle chicks. The bartender was stealing so much liquor that by the end of the summer Lennie Rosenfeld had to go into Chapter Eleven. Who had ever heard of a bar on Cape Cod that was losing money? The head bartender was a sleepy-eyed Rhode Islander named Clipper Jones, with a low-keyed and knowing manner that invited confidence. By the end of the summer he had stolen enough liquor to open his own place. I saw how it was done, but I couldn't go blabbing to Lennie. It was the kind of thing he had to find out for himself. I made the mistake of telling Clipper Jones where I kept the money I had saved, and one morning I woke up and found it gone. I confronted him that evening during the Happy Hours at the Hunt Club in Falmouth, before we went on duty. His expression of consternation was Academy Award material. Consternation gave way to pure grief. He shook his head slowly, as if reminded of a painful memory, and said: "How can you think that, man? When I was in Korea, my dead buddies were lying next to me in the trenches, and I never touched their wallets." He was so convincing that I ended up apologizing. Later, I learned that he had never been in Korea. He eventually went to jail for passing bad checks. With such remarkable con men, how can this country fail?

Clipper Jones was by no means unique. One of the waiters, a fast-talking Californian named Homer Loach, could have sold suspenders to paraplegics. He planned to be a lawyer, sensing that in the legal profession there was ample opportunity to exercise his talents for chicanery. Homer had a nose for finding willing women. It was he who first noticed the prim and rather schoolmarmish woman in her thirties who played the piano at the cocktail hour. "That's where the action is," he told Perry Silverman, who said: "You've got to be kidding. That old maid?" Homer pointed out that every afternoon there were one or two officers from the nearby air force base in attendance. "They're all banging her," he said. It turned out that he was right. There was a lot of camouflage in the fifties. It was hard to tell who was who, or what was what.

Beneath his circus-barker expansiveness, Homer had a hard and ungenerous view of life. He had hitchhiked around the country several times. He told me that he had no equal at thumbing rides. He never had to wait more than five minutes, not even in the middle of the Arizona desert. I hitched with him a couple of times on the Cape and saw what he meant. Leaning out into the road, jiggling his thumb back and forth at high speed, he gave off such a high energy level, he wanted that ride so badly, that he compelled the driver to stop. The listless hitchhikers of today, who seem not to care whether one stops or not, belong to a new and fatalistic era of thumbing, influenced by Eastern philosophies and vague notions of karma. Justin was a "make it happen" hitchhiker. And yet this master thumber had sworn that "when I get a car, I'm never going to take riders." Perry Silverman was a con man too, but not a thief. He used his powers of persuasion as a form of amusement. I was with him one night in Hyannis when he picked up two girls by telling them we were jet pilots on forty-eight-hour leave from the Korean front. His account of a pilot's life over the 38th Parallel was so gripping that by the end of the evening, when Perry said we were going back the next day, the girls broke into tears, pleading "don't go, Perry, don't go." Wherever you are, Perry Silverman, I hope you ended up like the rest of our most gifted liars, running for office.

The Newspaper Game

After graduating from Yale, in 1954, I went to the Columbia School of Journalism. I did not have a childhood vocation, like the twelve-year-old kid with the newspaper route who knows in his heart of hearts that someday he is going to be White House correspondent. With me, it was a process of attrition. I went down the list of things I did not want to do. Diplomacy more than ever seemed like a branch of domestic service. The ambassador and his butler were brothers under the skin. I did not want to go into business. It's impossible to shed the family tradition completely, and one of my subliminal beliefs, inherited from my de Gramont ancestors, was that commerce is crass. My brother George, who became an executive for Lipton's, at first had feelings of ambivalence about the corporate world because he had been brought up in a family where business was not considered a worthwhile pursuit. He had to work hard to develop the self-confidence and assertiveness necessary to succeed in his chosen field. I did not want to be a doctor or a lawyer, because I did not want to have patients or clients. I liked the idea of writing for a living, of being paid to use the language, a natural resource that was there for everyone. I also had a voyeuristic side to my nature, which preferred reporting on events to being involved in them. Journalism permitted detachment, it required placing a certain distance between oneself and one's subject. That distance, called objectivity, was part of one's professional equipment. In those days, foreign correspondents were still glamorous, and I thought I might become one someday. Finally, I remembered Clemenceau's phrase: "Journalism leads to everything, so long as you get out of it."

At Columbia, we were sent out to cover stories, and the funny thing is that I scored one of the few clean scoops of my entire career while I was at the school. I was sent to the United Nations one morning and ran into a member of the French delegation, Charles Lucet, who had been a friend of my father's. He took me aside and told me that the chief Soviet delegate, Andrei Vyshinsky, had died during the night but that the Russians for some reason were holding off the announcement. If I had been working for the *World Telegram* or one of the other afternoon papers, I could have made banner headlines. Instead, my scoop expired in the foreign-reporting seminar. Another time, whoever was playing city editor for the day sent me to the UN to interview Dag Hammarskjöld. This was in the nature of a merry prank, since I wasn't expected to get past the security guards. Again with the help of Charles Lucet, however, I got in to see Hammarskjöld, a dour and prickly Swede who carried the weight of the world on his bony shoulders, and I brought back a story. I learned the first rule of journalism: knowing somebody who can get you in to see somebody. I learned the second rule of journalism, which is also the first rule of ice-hockey goaltenders: I'd rather be lucky than good.

Newspaper editors came to Columbia each year to interview graduating students. They could hire trained youngsters at beginner's salaries and liven up their coverage. I was hired by Frank Murphy, the managing editor of the Worcester *Telegram* in Massachusetts, a hard-bitten editor of the green-eyeshade school. My salary was $52 a week. I lived in a boardinghouse and ate in diners. It was a drab life in a drab city. But all that was made up for by the fact that I was getting by-lines. Very few readers pay any attention to the by-line, but for the reporter it constitutes proof of existence. It gives him his daily sense of worth. He has made something he is responsible for and signs it, like an eighteenth-century cabinetmaker. I was off at six, but when I had a story in the paper I hung around the city room until midnight, when the first edition came up in piles that smelled of printer's ink, to look at the familiar arrangement of letters stretching across one or two columns of newsprint. It sounds ridiculous that the by-line should be so important, but there it is. Later, when I worked on night rewrite for the *Herald Tribune*, I was popular with the borough police reporters who phoned in their stories because I always gave them the by-line (I thought double by-lines looked cluttered).

As a newcomer on the *Telegram*, I was stuck with a front-page box called "There's Always Good News." The idea was that since most of the news was depressing, the readers wanted something upbeat as an antidote to all the mayhem and disaster. I would rather have been tortured on the rack than go through the daily agony of hunting down cheerful items. Good news by its nature usually went unreported, unless someone won a lottery or was dramatically rescued. There were no records kept for right-doing. I fell back on the weather, making the most of the Worcester sunshine, and pirating Bartlett's for quotable phrases. I don't think anything I ever wrote was more sickening.

I volunteered to work nights to escape the "Good News" column. One night the city desk got a call that a Worcester boy away at summer camp had drowned. The parents had no phone and could not be informed. This was a front-page story in the middle of a dull summer. I was assigned to get additional information from the parents, and a photograph. The pendulum had swung from "There's Always Good News" to an assignment where I not only had to write bad news, I had to be the bearer of bad tidings. I began to think I was in the wrong profession. I rang the bell, and when a man in shirt-sleeves answered, I identified myself and told him why I was there. His wife stood behind him, and started weeping, and he put his arms around her to comfort her. The wife regained her composure and offered me coffee. I said I hated to disturb them, but that I needed some additional facts, and a photograph. The wife took a photograph album from a bookcase and spread it open on a coffee table. She and her husband sat on a couch and began to look through it and discuss which picture they thought should be used. It was as if their grief was forgotten. I had expected them to throw me out like the vulture I was, or at least to ask to be left alone. Instead, they were completely engrossed in selecting the snapshot that would appear alongside their son's obituary, on the front page of the Worcester *Telegram*. I wondered whether this was shallowness of feeling or the power of the press. I decided that it was a way to adjourn grief. It was a very American thing to do, to involve oneself in the task at hand, and, although I was startled at the time, and thought their reaction was callous, I later decided it was life-affirming. Years later, I realized what I should have done when I heard a story about an old-time police reporter at the *New York Times*, Manny Perlmutter, who was sent to interview the widow of a slain Mafia figure. It was a walk-up in Little Italy, and when Manny got to the apartment, he heard, behind the door, a woman sobbing, and a child saying "Mama, please don't cry." Manny went back to the *Times* and told the city editor: "There was no one home."

As time went on, I got better stories. In August, there was one of the worst floods in Worcester's history, and we covered the city by boat. I covered the flood until my brain was waterlogged. I was involved in the life of Worcester, its disaster was my disaster. I felt more clearly than ever that my French background was behind me. I decided that I would stay in Worcester for a year, and then take my clippings to New York.

This Is the Army, Monsieur Dupont

One day in September, an official-looking envelope from France arrived in the mail. I was asked to report to a barracks in Normandy by October 15 for induction. France does not have a draft, it has a system of conscription going back to the days when Napoleon bled the country white to invade the rest of Europe. You were supposed to go in when you were eighteen, but I had been deferred to finish my studies. Now, the French army was crooking its finger at me. I could have stayed in Worcester, taken out my American citizenship, and forgotten about the whole thing. But the more I thought about it the more I felt I should go. It was my last debt to my father. He had done his duty in World War II and been killed. I was now being called up in a war in Algeria that I had no sympathy for, but I felt that if I went my account with my father would be settled, whereas if I didn't go my life in America would be tainted by evasion.

The next day, I went to see Frank Murphy. I showed him my conscription notice and explained what it was. He stared at it for about a minute, then shook his head and said: "I've lost a lot of men for a lot of reasons, but this is the first time I've ever lost one to the French army."

In Paris, I had a talk with Antoine, who was no longer my guardian, since I was over twenty-one, but who continued to dispense advice. He showed me the copy of a Braque still life that he was quite pleased with. "Several of my friends have mistaken it for the original," he said. Antoine gave me a little lecture on army life. "Of course you will meet young men from all walks of life there," he said, "but that is not necessarily a bad thing." I told him that I had two alternatives, either to remain a *troufion* (simple soldier), in which case I would probably be shipped out to Algeria quite soon, or to apply for officers' training, which would mean spending at least a year in France.

"In the first place," Antoine said, his hands folded over his crossed knees, "you don't have two alternatives, you have one alternative, offering a choice between two possibilities, so that if one is taken the other must be left." No sooner was I back in France than I was tripping up on the language. "In the second place," Antoine went on, "this war is regrettable, of course, but it should be over in a year or so. It is really a matter of convincing the Algerian people, most of whom are grateful for all that we have done for them, that they are being misled by a few fanatics." I felt that Algeria was a lost cause, and should be given its independence, but there was no point in arguing with Antoine.

On the day before I left for basic training, Antoine took me to Vallière to have lunch with his father Armand, the duc de Gramont, the one on whom Proust had supposedly modeled Saint-Loup. In front of each plate there was a small glass slate with the menu written in a kind of chalk. There was an hors d'oeuvre, an entrée, a main course, cheese, dessert, and fruit. "We never varied," Armand said, "not even during the war." He told me that the Germans had occupied Vallière and drunk up the wine cellar, but that he had saved thousands of his best bottles by putting up a false wall just before their arrival. He broke out a vintage champagne in my honor, since I was the first Gramont to be leaving for this particular war, and reminisced about his World War I experiences. He had gone to the front in a Rolls-Royce, thanks to which he was appointed aide-de-camp to a British general. When I left, he asked me to sign the guest book and wished me good luck.

I was surprised when I took my medical at how spindly and under-nourished most of the recruits were, in spite of Mendès-France's widely publicized attempts to get the French to drink milk. I was a foot taller than most of them, and they had to call Paris to find a uniform that fit me. I was given the same nickname that de Gaulle had in the army, "the big asparagus." I was also frequently asked the French equivalent of "How's the weather up there" — *"Eh, il fait bon là-haut?"*

Among these stunted Gallic conscripts, who had not grown one inch taller than their great-great-grandfathers who had fought at Austerlitz and their grandfathers who had fought at Verdun, I was a giant. In America, I would have needed seven feet to qualify, like Chicago's basketball star Tom Boerwinkle, who felt a tug at his coat one day and saw a tiny girl looking up at him and asking: "Baby, how many feets is you?"

There was an almost total lack of enthusiasm among the conscripts for the war in Algeria. Barracks talk centered on various *combines* (schemes) to avoid going there. There was no strong feeling against the war either, certainly not in the sense of conscientious objection. The prevailing attitude, probably as old as the French army itself, was *"faut pas chercher à comprendre"* (don't try to understand). It was the attitude of an individual caught up in a situation so absurd that the best he could hope for was to save his skin and thereby outwit the system, which was designed to do him in. It was also an attitude of bone-deep resignation toward the adverse forces of history, which had taken a thousand years to ripen. I opted for officers' school, thinking that, by the time I graduated, my eighteen months would be over. Owing to the war, however, the period of service was extended, and I ended up serving twenty-seven months.

After six months of basic training, I went to corporals' school in Metz, sergeants' school in Versailles, and officers' school in Saint-Maixent, in southwest France. Many of our instructors in officers' school had served in Indochina. They felt that the revolving-door governments of the Fourth Republic were corrupt and that the war in Algeria would be lost, like the war in Indochina, unless the regime was overthrown. As part of our training, we were lectured on sedition. I remember the paratroop colonel who commanded our battalion telling us on one occasion that "we don't even have to take power, we just have to pick it up." Already then, in the summer of 1956, more than a year before the coup that brought de Gaulle to power, the army was in open revolt. I was on to another scoop, but there wasn't much I could do with it.

At the end of six months, we gathered in a large auditorium to choose our regimental assignments as second lieutenants. Depending on your *rang de sortie* (your grade in the final exam), you could take whatever available regiment remained. The cadets who had graduated at the top of the class of 1000 and were supposed to be the finest examples of the French fighting man were expected to be eager to go to Algeria. In charge of the assignment board was the same paratroop colonel who was in the habit of making inflammatory speeches about overthrowing the republic. Each cadet rose when his name was called and shouted out the regiment he wanted and its location. Each of us had a list of available regiments, which were also posted on a large blackboard, and we crossed them off as they were taken. The valedictorian of our class chose a supply regiment in Paris. The next ten cadets also chose regiments in the Paris area. No one, it seemed, wanted to go to Algeria. That extra effort to graduate at the head of the class had not been a sign of patriotic zeal, but a last chance to stay out of the war. To Algeria would be sent the cadets at the bottom of the heap. I was about 200th, close enough to the top so that there would still be a few places left in France by the time my name was called. The colonel in charge finally lost his temper and roared: "Goddamn bunch of wet hens! It won't do you any good. You'll wind up in Algeria anyway." When my turn came, I rose and called out: "Fifth Regiment of Colonial Infantry, Dreux." Dreux was a town about an hour from Paris that had somehow been overlooked. Not too long after my turn, the names of Algerian cities began to be called with funereal voices: Oran, Bone, Constantine.

The paratroop colonel was right. After three months in Dreux, I was transferred to a village called Champlain in the mountains behind Algiers, and put in command of a platoon of Senegalese soldiers (the Colonial Infantry, as its name indicates, was made up of troops recruited from France's far-flung foreign territories). I was against the war, and I was unhappy about being in Algeria, but it never occurred to me to desert or openly protest. I had a friend in officers' training named LeMasson, the son of an admiral. In his student days, he had joined the Communist party. He was admitted as a cadet even though the army knew he was a Communist, which shows how hard up they were for officers. LeMasson told me that if he was ever in combat in Algeria, he would refuse to give his troops the order to fire at the *fellaghas,* as the Algerian rebels were called. I later learned that he had been as good as his word. He was demoted to private in a public ceremony during which his lieutenant's bars were ripped from his epaulets by his commanding officer. This kind of open rebellion was beyond me. My only form of protest was that I wrote some articles on the war for the Worcester *Telegram.* Frank Murphy, who did not want me to get into trouble, signed these dispatches by his first war correspondent "Lt. Pierre d'Alzon," after the founder of the order of Holy Cross, which had a campus in Worcester.

My only objectives in the war were to survive, to keep my platoon of Senegalese intact, and to try not to kill any Algerians. I succeeded in all three. I maintained an attitude of extreme caution, like a Renaissance mercenary whose troops are too valuable an investment to waste in battle. We went out regularly on patrols, but did not run into any *fellaghas.* Fortunately, we kept different hours.

The noncoms in my platoon were not Senegalese, they were regular army. This was 1957, and some of them had been fighting nonstop since 1943. They had fought in Leclerc's army in World War II, and had marched into Paris. After that they had fought in Indochina, which they called *"l'Indo,"* against the *"Viets."* To them, any native who wanted to oust the colonial power, and this included the Algerians, was a *"Viet."* The French technique in Indochina was to recruit native troops, and the noncoms had led ragged bands of Cambodians and highlanders against the "Viets." They regretted "l'Indo," where they had been their own bosses, sometimes cut off from their base for months at a time. They made the Indochina war sound almost desirable. Each of them had several native wives. They lived off the land, quite comfortably. They contracted exotic venereal diseases, unknown in the Western world. One of these was graphically named "the rooster's crest." The main ingredient in their medical kit was penicillin, of which they gave themselves copious and regular doses. The way they told it, the real war had not been fought against the "Viet," but against the spirochete. All of my noncoms were heavily decorated (they called decorations "bananas"), but one had an unusual blue ribbon with a metal frame. I asked him what it was. *"Ça, c'est la deestaingwish,"* he said. He had won the U.S. Distinguished Service Cross while in the French battalion in Korea.

My Senegalese troops had special requirements. They ate their own chow, a mixture of rice and hot peppers. They had a passion for kola nuts. The commissary gave me a small supply, which I kept locked in a trunk under my bed and held in reserve as a reward for feats of heroism, such as saving one's wounded platoon leader under a hail of enemy fire.

Once a month I took them to the military brothel in Médéa. This expedition was written into the military code, on the advice of French army psychologists, who opined learnedly about the Senegalese's "robust sexual drive." The theory was that if they were not taken regularly to have their ashes hauled they would run amok. The brothel run turned out to be my most dangerous assignment. As the officer in charge, I had to stand in the open cab of an armored car as we drove along the canyon road between Champlain and Médéa, flag flying. The canyon teemed with snipers, and I was a perfect target, right out in the open. I imagined my mother getting a telegram saying that I had been killed in action, when all I had been doing was taking some Senegalese soldiers to get laid. Occasionally, we were fired on, and the Senegalese peppered the canyon walls with their submachine guns the rest of the way into Médéa.

The French army believed in what it called "the utilization of competences," and it came to someone's attention in Algiers that I had newspaper training. I was summoned to become co-editor of a newspaper run by the psychological warfare section, *Algerian Realities*. It was a weekly that published articles on all the fine things France was doing, such as building dams and planting vineyards. It was sold on the newsstands, but everybody knew it was a phony, and you couldn't give it away. I took the job because it sounded harmless, and it meant moving to Algiers, getting out of uniform, and not having to carry a weapon. It was practically a return to civilian life, and it lasted all of 1957, until I was sprung. We churned out our stories, which no one read except the psychological warfare people, who had an infinite capacity for self-delusion.

In the fall of 1957, with the schools about to open, the *fellaghas* called for a boycott by Algerian children. I was asked to come up with a special "Go to School" issue. I did it like a comic strip. I found a pretty little Algerian girl named Malika in a kindergarten and ran photographs of her with captions such as: "Malika at the blackboard," and "Malika eats lunch." A banner headline on the cover proclaimed "TOUS A L'ECOLE," (everyone in school). The issue was timed to appear on the day schools opened, and we were told to print twice our normal run of 25,000 copies. I suggested we drop thousands of copies over the Casbah by helicopter. I was assigned one of the army's six Alouette helicopters, and I went up with 5000 copies of

Algerian Realities. I dumped them over the side as we hovered over the Casbah's jumble of flat white roofs. At that very moment, a strong gust of wind from the south blew the copies out to sea, and I watched them flutter away, toward the harbor and out of sight. That was my finest contribution to the war effort.

Lewis Clark, the American consul in Algiers, was a friend of my family's, and I was often invited to the beautiful Moorish consulate in El-Biar, with its walls of inlaid tile and its keyhole-shaped windows. It was there that I met my commander in chief, General Jacques Massu, the man who had masterminded and won the Battle of Algiers. He was always accompanied by two large muzzled dogs, and once, upon arriving, he calmly informed Lewis Clark that the *fellaghas* had ambushed him on the way up and that his car was riddled with bullet holes. There had been reports that the French were using electric generators to torture prisoners. Massu decided to try the *"gegene,"* as the generator was called, to see how bad it was. He had it applied to his hand for about thirty seconds, and told Lewis Clark: *"C'est très supportable"* (it's very bearable). It would have been just as bearable to the prisoners who were tortured if they had only gotten it for thirty seconds on their hand.

The American diplomats in Algiers struck me as combining equal parts of guile and naïveté. They had private contacts with the *fellaghas,* while they ostensibly were sympathetic to the French and to the officers' groups. Whoever won, they had their lines out. I made friends with a political officer named Hans Imhof, who used to invite me to dinner. It was at Imhof's that I met a state senator from Massachusetts named Barclay ("Buzzy") Warburton, who had come to Algeria on a fact-finding mission and to write articles for the Hearst newspaper in Boston. He intended to refute the position taken by the junior U.S. senator from Massachusetts, John F. Kennedy, who had spoken out in favor of Algerian independence. He wanted to see something of Algiers, and I offered to take him on a tour of the Casbah. From the newspaper accounts he had been reading, he expected house-to-house combat, and was surprised to find it calm, although he kept saying: "Remember, I've got a wife and six children." Buzzy Warburton had led a sheltered life. A stepson of William K. Vanderbilt and a great-grandson of John Wanamaker of the Philadelphia Wanamakers, he had grown up on a 3000-acre estate, being elected to Porcellian at Harvard by birthright, and developing a love of the sea as a child on the family boat, where dinner was ordered from a menu. He was a gentleman farmer, a North

Shore legislator, and, now, a foreign correspondent. Wherever you are, Buzzy (the last I heard, he had bought a restaurant in Newport called The Black Pearl, whose waitresses were required to address him as "sir"), I want you to know that our little visit to the Casbah got me into a heap of trouble.

Warburton was being tailed by the French FBI, the DST (Département de la Sécurité du Territoire). When they saw me with him, they began to tail me, not realizing, since I was in civilian clothes, that I was an officer in the French army. They saw someone dark and Mediterranean-looking, and probably thought the senator was reconnoitering with a *fellagha* leader for a secret meeting in the Casbah. They must have been disappointed when all we did was stop in a restaurant for some cous-cous. The state senator went back to Boston and wrote his articles for Hearst, supporting the French line. I should have been commended for my efforts. Instead, I was tailed for weeks, without ever realizing it. One day my landlady told me that two men had been asking questions about me. I went to my room and flushed the copies of my Worcester *Telegram* articles down the toilet.

The next day, when I went to work at *Algerian Realities,* my boss, a dashing Gascon captain, took me into his office. I had never seen him so glum. "You're in serious trouble," he said. "Military intelligence was up here asking about you. They think you're an American agent. If you've done anything, tell me now, and I'll see what I can do for you." I could not understand how my visit to the Casbah had become such a melodrama, or how I could be an American agent. Was America an enemy power?

The following morning I was politely arrested at the office and taken to Military Intelligence headquarters, where I was politely questioned by several captains, on and off for 48 hours. It was my introduction to the paranoia of the intelligence community. It was their job to find conspiracies where none existed. Friendly powers were potential enemies, and social acquaintances were vestigial spies. Nothing was what it seemed to be. I was automatically under suspicion, since it was impossible to meet my interrogator's requirements of total recall. Where had I been on Tuesday the 19th of August at 1.30 P.M.? What had my conversation been with Lewis Clark at lunch at the American consulate on the first Sunday in September? Why had I said, at a party at the United States Information Service on the rue Michelet, that the war would continue five more years? Why was I constantly seeing Americans? Why had I taken an American secretary for a drive to Médéa? I argued each point for hours, until the interrogator was more tired than I was. I disputed the accuracy of his data. I drowned him in detail. My indignation was sincere. As for my true opinion of the war, this was not the moment to share it. For 48 hours, I did not sleep or eat. I did nothing but talk, and when one interrogator started yawning, another one was brought in. I must have been convincing, for I was released, and a week later my army service was over.

I left Algeria in December 1957, disgusted with a colonial war that would continue for five more years. We had been told that we were fighting to preserve a part of France. I came to realize that in fact we were protecting the property and the financial interests of the French minority there, the so-called *pieds-noirs*, or black-feet. Against the Algerian claim to independence, our cause was the maintenance of property rights. The rest was rhetoric. In the end, after years of wanton killing and destruction, de Gaulle was able to end the war by lying to everybody, and the French minority, numbering a million or so, came to France, an underpopulated country where they were easily absorbed. Passions abated, and soon there were most-favored-nation agreements between France and Algeria, which made the long war and the wasted lives seem all the more absurd.

It was with a lingering sense of the absurdity of colonial wars that I later covered Vietnam. In this case, there were not even the property rights of a white minority to protect. American troops fought for an abstraction, for the idea that South Vietnam should remain a free and democratic state. It took a phenomenal amount of killing and destruction to enforce those lofty principles. As an American officer remarked without irony at the time of the Tet offensive in 1968: "We destroyed the city in order to save it." It was an example of regeneration through violence, a basic American theme going back to the hunter-hero in a savage new world, struggling to displace the Indian. Vietnam was an application of that frontier myth to the Southeast Asian subcontinent.

When I went there in 1965 for the *Saturday Evening Post* to write an article on the Viet Cong, it was the year of the big American buildup. I was planning to spend a few weeks on a Michelin rubber plantation where the manager was a friend of a friend. It was being used by the Viet Cong as a base camp. On the first leg of my journey, I took a taxi from Saigon to Dalat, a town about ninety miles north. Two thirds of the way there we were stopped by a roadblock of little men in black pajamas. The driver, seeing the roadblock ahead, removed the watch from his wrist and put it in the glove compartment. Through the driver, I explained that I was a French journalist and that I wanted to write a story about them (it would have been unhealthy to say I was American). They were used to people fleeing them and were puzzled by the idea that someone wanted to accompany them. The leader chattered and shook his head rapidly, and the driver translated: "They say you too big to fit in tunnels." They had networks of tunnels, where they repaired to escape the B-52 bombs, which had not been designed for six-footers.

On the plantation, in the upper highlands, near the town of Banmethuot, there was an ostensible French authority and a real Viet Cong authority. The workers and their families were subject to Viet Cong recruitment and indoctrination. The French were not pleased about the situation, but what could they do? They were Michelin employees, whose job it was to get the rubber out. Passed off as a visiting relative, I was able to attend a Viet Cong indoctrination meeting in one of the Montagnard villages on the plantation. The man conducting the meeting spoke at some length to the patiently gathered villagers. To illustrate his point, he took an egg and broke it into his cupped hand. The white of the egg dribbled off his hand to the ground, while the yolk remained in his palm. There was no disagreeing with that central fact, and I returned from my tour of the Viet Cong–controlled area convinced that the Americans would leave Vietnam just as the French had left Algeria.

Since there was a certain amount of danger involved in this assignment, the *Post* agreed to take out war risk insurance. I named as my beneficiary the woman I was living with and later married, Nancy Ryan. In New York, *Post* editor Michael Mooney had to try six insurance companies before he found one that would write the policy. The other five told him that since the beneficiary was an unmarried woman not related to the policyholder, she qualified as a moral risk, presumably because a member of my family could contest the settlement. In later years, when the women's movement campaigned for the designation Ms., Nancy, ahead of her time, had long been known by the designation MR.

On the Franco-American Seesaw

My accounts with my father were settled. It had taken two years and three months out of my life. My army experience had served to unravel whatever remaining sense of allegiance I had toward France. I still had the name and the blue passport, and that was it. At that point in my life I felt no sense of allegiance toward any country. The one thing I felt I had was a profession, which I wanted to start working at. After a two-week binge in Paris, I went back to New York in January 1958, looking for a job in journalism. I went around to the various newspapers and wire agencies. In those munificent days, New York had four morning and three afternoon newspapers, but none of them wanted me. At the *Herald Tribune* I saw the managing editor, George Cornish, who was practiced in saying no. In any case, I could see that he mistrusted my foreign origins and funny-sounding name. The Associated Press said they would try me out. Sam Blackman, the New York editor, told me: "We don't want ordinary people, we want exceptional people." I said that I would do my best not to be ordinary. Blackman assigned me to City News, a service that gathered local news for the New York dailies that subscribed to it. Its editors were colorful holdovers from the Ben Hecht school of journalism. One of them asked me when I could start. I said that I was getting married and that I was going to Mexico for a two-week honeymoon and that I could start after that. The editor congratulated me and said: "You know the difference between a honeymoon and a 25th anniversary? On a honeymoon the wife goes in the bathroom and cries. On the anniversary, the husband goes in the bathroom and cries."

City News was a backstop service; it covered whatever the New York papers did not staff. In the words of Vince O'Mahoney, one of the veterans, "Every time a nigger stubs his toe in Harlem, City News is there." We went out and covered stories, hundreds of stories, no matter how inconsequential. It was good training. You had to phone the story in more or less the way it would go out on the wire. Speed was the thing. It clattered out to the subscribing papers, and if it was important enough, the AP picked it up for its regional or national wire. On a typical day, I covered a Lithuanian parade, a marble-shooting contest in Central Park, a League of Women Voters lunch, and a protest demonstration in front of City Hall. I loved it.

I felt that I was part of the city, involved in its lapses and small triumphs. I was often the only reporter at events, which, without me, would have gone unrecorded. We, the City News boys, were the historians of New York miscellanea. It was an education in urban odds and ends. Once I covered a dawn robbery at the supposedly impregnable Tiffany's. The gang had used diamond drills to puncture holes the size of an index finger in the display windows, and had retrieved the bracelets and rings with wire coat hangers. Such ingenuity did not go unrewarded. They were never caught.

Our stories went out without by-lines. The New York papers ran them without even crediting them to the AP. How would it have looked for them to be using wire copy on a local story? We were anonymous toilers, known only to our confreres. When we weren't out covering stories that might make a paragraph in the *Journal-American,* we were in the office taking dictation. There was a kind of low skill in this instant rewriting of the phoned report that often made the difference whether the story would be used or spiked. The police reporters in the shacks scanned the papers daily for examples of their craft. Even though these were unsigned, it made them feel good to see them, as the unknown makers of minor gargoyles in Gothic cathedrals must have felt. Since God knew they were doing it, they didn't have to sign it.

After six months on City News I was given the choice between Indianapolis and Newark. It was presented as a promotion but I was crestfallen. Faced with two forms of purgatory, I chose the one closest to home. After three months, I had had enough of Newark. My friends had warned me that it was the asshole of the universe. I would not go that far. The universe has multiple assholes, but surely Newark is one of them. I took a job working nights for the French Press Agency. I started at midnight and went home at eight in the morning, taking the subway uptown to sleep when everyone else was taking it downtown to work. It was like swimming against the current, a stationary life.

One of the police reporters at City News, Johnny Carroll, had a brother named Luke who had become managing editor of the *Herald Tribune.* Johnny Carroll had noticed that I had a good batting average on the items he phoned in to me. He wasn't going to steal a man away from his own outfit, but once I had gone to the French Press Agency, I was fair game. One day in 1959, when I was pondering my reverse-plated existence, he called and said there might be a job at the *Trib* on rewrite. Luke Carroll, a second-generation Irishman, had replaced the WASP George Cornish. Carroll, who had made his way up from Hell's Kitchen to an important position on a major newspaper, was a member of the hard-bitten school of journalism. He was interested in performance, not pedigree, and he gave me a job. Wherever you are, Johnny and Luke, I am grateful.

Rewrite on the *Trib* was four to midnight, an improvement over midnight to eight. I was slowly digging my way to daylight. The life had a wonderful simplicity. You worked from four to midnight. You unwound next door at the Artists and Writers Club (a wood-paneled former speakeasy) with your colleagues from midnight to three, when the place closed down. You slept from four to noon. You had lunch and got ready to go to work. It was like an animal's fixed routine, from the watering hole to the shade tree to the pasture. I loved it. With all due respect to the Newspaper Guild, I would have worked there for nothing. I loved being involved in the manufacture of a product that I could examine each day. The half-million readers who bought the product had no idea how it was put together, but I did. That information from all over the world could be gathered and written and edited and set in type and stereotyped and printed on a rotary press from a mat and sliced into newspapers and delivered in trucks and sold on newsstands, and that all these operations were successfully repeated seven days a week, seemed to me as miraculous as the multiplication of the loaves.

Like City News, night rewrite on the *Trib* was the land of trivia. Most of the big news happened during the day. At night you had an occasional crime, an occasional fire, an occasional speech, an occasional disaster, but nothing you could sink your teeth into on a steady basis. It was a diet of canapés. The three rewrite men sat at a "bank" at right angles to the city desk. Within easy reach there was a wire basket in which the night city editor threw releases that might make a couple of graphs, and yellow death notices from funeral homes, of people sufficiently prominent to deserve an obit. It was our task to convert the releases into "fillers" and to call the funeral homes and obtain the pertinent information for the obits. I must have written a thousand obits while I was there. Death became my field of expertise. Cause of death, time of death, place of death, and time of memorial service were my daily concerns. I felt that I was in a permanent state of mourning. Another chore was making "recoveries" when the first edition of the *Times* came up. Invariably, the *Times* carried front-page stories that we had missed, and it was our job to recover those stories for our Late City Edition, which often meant waking people up and asking them to repeat, with sleep-filled voices, whatever it was they had told the *Times*.

Even though there weren't many by-lines on night rewrite either, and the big story continued to be out of reach, I enjoyed the life, and I was planning to take out my citizenship when my residence requirement was up. But after two years on night rewrite, I was sent abroad, as number two man in the Paris bureau, a promotion so stunning and unexpected that it was impossible to turn down.

The irony was that I had come back to America to be a newspaperman, but somehow I could never get away from France. The pattern of my life, alternating between the two countries as a result of circumstance, was continuing. There was no way to escape my dual identity. I would always, it seemed, straddle the Atlantic, with one foot in the Hudson and one foot in the Seine, testing the water.

Things went well. I won the Pulitzer Prize in 1961, and was sent to Rome as bureau chief in 1962. The *Trib*, in its declining days, was short of correspondents, and I became their utility outfielder. I covered most of the wars of the sixties, including, in alphabetical order, Algeria, Cambodia, the Congo, Cyprus, the Middle East, and Vietnam. I got more combat experience than I had had as an officer in Algeria. As a correspondent in Algiers, I saw OAS gunmen shoot down Arabs in the street with a cold-bloodedness that made me sick to my stomach. It was a common sight when I left the Aletti Hotel in the morning to see an employee mopping up puddles of blood on the sidewalk in front of the entrance. My colleague Henry Tanner of the *New York Times* once received one of those idiotic queries from one of the green-eyeshade boys on the desk in New York: How do you tell a member of the OAS from an Algerian civilian? "One is holding a smoking pistol," Henry replied, "and the other is lying in a pool of blood."

In the Congo, I was shot by Swedish United Nations troops who had mistaken me and the other reporter I was with for mercenaries. In the town of Famagusta in Cyprus, I was caught in a gun battle between Greeks and Turks. I was with a Greek Cypriot, who, during a lull, pointed to a wall about 20 yards away where we could find cover, and said: "Now run, but FURIOUSLY." I realized that there was something to the old story about foreign correspondents who break Olympic records as they dive for cover. In Vietnam, on a helicopter tour of the Camau peninsula with a general, we took some sniper fire. I asked the general if rifles could do any damage to choppers. "Hit in the right place," he said, "the helicopter has the flying characteristics of a falling boulder." I left too many friends behind in Vietnam: George Syvertsen, with whom I had started out on AP local, Jerry Miller, who had been in Rome for the AP during the Vatican Council, and Bernard Fall, who, as an academic, did not have to take risks, but insisted on going out on patrols, and stepped on a mine. They had died for a headline, for footage on the evening news. The television reporters in particular were prodded by the home office to take risks because of network competition.

I did not have a death wish, and I began to think that there must be a better way to make a living than watching men kill one another. I was also getting tired of the repetitiveness and formula writing of daily journalism. My base was Rome, and in 1963 I covered the death of Pope John XXIII and the election of Pope Paul VI. Pope John, in his eighties and rotund, was a sturdy old peasant with a heart like a Calabrian ox. Each night I churned out columns of copy on the efforts being made to keep him alive. It was long after his death that I learned the truth, from the dean of the Vatican diplomats, Baron Poswick, the Belgian ambassador to the Holy See. He had been asked by the Vatican Secretariat of State to remain in attendance at the Pope's side and help them deal with an unprecedented situation. Pope John was in an oxygen tent. The world waited for him to die, but he did not die. It was an international crisis. How long could this situation be allowed to continue? Arrangements had to be made for the election of a new Pope. John, with his heart that would not stop beating, was holding up the works. Medically he was dead. The sensible thing to do, for reasons of state, was to put him out of his misery. After a week of waiting, they pulled the plug on the oxygen tent. It was a story that I could not write. Poswick would deny it, and so would the Vatican. Instead I wrote stories that began: "Pope John XXIII was reported sleeping peacefully tonight. Crowds kept vigil in St. Peter's Square as the 81-year-old holy father hung between life and death, etc." Frank Perry, who was in Rome showing his first film, *David and Lisa,* would say when we met: "Well, what did the eighty-one-year-old holy father do today?" He brought home to me the limitations of daily journalism, the stock phrases, the banality. The best part of what I saw somehow did not fit the news column format. If I wrote about my wife and I relaying each other waiting for the end, and about sleeping in a cot in the office waiting for a call from a Vatican informant (an irreverent *monsignore* who had once told me "everyone calls us father except our own children, who call us uncle"), some editor in New York would cut it out. In 1964, two years before its amalgamation as the *World Journal Tribune* and eventual demise, I quit the *Tribune* and became a contributing writer for the *Saturday Evening Post.* I stayed in Europe mainly because it was cheaper, and in 1968 I went to Morocco, which was even cheaper than Europe, to finish a book on the French and write a novel.

The book on the French, one of a series of opuses on national character like *The Italians* and *The Russians,* was taken by the Book-of-the-Month Club, and I went to New York in the fall of 1969 for a publicity tour. I felt uneasy about it because I knew I would have to play the Frenchman. It was back to an ethnic character-actor part. I did what I could to live up to my image. On the "Today Show," I rubbed Barbara Walters' knee under the table. During a pause for a commercial, Barbara asked me what I really thought of French women. I was the wrong person to ask, since I have had two American wives (one from Far Hills, New Jersey, and one from Short Hills, New Jersey, which indicates some kind of strange geographical fixation), but I thought she was indulging in idle chatter, and I said: "I think they're for the birds." No sooner were we on the air than she repeated my frivolous remark to her 20 million households and asked me to elaborate. Cheap shot, Barbara. I went into my theory of "the woman of iron and velvet," but the harm had been done. I don't know whether my appearance on the "Today Show" sold any books, but the number of letters I received from irate French women convinced me of the program's drawing power.

Worse, a woman editor working for my then publisher came up to me at a party and asked: "Who translates you into English?" As I have explained, I am unable to write in anything *but* English. If my publisher's own people thought I wrote in French, what must everyone else think? After ten years as a professional writer, that was a blow.

Cards of Identity

More than ever, I felt I was playing a part. Of course, I had cast myself for it by writing *The French.* Now that the book had a chance of being a commercial success, I had to peddle it convincingly. The irony was that over the years I had found that I used writing as a way of getting things out of my system. I had written the French to help me get the French out of my system, just as I had written *Epitaph for Kings,* a book on prerevolutionary France, to get the *ancien régime* out of my system.

After *The French* I wrote two novels, which, each in its own way, had a cleansing effect. The first one dealt with four members of a World War II resistance group in Paris, one of whom appears to have betrayed the others. It was called *Lives to Give.* When I saw my psychologist brother Pat, who, having just won his Ph.D., was now qualified to dispense clinical opinions, he told me: "You should have called it 'Pavanne for a Dead Father.' It's a text book example of trying to solve through fiction a situation that you've never been able to accept. The only one of the four resistance fighters who survives is the one who does not take an ideological stand. Our father died because he took one. The whole book is about the futility of commitment." In my next novel, the fictitious memoirs of a Count Gramont who sought his fortune at the court of Louis XV, I got the Gramont family out of my system so thoroughly that several of them refused to see me again after reading the book, in which I had depicted them in what I felt was their true period.

I found that, more than ever, I was suffering from a sort of malaise, which the dictionary defines as a morbid and indefinite feeling of uneasiness. The longer it lasted, the less indefinite it became. The definite origin of my malaise was that for forty years I had lived in a state of ambivalence. I was not quite French and not quite American. I had a French passport, but I worked for an American magazine and wrote books for an American publisher and an American audience, which thought of me as a foreigner who wrote about the French and was translated into English. My French family thought of me as more American than French. My friends thought of me as mixed up. What was I?

I felt no sense of kinship with the Gramonts. To me they were curiosities, part of what Hegel called "the historical lumber-room of old Europe." Their reaction to my personal life clinched my conviction that we were not living in the same century. I had married an American girl in 1958, but the marriage did not work. When the *Trib* sent me to Paris, she stayed in New York. I had been in Paris six months when I met Nancy Ryan, who was living in a tiny hotel room on the Left Bank. She captivated me at once by asking me to take her to see the Bastille. I broke it to her gently: the Bastille had been burned down as a symbol of royal despotism in 1789, the year of the French Revolution. Standing in its place was a memorial column.

Only an American, I thought, could feel secure enough to ignore the principal events of European history. Hoping to rescue her from her Left Bank squalor and a life of ignorance, I asked Nancy to live with me. She hesitated. She had come to Paris to write poetry and live the Bohemian life. She had seen one of my calling cards on my desk, not my *Herald Tribune* card, but the one that said Comte Sanche de Gramont. Confiding her problem to the mutual friend who had introduced us, she said: "I'm just a girl from New Jersey. I don't want anything to do with a French aristocrat. I didn't realize what I was getting into. These people are empty and indolent and won't let you into their homes. I'm a gypsy. We don't belong together."

"Don't be silly," the friend said. "He's letting you into his home, isn't he? This is just a form of reverse snobbery."

Nancy overcame her misgivings and moved out of her vest-pocket room. In 1962, she gave birth to a son. My first wife refused to give me a divorce. As far as the rest of the Gramonts were concerned, we were living in sin. With one or two exceptions, they boycotted Nancy. I was asked to dinners as an extra man, as if she did not exist. When one of them called and she answered the phone, they talked to her as if she were the maid. The Comtesse Antoinette, who had been my favorite aunt, said she wanted to see my son. If Nancy took him to the Bois de Boulogne at a certain hour near a certain bench, she would watch him play, but Nancy must not expect her to introduce herself. Poor Nancy had become a character in a medieval morality play.

Another thing that bothered me was the attitude of French women toward a foreigner. We would go to a dinner party, and the men and the women would separate afterwards (this custom, believed to be British, is faithfully followed in France). The men talked about de Gaulle and the women talked about de Givenchy. I would look over and see Nancy sitting by herself in a corner. Not one of these women made an effort to draw her into the conversation. She was a leper without a bell. It wasn't the language problem, because Nancy could get by in French. It was a collective decision to exclude someone who did not belong. In every French woman, there is something of Madame Defarge, taking pleasure in the discomfort of others. I couldn't help thinking that if the situation was reversed, and a French woman was with a group of American women, she would be made to feel included.

There were occasional breaches in the family boycott. Cecile de Rothschild, who was a distant cousin by marriage, asked us to dinner. She was a tall, rangy woman with close-cropped curly gray hair and a fierce independence of mind. A ranked golfer, she had once succeeded in playing at the Piping Rock Club in Long Island, a WASP establishment with a ban on Jews. She was a very determined lady. In any case, this was a formal dinner for eight, with a footman behind every chair and wine from the Rothschild vineyard of Château Lafite. On the walls of eighteenth-century paneled wood hung Fragonards and Hubert Roberts. Nancy was not impressed. She had never heard of Fragonard. She liked the New York action painters.

The first course was *bar,* a sort of sea bass. The *bar* is a rather large fish, and a footman brought in two on a silver tray. Nancy was the first to be served. I don't think she had ever seen a *bar* before, but they must have looked good, because she took a whole one and put it on her plate. The fish was bigger than the plate, and its head and tail hung over the rim. The footman hesitated, but said nothing, and continued to serve the other guests. Cecile, whose eyes had a natural tendency to bulge, stared at Nancy's plate. With one remaining *bar* for seven persons, our portions were modest, although I must say to Nancy's credit that her *faux pas* (I don't want to commit any fox-paws, she had told me before the dinner) did not prevent her from enjoying her meal. Cecile de Rothschild complimented her on her appetite, and we were not asked again.

In 1968, my first wife decided that she wanted to get remarried, and gave me a divorce. Some months later, after she had satisfied the numerous requirements of French bureaucracy, Nancy and I were married at the *mairie* of the sixth *arrondissement.* The lady mayor, a tricolor sash bisecting her ample bosom, gave a spirited talk on Franco-American rapprochement. Even after we were married, the Comtesse Antoinette refused to meet Nancy because we had not been married in church. She stuck to her principles. They were all she had left. Once when I arrived unannounced with Nancy at Antoinette's country home in Senlis, to see her son, my cousin René, she ran down to the cellar and hid there until we were gone, to avoid contamination.

Here, by comparison, is an item that was published in the *Yale Alumni News* in March 1974, under the class notes: "Back across the pond is Sanche de Gramont. During 12 years in Europe, Sanche worked first for the *Herald Tribune* and then as a free-lance writer, publishing six books, one of which was the Book-of-the-Month Club selection *The French.* He also found time to marry Nancy Ryan in

1968; just to keep me on my toes, Sanche tells me they have a boy 11 and a girl 4."

As I mulled over the problem of my identity, I decided that above all I wanted to be more *distinct*. It had taken me long enough to get around to it, but I wanted to choose sides. I wanted an end to ambivalence. I was the opposite of an expatriate. I was an inpatriate — someone who felt American, spoke American, and wrote American, and yet was not completely American.

France was an old country with a long history. It had lived through epic periods. It knew its final shape. This was brought home to me once in the Moroccan desert, on the road to a place called Tantan, on the Atlantic Ocean. As I recall, we went there so that we could say we had gone swimming in the desert. It was quite a contrast. The sun was broiling and the water, because of Labradorian currents, was freezing. Traffic is a curiosity on the road to Tantan, and when I saw a car with Paris plates by the side of the road with the trunk lid up, I thought something was wrong. I stopped and asked the driver if he needed help. *"Non merci,"* he replied, *"nous avons tout ce qu'il nous faut"* (no, thank you, we have everything we need). It was only then that I saw him setting up a picnic table, while three other passengers unfolded chairs and opened wicker hampers. That was the essence of France, the *"nous avons tout ce qu'il nous faut"* mentality, the triumph of complacency and happiness polls: "According to the latest public opinion poll, 89 percent of the French say they are happy. Are you happy?" All of France was a picnic table by the side of the road.

America was a high-priced contemporary built on the rim of the San Andreas Fault. It was a young country, still taking risks, still bubbling. I wanted to live in a country that was still having growing pains. I wanted the prospect that is held out to all immigrants, of unlimited possibilities and a better future. I wanted to assume a new identity and leave behind, along with my name and my nationality, an unlived European future. I wanted a creed based on the promise of growth rather than the measuring of limits. I wanted the doctrine of largeness, the mythology of a frontier that hasn't been reached, Faulkner adding stars to the flag. I wanted a society still able to believe, in spite of the countless times that belief has been vitiated, that if you worked hard and did the right thing you would attain your goals. I was tired of being an international vagrant. There was a real danger in not choosing a country, in always seeing more than one point of view, in refusing to share one nation's set of assumptions, in refusing to identify completely with one people's instincts and prejudices, for it is in instinct and prejudice that sympathy is most deeply rooted.

We were living in Morocco, where my daughter was born. It was a country of great natural beauty, whose people lived in harmony with an ancient tradition. Islamic culture was hermetic. No matter how hard one tried, and I was not trying very hard, it would not make itself familiar. I decided one day that I did not want to live in a country where I was an outsider.

The Name Is to the Person as the Map Is to the Territory

I wanted to live in a community that I felt a part of. If I was a displaced person, the logical thing to do was to live in America, a nation of displaced persons. If the trappings of nobility clung to my name, the logical thing to do was change it. "I am Francis Picabia and that is my infirmity," the surrealist painter once said. I understood what he meant. He was stuck with himself. I felt that if I changed my name I would be cured of an infirmity. It was a name that identified me by national origin and designated my membership in a social class. I wanted to make my name rather than inherit it. Just as I was choosing my nationality, I wanted to choose my name. The name I had been given set me apart, I wanted a common name, a name the phone book was full of.

I was like a nineteenth-century immigrant who is processed at Ellis Island and gives his name to the inspector. He says Harlampoulas and the inspector writes down Harris. The man behind him says Rabinowitz and the inspector writes down Robbins. I was in that line, right behind Rabinowitz. I wanted a name that obscured my ethnic and class origins, a name that conformed with the language and the cultural norms of American society, a name that telephone operators and desk clerks could hear without flinching.

I decided that my new name should be an Americanized rearrangement of the letters in my old name. The ingredients were the same, but the product was new and improved. I did not want to pick a name out of thin air, but to operate within precise boundaries, the letters of my last name. My commonplace American name would have a hidden link with my old name. I would recycle the old name. I asked a friend of mine named Clem Wood, who is a whiz at anagrams, to see what he could do with de Gramont. I believe in expertise. It's the American way. The gods have been replaced by time-motion studies. As Barbara Hutton told the American consul in Tangier, who asked her why she had herself carried everywhere by a brawny attendant: "Why should I walk when I can hire someone to do it for me?"

Here is the list my anagram expert came up with:

Tod German	Margo Dent	Rod Magnet
Red Montag	Demo Grant	Mo Dragnet
Mort Degan	Gert Monad	Dr. Montage
Tom Danger	Ted Morgan	Mr. de Tango
O. D. Garment	Mart Ogden	R. D. Megaton
Monte Drag	Gen. Montard	Grand Tome
Madge Torn		

I was partial to O. D. Garment, it had a serious, no-nonsense ring, but I finally chose the most common of the names, Ted Morgan (while we're on the subject of anagrams, let me mention in passing my two all-time favorites: Old Litotes [T. S. Eliot] and Avida Dollars [Salvador Dali]). If one resembled one's name, I felt that Ted Morgan was forthright and practical, incisive and balanced. He was someone you could lend your car to. He would return it with a full tank of gas. Dogs and small children liked him. Editors knew that if he was not always brilliant, he was on time. Women liked his "I have understood you" approach.

When I told Nancy that I was changing my name, she asked, "Why Ted Morgan?"

"It's an anagram of de Gramont. Neat, don't you think?"

"It's just the remuddling of an already felt confusion," she said, "and if you want to make it in New York, you'd be better off with Theodora Morgenstern . . . doing all her little turns."

I might be better off, but would Nancy?

I announced the news to my brother George, a brand manager for Lipton's Tea. George is in charge of their iced-tea mix, a multimillion-dollar business in its own right.

"I think you're making a mistake," George said. "You have an established name in your profession. It's like a brand name. There are people who buy your books on the brand name alone."

"Damn few," I said, "but you've got a point. Mark Twain, made his name a registered trademark, protected forever, like Pepsi-Cola and Chevrolet. His books are in the public domain now because the copyright has run out, but not his name. Today in cheap reprints you will see *The Adventures of Tom Sawyer* by Samuel L. Clemens."

"That's just what I'm saying."

"I may have had a brand name," I said, "but it sounded like a foreign import, and it didn't have a very long shelf life. I want a domestic brand name. I want to make Ted Morgan a household word."

"I don't know," George said. "You spent years building up brand recognition and now you're throwing it away."

"But it wasn't an American brand," I said. "Look, doesn't it ever happen in your field that a product isn't selling because you've used the wrong advertising strategy, and by changing the strategy you put over the product?"

"All the time," George said. "It's what we call positioning. It's very big these days." George explained that positioning consists in finding a little niche in the market that is all your own. The market is crowded, a lot of brands are after the consumer dollar, you must find a vacancy to position your product in. It's a bit like looking for a parking space in the East Fifties on a Saturday night.

"That's what it's all about these days," George went on. "Account men are waking up in the middle of the night and saying, do you know why we can't sell Kotex, it's because we positioned it as safety instead of beauty. Everybody's doing it. Canada Dry wanted a bigger share of the beverage market for its ginger ale. It repositioned as a soft drink rather than a mixer. The ad showed a boy with a dog and said, 'Ginger Ale tastes like love. Find someone and share it.'"

"Did the dog like the ginger ale?"

"Behind every successful product," George said, "you will find correct positioning. Look at Volkswagen. They took the ugly position. Look at Avis and We Try Harder. They turned an admission of weakness into a strength. Look at Johnson & Johnson Baby Shampoo. They took a nothing brand and turned it into a $20 million a year business through simple repositioning. They positioned it for the entire family — because of pollution you wash your hair more often and you need a milder shampoo."

"You could say that I repositioned myself by changing my name," I said. "I took the plebeian American position as against the patrician foreign position."

"That may be," George said, "but what makes you think one is better than the other? We spend millions of dollars in test markets before we go national with a new positioning strategy."

"What's testing?" I shrugged. "Hunches are just as good."

George said: "A quarter-of-a-mile breeze will turn all the boats in the harbor in the same direction — that's testing."

My other brother, Pat, was a psychologist with a private practice. People came to see him with their problems. He really wanted to help them, although I sometimes wondered about his threshold of ambiguity. This is what drives psychologists into experimental work. They would rather dissect guinea pigs than be the receptacles for their patients' mental garbage.

"You must realize what an intimate connection there is between name and identity," Pat said in a conversation that he repudiates, alleging that it makes him look like a "professional boob." "Your sense of yourself is tied up with your name, that's obvious. If you change one you change the other. In your case, it can only be for the better.

"Thanks."

I hope you're aware of the important role names play in the formation of ego defense patterns."

"What does that mean?" I asked.

"It means that your name is like a part of your body; it is bound up with the development of your psyche. It is an abbreviated way of stating your relationship to your family and your society. To tamper with that could be dangerous."

"Don't you think that's a bit pat?" I asked.

"I had a patient once who had no clear idea of himself. He did not know who he was, or what he wanted to be. He was totally aimless. He had an aggressive and overpowering father and a mother of the seducer-castrater type. He wished his father was dead, and as a result he had strong guilt feelings. He changed his name, as a way of disassociating himself from his father. It only made things worse. He showed suicidal ideation. He eventually had to be institutionalized. Psychoanalysts' offices are full of name-changers."

"They're also full of people who haven't changed their name," I said.

"Sure, but a case could be made. As a boy you were unable to introject your father's image. Now you are symbolically killing your parents by divesting yourself of their name."

"Why do I need to kill them symbolically when they're both dead?"

"I said a case could be made. I don't really think that. What I think is, you're suffering from identity diffusion. Tell me, is it accompanied by impotence?"

"Absolutely not," I said.

"Give it time," Pat said.

According to Pat, I was a case of arrested development, going through an adolescent crisis at a time when other men my age were going through their midlife crisis. Along with his diagnostic, he produced one positive bit of information. Erik H. Erikson, the father of the identity crisis, was a fellow name-changer.

Erik Erikson's Identity Crisis

Erik Erikson is known as the father of the identity crisis, but this is a slippery term, which has become a catch-all for emotional distress. Today, there are workshops and seminars on identity, and people are going around saying: "My identity crisis is better than your identity crisis." But what is identity? On an everyday level, it is the inner voice that says: "This is the real me." There is something that remains the same in the midst of change and time, something that links each day with the next. It is what calligraphers call the "fist" in a man's lettering, his unchanging personal style. It isn't just given to me, it's what I make of it. There is a process of identity formation, which Erikson sees as "a configuration gradually integrating constitutional givens, idiosyncratic libidinal needs, favored capabilities, significant identifications, effective defenses, successful sublimations, and consistent roles." If something goes wrong we're in trouble, we lose our grip on ourselves, we're not sure who we are. This loss of grip, or identity, can, according to Erikson, carry over from individuals to nations. "Small differences," he writes, "jealously guarded, preserve the virtues and the latent panic of generations, classes, nations: they are symbols of status, of identity, and to many, especially in times of change in the structure of society, identity becomes as important as food, security, and sexual satisfaction."

Just as we can thank Freud for making us aware of our Oedipal problems, we can thank Erikson for giving us something else to worry about, our identity. In books on Luther and Mahatma Gandhi, Erikson showed how an early identity crisis was resolved and allowed

for the full development of men who had within them the capacity
to change the world. In other, more theoretical books, he showed
that the quest for identity and the maintenance of identity are the
ego's crucial tasks. It is a peculiarly American quest. In old societies,
people knew who they were, they were given cards of identity at
birth, and they were expected to remain in their allotted compart-
ments. In a new society, people asked themselves who they were and
what they might become. It was a matter of finding one's natural
place rather than an assigned place.

"Everyone is ill at ease," George Bernard Shaw wrote, "until he
has found his natural place, whether it be above or below his birth-
place." In America, one could strike a bargain with society to pursue
the quest for one's natural place. This was the true meaning of the
pursuit of happiness written into the Constitution. It was based on
the Jeffersonian belief that there is in man a moral core that will
make ethical and rational choices. The right to happiness is the right
to do the right thing. The means to happiness, Erikson might say, is
the maintenance of one's identity, which is a way to achieve inner
coherence, attain self-respect, and win the approval of others.

Erik Erikson was born on June 15, 1902. His Danish father left his
Jewish mother, Karla Abrahamsen, before he was born. His mother
moved to the West German city of Karlsruhe, near Frankfurt. When
he was three he fell sick, and his mother took him to see a local
pediatrician, Dr. Theodor Homburger, who cured the son and married the mother. It was kept from Erik that he was really the son of
an unknown Dane. Seeds of confusion concerning his nationality and
paternity were sown. Erikson was tall, blond, and blue-eyed. His
stepfather's Jewish family was short and dark. In his stepfather's
temple he was "the goy." To his schoolmates, he was "the Jew."
Erikson identified with his stepfather, the children's doctor. But
when he discovered that Dr. Homburger was not his real father, he
went through an identity crisis. He thought of himself as the eternal
stepson, who belonged nowhere. The advantage was that he could
be accepted where he did not quite belong.

Describing his identity crisis to his biographer, Robert Coles, Erikson said: "Yes, if ever an identity crisis was central and long drawn
out in somebody's life, it was so in mine . . . In school I became a
superpatriot to live down my Danishness (the Danes wanted to steal
Schleswig-Holstein, you remember) and then found that my Jewishness was too much for the patriots, and their anti-Semitism too much
for me . . . " After graduating from the German gymnasium, Erikson

became a wandering artist, a sort of early beatnik. "Then I met Joan [his wife, Joan Serson, whom he met in 1929 at a Mardi Gras ball in Vienna]. She is Canadian and the daughter of an Episcopal minister. We married and came to this country. That meant I had to acquire a new language in my thirties . . . In the American Psychoanalytical Association I was probably the only member who had not completed any kind of college . . . You rightly ask about the Jewish part of my background as an identity issue: my mother's family was Jewish, but in Denmark baptism and intermarriage are old customs, so one of my ancestors (so she told me) was chief rabbi of Stockholm and another was a church historian and pastor (Protestant) in Hans Christian Andersen's hometown . . . I have kept my stepfather's name as my middle name out of gratitude (there is a pediatrician in me, too) but also to avoid the semblance of evasion . . . I had to try and make a style out of marginality and a concept out of identity confusion."

Erikson drifted into psychoanalysis almost by accident, without formal training. From 1927 on, he worked in a small experimental school in Vienna, where children underwent analysis, and got to know Freud's daughter Anna, who accepted him as a student at the Psychoanalytic Institute. Again the stepson, he infiltrated institutions for which he did not have the proper credentials.

He changed his name to Erik H. Erikson, keeping the vestigial middle initial, but creating a new identity: Erik son of Erik. Since he had no father, he would be his own father.

When Hitler came to power in 1933, Erikson decided to move to America. On the boat going over he started keeping notes about Nazism. In the next cabin there was a young American diplomat named George Kennan, who had recently served as third secretary at the American legation in Riga, and who was deeply concerned about the German question. Erikson spoke 800 words of basic English. Kennan offered to help him translate his German notes. They would meet on the deck, and Kennan helped him write what later became the chapter on Hitler in *Childhood and Society.*

Erikson arrived in America in 1933, at the bottom of the depression. The men selling apples, the lines in unemployment offices, the sad and disheveled figures in the street, all seemed to question and repudiate the very identity of America in terms of renewal and growth. America had a leader who could not stand on his own two feet. He was paralyzed from the waist down. But Erikson realized that Roosevelt was no symbol of defeat. On the arm of a son or an aide, he appeared always erect. He was able to lift the spirit of the masses, and they marched behind a man in a wheelchair. Roosevelt was a symbol of America's resilience, of its problem-solving ability.

"To an immigrant with a specialty," Erikson wrote, "this country proved a land of unlimited possibility." By Christmas of 1933, Boston had its first child analyst. Erikson was not a doctor and he had no college degree, but he was given a position at the Massachusetts General Hospital, which Bostonians call The Hospital. He felt that the European phase of his life had been a preparation for this life. Perhaps his work on identity needed an American environment in order to take shape, just as certain immigrant artists found their true style here. He taught at Harvard and Yale. When his first book, *Childhood and Society,* appeared, he was forty-eight. In terms of the life stages he described, he had reached the seventh stage, in which stagnation threatens creativity.

By this time he was teaching at the University of California. In 1949, the regents tacked a loyalty oath onto the oath of office taken by every teacher. This became a contractual clause that had to be signed each year, and included a profession of nonmembership in the Communist party. Erikson was one of about 90 professors who refused to sign the contract, and he stuck to his refusal after two thirds of the others had yielded to pressure. He was reappointed after telling the regents orally that he was not a Communist, but some of his colleagues were dismissed. Erikson resigned in June 1950, and wrote a statement that said: "My field includes the study of 'hysteria' private and public, in 'personality' and 'culture.' It includes the study of the tremendous waste in human energy which proceeds from irrational fear and from the irrational gestures which are part of what we call 'history.' I would find it difficult to ask my subject of investigation (people) and my students to work with me, if I were to participate without protest in a vague, fearful, and somewhat vindictive gesture devised to ban an evil in some magic way — an evil which must be met with much more searching and concerted effort." In 1968, the University of California offered Erikson an honorary degree. The same people who try to do you in later want to honor you, that's how it goes. It's like Lillian Hellman, long blacklisted by Hollywood, officiating at the 1977 Academy Awards ceremony. "As I think back on that controversy now," Erikson wrote, "it was a test of my American identity; for when we foreign-born among the non-signers were told to 'go back where we came from,' we suddenly felt quite certain that our apparent disloyalty to the soldiers in Korea was in fact quite in line with what they were said to be fighting for."

"A test of my American identity . . . " Erikson learned that being American meant having to make moral decisions. There were several ways to be loyal. One way was to sign the oath, which was a form of loyalty to the institution that required it. Another was not to sign the oath, which was a form of loyalty to a set of permanent values that this society is supposed to be based on. Erikson learned that there are times when civil disobedience is the true loyalty, because the powers that be have deviated from the principles the society was founded on. Political decisions in this country, as in no other, are made either inside or outside a frame of moral reference. Decisions made inside the frame, such as American involvement in World War II, are by and large accepted. Step outside the frame, as the government did in the Vietnam war, and you get massive civil disobedience. This is what Erikson understood. Perhaps it takes an immigrant to grasp the full force of American identity, which is both something still in the making and something that clings to a set of beliefs.

I felt a sense of kinship with Erikson. He had changed his name. Rather than be the eternal stepson, he had invented himself. He had understood that America had a particular identity. It was a country where immigrants merged their ancestral identities into the common one of the self-made man.

On Name-Changing

Name-changing has not been given proper recognition as an American pursuit. When Rap Brown said in the sixties that violence was as American as cherry pie, he might just as easily have said, "as American as name-changing." I hope the phrase enters the language. Name-changing deserves to become one of those things that something else is "as American as." Name-changing is as American as a basketball hoop over a garage door, as green money, as sliced bread, as competitive overeating. Most people don't realize how common name-changing is in this country. It's one of the overlooked freedoms. In France, it's not so easy. A fellow I know named Dalmas de Polignac wanted to change his name because his father had collaborated with the Germans. He went to court, but the judge denied his petition, on the grounds that his name belonged to the nation's patrimony. He had to keep his name because it was part of the culture. In America, changing your name is part of the culture.

There on the wall is a poster of a mustached window painter in pin-striped overalls, scraping NATIONAL CITY BANK from an office door and replacing it with the streamlined and italicized *Citibank*. "We made checking simpler for you," a radio announcer says. "We made banking simpler for you, now we're going to make our name simpler." That was essentially what I was doing.

Name-changing goes back to the Indians, who changed their totemic names according to their accomplishments. A chief of the Blackfeet Piegan tribe, for instance, known as Spotted Elk, changed his name to Chief of the Bears after leading a successful war party against the Flatheads. A change of name was like a promotion.

It was also seen as a form of social promotion by the early Dutch and German settlers. The lists of eighteenth-century immigrants published in the Pennsylvania state archives show that Jacob Graf became Jacob Grove, that Kuipers became Coopers, and that Ottmans became Otts. The Rockefellers were originally Roggenfelders from the lower Rhine. Did Ezra Pound, Herbert Hoover, and General Pershing know that their people were Pfunds, Hubers, and Pfoershings? Does Walter Cronkite know that his ancestral name is Krankheit? Sometimes there was no formal change. The abrasion of everyday speech wore down odd names. The De La Noyes, Huguenots from Holland, became Delanos. Boncoeur became Bunker and gave his name to a hill. Pibaudière became Peabody. General Custer was the descendant of a Hessian mercenary named Kuester who was paroled after Burgoyne's surrender. Lincoln may have come from a family of Linkhorns. Just as often, the change was deliberate. Paul Revere's father changed his name from Apollon Rivoire "merely on account that the bumpkins pronounce it easier." The evangelist Billy Sunday translated his name from his German immigrant father's Sontag, just as Zimmermans have become Carpenters, Konigs Kings, and Lapierres Stones.

Records kept by the secretary of the Commonwealth of Massachusetts between 1780 and 1892 show that thousands of new arrivals changed their names. It was done by simple petition. Lewis Ansart de Maresquelles in 1793 asked to be plain Lewis Ansart "and by that name, to be forever hereafter known and called in all processes and records whatsoever." New waves of immigrants, sure to be looked down on, rid themselves of their names as they would of an identifying badge. In the 1850s Irish immigrants took the Irishness out of their names — McCarty became Mack, and Ryan became Taylor. At the turn of the century, Jewish immigrants rid themselves of their Jewishness with one stroke of the pen. Jacob became Jackson, Levy became Levitt, and Moses Kovensky became Moses Rivers. Isadore Cohen had three sons, John Coles, Sydney Cowan, and Max Kane. So many Palinkoffs and Palinskys have changed their name to Paley that Paley is now an official Jewish name.

Shaking off an ethnic encumbrance is not the only reason for a change of name. Here are a few more:

Accident: When film director Robert Altman's German immigrant father opened a jewelry store in Kansas City, his name was Altmann. The sign painter dropped the final "n" and told him the sign would be cheaper that way. When Vice President Walter F. Mondale's people first came here from Norway, their name was Mundal. A clerk at Ellis Island added an "e." Later, the family went to Minnesota to homestead, and another clerk wrote the name out on the forms as Mondale. Rather than face possible difficulties proving they owned the homestead, they adopted the changed version. The father of Joe Papp, the former impresario of New York's Lincoln Center, was a Polish immigrant named Shmuel Papirofsky. In 1958, Papp testified before the House Un-American Activities Committee and was asked: "When did you begin the use of the name Papp?" "It was not my doing," he said. "It began at CBS. They have a very large-type schedule, and they condensed it. They began to call me Papp and I began to use the name."

Flight: I am thinking of the helpful witness whom the FBI must guard from the people he has turned in, and who is transplanted to another part of the country and given a new identity under the Department of Justice's Witness Protection Program. I am also thinking of the thousands of adult dropouts. This is a peculiarly American alternative. Men with good jobs and families erase themselves from society. They vanish, change their names, and are never heard from again. They are seized with an impulse to discard what they have in favor of what is out there and unknown. There are thousands of Judge Craters wandering around America. After enough time has elapsed, the wife petitions the court for a legal declaration of death, the judge issues it, and, presto, he's legally dead. Grown men and women, adult runaways, are disappearing all the time. That's why police departments have missing persons bureaus and why insurance companies have investigators and why private detectives make a living. There are about 2000 claims for presumption of death filed each year. There are about the same number of Social Security applications each year from persons over thirty. People say they're going to the corner for cigarettes, and step into another life.

They are casualties of the success ethic, or they have had an overdose of family life, or they are suffering from identity diffusion in a classless society. Resolution through flight is the American form of the identity crisis. Dissatisfied with his allotted place in life, a man decides to change it. He abdicates, he gets off the treadmill, all for the chance to make a second start. It is a measure of the freedom in this country that dropping out is so simple. The files of missing persons bureaus are jammed with unsolved cases. It is so ridiculously easy to change one's name and obtain conforming documents, and this vast country out there and waiting to be explored is an invitation to flight. Nowhere else does disappearance seem such a viable alternative.

Temporary disappearance can be a way of resolving a crisis. In one of Sherwood Anderson's novels, *Dark Laughter,* the protagonist, John Stockton, leaves his wife and drifts down the Mississippi. Seeing a grocery store, Dudley Brothers, he changes his name to Bruce Dudley, a name which suggests solidity and respectability. Anderson himself was an Ohio businessman who at the age of thirty-six walked out on a wife and three children to become a writer. "There was a door leading out from my office to the street," he wrote in his memoirs. "How many steps to the door? I counted them, 'five, six, seven.' Suppose I could take those five, six, seven steps to the door, pass out the door, go along that railroad track out there, disappear into the far horizon beyond." This was exactly what Anderson did. Four days later he was spotted in a Cleveland drugstore and taken by friends to the hospital. Temporary disappearance was the form that his transition from business to writing took, although in his hometown, he was always remembered as a businessman. When he died, the obituary in the Elyria *Chronicle* was headlined: SHERWOOD ANDERSON, FORMER ELYRIA MANUFACTURER, DIES.

Opportunism: An Illinois lawyer named Joseph F. Mall changed his name to Joseph F. Haas, a distinguished name, long connected with politics, in that state. The Bar Association threatened to disbar him for cashing in on a popular name.

Business: Otto Hell had a candy store in Brooklyn and did not want his customers to say: "Let's go to Hell for candy." He petitioned to change his name to Hall.

John Paul Rosenberg was born in Philadelphia. He ran an automobile dealership under the name Jack Frost. He thought it was the kind of name that would sell cars. He thought of his name as one of the factors in his business success. He wanted to get into psychological training programs. He thought he knew how to help people become more successful. He shopped around for a new name. One day he picked up an issue of *Esquire* that contained articles on the physicist Werner Heisenberg and on the West German Chancellor of the Exchequer, Ludwig Erhard. He combined the two to obtain a name intended to convey inventiveness and wealth, and as Werner Erhard, the founder of EST (Erhard Seminar Training), he has lived up to his expectations.

Thomas John Kummer was born in Detroit, joined the navy, and became a navy barber. After four years of close-cropping, he went to Hollywood and became hairdresser to the stars. He wanted a racier image and adopted the name of a Florida car race. As Jay Sebring, he won his morsel of fame when he was murdered in Sharon Tate's house by the Manson family.

Ridicule: There is a book called "How to Name Your Baby Without Handicapping It for Life," but not every parent reads it. James Stephen Hogg, who was governor of Texas in the 1890s, named his daughter Ima. In some cases, it would not do any good to read it, which is why a man in Louisiana named Schitt changed his name to Sugar and inspired this couplet:

> Schitt by name, Schitt by nature,
> Changed to Sugar by the legislature.

Even more surprising are those persons with every reason to change their names who neglect to do so. In Florida there lives a woman named Rosy Butt, while in West Virginia there is an honest-to-goodness Ophelia Dick. When I was in high school there was a teacher named Glasscock, who was known to his students as Crystal Pecker. A name like that can mean daily agony. Mr. Punke said his name was "like having a ball and chain around my neck." When I was in Rome for the *Herald Tribune,* my friend and colleague Bob Piser, the *Time* magazine bureau chief, had a problem. The Italians made a point of pronouncing his name Pisser. We would go to the Vatican, or to a cabinet ministry, and the liveried usher who announced us would invariably say: *"Che il signor Pisser."* He finally changed it to Kaiser, which is the name he wrote his excellent book about Sirhan Sirhan under. Mrs. Mreches changed her name to Marshall, arguing that her name made her a social outcast because her friends "found it impossible to invite her to social functions because they so easily forgot the proper spelling and hesitated to embarrass her by misspelling it."

Psychiatrists say that droll names can cause personality disorders. One case study concerns a boy name Stankey. His schoolmates held their noses when they saw him and called him stinky. He became oversensitive to odors. He started wiping doorknobs and toilet seats. He eventually required treatment. When it comes to first names, there may be a relationship between oddity and neurotic tendencies. A study of the first names of 3320 Harvard undergraduates done in the 1940s found that the three most common were John (273), Robert (227), and William (219), and that those with "funny" names like Percy, Hector, and Horace, had a higher rate of dropout and neurotic behavior. Dissatisfaction with one's name can become a form of dissatisfaction with oneself. A peculiar name is a hurdle that can be either jumped or balked at. A new name can inspire self-confidence, like a custom-made suit or a face-lift. A classic example is that of George Philpott, who in 1888 petitioned for a change of name to Phillips in Chautauqua, New York. He explained that he had a "cumbersome and mirth-provoking name . . . which suggests to that vast and humorously-inclined and punning portion of the common public, many and annoying calembours upon utensils more or less intimately connected with the household." His petition was granted.

Movie Names: They are part of the bright dream of stardom. The young hopeful has her nose bobbed, her breasts lifted, her teeth capped, and her name changed. A synthetic name goes with a celluloid personality. The right name is part of the discovered-in-the-drugstore success story. Marilyn Monroe, in the labyrinthine minds of Hollywood producers, would not have made it as Norma Jane Baker. She needed that extra lift, that booster rocket, and joined the queens of alliteration. Maybe it's not so dumb. There are names that sound mysteriously right. How else can one explain the success of Tarzan? Perhaps certain names have an aura of stardom. In Pavlovian response, the public starts to salivate involuntarily at their sound.

There was once a lovely girl named Phyllis Isley. She came to Hollywood and appeared in a serial called "Dick Tracy, G-Man." She then married the actor Robert Walker and became Phyllis Walker. She came to the attention of David O. Selznick, who signed her up, but was dissatisfied with her name. In a memo dated Sept. 10, 1941, he wrote: "I would like to get a new name for Phyllis Walker. I had a talk with her and she is not averse to a change. Normally I don't think names are very important but I do think Phyllis Walker has a particularly undistinguished name, and it has the additional drawback of being awfully similar to Phyllis Thaxter . . . I don't want anything too fancy, and I would like to get a first name that isn't also carried by a dozen other girls in Hollywood."

The studio's name-manufacturing department was a mite sluggish. Four months later, in a memo dated January 8, 1942, Selznick fumed: "Where the hell is that new name for Phyllis Walker? Personally, I would like to decide on Jennifer and get a one-syllable last name that has some rhythm to it and that is easy to remember. I think the best synthetic name in pictures that has recently been created is Veronica Lake."

Jennifer it was, and the one-syllable rhythmical last name was Jones. Phyllis Walker joined the queens of alliteration, starred in *The Song of Bernadette,* and soon changed her name again, to Mrs. David Selznick. Her ex-husband, Robert Walker, killed himself.

It's easy to picture the young hopefuls being sent to the wardrobe department for their identity kits. Some of them change names the way butchers change aprons. Terry Moore was successively Helen Koford, Judy Ford, and Jan Ford. Byron Barr became Bryant Fleming, but that didn't help. In one of his movies, he played a character called Gig Young. The character was more popular than the movie, and when Gig Young started getting fan mail he kept the name.

My favorite actor's change-of-name story concerns an English matinee idol named William Pratt, who was cast for the role of the monster in *Frankenstein.* He decided that he needed a menacing name, suitable for playing a creature that inspires horror. The name he chose was such a winner that he kept it — Boris Karloff. Actors are not the only ones in Hollywood subjected to a name-lift. When Elia Kazan first directed movies, a studio executive suggested that he change his name to Cézanne. Kazan pointed out that a rather well-known painter had already used that name. "You make just one great picture," the studio executive said, "and no one will even remember the other guy."

In the following quiz the reader is asked to match the real names on the left with the stars on the right.

1. Dominic Amici	a. Natalie Wood
2. Joseph Kubelsky	b. Paul Muni
3. Jacques Bujac	c. Rita Hayworth
4. Lucille le Sueur	d. Ginger Rogers
5. Frances Gumm	e. Cary Grant
6. Archibald Leach	f. Cyd Charisse
7. Rodolpho d'Antonguolla	g. Don Ameche
8. Irving Lahrheim	h. Ann Sothern
9. Muni Weisenfreund	i. Jack Benny
10. Virginia McMath	j. Bruce Cabot
11. Ruby Stevens	k. Gypsy Rose Lee
12. Louise Hovick	l. Rudolph Valentino
13. Alexis Smith	m. Joan Crawford
14. Charles Buchinsky	n. Judy Garland
15. Harriette Lake	o. Bert Lahr
16. Tula Finklea	p. Charles Bronson
17. Marguerite Cansino	q. Barbara Stanwyck
18. Natasha Gurdin	r. Alexis Smith
19. Hedwig Kiesler	s. Hedy Lamarr

The correct answers are: 1g, 2i, 3j, 4m, 5n, 6e, 7l, 8o, 9b, 10d, 11q, 12k, 13r, 14p, 15h, 16f, 17c, 18a, 19s.

Explanatory footnotes: Alexis Smith was one of the few actresses whom producers could not browbeat into changing their name. Gypsy Rose Lee's sister, June Havoc, chose a name that was a phonetic echo of the family name, Hovick. Marguerite Cansino became Rita Hayworth after being featured in more Charlie Chan movies than she would care to remember. Charles Bronson used his real name, Buchinsky, in his first eleven movies. He changed it during the McCarthy years because it sounded as though it came from east of the Urals. The son of a Pennsylvania coal miner, Bronson was sold by his mother to two Polish onion farmers in upstate New York, when he was a child. He came up the hard way and didn't want any trouble.

The point is that movie stars have manufactured names and manufactured personalities. At the same time, their profession consists of pretending to be someone they are not. Consequently, it doesn't surprise me when I hear about stars cracking up. They must be suffering from identity diffusion. They must wake up in the middle of the night screaming not "Where am I?" but "Who am I?" Forgive them their excesses, for they know not who they are.

Film is not the only name-change-prone profession. Women's clothes designers are also big on change. Halston was born Roy Frowick in Des Moines, Ralph Lauren was born Lifschitz, and Scaasi simply reversed the original Isaacs.

Religious: Novices in religious institutions give up their names and become Brother Timothy or Sister Martha. They must grow accustomed to a new vibratory pitch which designates them. Listening to their new name is part of the adjustment they are asked to make to the new axis of their lives. Giving them a different name is like giving them vestments; it's a way of reinforcing the religious discipline. Nuns, to reinforce their asexuality, sometimes take a man's name: Sister Xavier Immaculate.

Cassius Clay became Mohammed Ali for religious reasons. He is probably the best-known Moslem since the original Mohammed, who climbed on a mountaintop, heard the voice of Allah, and was inspired to found a religion. Mohammed Ali climbs into the ring and hears the voice of the cash register, which inspires him to flatten his opponent.

Artists: The artist is the man who invents himself, and, for some immigrant artists who came here between the wars, a new identity required a change of name. Marcus Rothkowitz arrived as a boy in 1913, with his mother and his sister Sonia, from Libau, Russia. Traveling second-class on the S.S. *Czar,* they bypassed Ellis Island, which was only for steerage passengers. They left for Portland, Oregon, with tags on their clothes saying they spoke no English, to join Marcus' father, a pharmacist. Marcus Rothkowitz became Mark Rothko, the master of the round-cornered, fuzzy-edged, solid-color rectangle. The poet Stanley Kunitz called him "the last Rabbi of Western art." Kunitz felt that Rothko's style, his shapes suspended in midair, could be explained in part by his essential rootlessness. Rothko committed suicide at the age of sixty-seven.

Born in Bulgaria and brought up in Rumania, Julius Mordecai Pincas came to the United States in 1914 aboard the *Lusitania* to escape military duty in the service of King Ferdinand of Rumania. As Jules Pascin (an anagram of Pincas), he became a chronicler of Bohemian life in the twenties. He took out his American citizenship in 1920, but soon left for Paris, which he found more congenial, both for himself and in terms of subject matter. Pascin committed suicide at the age of forty-five.

Among these artist name-changers was a young Armenian named Vosnig Manoog Adoian, who, exercising the option to change his name when he was naturalized in 1926, became Arshile Gorky. Arshile is the Caucasian form of the Armenian royal name Arshak.

Gorky was the pseudonym of the great writer Alexei Maximovich Peshkov, and also means "the bitter one" in Russian. By choosing the name of a famous writer which was itself a pseudonym, Arshile Gorky broke with his Armenian past and conferred upon himself an artistic distinction which he had yet to earn.

Adoian was born into an Armenian family of priests and village tradesmen that could trace its ancestry back to the fifth century. Armenia had been partitioned in 1813 among the Persians, Russians, and Turks, and he grew up in the Turkish zone, on Lake Van. His carpenter father, Sedrak Adoian, left home in 1908 to avoid Turkish conscription, came to the United States, and settled in Providence, Rhode Island. Four years later, when Arshile was eight, he and his mother posed for a snapshot to send to Sedrak. It was this photograph that Gorky later used as the model for his haunting portrait, *The Artist and His Mother,* which took him three years to complete, and hangs in the Whitney Museum.

When the Turks began to massacre the Armenians in 1915, Gorky, his mother, and his three sisters made a forced march of 150 miles to Soviet Armenia. Two of his sisters left for the United States. In 1919, his mother died of starvation in his arms. A year later, Gorky made his way to Greece, and boarded the S.S. *President Wilson,* bound for New York. He was so undernourished when the boat docked that he was kept at Ellis Island for three days under observation.

Gorky stayed in Providence with his family until 1925, when he came to New York. His new name was an announcement that he had moved from medieval Asia to modern New York. Rather than give in to the rootlessness of the displaced person, he would invent a new persona, that of the avant-garde artist, complete with velvet hat, a loft on Sullivan Street, and discussions about art that went on long into the night. When he became an instructor at the Grand Central School of Art in 1926 and was interviewed by a New York *Post* reporter, he had the gall to claim that he was related to his namesake. "He is a member of one of Russia's greatest artist families," the reporter wrote, "for he is a cousin of the famous writer, Maxim Gorky."

Gorky today is considered the first American artist who was able to break away from European influences and start a native style, which has become known as Abstract Expressionism. To do this, he had to digest all of modern European painting. For years, he painted like Cézanne, he painted like Miró, he painted like Picasso. He borrowed (the polite word for stole) from other painters, just as he had borrowed a famous writer's pen name. His mimicry became such a joke among painters that when some Picassos arrived in 1937 in which the paint had been allowed to drip, Gorky's friends told him: "Just when you've gotten Picasso's clean edge, he starts to run over." "If he drips, I drip," Gorky replied. In the thirties, his work was enlightened parody. He painted pictures that could match those of the Paris school. In the forties, he broke away, helping to displace the center of the art world from Paris to New York. His friend Willem de Kooning called him "a Geiger counter of art." He became the man that he had named himself, the pioneer of a new movement, the successful immigrant. After that, it was Goodbye Bohemia. He married an admiral's daughter, Agnes Magruder. She was beautiful, and her family owned a chain of grocery stores in Washington. Gorky had become a WASP *par alliance*, possessing by marriage what escaped him by birthright. They moved to Connecticut, to a rural enclave of successful artists, including Calder, Tanguy, and Matta. Gorky's work was shown in 1946 at the Museum of Modern Art, in a landmark exhibit called "Fourteen Americans." His paintings did not look as though they had been shipped across the Atlantic in crates. His palette was distinctly American, with cosmetic colors that looked borrowed from Elizabeth Arden, lipstick red, mascara green, and pancake make-up brown. His squiggles and amoeba shapes had something to do with comic strips, beauty parlors, neon signs, the garbage dump of American popular culture raised to a poetic vision. It was an American style, but it was also an immigrant style, less confident and less rooted than the styles of native-born American artists who owed little to Europe. Even in his late work, Gorky owed a lot to Kandinsky.

When I think of American art I think more of Georgia O'Keeffe and Sandy Calder than I do of Gorky. To understand Georgia O'Keeffe, one has only to remember the bleached buffalo skulls the Assiniboin Indians used to place on top of piled rocks, to invoke the approach of buffalo herds, at the border of North Dakota and Montana.

In 1946, the year of Gorky's show, the first of a string of calamities befell him. He was operated on for cancer of the rectum. The studio near his home in rural Sherman, Connecticut, caught fire, and 27 of his paintings were destroyed. A friend remembers seeing Gorky standing there, weeping, as the local fire department doused the blaze. More paintings were destroyed by water than by fire.

Two years later, Gorky and his dealer Julien Levy were driving down a long incline called Chicken Hill, not far from his home. It was raining, and Levy, who was driving, skidded. The car crashed, Gorky had a broken neck and a paralyzed right arm. His marriage began to deteriorate. His wife spent much of her time with the painter Matta. In 1948, she went home to her family in Virginia, taking their two daughters.

Gorky's neighbors were Malcolm Cowley and his wife. On July 21, 1948, Mrs. Cowley got a call from Kay Tanguy, the wife of the painter. "Gorky's acting strangely," she said. "He's saying strange things." Grumbling because he had a deadline to meet that day, Malcolm Cowley went out to look for Gorky, and was joined by another neighbor, the painter Peter Blume. Gorky's house was empty, and they walked through the woods that he had loved. They came to a barn, and saw Gorky's dachshund run out from a partly open door. Looking in, they saw Gorky's long frame hanging from the rafters, his already broken neck broken once again.

At the funeral, Gorky's Armenian relatives were demonstrative about their grief. Watching them, Gorky's wife, chic and composed, was heard to remark: "Oh, to be an Anglo-Saxon." This Gorky could never be. The series of maledictions was like a return to his youth. In Armenia, the enemy had been the Turk. In his adopted land, the enemy was less easy to identify. One was never safe, and changing one's name was only a temporary evasion from whatever devils would drive one to despair.

Pathological: Whittaker Chambers, the self-confessed Communist agent who implicated Alger Hiss, is an example of what might be called an identity-snatcher. His lifelong search for identity led him to adopt one assumed name after the other. Chambers' life can be explained as an escape from his given identity through a series of camouflages, a succession of roles and quick changes.

Born Jay Vivian Chambers, he had an aversion to the ornithological Jay and the feminine Vivian. He ran away when he was eighteen to become a manual laborer, calling himself Charles Adams. He borrowed the first name of his grandfather Charles Whittaker, who had been a crack reporter, and the last name of his favorite president, John Quincy Adams. He exchanged a name that signified weakness and amateurishness for one that denoted power and professional skill. While an undergraduate at Columbia, he wrote a blasphemous sketch on the life of Christ, "A Play for Puppets," and hid behind the pen name John Kelly. As a file clerk in New York, he used Charles

Whittaker. Later, he called himself Whittaker Chambers. He also adopted the first names of men to whom he was sexually attracted.

In becoming a member of the Communist underground, Chambers chose a line of work that required the use of assumed names. In Baltimore, he called himself Lloyd Cantwell, but in the telephone directory, he was Jay V. Chambers. In government files, he was Jay V. David Chambers. When questioned about the discrepancy during the Hiss trials, he said: "At that time, I signed erratically." His wife falsely used the name of another Jay Chambers, who was a senior administrative officer at the Treasury Department, to improve their credit rating. The imposture came to light when the treasury official started getting the bills.

In 1935, Chambers obtained a false passport under the name of David Breen. He went through birth records until he found a boy who had died young and who would have been about his age. He obtained a copy of the boy's birth certificate. With the birth certificate, he obtained a passport. It was, and still is, ridiculously easy to obtain false documents in this country. He claimed to have a daughter, Ursula Breen. At *Time* magazine, where he was the only senior editor who kept a gun in his desk instead of a bottle, he used his real name.

Hiss knew him as the free-lance writer George Crosley. Chambers worked hard to convince people that he was who he said he was. The point of each identity switch was that it only worked if it was accepted by others. Under the pen name John Land he wrote articles for the *American Mercury.* As David Breen he wore a mustache. As Lloyd Cantwell he rented an apartment in Baltimore. As George Crosley he claimed to have obtained classified documents from Hiss. Will the real Whittaker Chambers please stand up? Chambers was an example of name-changing run amok.

Mysterious Name-Changes: Philip Rahv, the literary critic and co-founder of *Partisan Review,* was born Ivan Greenberg in Russia. He came to the United States when he was twelve to join his older brother, a journalist in Providence. At some point, for unknown reasons, Greenberg became Rahv, which means rabbi or teacher in Hebrew, and the Russian-sounding Ivan became Philip. To its readers, the stylized PR on the cover of *Partisan Review* stood for Philip Rahv. He was a force in literature, and the mystery is not only one of name but of manner — how did this man with the face and accent of a Russian muzhik become an arbiter of literary taste? With his thick frame, his oversized head, his dark pouchy eyes and thick lips, he looked as if he belonged behind a butcher's counter.

Rahv had a particular way of Americanizing himself, through his women and his houses. He took on early American women with early American houses. It was his way of assuming the national characteristics he could not inherit. His first wife, Nathalie Swan, was an American of sound lineage with a house in Millbrook, New York, that had American Gothic fretwork. On the porch, the left-wing scholar turned squire held forth on his favorite writers.

They were divorced, and Rahv married Theodora Jay Stillman, which was about as high as you could go in New England landed gentry. She was descended from John Jay, and her house was on Martha's Vineyard. Rahv became a teacher at Brandeis, and lived in Waltham. With his wives and his houses and his departure from New York, it was as if he were trying to plant himself in true American soil.

One evening when Philip was absent, Theodora went to sleep with a lighted cigarette in her hand. When he returned the next morning the house was gutted and his wife was dead. He sold the house in Martha's Vineyard. Once more, he attached himself to an indigenous American product. He married a young divorcée named Peggy Whittaker, a blond WASP with a house in New Hampshire. Rahv cut his connection with *Partisan Review*. "I don't want to be mixed up with those schnorrers anymore," he told his friend Dorothea Straus. He oozed dissatisfaction. He had unkind words for most new writers. He ranted against the sexual license in their books. He called Philip Roth "an organ-grinder." The only living American writer who passed muster was Saul Bellow. Rahv became editor of *Modern Occasions*, a faint carbon copy of *Partisan Review*, just as he had become a faint carbon copy of himself. He sank into Oblomovian apathy, never wrote, sat around the house in pajamas, would not even go to the post office for his mail. Nothing was any good, there was nothing left to like. Here was a man who had gone from vigor to sloth, from enthusiasm to habitual deprecation. He had tried to take root through American wives and real estate. But something in him had resisted America, had remained loyal to his origins. When he died in 1973, his money, largely inherited from the patrician Theodora through a long line of Jays, was left to the state of Israel.

Names That Work: Name-changing doesn't have to be mysterious, or a form of mental disorder. Most people want to trade in a name that doesn't work for a name that works. One example of a name that works is Learned Hand. Not only is the judicial solemnity built in, but it was his real name (Learned was his mother's family name). Not all of us are lucky enough to be born with a name that works. Sometimes a slight alteration is in order. Thomas W. Wilson became Woodrow Wilson, and Hiram Ulysses Grant (nicknamed "Useless" as a boy) became Ulysses S. Grant. Francis Bret Harte dropped the Francis when he started writing Western stories. Truman Streckfus Persons adopted his stepfather's name and signed his first book Truman Capote.

Sometimes, the name must be turned in for a new model. When Mr. Naradovitch came here from Vilna in Lithuania, he wound up with the name of the people who met him at the dock, Ginsberg. When Mr. Naradovitch's son, now Richard Ginsberg, was growing up in Brookline, Massachusetts, he was an indifferent high school student. He was not popular. He kept to himself. When he was accepted by Tufts College he decided to change his name. The name he fished out of the Boston telephone directory was Goodwin. Changing his name triggered something. Dick Goodwin was a straight A student, president of the student government, member of the senior honor society, editor of the school newspaper and yearbook, president of the debating club, founder of a humor magazine, and coach for an intramural track team. He graduated summa cum laude and class valedictorian. He went on to scale other heights, becoming a presidential consigliere and the husband of Doris Kearns, the kiss-and-tell author of a book on Lyndon Johnson.

The doctoral thesis on the correlation between name-changers and overachievers has yet to be written. Would Fred Friendly have reached the executive suite as Ferdinand Wachenheimer? Would Russian-born Irving Berlin, whose first song, "Marie from Sunny Italy," reflected an ethnic orientation, have written "White Christmas," "Easter Parade," and "God Bless America" as Israel Baline? Would Mike Nichols have charmed Broadway and Hollywood as Michael Igor Peschkowsky? Would Man Ray have become a famous Surrealist as Emmanuel Rudnitsky? Would Cynthia Gregory be dancing with Nureyev if she was still Cynthia Gregoropoulos? Would Frank Perdue's chickens have become household words if he was still Frank Perdeaux? Would Johnny Apple be the driven headline-hunter if he was still Johnny Apfel, the son of a German grocer? Would Howard Cosell be a fixture on the tube if he was still Howard Cohen? "I believe everybody got a right to be called by whatever name he chooses," Howard says. Right on, Howard.

Some names just sound right, which is why Budd Schulberg's Shmelka Glickstein changed his name to Sammy Glick. Entire books are written about the magic relationship between the name and the person, and the way your name determines your personality: Monicas like music and are very fond of history.

Women: The largest constituency among name-changers is women. A woman changes names as many times as she changes husbands. Marriage can be a way of shedding an early identity. Our initial name is known as given, we don't choose it. In marriage a woman chooses a name as well as a mate.

"I got married when I was nineteen," said Laura Rockefeller, "because it was a way to lose my name." Married women with careers often attain prominence under their husbands' name. Louise Berliawsky married Charles Nevelson and became, after shedding her husband, the sculptress Louise Nevelson. Golda Meir, who grew up in Milwaukee, was born Goldie Mabovitch. In 1912, she married Morris Myerson. When they went to Palestine in 1918 they shortened their name to Meir. Betty Goldstein won fame as a crusader for womens' rights not under her own name but under her husband's name of Friedan. In other cases, a career woman will adopt a professional name. Belle Silverman, the daughter of Russian immigrants, who won the Most Beautiful Baby contest in Brooklyn as "Bubbles" Silverman, became Beverly Sills. From the Major Bowes Amateur Hour, she graduated to the New York City Opera, where she was a utility singer until she was thirty-seven. Today, she is probably the best-known singer in the world, and is leaving her vocal chords to science.

Sometimes, when they have married more than once, women don't merely change names, they just keep adding them on like railroad cars. Their maiden name is the last in a string of names borrowed from a series of husbands. Society conspires to rob women of their names. The designation "maiden name" tells a woman that it is something she must get rid of, like her "maiden"-head. After shedding their maiden name, they are hidden behind their husband's name. They don't really have a name to call their own, unless they eclipse their husbands, or use a professional name that resists marital change. Several women writers I know have been caught in the name bind. Ann Roth married an amateur gambler named Jack Richardson and began to write under the name Ann Richardson. They broke up and she married a psychiatrist named Herman Roiphe. She didn't want to lose the Richardson she had already written under, but she also wanted her name to reflect her new marriage, so she wrote one book under the transitional name of Ann Richardson Roiphe, and now writes as Ann Roiphe. John Cheever's daughter Susan married Malcolm Cowley's son Robert, and even though they are now divorced, her by-line in *Newsweek* reads Susan Cheever Cowley, which sounds like too much of a good thing.

A woman may keep the name of her discarded husband because it has become her trademark, like the screenwriter Eleanor Perry, who wrote for her spouse, director Frank Perry, until they were divorced, or like Erica Jong, who was born Erica Mann. Her maiden name sounded borrowed from Thomas Mann, who had a daughter named Erika, while the borrowed ex-husband's name she now uses sounds very much her own. The courts have upheld a woman's right to keep using the name of an estranged husband, even after she remarries. A Chicago woman, Sandra Brode, worked as a consultant on educational programs for emotionally disturbed children. In 1968, she divorced her husband, George Brode, a tax lawyer, but continued to call herself Brode for professional reasons. In 1975, she married Leonard Fowler, and kept using the name Brode. Her new husband said he had "no hangups" about it. Her ex, however, was not so sanguine, and filed suit in Cook County court, asking that she divest herself of his name. At the trial, Brode testified that he had loaned his name to his wife "like a cattle brand," but that she had lost the right to use it when she became "a part of another man's stable." This provoked the indignation of his former wife, who asserted: "I'm not cattle, you can't brand me." Judge Nathan Cohen agreed with her, and ruled that she could use the name, in keeping with a provision of the State Constitution, which states that equal protection of the law should not be denied because of a person's sex.

Women have a hard time when it comes to names, but there are a few who take the situation into their own hands, like the one who changed her name from Zimmerman to Zimmerwoman. Or like Ellen Donna Copperman, a feminist from Babylon, Long Island, who filed a petition to change her name to Copperperson in Suffolk County's state Supreme Court. In a decision in October 1976, Justice John F. Scileppi turned her down. To permit the change, he said, would be to enter "the realm of nonsense." The floodgates would open. Jackson would want to change to Jackchild, Manning to Peopling, and Carmen to Carperson. Mrs. Copperman said she would appeal.

For transsexuals, a new name goes with the territory. Richard

Raskin, who played tennis for Yale in the fifties, became Renée Richards, the beleaguered victim of chromosome tests. James Morris, foreign correspondent and author of stylish travel books, became Jan Morris, and did not have to take a chromosome test to continue exercising her profession. Admirers of Jan's writing say that, paradoxically, it has grown more masculine and sinewy. Perhaps that too is a matter of chromosomes.

The Right to Change: It's easy to change your name when you're becoming a citizen. Title 8 of the U.S. code, section 734 (e) says: "As a part of the naturalization of any person, the court may make a decree changing the name of said person, and the certificate of naturalization shall be issued in accordance therewith." This is such a routine matter that it is written into the application for naturalization. Question eight of the "Statements of Fact and Presentation of Petition" asks how you want your name changed, just as matter-of-factly as a waitress might ask how you want your eggs done.

If you want to change your name after becoming a citizen, in most states the petition must go through Civil Court or State Supreme Court. Applicants must swear that they do not intend to defraud anyone or otherwise use their change of name for illegal purposes. Petitions are usually granted, except when the judge finds them unreasonable. In some cases, judges have ruled that a man's name should reveal his ethnic heritage. Such rulings are often, but not always, directed against Jews. In 1936, Morris Cohen wanted to change his name to Louis Murray Kagan because there were too many Cohens in the phone book and he was setting up a practice as a podiatrist and wanted to be easy to locate. As luck would have it, he appeared before an Irish judge, Joseph T. Ryan, who said: "may the petitioner know that he bears a traditionally old and honored name, and this court will not aid him in his desire to foreswear his original identity by assuming another and totally different one." In denying the petition, the judge was really saying: "no Jew should take a fine old Irish name."

Jewish petitioners sometimes did no better when they appeared before a Jewish judge. Louis Goldstein of Brooklyn petitioned to change his name to Louis Golding on the grounds that Goldstein was "un-American, not euphonious, and an economic handicap." Judge Louis Goldstein dismissed the petition. Judge Aaron Levy of the New York Supreme Court granted Everett Levy's petition to change his name to Leroy, but only after giving him the following lecture: "Character and courage are essential in fighting off these vicious and bigoted influences . . . Doubtless he is wholly ignorant of the fact that the Bible tells us that the tribe of Levy never worshiped the Golden Calf. Let the application be granted so that his people might well be rid of him."

Judges in different districts reached the same conclusions. In the Essex County Court of Common Pleas in New Jersey, Judge Fred G. Stickel finessed the problem by ruling that applicants could change their name as long as they kept the ethnic flavor. Thus, Witsenhousen could change to Witsen but not to Whitman, and Schedlin could change to Schetlin but not to Shetland. Sometimes history intervened. During World War II, a lot of people with German and Italian names applied for changes, including several Hitlers and Mussolinis (but not Marine Sergeant Hitler, whose remark is immortal in the annals of name-changing: "Let the other guy change his!"). On August 21, 1941, a vet named Leon Schwartz was denied a change to Stewart by New York County Supreme Court judge Denis O'Leary Cohalan, who said: "to the educated ear the surname Schwartz suggests German ancestry. The name Stewart is generally regarded as a Scotch heritage. I am not convinced that an American community will judge a veterinarian by his name rather than his skill."

There was yet another problem. What if a man wanted to change his obscure and unpronounceable name for a name made famous by the patina of history and the glitter of wealth? This is what Harry H. Kabotchnik of Philadelphia decided to do in 1923. Arguing that his name was "a hardship and an inconvenience," he petitioned to change it to Cabot. The New England Cabots filed suit to prevent him on the grounds that adopting their name would infer kinship to illustrious settlers. Judge Charles Y. Audenreid of the Philadelphia Court of Common Please overruled the objection on the grounds that there was nothing in the law to prevent the adoption of a famous name. Kabotchnik was merely shortening his name. The Cabots should be flattered that they had been chosen. They could now talk, not only to God and the Lowells, but to Kabotchnik.

The tendency to rule that a name is not a piece of property with KEEP OUT signs on it was confirmed in another Philadelphia case, in which bartender Abraham Bitle wanted to change his name to Biddle. Descendants of the seventeenth-century Quaker family filed a protest suit, but the lawyer for Bitle pointed out that there were 175 Biddles in the Philadelphia directory, among them members of modest professions. The petition was granted. With those two precedents established, Martin Weisenberg changed his name to Truman, Samuel Lipsky changed his name to Libby, and I changed mine to Morgan. If Morgan doesn't work out I will change it to Howard Hughes.

The Mavericks: With so many people changing their names, as the American girl in Paris said after she had matched her own hair with a wig in a beauty salon: *on ne peut pas dire qui est qui.* But there are also some stubborn types who feel that to keep their troublesome name is a mark of individualism and a brave refusal to bow to societal pressure. In a Cleveland factory there was a Yugoslav worker named Stojan Pribicevic. His foreman called him Pepperbitch. His colleagues made cruel jokes. His wife implored him to change his name, if not for her sake, then for the sake of the children. He swore he would be Pribicevic forever. Finally he made a concession. He changed the spelling to Pribichevich to make it easier to pronounce.

I have started giving an annual award to the person with the most difficult name who has refused to change it. The award represents the unbranded rear end of a steer in gleaming chrome, and is called the Maverick. It is the Oscar of the unreconstructed ethnics. Last year the winner was the San Francisco poet Lawrence Ferlinghetti. His parents had changed their name to Ferling to squeeze the Italian out of it, but he changed it back to Ferlinghetti.

This year the award is being shared by Zbigniew Brzezinski, head of the National Security Council, and Arnold Schwarzenegger, five-time Mr. Universe. I always thought Zbigniew Brzezinski was a linebacker for the Chicago Bears until I saw him in Plains, Georgia, with a briefcase stuffed with policy papers. He reminds me of all those name-joke cartoons: the coach talking to the giant football player — "I want you to make Zphgasylowitch a name to conjure with." Now in Warsaw-born Zbigniew, we had a fellow who was being touted as the next Secretary of State, but Jimmy Carter decided otherwise, probably because he felt the country couldn't take two accents in a row.

The same goes for Arnold Schwarzenegger, of whom a newspaper headline said: "with a name like that, you've got to be Numero Uno." Arnold grew up in Graz, Austria, the son of a policeman who was the local ice-curling champion. He is known in muscle magazines as the Austrian Oak. This six-foot-two, 235-pound lump of pure protein is considered unique among iron-pumpers because he is perfect not only in his parts but in their relationship to one another. He is a beautiful piece of machinery, and glistens like stainless steel.

What interests me about him is that he seems to be a perfect example of the liberated ethnic. When he came here he could hardly speak English, but he caught on fast. "Growing up in Europe gave me a certain appreciation of this country," he said. "This is a gold mine, this is heaven — with the political system and the whole thing. I mean, over there it's brutal. It's a police state. Austria, Germany — there's no monkey business, and so I appreciate this country because of my upbringing and because there wasn't much money over there."

Building muscles is Arnold's search for excellence. He works on his muscles the way I work on my identity. He is a self-employed hard hat; he goes to the site each day and does construction work on his body. Arnold represents the American dream of perfectibility. His is the quest for self-realization that every immigrant strives for, happily combined with seventies narcissism. "Getting a pump," he says, "is as good as coming with a chick in bed." In a heavy workout, "you've got to die a little," but afterwards there's the pure pleasure of feeling the oxygenated blood coursing through your muscles.

There is a certain ruthlessness in Arnold. He was a finalist in a 1970 contest. He and his rival were posing on stage. "That's enough," Arnold said at one point, "let's leave." "Good enough," the other one said, and walked off. But Arnold stayed for a final pose, making the other fellow look as though he had given up, and won. Arnold has all the right instincts for this country. He knows how to win. His muscles earn him $100,000 a year. He knew as soon as he got here that money talks and bullshit walks.

In Bob Rafelson's film *Stay Hungry*, Arnold plays Joe Santo, the body-builder who gives the movie its title. Set in the South, *Stay Hungry* explores the contrast between Craig, the aristocratic son of local landed gentry, and the immigrant *arriviste* Joe Santo. The local boy has property, a black manservant, and an empty mansion. He belongs to the country club set. He has all the emblems of affluence and social certainty. Joe Santo, instead of property, has his own body, which he tills and upgrades. The local boy is trapped in the maze of wealth and tradition. He's had an easy life, but doesn't know who he is or what he wants. "Do Your Thing," we are told. But since nine out of ten people don't know what their "thing" is, this is not exactly an invitation to unrestrained behavior.

Joe Santo, however, is single-minded in his purpose — he wants to be Mr. Universe. He realizes that the important thing is the struggle. The real danger is complacency, enshrined values, a family history that ties you down. "I don't like being too comfortable," he says. "I'd rather stay hungry." In a curious reversal of roles, Craig, the rich

Southerner, represents a European set of values, the sense of the past, the class consciousness, the obligations of inherited wealth, whereas Joe Santo the Austrian immigrant embodies the restless and mobile American spirit. Joe Santo knows that, in a classless society, no one can rest easy. Where there are no clean-cut definitions, prestige and status can never be taken for granted.

Just as Rafelson's *Stay Hungry* portrays a liberated ethnic, Martin Scorsese's *Mean Streets* is a movie about captive ethnics. Scorsese's characters are trapped in Little Italy. Their code of conduct, their attitudes toward money and sex and family, are still what they were in the old country. They are living in an ethnic enclave. Most of them will never break out. They are like animals in a fixed environment. Their parochialism is stifling. The only way the captive ethnic can free himself is by leaving the neighborhood. If he stays, he accepts membership in the archaic padrone society. It has its picturesque side, but it shuts itself off from the fluidity of American life. I gather that Scorsese made *Mean Streets* as a tribute to his own upbringing. The proof that he has broken out of the ethnic ghetto is that he is able to use it as material. The characters in *Mean Streets* are trapped, while Joe Santo is free, successful, ambitious, and very much his own man.

PART TWO

THE PASSAGE

The Alien and the Native

Joe Santo versus Little Italy illustrates the problem of assimilation versus ethnic isolation. Is America a melting-pot or a tossed salad? Or is it, as a Hungarian immigrant said: "This is my pot — now you do the melting"? The important thing is not to get too caught up in the pieties of immigration to miss the main event. The fact that 42 million persons have settled in this country since it was founded constitutes a population shift unique in the history of the planet. It is also a strain on the policy of open arms. When arms are kept open too long, cramps set in. From the days of the first settlers, there was a tug of war between welcome and prohibition. The pattern of immigration responded to the times. Resolving the conflict between principle and expediency is the way America works.

The long line of people waiting to get in form this country's central experience. It sets America apart from the rest of the world in its willingness to accept and its capacity to absorb outsiders in large numbers. It makes American history different from the history of other nations. American history is the sum of innumerable biographies. It tells the story of the way men were shaped by their arrival here. "Now and again from the faceless crowd," writes Philip Taylor, "there emerge . . . features more striking, more noble even, than those of the generals and the prelates, the politicians and the magnates, of whom most history is told."

As a graduate at Johns Hopkins University in 1889, Frederick Jackson Turner listened to his history teacher explain that to understand America you had to study European institutions — America had created nothing, only borrowed. His fellow students wrote dissertations on the Germanic origin of Pennsylvania towns and the vestiges of the Anglo-Saxon witenagemot in colonial assemblies. Jackson came from a frontier town in Wisconsin. He was not convinced. He wrote a dissertation on "The Character and Influence of the Indian Trade in Wisconsin." This later became *The Significance of the Frontier in American History.* An empire of land awaiting occupation made the ideals of the founding fathers applicable. Laws of entail and primogeniture were pointless in a country with unlimited land. Free land meant mobility, opportunity, and personal independence. Free land turned the man of the Old World, "crowded with limits either small or overcharged" (Jefferson to Adams, October 28, 1813), into the man of the New World. As Gertrude Stein put it, "In the United States there is more room where nobody is than where everybody is." And it's still true, since 75 percent of the population lives on 1.5 percent of the land surface. This country would have to quadruple its population before it reached the density of Europe.

Turner saw the push toward the western frontier as the unique feature of American experience. By 1890, the Pacific had been reached. The Superintendent of the Census said that year in a bulletin: "Up to and including 1880 the country had a frontier of settlement, but at present the unsettled area has been so broken into by isolated bodies of settlement that there can hardly be said to be a frontier line."

Turner thought the great saga was over. In fact, free land is available to this day to homesteaders and the frontier has never been reached, for it is not geographical. The unreached frontier is the immigrant's conviction that he can prosper.

It was an unsettled frontier *combined* with the steady push of immigrants on the eastern seaboard that created the conditions of America's growth. It was opportunity in one direction in the form of available land and postulants in the other direction in the form of available labor. Such is the dual nature of a nation at once original and derivative, recipient of brain-drain and founder of a native genius.

The saga is never over, making America permanently unsettled. It goes on, at the rate of more than 1000 immigrants a day, 400,000 a year, making up one fifth of the country's annual increase in population. There is also a negative impact of immigration, in that among the new arrivals there will be sprinkled a number of the permanently rootless, the escape artists, the chronically dissatisfied, and the self-aggrandizers, who find in America's open society the perfect environment to express themselves. But freedom cannot be limited to the top half of the class. The same road can lead to self-realization or self-destruction, and it is pointless to blame the road.

Immigration is America's seal of success. Forget for a moment the anointed nay-sayers, the federally funded Cassandras, the boys who pile up foundation grants by predicting the imminent demise of industrial society, the editorial writers whose status in the media depends on the quality of their pessimism, the whole my-God-we're-going-down-the-drain chorus, and remember this simple truth: This country is a success, in the same way that a Broadway show is a success. People are lined up at the box office for tickets of admission. In the Soviet Union they are lined up to get out, and if they can't buy a ticket they'll go down a fire escape or jump out the window. It is useful sometimes to remember the obvious. Svetlana Alliluyeva, Stalin's only daughter, lived in Princeton, which is roughly comparable to Margaret Truman living in a *dacha* outside Moscow. Mstislav Rostropovich, the great Russian cellist, is director of Washington's National Symphony Orchestra. Russia's two greatest male dancers, Nureyev and Baryshnikov, are dancing in New York. Solzhenitsyn, Russia's greatest living novelist, hounded out of his country, is living in Vermont. The number one Czech tennis player, Martina Navratilova, who defected in 1975, says: "Americans don't know what they've got. Anybody who complains about life here should go to a Communist country." Once that has been said, we can all go back to picking the lice out of our own hair.

The Skills Quota

I was admitted to this country in 1973 under a bill that did away with the national-origins quota system in force since 1920. Under the new system, the spouses of American citizens are given the top priority, after which there are seven preferences. Beyond these preferences, applications are handled on a first-come, first-served basis, with no one country able to receive more than 10 percent of the annual ceiling of 170,000 from the Eastern Hemisphere (Europe and Asia) and of 120,000 from the Western Hemisphere.

The new system is heavily weighted in favor of the families of American citizens, making up for some of the absurdities of the quota system, under which the daughter of American parents born in

Egypt, for instance, would have to wait for years for admission on the oversubscribed Egyptian quota. Four of the seven preferences are for the relatives of citizens and the spouses and unmarried children of resident aliens. Two others are for professionals and persons of exceptional ability in the arts and sciences, and for immigrants who can do work for which there is a shortage of available labor. Thomas Finletter, former Secretary of the Air Force, wanted to bring a Spanish maid to America. He was told that she could not qualify under the sixth preference. He made another application, specifying that the maid "must be able to entertain foreign dignitaries," and got her in. The seventh preference is for refugees, more than a million of whom have been admitted since 1965. If there are any leftover numbers, they go to "new seed" immigrants. Most immigrants today come from Mexico (more than 60,000 in 1975), followed by the Philippines (more than 30,000) and Korea (more than 25,000). The complexion of immigration has changed, away from Europe and in the direction of South America, Asia, and the Caribbean. More brown and yellow are being added to the blender.

It was John Fitzgerald Kennedy, whose great-grandfather, a farmer from County Wexford in Ireland, had come to America and worked as a cooper in East Boston, who proposed the legislation doing away with the quota system. Kennedy could not get his bill through Congress. He was fought by the chairmen of the immigration committees of both houses, Senator James O. Eastland of Mississippi and Representative Michael A. Feighan of Ohio. This was the same Feighan who in 1964 convened a subcommittee of the House Judiciary Committee to consider opposing the admission of Richard Burton to the United States. Burton at the time was playing Antony to Elizabeth Taylor's Cleopatra, off-screen as well as on. In hearings that lasted several days, Feighan tried to determine whether the moral turpitude clause applied to Burton. But he would not hold hearings on the new immigration bill.

When Kennedy was killed, supporters of the bill wondered which way Lyndon Johnson would jump. He had voted for the restrictive McCarran Act in 1950, and he had voted to override President Truman's veto. But in his State of the Union message on January 8, 1964, Johnson said: "A nation that was built by immigrants of all lands can ask those who seek new admission: what can you do for your country? But we should not be asking: in what country were you born?"

Johnson supported the bill, and with the help of his attorney general, Bobby Kennedy, got it through Congress and signed in a little less than two years. In July 1964, the House Judiciary Subcommittee on Immigration and Nationality held hearings, and Bobby Kennedy said that the present method of selecting immigrants was "a source of embarrassment to us around the world. It is a source of anguish to many of our citizens with relatives abroad."

On July 2, the day before he was due to testify, Secretary of State Dean Rusk called one of his colleagues at the State Department and expressed his misgivings about the whole thing. "I'm not inclined to testify on the immigration bill tomorrow, because I'm a reluctant witness," he said. "You don't really think we should let in people like the . . . . [fill in your least favorite people] on a world-wide competitive basis, do you? After all, we are an Anglo-Saxon country." Rusk overcame his misgivings, however, and was a persuasive witness in favor of the bill.

In February and March of 1965, further hearings were held before the Senate Judiciary Committee's Subcommittee on Immigration and Naturalization. Lovable Senator Sam J. Ervin, Jr., of North Carolina, the folk hero of the Watergate hearings, turned out to be the most stalwart defender of the McCarran Act. It's worthwhile to look at these hearings in some detail, for Ervin provided a veritable anthology of nativist thought, while the bill's supporters fell into several traps of their own making.

Attorney General Nicholas de B. Katzenbach gave examples of inequities under the quota system. A brilliant surgeon from India urgently wanted by an American hospital would have to wait for years under the tiny Indian quota of 100. A half-Chinese Colombian woman was considered to be under the Chinese quota of 105 a year and her turn would not come until the year 2047. Under the national origins system, deserving persons were kept out, while the quotas of favored countries went half-filled.

Ervin pointed out that under the new law there would be discrimination between the skilled and the unskilled.

Katzenbach: "Do you think, Senator, that a maid from Ireland really will contribute more to the United States than a trained doctor from an Asian country?"

Ervin: "Frankly, if it comes down to the choice of people from the Congo and those from Ireland, I am going to discriminate in favor of the people from Ireland because they have made the greater contribution."

Ervin had a point. Choosing only the highly qualified was just as much of a discrimination as preferring the inhabitants of Anglo-

Saxon countries. But it was a more advantageous and less racist form of discrimination.

Ervin had another point when he asked: "Do you not think the United States discriminates against the rest of the world when it seeks to take from them their brilliant people?"

Katzenbach: "We say, if they wish to come, we would like the best that you have."

Ervin: "Instead of taking those we talk about when we get oratorical, the tired and the poor and the despised, we take the brilliant . . . Now aren't we chasing ourselves around in a circle, when we send the Peace Corps abroad in order to lift those people up, and we are spending money for helping undeveloped countries, and then we admit to this country their most skilled people, aren't we leaving them in the fix from which we are trying to extricate them?"

Ervin also pointed out that the United States is the only country in the world that has developed a guilt complex over selective immigration. The other great powers, Russia and China, don't have much of an immigration problem. Their problem is getting their citizens to stay put. England keeps out members of Commonwealth countries like Jamaica, and Israel keeps out non-Jews, without agonizing over it. America admits one third of all the people in the world who change their residence, and worries about the others.

Ervin argued that the McCarran Act rightly discriminated in favor of those ethnic groups, the English and the Germans and the Scandinavians, who had done the most for America. Letting them in was a sort of gold star for past excellence. "The reason I say this bill is discriminatory against those people," he said, "is because it puts them on exactly the same plane as the people of Ethiopia are put . . . and I don't think — with all due respect to Ethiopia — I don't know of any contributions that Ethiopia has made to the making of America."

Dean Rusk: "Senator, the issue is not, as I see it, whether they come from Ethiopia, but who is the man, what is he like, what is his character, what are his capabilities, will he make a good citizen — not whether he came from Britain or Ethiopia, but what can he contribute here, and whether he would make a good citizen."

Ervin shifted his ground. There were other arguments, many of them. We must protect ourselves from overcrowding; we have many jobless and the immigrants take jobs.

Senator Hugh Scott of Pennsylvania replied that in his experience immigrants had contributed to employment through setting up new business. "As to Congressman Walter" (co-author of the McCarran Act), Scott went on, "while I ought to say de mortuis nil nisi bonum, it was always my impression that Congressman Walter did not want to admit any foreigners into this country at all if he could avoid it."

Ervin: "Do you not believe that it is much easier to assimilate into our nation people who bear a likeness to those who are here?"

Scott: "I do not know what a likeness is. Does the Senator mean two eyes, a nose, a mouth, or what other likeness does the Senator have in mind?"

Ervin: "To specify, do you not believe it is much easier to assimilate into this nation people who have, more or less, similar ideas in respect to government, and in respect to philosophy?"

Scott: "We could have said that the people who helped us from the Kingdom of Poland, including Kosciusko, did not have the same cultural background perhaps. It was a Slavic monarchy . . . I am afraid that I feel that a variety of cultural backgrounds is better for America than any attempt at a drab unitarianism."

Ervin: "I do not think by extending the provisions of this bill to people like those in the Congo we are going to get highly skilled people."

Scott: "I must say to the Senator, also having been born in the South, I marvel at his ability to retain the simplistic views of my youth."

But when Bobby Kennedy castigated the folly of a system that was excluding a Japanese microbiologist and a Greek chemist while it was letting in innumerable Northern European housemaids, he proved Ervin's point that one form of unfair selection was replacing another. The new bill was no more egalitarian than the McCarran Act, but it was more humane in that it made it much easier for the relatives of American citizens to get into the country.

A great many witnesses representing a great many groups appeared before the committee. There were ethnic groups like the Order of Ahepa (Greek), the Order of the Sons of Italy, and the Japanese American Citizens League. There were various senators representing various regions. There were spokesmen for farmers and workers, and patriotic groups, and chambers of commerce.

There was Mrs. William Henry Sullivan, Jr., president general of the Daughters of the American Revolution, who declared that 30 to 40 percent of the Iron Curtain refugees were either subversives or criminals or both. She was concerned about letting in Orientals. "The potentialities are incalculable," she said. She was concerned about "the lack of assimilability" of Mexicans, "best illustrated by the fact that the State Legislature of New Mexico is now officially bilingual." "Why should this nation subscribe to the fallacious theory that immigration is an alien's right rather than his privilege?" she asked. I was reminded of Franklin Roosevelt's celebrated speech to the DAR, ending with these words: "Remember, remember always, that all of us, and you and I especially, are descended from immigrants and revolutionists."

There was Anthony J. Celebrezze, Secretary of Health, Education, and Welfare, who was there to show Senator Ervin that not all Italians are organ-grinders. Celebrezze was one of the thirteen children of poor Italian parents, and the seventeenth member of the Cabinet to have been born on foreign shores. His parents had settled in Cleveland with many other immigrant families. "They could not even say hello in English when they came here," Celebrezze said to Ervin. "They were known as Hunkies, Dagoes, Wops and all these other names for nationalities . . . just give them some credit, Senator."

Celebrezze's father was a track walker who started out at twelve cents an hour. For forty-two years, he worked for the Wheeling & Lake Railroad. Celebrezze put himself through school and became mayor of Cleveland. "You do not contribute to America," he said, "to the good of this country, by numbers alone. One person of Polish ancestry can contribute much more in certain instances than 100 people of English origin."

Senator Ervin's views did not prevail, although with the help of his colleague Everett Dirksen of Illinois, he was able to obtain a ceiling on Western Hemisphere immigration. The wetback's best friend he was not. Both houses of the 89th Congress passed the bill, and it was voted into Public Law 89236 by President Johnson at the foot of the Statue of Liberty. The President proclaimed that it was a great humanitarian act in the best tradition of Emma Lazarus' poem. But her lines would now have to read: "Give me your doctors, your chemists, and your scientists, your huddled Ph.D.s yearning to be rich." It was a brain-snatching act, looting the developing world of its qualified people. This was a law that profoundly changed the pattern of immigration. As the attorney general suggested, there would be fewer Irish maids and more Filipino doctors. Under the quota system, Britain and Ireland and Germany had had 70 percent of the total. Under the 1965 law, no one country could claim more than 10 percent of the total. It was a law that combined an idealistic impulse with a canny awareness of national self-interest. America could skim the cream off the immigrant bucket, and be congratulated for it by the rest of the world.

Complicated Attitudes

America has always had mixed feelings about immigration. The first impulse of the pilgrims was exclusionist. They were Church of England dissidents who wanted a one-on-one relationship with God. They did not welcome outsiders who could not match their standards. They called the Quakers "a cursed set of hereticks lately risen up in the world." The Puritans were a chosen people, the original Know-Nothings. In 1636 they founded Harvard College. In 1637 they passed a law prohibiting strangers from settling in Massachusetts without permission. They believed that idle hands did the devil's work, that hard labor was rewarded by profit, that wasting time was a sin, that material success was a sign of virtue, that without an education you could not read your Bible, and that foreigners were no good.

The nonsectarian counterweight came from the Quakers. When the British Crown gave William Penn land in 1681, he proposed religious tolerance. He let in the Germans, which led to Benjamin Franklin's outburst in his "Observations Concerning the Increase of Mankind" in 1751: "Why should the Palatine Boors be suffered to swarm into our settlements, and by herding together establish their language and manners to the exclusion of ours?" Sam Ervin, shake hands with Ben Franklin.

Other settlements put up WELCOME signs like Pennsylvania, rather than KEEP OUT signs like Massachusetts. Virginia offered "head rights" of 50 acres to each settler. The first Jews arrived in New Amsterdam in 1654. The Dutch let them in. Most of them were refugees from the Spanish Inquisition who had fled to Holland and the Dutch West Indies. By 1730, they had built their first synagogue.

Another group of immigrants had arrived in 1619 in Jamestown, a swampy, mosquito-infested island in the James River in Virginia that had been settled in 1607, making it the first permanent white settlement in America. These immigrants were black and they had not come by choice. They arrived one year ahead of the *Mayflower,* and were sold not as slaves but as indentured servants. "In August," wrote Robert Beverley in his history of Virginia, "a Dutch Man of War landed Twenty Negroes for Sale; which were the first of that kind that were carried into the Country." Negroes made ideal slaves: they were in plentiful supply and easy to identify.

Enough newcomers arrived to warrant the passing of a naturalization act in England in 1740. The law provided that after seven years an immigrant could become a citizen of British America but not of England. They would be given full civil rights and usually had the right to vote and own land. Catholics were excluded. The colonies were not founded on religious freedom, quite the opposite. But by standards in Europe, where aliens could not own property and naturalization was long and costly, the 1740 act was liberal. Individual colonies expanded this liberal law to attract settlers. South Carolina offered tax exemptions to immigrants.

In 1774, however, England put a stop to naturalization, fearing that the added influx would strengthen the movement for independence. It was the start of a long habit of changing the immigration laws to suit the political climate. It was this interference by the Crown in a policy of unrestricted immigration that was condemned in the Declaration of Independence.

The relevant passage in the Declaration reads: "He (George III) has endeavored to prevent the population of these States; for that Purpose obstructing the Laws for Naturalization of Foreigners; refusing to pass others to encourage their migrations hither, and raising the conditions of new Appropriations of Lands."

There was thus a strong mandate in the Declaration of Independence for unrestricted immigration. This was only natural, since at the time of the revolution, the population of the colonies was about two million. But already, among the founding fathers, there was a dual attitude. Would it be the public park or the country club? Would it be America as a sanctuary, and a place for foreigners to make a new start? Or would it be America for members only, a land of special character that must be preserved from being spoiled by outsiders? Benjamin Franklin, who was aware of the danger, and wrote his friend Peter Collinson in 1753 that the German immigrants were "generally the most stupid of their own nation," could also write, in a more amenable mood: "The only encouragements we hold out to strangers are — a good climate, fertile soil, wholesome air and water, plenty of provisions, good pay for labor, kind neighbors, good laws, a free government, and a hearty welcome."

Jefferson saw the inconsistency of having been allowed to settle a new land and then refusing to pass on that chance to others. "Shall we refuse to the unhappy fugitive from distress," he asked, "that hospitality which the savages of the wilderness extended to our fathers arriving in this land?" But, like Franklin, he feared the danger of being overrun. He did not want immigrants in America to "warp and bias its direction, and render it a . . . distracted mass."

This was the dilemma: that it was part of America's special character to be a haven, but that by being a haven America might change beyond recognition. In theory, it was fine to let anyone in, but in practice it was dangerous. It was like some of the other principles of the founding fathers. Equal rights was a fine idea, but in American society there were groups — slaves, indentured servants, women, Catholics, Jews — who were excluded from those rights. As Dr. Johnson remarked: "How is it that we hear the loudest yelps for liberty among the drivers of Negroes?" And even forgetting those disenfranchised groups, what were equal rights but a vague promise that the state would not conspire against its citizens? As the eighteenth-century British legal theorist Sir William Blackstone put it, to say that men were equal in respect to their rights amounted "to nothing more than to the identical proposition, that all men have equal rights to their rights; for when different men have perfect and absolute rights to unequal things, they are certainly equal with regard to the perfection of their rights, or the justice that is due to their respective claims. This is the only sense in which equality can be applied to mankind. In the most perfect republic unequal industry and virtues of men must necessarily create unequal rights." In other words, it is illegal for the rich as well as the poor to ride the rails, and the deaf-mute enjoys the same First Amendment rights as Billy Graham.

In certain cases, the rights were not even equal in theory. The founding fathers limited the office of President to the native-born. Naturalized citizens could serve in every other position of government. Why not President? If Franklin Roosevelt had been born on Campobello Island in Canada, where his family spent the summers, instead of Hyde Park, he would have stayed governor of New York, according to Article II, section 1 of the Constitution, which reads in part: "No person except a natural born Citizen, or a Citizen of the United States, at the time of the adoption of this Constitution, shall be eligible to the Office of President; neither shall any Person be eligible to that Office who shall not have attained to the Age of thirty-five years, and been fourteen Years a Resident within the United States."

I asked my son Gabriel, who was born in Rome, how he felt about the matter. He said he did not want to be President because "I don't want my head chopped off." But, really, why should the office of President be any different from a cabinet post or that of a justice of the Supreme Court? In 1972, Henry Kissinger was number one in the regard of his fellow Americans, according to a Gallup Poll. He was more popular than the President. And yet the little scholar from Württemberg could not run for the highest office, not even if he went to speech class. A concerned Congressman, Jonathan Bingham of New York, introduced a constitutional amendment to repeal the native-born clause. He wasn't endorsing Henry for President, he just felt that the Kissinger case highlighted the constitutional problem. Kissinger's popularity has since dropped, and Mr. Bingham's amendment is no longer mentioned.

After the revolution, this country's first naturalization law, in 1790, encouraged immigration, but limited it to "free white persons." There was only a two-year waiting period. But even in those early days of childlike optimism, when an honest man could make a good living, and a clever man could make a fortune, there were nativist fears. When refugees from the French Revolution began arriving in substantial numbers, in 1795, the waiting period was extended to five years. That same year, George Washington, in his Thanksgiving Day proclamation, asked all Americans "to render this country more and more a safe and propitious asylum for the unfortunate of other countries."

In 1798, a Federalist Congress took advantage of anti-French hysteria to extend the residence requirement to fourteen years (you could die waiting) and to pass the Alien and Sedition Acts, which allowed the President to deport foreigners "dangerous to the peace and safety of the U.S.A." It was the first law to be directed specifically against immigrants. The immigration issue was now split along party lines. The Federalists were alarmed at the invasion. They feared that America would drown in its new blood. The Jeffersonians had faith in America's ability to sponge it up. This faith was usually expressed in do-gooder terms. "Shall oppressed humanity find no asylum on this globe?" asked President Jefferson. The truth was that America needed muscle, and that the immigrants had come to work. The word immigrant, by the way, is of American coinage. It is mentioned in Jedidah Morse's *American Geography* of 1789: "There are in this state (New York) many immigrants from Scotland, Ireland, Germany, and some from France." An English traveler in 1809 wrote that "immigrant is perhaps the only new word of which the circumstances of the United States has in any degree demanded the addition to the English language."

Returning to power, the Jeffersonian Republicans restored the five-year residence rule in 1802, and established many of the naturalization requirements that are still in force today: good moral character, attachment to the Constitution, and giving up titles of nobility among them. For much of the nineteenth century, easy immigration was the rule. It had the dual advantage of letting the nation live up to its reputation as a welcomer of refugees and of providing cheap labor for a country that needed settling.

"The happy and powerful do not go into exile," wrote de Tocqueville, "and there are no surer guarantees of equality among men than poverty and misfortune." I guess he was right in a way, and that many of these nineteenth-century immigrants were exiles from a continent where they would never be given a chance: the splitaway sects from Swedish Lutheranism, the Hungarian peasants who could do nothing about the concentration of land in the hands of the Magyars, the Norwegian small farmers whose land was subdivided by inheritance laws, the Czech farmers reduced by mortgages to the rank of laborer, the thousands expelled from Russia after the assassination of Alexander II, the wretchedly poor of Ireland and Italy. They left the real for the mythic, and a rooted past for a fluid future. They came from places where nothing would ever change. Read the German writer Peter Handke, writing in 1970, in *A Sorrow Beyond Dreams.*

"It began with my mother being born more than fifty years ago in the same village (in West Germany) where she had died. At that time all the land that was good for anything in the region belonged either to the church or to noble land-owners; part of it was leased to the population, which consisted mostly of artisans and small peasants. The general indigence was such that few peasants owned their land. For practical purposes, the conditions were the same as before 1848; serfdom had been abolished in a merely formal sense . . . Nevertheless, my grandfather's brother inherited enough money to buy a small farm. And so it came about that my grandfather was the first of his line — generations of hired men who had been born and who died in other peoples' houses and left little or no inheritance because their one and only possession, their Sunday suit, had been lowered into the grave with them — to grow up in surroundings where he could really feel at home and who was not merely tolerated in return for his daily toil." This was the simple dream of thousands who came over here: to die in one's own house.

The Builder of Bridges

Nor were all the immigrants poor and miserable and unskilled. Take John Roebling, America's greatest builder of bridges. He was born in Mühlhausen, Germany, in 1806, and attended the Royal Polytechnic Institute in Berlin, then the world's best engineering school. Hegel was one of his teachers. They became friends. Hegel told him that America "is a land of hope for all who are wearied of the historic armory of old Europe. The deepest law of politics is freedom — the open avenue to change. History is the growth of freedom, and the state is, or should be, freedom organized."

Freedom organized. It seems a paradox. Roebling listened. He was a civil engineer, working for the state. The pettiness of German officialdom was heartbreaking. Nothing could be done, he wrote in his diary, except with "an army of councilors, ministers, and other officials discussing the matter for ten years, making long journeys, and writing long reports, while the money spent in all these preliminaries comes to more than the actual accomplishment of the enterprise."

A boyhood friend who had been to America told him that the restraints of tradition did not exist there. At that time, there was a crackdown in Germany on emigration. Skilled workmen could not leave the country without a permit. One of Roebling's friends was jailed for encouraging people to leave. With the help of his brother Carl, Roebling left Germany secretly. "The decision to settle in America must come from a man's own power of will and deed," he said. "Otherwise he is not suited for America." The decision to leave was in itself an indication that one was suited to America. Those who stayed behind, unventuresome, rooted, would have adjusted with greater difficulty.

Roebling arrived in Philadelphia in 1831. He was twenty-five years old. He was not the wretched immigrant who came in steerage without funds or prospects. He had $400 in his pocket and he knew

how to build suspension bridges. The time was right. The Erie Canal
had just been opened. The first steam locomotive had made its first
run. Roebling wanted to try the life of a settler, and became a farmer
in Saxonburg, Pennsylvania. He married the daughter of a tailor,
which in Mühlhausen would have been marrying beneath him. He
called his first son Washington. In 1837, he appeared in Butler, Pennsylvania, in the Court of Common Pleas, and became a citizen.

America broadened Roebling's vision. In Germany, he had gone to
Bamberg to see a "miracle" bridge over the Regnitz, a small span
suspended from four iron chains. Here, new methods had to be
devised, for nature was on a different scale. He invented a rope made
from strands of wire, ideal to span America's wide rivers. By 1850,
Roebling had built six suspension bridges, including one at Pittsburgh over the Monongahela, and one at Cincinnati over the Ohio.
He had to fight politicians and vested interests, but he got them built.
In 1855, he built a suspension bridge over the Niagara. He spun the
cable in place so that each strand of wire carried its share of the
weight load. He kept working during a cholera epidemic, willing
himself immune. "Keep off fear," he said, "this is the great secret."
On March 16, 1855, for the first time in history, a train crossed a
bridge suspended from wire cables. It was the most talked-about
bridge in the world. The Prince of Wales, touring America in 1860,
left his parlor car to study its construction.

In 1866, New York had a memorable winter. The East River was
so choked with ice that the ferry between Manhattan and Brooklyn
was useless. A public clamor arose for a bridge. Roebling was made
chief engineer, at $8000 a year. He would build the world's greatest
bridge, with a span of nearly 1600 feet. When you plan on a grand
scale, you get problems on a grand scale. Not the petty bureaucracies
of Europe, but dishonest contractors, a shortage of public funds, and
on-the-job accidents. Sandhogs, most of them immigrants, worked in
the caissons with calcium lights, the electric light not having been
invented. They breathed compressed air and were stricken, sometimes fatally, by airsickness. Boom derricks laid the stone above the
caisson, granite from Maine and limestone from Canajoharie.

On July 6, 1869, Roebling was taking observations to determine the
location of the Brooklyn tower. He was standing on a cluster of piles
at the rack of the Fulton ferry slip. Absorbed in his work, he did not
notice a ferry crowded with passengers entering the slip. It heaved
into the fender, which was forced against the piles. Roebling's foot
was caught and crushed between the timbers. The toes of his right

foot were amputated. He contracted lockjaw. Refusing to see doctors, he prescribed his own treatment. Incapable of inactivity, he designed a device to lift him in and out of bed. Death overcomes all stubbornness, and on July 22 Roebling expired.

His son Washington finished the bridge. In 1872 he was paralyzed by what had then become known as caisson disease. But the work went on, in spite of a crooked contractor who was palming off rejected wire as good, so that whole sections had to be restrung, in spite of funds being cut off, in spite of twenty workers losing their lives. Each of the two main towers took five years to build, one to sink and fill the foundations, four to complete the masonry. The bridge was finished in 1882. It had taken thirteen years to build. With its vaults and soaring design and buttresslike webs of steel cables, it recalled the Gothic architecture of Roebling's native Mühlhausen. It had, said one of its admirers, the latent poetry of the mathematician. It was a bridge made of granite and steel and the vision of a German immigrant.

In 1931, the historical society of Mühlhausen proposed an official celebration in honor of Roebling on the 100th anniversary of his departure for America. The city fathers vetoed the project. Roebling's wire rope had been a weapon against Germany in World War I. The Roebling wire works had supplied the navy with 84 million feet of steel rope for the North Sea mine barrage, which turned that body of water into a graveyard for German submarines. The Germans admitted that Roebling's cables had netted 23 of their U-boats. Roebling was long since dead, but he could not be forgiven for the use of his invention against his own people. In Germany he was a traitor, in America he was a patriot.

The Thing and its Opposite

At about the same time that Roebling was starting to make wire rope, a Massachusetts portrait painter returning from a trip to Europe had a brainstorm. What if you sent a current of electricity through a wire so that when it reached the other end it magnetized a piece of iron, which would attract a swinging metal armature and strike with a clicking sound? With longer or shorter clicks you could send coded messages long distances. His name was Samuel Finley Breese Morse, and he was the son of the Jedidah Morse who coined the word "immigrant" in his *American Geography* of 1789. He was, of course, the inventor of the telegraph, and he built the first model on one of his portrait frames. A lot of people thought it was a crazy idea. It took years before Congress gave Morse the money to build a line between Baltimore and Washington. One of his assistants explained how it worked: "Suppose you stretch a dog from Washington to Baltimore. If you step on the dog's tail in Washington, he will yelp in Baltimore. Well, the telegraph responds in Baltimore to something done to it in Washington. However, it's a lot easier to lay a telegraph wire than to stretch a dog." On May 24, 1844, Morse sent his first clear message: "What hath God wrought?"

That was a good question, and Morse did not really know the answer, since inventions have a way of straying beyond the intentions of their makers. The true importance of the telegraph was not the singing telegram, it was not the Zimmermann telegram, it was the creation of the wire service. Until the 1830s newspapers were owned by political parties and were notable for distortion and invective. The telegraph made the wire service possible. The Associated Press was founded four years after Morse sent his first message. The AP, wishing to sell its service to the widest possible number of clients, had to provide a nonpartisan product. News as polemic was replaced by news as a commodity, to be sold by the yard, like cloth. For the wire service, reporting the news impartially was a condition of business success. Our free press owes more to technology than it does to ideals. Besides the telegraph, the Fourdrinier machine, producing paper in one continuous strip rather than in sheets, and the Hoe press, which could turn out 144,000 16-page newspapers an hour, made the large-circulation newspaper with plenty of advertising possible.

In any case, Roebling and Morse were men of similar bent, inventive, single-minded, and capable of conceiving an idea and seeing it through to its execution. But if they had met, Morse would not have liked Roebling, because he had it in for immigrants, and in fact had written a pamphlet published in 1835, entitled: *Imminent Dangers to the Free Institutions of the United States through Foreign Immigration.* Morse wanted a law passed denying immigrants the right to vote.

Morse wrote: "It is that anomalous, nondescript . . . thing, neither foreigner nor native . . . against whom I was; a naturalized foreigner, a man who from Ireland, or Germany, or France, or other foreign lands, renounces his native country and adopts America, professes to become an American, and still, being received and sworn to be a citizen, talks for example of Ireland as 'his beloved country,' resents anything said against the Irish as said against him, glories in being Irish, forms and cherishes an Irish interest, brings hither Irish local feuds, and forgets in short, all his new obligations as an American."

Samuel Morse was not an isolated crank. His views were shared by many cultivated men, who held the immigrants responsible for pauperism and crime. A deep and genuine dislike of the immigrant ran across class lines. Rural folk saw the city as a hive for the foreign-born. Workingmen saw the immigrants offering to work for less, and taking their jobs. Protestants were infuriated by the Catholics' practice of setting up their own schools.

Anti-immigrant groups were founded, among which the best-known was the Know-Nothings. Apparently its members were instructed to answer "I know nothing" when asked about their activities. The Know-Nothings became a national political party that elected six governors and 75 Congressmen in the 1854 election. Part of its platform was a 25-year residence period for naturalization. A Swiss girl in the 1850s in Missouri was taunted by Know-Nothing children on the way to school. Her name was Elise Isely. "Yoah, see the Dutch girl," they said. "Dutch is better than you," she responded. In those days, an immigrant was either Irish or Dutch. They would not let her brother draw water from the well. They beat him up and yelled "Bawl, you Dutchman, you."

When the Civil War came, there was one place where the immigrants were welcome, the army. One of the strangest chapters in the story of immigration is that of the alien just off the boat, not speaking the language, knowing nothing about the nature of the war and the issues involved, and being recruited into the Union army. There was a recruiting office across the street from Castle Garden, where immigrants landing in New York began to be processed in 1855. A poster said: "30,000 men wanted. U.S. Army. County bounty $300. U.S. bounty $300. Total bounty: $600." Thousands of immigrants were thus inducted. They would be given a land bounty if they survived the experience. The army was one of those places where the ingredients in the pot melted. Meals and haircuts and uniforms were alike; they marched in step, they fought alike and they died alike, with identical white wood crosses in military cemeteries.

The Know-Nothings had supported slavery, an issue which soon became irrelevant. The party died out. America was too complex for a party to succeed on the single issue of nativism. The government did not respond to nativist pressure. Immigrants continued to enter the country freely. The only federal regulations were the Passenger Acts concerning the health and welfare of new arrivals.

As immigrants arrived, America expanded, and the number of states was in the process of quadrupling from the original thirteen. The inland states competed for migrants, vaunting their climate, their opportunities, their political freedom, and the full rights of aliens. Nowhere on earth, said a pamphlet, could "unaided muscle" do better than in Minnesota. Missouri claimed that for $50 an immigrant could reach a state where "forty million people can subsist in plenty and comfort." Colorado called itself "the Switzerland of America," where "garden vegetables attain an enormous size." Georgia claimed that its death rate was half that of Michigan. States sent agents to Sweden and Germany to recruit some of that good Nordic stock.

The greatest lure of all was the promise of free land. To tenant farmers in Ireland or Austria-Hungary, scratching a living from a couple of acres that did not belong to them, free land meant emancipation. President Lincoln, in signing the Homestead Act on May 20, 1862, freed thousands of European serfs. The Homestead Act defined America as a country which gave away surveyed land. Circulars from the General Land Office explained how to apply. The applicant signed an affidavit before the Receiver at the Land Office that he was head of a family, over twenty-one, and that the land was for settlement and cultivation. The right of purchase was conceded to one quarter section, 160 acres, at 25 cents an acre, or a total of $40 (there are still parts of America where land is measured in sections). After five years, the homesteader had to submit "final proof" that residence and cultivation requirements had been met, and that a suitable house had been built. If the final proof was accepted, the land was his. Between 1868 and 1961 there were 1,622,107 final homesteading entries recorded by the Bureau of Land Management, for a total acreage of 270,216,874 acres. If all these homesteads were laid end to end, they would cover a strip 125 miles wide from Boston to San Francisco. America conducted the greatest land reform in history, by giving away more than 270 million acres.

The homesteading act is still in effect. From what was once a billion and a half acres of public land, about 350 million acres remain, most of it in Alaska. Land that is frozen eight months of the year, or is covered with thick stands of spruce and birch, is hardly ideal for homesteading. Half of the people who start homesteads in Alaska abandon them. The Bureau of Land Management tells applicants to think long and hard before moving there. But the dream of free land, the actualization of myth, can still, in principle, be realized.

America was the sum of and the tension between the often contradictory experiences of the settlers. America was the contrapuntal march, the yin and the yang of hope and disappointment, the cluster of opposites that somehow interlocked to make a civilization. The arriving immigrants had this in common: they were starting at the bottom of the ladder. Often they did not know the language. They were easy to cheat. They thought they were in Eden, bit the apple, and tasted failure. It was a way of discovering one's true worth.

Their experiences could be summed up as a series of paired opposites, such as the square deal against the raw deal. In America you could believe what you were told and expect fairness. The "Sloopers," the Quakers of Southwestern Norway who migrated in the 1820s for religious reasons, were fined $3150 on arrival in New York harbor on October 9, 1825, for violating a federal law that permitted only two passengers for every five tons of a vessel. They were so obviously well intentioned, however, that a month later they were pardoned by the President himself, John Quincy Adams, and went upstate to found a settlement. But where there was free land there was speculation, so that America was also a country where you could be bilked outrageously. Dickens had Martin Chuzzlewit buy a tract of land called Eden and arrive to find he had been sold a piece of Illinois swampland.

There was the language problem. "Our son attends the English school and talks English as well as the native born," wrote one of the Sloopers who founded the Kendall settlement on Lake Ontario, 35 miles from Rochester. The foreign tongue was like a girdled tree. The words withered and dropped away. But in other cases the foreign tongue was like part of one's anatomy, and could not be severed. A Polish immigrant went to Montana as part of a section gang rebuilding tracks for the Great Northern Railroad. Ten years later he still expressed old-country thoughts in his old-country language.

There was the matter of principles as they are enunciated in the Constitution and carried out in practical politics. "The vote of the common man," another Kendall settler wrote, "carries just as much authority and influence as that of rich and powerful men." But this touching faith in one man, one vote, was being laid to rest by other immigrants in large cities. "Stand together," Tamanend, the Delaware Indian chief who became the patron saint of Tammany Hall, is purported to have told his tribe, "and you will be a mountain." Tammany bosses made naturalization a tool of machine politics. They were the new autocrats, who knew how to exploit an open society, the men who have the inside track, who use free enterprise as a permit to plunder, who exploit the absence of regulation intended to give greater freedom to honest folk. Two New York judges once naturalized 1147 immigrants in 23 days, which qualified them to vote. Boss Richard Croker boasted of having voted seventeen times for a constable in Brooklyn, "so enamored was I with participating in the democratic process." Boss Tweed argued that America's diversity made dishonest practices necessary. "This population is too hopelessly split into races and factions," he said, "to govern it under universal suffrage, except by bribery or patronage." The immigrant who had fled the corrupt aristocracy of the Old World was welcomed by the corrupt bosses of the New. The struggle continues between the poor slob with his single vote and the new autocrats with their powerful apparatus to steal an election or otherwise fix things. There is so much freedom in this country that we don't always recognize the latest shape that the autocrats have taken (industrial polluters of rivers, fixers of prices, sponsors of new weapons systems that will never see the day, Medicaid "ping-pong" specialists, are among a few of the recent incarnations of the type).

Abundance and scarcity was another set of opposites. "The United States owns an untold amount of land which is reserved by law at a set price for the one who first buys it from the government," one immigrant wrote home. But another found that it filled up fast: by 1838, "there is now no more land to be had in the entire state (Illinois), and therefore we must move Southwest to Missouri. Land can still be bought there at Congress prices."

Slowly they were learning. The mist of a virtuous nation was burning off. "Nobody here can take anything away from you by force," said a letter home, "but he can do this by cunning, power of money, and forestallment." There were no privileged classes, but power of money could work wonders.

Another pair of opposites was sedentary-migratory. There was no place like home, but it was always being left behind. If you could see your neighbor's chimney, it was time to move on. People moved west, grew prosperous, and their grandchildren went back east to Ivy League schools. Listen once again to Stephen Vincent Benét's prelude to "Western Star":

Americans are always moving on.
It's an old Spanish custom gone astray,
A sort of English fever I believe,
Or just a mere desire to take French leave,
I couldn't say. I really couldn't say.
But when the whistle blows, they go away.

The immigrants could say. They moved on, not because they were rovers, but to look for better land. "The poor method of building," wrote one, "comes from the American's bent and necessity to move from one place to another. When a person has got a piece of land cultivated enough so that he can earn a little from it, he sells it and begins on a new place. Fear of loss has in this way made it necessary to build simply."

There were just as many who didn't move because they were on to a good thing. The price of wheat soared during the Civil War, and made immigrant farmers rich. They moved their families from log cabins to frame houses. "Here you can work ahead to success and get to own a good deal of property, even though you did not have a penny to begin with," a successful farmer wrote.

By 1860, the first year the census distinguished between native and foreign-born Americans, the population was 31,500,000, including 4,136,000 foreign-born, who were spread out everywhere, doing everything: Irishmen digging a canal from the Mississippi to Lake Pontchartrain, Italians in the mines of Calumet, Michigan, Welshmen laying the tracks of the Santa Fe Railroad; and farmers — Sloopers in Wisconsin, Scotch Presbyterians in the Carolina Piedmont, German Mennonites in Pennsylvania, Italian Waldensians in New York. There were still waves of political refugees, like the German Forty-eighters, but there were just as many who came out of a practical desire for well-being.

In certain immigrants there was a yeasty quality that made them rise. Carl Schurz came to America in 1851. He supported Lincoln for the presidency, going on a 21,000-mile speaking tour to win the German vote. He fought in the Civil War and attained the rank of major general, and was elected Senator from Missouri in 1869. He later became Secretary of the Interior, and editor of the New York *Evening Post*. Where else would such a meteoric career have been possible? It was possible because the German community resisted assimilation and could only be reached by one of their own. They had come to Germanize America with kindergartens, singing societies, and sauerkraut.

Migrants and Feds

By 1850, Clyde-built iron-screw steamers like the *City of Glasgow* and the *City of Manchester* were making the Atlantic crossing in ten or fifteen days, and charging eight pounds fifteen shillings for steerage to New York. Improved transportation brought increased immigration. An organized processing of the daily influx became necessary. There was a round stone building at the tip of the Battery that looked like a Spanish bullfight arena. It had been built as Fort Clinton to defend Manhattan in the War of 1812. In 1823, it had been renamed Castle Garden and used as a concert hall. Daniel Webster gave speeches there. Morse's telegraph was demonstrated there. Jenny Lind sang there, and gave her $10,000 fee to charity. Castle Garden's longest-running act, the processing of immigrants, opened in 1855.

Between 1855 and 1890, when it closed down, only to reopen a few years later as an aquarium, the Castle Garden depot processed 8,280,917 immigrants. They were brought from the ship's dock to the depot along a narrow gangway. The idea was to get them out fast and on their way inland. The process was as follows: medical check, baggage check, money check, destination check, and mandatory bath with soap and towels in a communal tub. Thus cleansed and checked, they were ready to greet the new world. Their first experience was usually with crooked runners who tried to sell them a counterfeit train ticket or a nonexistent hotel room. The runners spoke the language of the immigrants. The first lesson the immigrants learned was that in America they would be cheated by their own.

Made uneasy by the truly monumental scale of arrivals, the federal government timidly got into the act. In 1875, a federal regulation banned criminals and prostitutes. In 1881, the Chinese Exclusion Act was voted. In 1882 it was the turn of "any convict, lunatic, idiot, or any person unable to take care of himself or herself without becoming a public charge." In 1885 contract labor was banned. In 1888, the terms of exclusion were made to include "undesirable aliens," which could cover a multitude of sins.

A new wave of xenophobia, based on the theory that the current wave of migrants from Eastern Europe and the Mediterranean was far more dangerous than the Irish and Germans, was expressed by a Protestant clergyman from Pennsylvania in 1888: "I have stood near Castle Garden and seen races of far greater peril to us than the Irish. I have seen the Hungarians and the Italians and the Poles. I have seen these poor wretches trooping out, wretches physically, wretches morally, and stood there almost trembling for my country, and said, what shall we do if this keeps going on?"

Among the wretches that the Pennsylvania clergyman could have spotted as he stood near Castle Garden watching them make their first steps in the new land were the following, who provided from immigrant backgrounds contrasting experiences: Edward Bok, Achille and Irene LaGuardia, and Emma Goldman.

The Algerization of Edward Bok

Edward Bok's life is too good to be true. It has the simplistic virtue of a fable. He happens to be real, but he could just as easily join the list of Horatio Alger heroes like Tom the Bootblack and Ragged Dick. Bok was six when he passed through Castle Garden in 1870 with his parents, who had come from Den Helder, Holland. He spent the next twenty years of his life in Brooklyn. He dropped out of school at the age of thirteen to contribute to the family kitty and went to work at Western Union at $6.25 a week. He saved his lunch money and walked five miles to work so that he could buy Appleton's *Encyclopedia,* where he read about successful men and was inspired by the discovery that some had had beginnings as humble as his own.

Bok decided to test the accuracy of the biographies. He wrote James A. Garfield, a Congressman who was being mentioned for the presidency, and asked whether it was true that he had once been a boy on the towpath. Garfield replied that it was. Elected officials feel that it is part of their duty to answer the letters of children who may one day grow up to be voters. Bok showed Garfield's letter to his father, who told him to hang on to it because it might be worth something someday. The wheels in Bok's teen-age mind began turning. If one letter was worth something, what would one hundred be worth? He had made, at the tender age of thirteen, the move that is essential in a capitalist society, from disinterested enthusiasm to an entrepreneurial mentality. He now wrote letters to the famous not only because he wanted to learn, but because he wanted to profit. He became a celebrity hound. He would find out where important men were staying and pursue them in their hotel rooms. He went to see Jefferson Davis at the Metropolitan Hotel, and Davis promised to get him a letter written by each surviving member of the Confederate cabinet. He went to Boston to see Oliver Wendell Holmes, who gave him an inscribed set of his poems and a letter of introduction to Longfellow. Longfellow told him how he came to write "Excelsior." Tennyson wrote out a stanza or two of "The Brook," on condition that Bok never use the word "awful," which the poet said was slang for "very." "I hate slang," Tennyson told him. Bok prevailed upon General Grant to sketch on an improvised map the exact spot where General Lee had surrendered. He had such an impressive collection of letters that he was interviewed by the Brooklyn *Eagle*.

Bok took a course in shorthand at the YMCA, and learned the art of "pothooks." The course paid off. In 1880, when he was sixteen, the Brooklyn *Eagle* assigned him to cover a political dinner at which President Rutherford B. Hayes was speaking. Bok had been instructed to take the speech down verbatim, but Hayes spoke too fast. Bok had the wine glasses removed from his place. He wanted to concentrate on the speech.

After the speech, Bok went up to the President, explaining that he was on his first assignment, and asked for a copy of the text so that he could beat his competition. Hayes told him to wait, and was back in fifteen minutes. "Tell me, boy, why did you have the wine glasses removed from your place?" he asked. The President had seen the gesture as proof of sterling qualities. Bok explained that he could write faster that way. Hayes reached for a place card and said: "Suppose you write your name and address on this card for me.

"Now I am stopping with Mr. A. A. Low on Columbia Heights," Hayes went on. "Is that in the direction of your home?"

Bok assented vigorously, although it was not.

"Suppose you go with me, then," Hayes said, "in my carriage, and I will give you my speech." Hayes gave Bok his handwritten copy.

The next day, a note arrived for Bok at his home. "My dear young friend," it said, "I have been telling Mrs. Hayes this morning of what you told me at the dinner last evening, and she was very much interested. She would like to meet you, and joins me in asking if you will call upon us at 8:30. Very faithfully, Rutherford B. Hayes."

When Bok got there, the butler said to the sixteen-year-old immigrant: "The President and Mrs. Hayes are waiting for you." Those were words to make one giddy. The story is pure American myth — the accessibility of powerful men, virtue and determination rewarded, the highest elected official taking interest in a humble non-voter. It also happens to be true. Bok and Hayes continued to exchange letters, and remained friends.

Bok noticed that women were restless during theater intermissions. He published a program. He published the *Brooklyn Magazine*, which later became *Cosmopolitan*. He launched a syndicate. He went to work for Scribner's. In his autobiography, written in the third person, he said that "he found every avenue leading to success wide open and certainly not overpeopled . . . it was not long before Bok discovered that the possession of sheer merit was the only real factor that actually counted."

On a trip to Philadelphia, Bok met Cyrus H. K. Curtis, the owner and publisher of the *Ladies' Home Journal*. Curtis told Bok he was looking for an editor and asked him whether he knew of any. "Are you talking at me or through me?" Bok asked. "Both," Curtis replied. Bok left New York in 1889 for Philadelphia, against the advice of his friends, who said he would be buried there. He reasoned that cream rises to the top anywhere. In 1896, after a four-year engagement, he married the boss's only child, Mary Louise Curtis. Bok seems to have thought that the boss's daughter went with the job. One searches his autobiography in vain for a word about his feelings. In his laconic Dutch way, he sums up the romance like this: "He had now turned instinctively to the making of a home for himself."

Bok remained editor of the *Ladies' Home Journal* for thirty years, and raised the magazine's circulation first to a million, then to two million. For years, he fought a crusade against patent medicines. He made the makers of Mrs. Winslow's Soothing Syrup admit that there was morphine in it. He published the names of 27 medicines with their ingredients, which included opium and digitalis. He published an ad saying, "Mrs. Pinkham is able to do more for the ailing woman in America than the family physician," next to a photograph of Mrs. Pinkham's tomb in Lynn.

He was a great magazine editor in an age when magazines counted, and yet there is something disappointing about Edward Bok's career. He did not live up to his youthful exploits. At some point in his life, he ceased to be adventurous, and settled comfortably in his editorship. He continued to be exactly what he had been as a boy — someone who knew great men.

The Triumph of the Hybrid

Baron von Hubner, of the Austrian foreign service, visited America in the 1870s and subsequently wrote that he had met Italian peddlers from Turin in the Pacific states. Their original plan had been to make money and go home. They made money and went home, but they came back to California. America did that to immigrants. It made them outsiders in their own country. "You see," the peddlers explained to von Hubner, "in Europe we can't associate with the gentry and we can't live with our equals above whom we have unconsciously raised ourselves. We feel therefore like fish out of water, and so, we give up the dream of living in our native land and return to America."

Among the tens of thousands of Italian immigrants who came through Castle Garden in the 1880s were Achille Luigi and Irene LaGuardia. Achille Luigi was a successful musician who had first visited America in 1878 as the accompanist for the great singer Adelina Patti. He liked what he saw, and decided to settle there, returning two years later with his wife Irene. She came from a Jewish family named Coen who were merchants in Trieste. In 1882 she gave birth to a son who was named Fiorello.

Fiorello LaGuardia was not, technically speaking, an immigrant. He was born in New York. When he was sixteen, however, his parents took him back to Italy, and it was by choice that he returned to America. He was the outsider, the foreigner trying to make a place for himself. His career as a congressman and as New York City's greatest mayor was a running battle against vested interests.

LaGuardia was the marginal man, who lives on the edge of many cultures. He could no more identify with old American stock than he could identify with a single ethnic group. He was half Italian and half Jewish, and worshiped as an Episcopalian. He summed up in his background the ethnic diversity of the city he would one day govern.

Edward Bok believed in the open society which made a place for deserving young immigrants. It did not occur to him to question the principles of the politicians whose autographs he collected. He was an Uncle Tom of immigrants. He did not rock the boat because he had been given a berth on it. LaGuardia's way was to rise within the system by combating its injustices. He was a reformer by instinct, but also because he was an immigrant determined to command respect, a new boy who would not give in to bullying. Edward Bok concentrated on his own success. The fact that he could make it was proof that the system worked. LaGuardia somehow developed a social conscience. He saw his own rise in the context of what he could do for those who were being exploited by special interest groups. He was compulsively ambitious, but he was equally compulsive in his need to serve.

When Fiorello was three, his father joined the army as a bandmaster. He was the leader of the 11th U.S. Infantry Band in Whipple Barracks, near Prescott, in the Arizona territory. Fiorello grew up as an army brat. Instead of living in the East Side Italian ghetto of New York, he lived amid the scenic beauty of the sparsely settled Southwest. His landmarks were not Mott Street and the Bowery, but Thumb Butte, Point of Rocks, Granite Hell.

You did not have to live on the lower East Side to meet social injustice. It was just as apparent in a frontier town. LaGuardia's loathing for professional politicians originated with the patronage-appointed Indian agents he saw in Arizona. These rural ward heelers were paid by Washington to feed the Indians, and raked off part of the funds. He saw his father's regiment protecting the property of the Acheson & Topeka Railroad during a Pullman strike. Why, he wondered, was the army siding with the employer against the workers?

One day an Italian organ-grinder with a monkey came to Prescott. Fiorello and some school friends saw the man. "Hey," the friends said, "a dago with a monkey. Hey, Fiorello, you're a dago too. Where's your monkey?" Fiorello's shame was profound. It was compounded when his father came along and started chatting Neapolitan with the man, and asked him home for one of his mother's famous macaroni dinners. Fiorello saw the organ-grinder as one of several disreputable Italian stereotypes. They were unassimilated ethnics, whose success was predicated upon emphasizing their separateness from other Americans.

One of LaGuardia's first acts as mayor of New York was to ban organ-grinders from the city streets as nuisances to traffic. Cornelia Otis Skinner wrote him a letter saying that he had no soul and that she would not vote for him again. She did not realize, LaGuardia replied, that the organ-grinder's instrument was rented from a padrone at exorbitant fees.

Corrupt contractors supplied the army with diseased meat, known in the trade as "embalmed beef." The meat made Fiorello's father so ill that he had to be discharged for "disease of the stomach and bowels, catarrh of head and throat, and malarial poisoning." The family returned to Trieste in 1898 and lived on his father's meager pension. In 1901 his father died. Fiorello was convinced that it was the meat. The American government would not give his mother a pension because she could not prove that her husband's death had been caused by a service-incurred disability. When Fiorello became the first Italian-American to serve in Congress, he introduced a bill in 1917 providing the death sentence for contractors who supplied defective food or equipment in wartime. The bill died in committee.

Fiorello got a job as clerk in the American consulate in Budapest. He was useful because he was multilingual. The consul, Frank Dyer Chester, was a Harvard-educated Boston snob. He told LaGuardia that because he had not gone to Harvard he would never rise above clerk. When he introduced Fiorello he said: "This is our amanuensis." It was an opportunity to show off his Harvard education.

Fiorello was promoted to consular agent in Fiume, at the age of twenty-one. Two thousand emigrants were departing the Austro-Hungarian empire from Fiume every two weeks via the Cunard and Adria lines. LaGuardia decided that it made more sense to hold the medical examination at the port of embarkation than to have people turned back at Ellis Island. The shipping people had to comply. If they didn't, he would not sign the Bill of Health they needed when they landed in New York.

The sight of emigrants embarking in steerage was an amusing spectacle for visitors of high rank, who were given passes to watch them from the first-class deck. In the spring of 1904, Archduchess Maria Josefa of Austria visited Fiume. About 500 emigrants were waiting to sail aboard the S.S. *Panonia*. The city authorities decided to have them board even though the ship was not due to sail for three days. The sight of these creatures trudging up the gangplank dragging their luggage and their children would entertain the Archduchess. The emigrants could not board without LaGuardia's Bill of Health, which LaGuardia refused to sign. He would not allow them to be herded into steerage three days before sailing time for a frivolous reason. Fiorello was already playing his assigned role: defender of the people against special interests.

There was no future for him in the consular service. He had offended too many people. "Look here, Mother," he said in 1906, "I'm going back to America to become a lawyer and make something of myself." He worked as an interpreter at Ellis Island and went to law school nights.

He hung out his shingle as Fiorello H. LaGuardia. The H. was for Henry, the Americanization of his middle name, Enrico. LaGuardia saw that the way for his clients to stay out of jail was to bribe Tammany appointees. Machine politics had become a special branch of laissez-faire capitalism. In New York the machine was Democratic. It was so powerful that the cartoonist Thomas Nast portrayed it as a tiger. Fiorello became a Republican. He read the *Congressional Record* and legislative history. He wanted to be a congressman so badly it hurt. He was an election district captain and hung around the 25th Assembly district. In the late summer of 1914 the boys were filling in the printed petitions for the nominations for Congress. Someone shouted: "Who is the candidate for Congress?" The district leader echoed from his backroom office: "Who wants to run for Congress?" It didn't matter who it was. The Republicans had never elected a congressman in that heavily immigrant district. "I do," LaGuardia said. "O.K.," the district leader said, "put LaGuardia down." Destiny never took a more casual turn. The man filling in the blank said, "Hey, LaGuardia, what's your first name?" "Fiorello." "Aw, hell, let's get someone whose name we can spell." LaGuardia told him how to spell it.

He ran against Michael Farley, a saloonkeeper who was president of the National Liquor Dealers Association. Not only was he not a good congressman, LaGuardia said, he wasn't even a good bartender. Farley was re-elected by a small margin. Fiorello ran again in 1916. He covered every street corner in his secondhand Ford, dismembering the Hapsburg empire on the East Side and recounting the history of Ireland on the West Side. He won by 357 votes. It was the first time a Republican had been elected to Congress from below 14th Street since the foundation of the Grand Old Party.

In 1916 Woodrow Wilson was re-elected with a "he kept us out of the war" campaign, and a year later he put America in the war. LaGuardia enlisted as a Signal Corps pilot and bombed an Austrian aviation camp. He reached the rank of major. After that, he always wanted to be called Major.

LaGuardia remained in the House for fourteen years. He felt comfortable in an adversary role. He was a Republican who sniped at his party. He was a lawyer who called lawyers "semi-colon boys who have retarded civilization more than cancer and smallpox combined." He viewed history as a succession of crooked deals, a reenactment of his father being poisoned by tainted meat. Alexander Hamilton was the villain of America's infancy, who had redeemed the Continental currency at par and cut himself in on the deal. Henry Clay was no better, and Daniel Webster was paid hard cash for introducing legislation. He knew the inside stories of railroad scandals and hated lobbyists who were "pimps for Wall Street." He bubbled along in a permanent state of moral outrage. His great enemy was Treasury Secretary Andrew Mellon. Fiorello called for Mellon's impeachment on the grounds that there was a conflict of interest with his directorship of companies. Herbert Hoover appointed Mellon ambassador to England. In her reminiscences, Fiorello's wife wrote of her husband: "It was like he owned the United States. Nobody should do anything to it."

Franklin Roosevelt's 1932 victory affected Fiorello in two ways. He lost his congressional seat, but Jimmy Walker, under investigation for corruption by the new administration, resigned as mayor of New York City. There was an election in 1933 and LaGuardia won. He was sworn in as the 99th mayor of New York on January 1, 1934, and remained in office for twelve years. The first thing he did was order the arrest of a fellow Italian, Lucky Luciano. The beauty of LaGuardia, this fat, jowly, messy, five-foot-two man with the ridiculous black Stetson, was that he had ties to all groups but belonged to none. He spoke seven languages and used them all. His enemies called him "a half-Jewish wop." His was the triumph of the hybrid. New Yorkers could recognize themselves in him. He had their sense of humor based on irreverence. When Cuban dictator Fulgencio Batista arrived, LaGuardia met him at the airport with the words: "Hi, Sergeant, have a good five-cent cigar." He had their resourcefulness that borders on sharp practice, as when he dealt with the women laundry workers' strike. The laundry owners wanted the city to remain neutral. Fiorello asked them to make the request in writing. When he got it he announced that the application for municipal neutrality had been granted, and that, as a first sign of it, the Water Commissioner would turn off the water in all the laundries. The ladies got their raise. He had the New Yorker's manic energy and flamboyance, racing his firemen to fires, taking Toscanini's place on the podium of the New York Philharmonic, reading "Dick Tracy" over the radio during a strike of newspaper delivery men, asking kids whose fathers bet on the horses to snitch on them, banning the sale of dirty magazines under the "power of sewage," and waiting for his legend to catch up with him.

He wasn't just a comic opera mayor. He did the things mayors are supposed to do; he added parks, highways, and subways, put the poor on relief, created jobs, and built low-rent housing. But there was a special quality to life in New York when he was mayor. He brought fervor to government. He did not want to run for a fourth term in 1945, and William O'Dwyer was elected. New York went back to its sleazy ways. LaGuardia's life was spent. On the morning of September 20, 1947, the number five bell rang four times on the signal system of the New York City Fire Department. This is the traditional announcement of mourning that marks the passing of a fireman in the line of duty or an important city official. LaGuardia was dead at sixty-four. Forty-five thousand New Yorkers walked by his bier in St. John the Divine Cathedral. Nine thousand five hundred persons attended his funeral service. One thousand seats were reserved for close friends, diplomats, and city, state, and federal officials. The other eight thousand five hundred were for ordinary people.

The Americanization of Emma Goldman

Emma Goldman, another Castle Garden immigrant of the 1880s, gained some prominence in her devotion to the cause of anarchy. As Edward Bok is an example of working with the grain of the system, and LaGuardia is an example of working against it, Emma Goldman is an example of working outside the system. Arrest and jail were her occupational hazards, and she was eventually deported.

It was in Lenin's Russia that she came to regret the freedom she had enjoyed in America. She also regretted her notoriety as Queen of the Anarchists. In America she had made a career out of denouncing the system that allowed her to operate. In spite of police harassment, she functioned for a quarter of a century as a professional revolutionary, and made ample use of her First Amendment rights. Russia was unbearable because there was no opposition role to fill. She was relegated to the anonymous masses.

Emma Goldman came to America from Russia in 1885, and went to Rochester. In 1889, when she was twenty, she moved to New York. She had five dollars and a sewing machine. She became the mistress of Alexander ("Sasha") Berkman, who in 1892 shot but did not kill the distinguished captain of industry, Henry Clay Frick. A symbol of capitalism's excesses, Frick, the Coke King, had built a palace on Fifth Avenue, where, flanked by a Van Dyck and a Rembrandt, he sat on a Renaissance throne reading the *Saturday Evening Post* while his private organist played "Silver Threads Among the Gold." Berkman wanted to kill Frick as Charlotte Corday had killed Marat, to put an end to ostentatious tyranny, but he was less successful, not having caught Frick in his bath. He was sentenced to a 21-year prison term, of which he served fourteen.

Emma became a militant. She was good copy, a city editor's dream. The newspapers dubbed her Red Emma. She was one of the media creations of the 1890s. The police began to attend her lectures. In 1893 she made an inflammatory speech to striking New York garment workers and was convicted of "inciting to riot and unlawful assembly." She was sentenced to a year in jail on Blackwell's Island. When she was released she resumed her political activities. Her life from then on would mingle the lecture circuit and the arrest circuit. Emma spoke across the country, arousing secret sympathies. In those days there were anarchist cells in most large cities. She talked about injustice, and police violence, and the true despotism of republican institutions. But when she was arrested, she was acquitted in the courts.

On September 6, 1901, an anarchist named Leon Czolgosz stood in a line to meet President William McKinley, with a gun wrapped in a handkerchief in his hand. His turn came and he shot the President, who died eight days later. McKinley was the second president to be assassinated by a lunatic with a foreign name. The first was Edward Bok's hero, James Garfield, on July 2, 1881, four months after taking office, who was shot as he was boarding a train to attend commencement exercises at Williams College by Charles J. Guiteau, a disgruntled office-seeker. Czolgosz, before being put to death in the electric chair on October 29, 1901, said that Emma had incited him. Emma had never met him, and no evidence was ever found to connect her with him, but the press said that she was the woman behind the man behind the gun. Emma sought out unpopular causes. She defended the assassin in her speeches.

After McKinley's death, a new immigration law was passed, in 1903, adding anarchists to the list of the proscribed. Emma could flatter herself that she had contributed to an important piece of legislation. She could not have done a better job if she had been hired by the anti-immigration lobby. The new law excluded "persons who believe or advocate the overthrow by force or violence of the government of the United States, or of all governments, or of all forms of law, or the assassination of public officials." It was the law under which Emma would herself be deported. Anarchists were unpopular. Senator Hawley said he would pay $1000 for a shot at one. A cartoon showed Uncle Sam looking at German nihilists and Russian anarchists parading in the streets of New York and saying: "The American nation, a pretty darned crew." Emma had to adopt an assumed name, Miss E. G. Smith. No landlord would rent a room to Red Emma. She wanted to work as a nurse, but no doctor would hire Red Emma.

As Miss E. G. Smith, she nursed a woman who said to her son, "If I got hold of Red Emma I would soak her in kerosene and burn her alive." The woman told her son: "Miss Smith is a wonderful nurse." "Do you know who she really is?" the son asked. "It's the terrible Emma Goldman." "My God," the woman cried, "I hope you have not told her what I said about her." The son admitted that he had. "And she nursed me so fine? Oi, a wonderful nurse."

Emma lectured in Chicago on conditions in czarist Russia. The police attended but did not interfere. "We believe in freedom of speech as long as Emma Goldman talks about Russia," they said. At the railroad station in Chicago, she was arrested with her lover, Ben Reitman. "On what grounds were we arrested?" she asked. "Just on general principle," the desk sergeant said. "Your principles are rotten," Emma said. "Go on, now," said the desk sergeant, "you're Red Emma, ain't you? That's enough." Being Emma's lover took courage. In San Diego, Ben Reitman was tarred and feathered. At some gatherings when Emma spoke, there were more policemen than civilians. She always carried a book in her purse in case she should have to spend the night in jail.

At a meeting in San Francisco in 1907, she spoke on patriotism. "Leo Tolstoi, the greatest anti-patriot of our times," she said, "defined patriotism as the principle that justifies the training of wholesale murderers." After the talk, people threw their hats in the air, stamped their feet, and yelled. A soldier in uniform came up and shook her hand. Detectives followed the soldier to his barracks and reported him to the military authorities. His name was William Buwalda and he was placed under arrest to await court-martial. Emma organized a committee for Buwalda's defense, which probably aggravated his situation. Buwalda was a career soldier, who had already served fifteen years. His record was spotless. General Funston, who served on the court-martial board, described his crime as having "attended Emma Goldman's meeting in uniform, applauding her speech, and shaking hands with that dangerous anarchist woman." It must have been serious, for Buwalda was sentenced to five years in Alcatraz.

When asked at his court-martial what Emma had done for him, Buwalda replied: "She has made me think." Theodore Roosevelt pardoned him. It was clear to this man of common sense that five years in jail for a handshake was a little expensive.

Emma toured America, preaching anarchy. In one month she was stopped by the police in eleven different places. When she lectured on Ibsen as part of a series on drama, members of the Anarchist Squad were there. They told her to stick to the subject, and when she did not they emptied the hall by pulling the chairs out from under the audience.

Emma was a feminist, but she argued that woman's inhumanity to man keeps him what he is. "The inconsistencies of my sex," she wrote, "keep the poor male dangling between the idol and the brute, the darling and the beast, the helpless child and the conqueror of worlds."

She was always in the lion's den, talking atheism to theologians and birth control to orthodox Jews. Wherever there was an arena, she jumped in. Margaret Sanger had been arrested. She had been tricked by a woman detective posing as a mother of four. It is amazing to think that sixty years ago you could go to jail for giving someone a contraceptive. Emma lectured on birth control and was arrested. She took her own defense at her trial and turned it into a forum. Judge O'Keefe sentenced her to a $100 fine or fifteen days in the workhouse. She chose the workhouse.

Emma had a true gift for embracing unpopular causes. In 1917 she spoke out against conscription, which was not a good idea just as America was entering the war. A Selective Service Act had been passed and declared constitutional. Emma was convicted of violating that law and was sentenced to two years in jail and a $10,000 fine. The judge recommended that she and her lover, Berkman, who had served his sentence for the Frick shooting and been released in 1906, be deported. Emma was sent to Missouri State Prison in Jefferson City.

"Any disease?" the head matron asked her.

"No complaints," she replied, "except that I need a bath and a cold drink."

"Don't be impudent and pretend you don't know what I mean,"

the matron said. "I mean the disease immoral women have. Most of those delivered here have it."

"Venereal disease is not particular whom it strikes," Emma said. "The most respectable people have been known to be victims of it. I don't happen to have it, which is due perhaps more to luck than to virtue."

Emma spent her fiftieth birthday, June 27, 1919, in the Missouri jail. "I felt as if I had five hundred on my back," she said. With time off for good behavior, she served 20 months, and was released in August 1919. She went straight from jail to her deportation hearing, where immigration officials sat behind desks piled high with anarchist publications and transcripts of her speeches. A new and more stringent alien-expulsion law had been passed in 1918, calling for the "exclusion and expulsion of all U.S. aliens who are members of the anarchistic and similar classes."

Emma's deportation occurred in the context of a curious example of collective hysteria that became known as the "red scare." In May 1919, sixteen packages were intercepted by a vigilant New York mail clerk, not because they looked suspicious but because they were short on stamps. They were sent to the Short Payment Division in the basement of the main Post Office Building. One undetected package, however, reached its destination. It arrived at the home of ex-Senator Thomas R. Hardwick of Georgia, who, as chairman of the Senate Committee on Immigration, had proposed restrictions to keep out Bolsheviks.

Opened by a black maid, it exploded, blowing off both her hands and severely injuring Mrs. Hardwick, who was standing nearby. Attention focused on the packages in the Short Payment Division, which also turned out to be bombs, addressed to prominent politicians and businessmen. It was right out of the gang that couldn't shoot straight. The terrorists who made the bombs did not put enough stamps on the packages and did not stop to think that the powerful men they wanted to kill never opened their own mail.

Only one bomb had exploded, but the newspapers turned the story into a national disaster. "A desperate band of anarchists who would stop at nothing" was at work. The bomb squad was investigating "sleeplessly." It was a "gigantic conspiracy." "The net was tightening." On June 3, there were more explosions in seven cities. A bomb went off in front of the residence of Judge Charles C. Nott in New York, and a watchman was killed. In Washington, a bomb exploded in front of the residence of Attorney General A. Mitchell Palmer.

Pent-up nativist fears were released. It was one year after the end of World War I, the first time in history that Americans had fought on European soil. Part of the backlash of the war was this kind of thinking: not only does Europe send us its social dregs, but when they start a war we have to bail them out. World War I was the end of the illusion that America could remain aloof from the affairs of Europe, that there was a real break between the Old World and the New. It was the beginning of the end of American innocence. Not only that, but in 1917 the Russian czar had been overthrown and the Bolsheviks had come to power. They had withdrawn Russian armies from the war. We, the Americans, were sending men thousands of miles to fight for Europe, and the Russians, with the war on their doorstep, were backing off. And these same Reds who wanted us to fight their war were agitating in America and throwing bombs. The nation's diffuse resentment, the feeling that America was no longer a refuge from the turmoil of Europe, focused on the "red agitators." With the press milking the story, it became plausible to believe that there were anarchists everywhere, that foreigners were reds and reds were terrorists. They had to be stopped.

The man who championed these fears was Attorney General A. Mitchell Palmer, "the Fighting Quaker." On June 12, 1919, in a speech asking Congress for appropriations to deal with the red menace, he warned that these same "wild fellows" would try to destroy the government "at one fell swoop." As the Baltimore *Sun* noted, Palmer seemed to scent "a Bolshevist plot in every item of the day's news." Congress gave Palmer $2,600,000 for his anti-red crusade, and he hired a private detective named William J. Flynn as his anarchist expert. Palmer and Flynn would demonstrate that our liberties are threatened not by those who oppose them but by those who, pretending to uphold them, disregard them in the name of some higher principle.

This was no longer a matter of closing the door on immigrants. It was a question of throwing out the ones who were already here but who held unpopular views or belonged to certain organizations. In so doing, most of the principles that this country is based on, such as the Bill of Rights, and due process, and the right to a fair trial, went down the drain. It seems that whenever something awful happens in this country it is because of a deviation from the government of laws. And after these more or less brief spasms, there is a correction. The red scare is important because it was the first time that "Communist influence" (in this case Bolshevik influence) was used as an excuse for the illegal prosecution of vulnerable persons and groups. In the next 50 years the red scare would go through other incarnations — McCarthyism, the hounding of people in the State Department and the entertainment industry, and the harassment of Martin Luther King, Jr., by J. Edgar Hoover, to name a few.

On November 7, 1919 (the second anniversary of the Bolshevik revolution), Palmer and Flynn conducted simultaneous night raids on meeting halls in eleven cities. On December 21, 247 aliens arrested in the raids were deported, by executive order. They were not convicted of any wrongdoing. They were simply detained and thrown out, as they might have been under any *ancien régime* king, in complete violation of their rights. Two others, not arrested in the raids, were deported with them: Emma Goldman and Alexander Berkman.

There would have been far more deportations had it not been for Louis F. Post, the Assistant Secretary of Labor. Post was a champion of free speech and the one-time editor of a liberal weekly. Immigration was under the Department of Labor, and it was Post's job to rule on the deportation cases. In many patently unfounded or borderline cases, he refused to deport. As a result, the House Committee on Immigration and Naturalization tried to impeach Post. Its chairman, Albert Johnson of Washington, said he was too easy on the Reds. People who think the McCarthy years were something new in American history should look back to the red scare of the 1920s, where the hysteria of McCarthyism was already in full flower. Post appeared before the House Rules committee in May 1920 to defend his actions, and emerged as the custodian of American principles, while Palmer and his colleagues were revealed as the trodders over them. After Post testified the impeachment drive collapsed.

Ironically, it was Louis F. Post who signed the deportation orders for Emma Goldman and the other 248 "radicals" who were sent back to Russia in December 1919. Emma had been a guest at his home. They had discussed anarchism and Post had admitted its idealistic intent. She felt that a friend had betrayed her. But he had to apply the law, and the law said that anarchists were subject to deportation. For Post, the only question was whether she believed that no government was better for human society than any kind of government. If she did, as the record of her hearing confirmed, she was an anarchist.

On December 21, 1919, four days before Christmas, Emma and Berkman and the 247 other "deportees" boarded the S.S. *Buford,* an army transport that had seen service in World War I. The press dubbed it "the Soviet Ark." Newspapers made the deportees sound like convicted bomb-throwers. One New York newspaper wrote that they were "249 blasphemous creatures who not only rejected America's hospitality and assailed her institutions, but also sought by a campaign of assassination and terrorism to ruin her as a nation of free men." The actual terrorists were never found.

The S.S. *Buford* was to land at Libau in Western Latvia, but there was fighting between the Whites and the Reds on the Baltic front. On January 16, 1920, four weeks after leaving behind her the Statue of Liberty in New York harbor, the S.S. *Buford* reached the Finnish port of Hango. A special train drew up to the dock, and the deportees were locked in sealed railroad cars with three days' rations. In Russia, they were received with military honors. Some of them knelt and kissed the snow.

Postrevolutionary Russia was the promised land to Emma, but she was quickly disillusioned. She was shocked at the rations, the lines, and the favoritism (model schools and special shops). She was told of the wholesale executions, the persecution of anarchists, the thousands in jail. She was driven crazy by the bureaucracy. You needed permits and passes to go anywhere. She had a talk with Gorky, who blamed the problems of the revolution on "our poor Russia, backward and crude, her masses, steeped in centuries of ignorance and darkness, brutal and lazy beyond any other people in the world." Gorky's appraisal shocked her. Where was the just and egalitarian society that the revolution had been fought for?

Emma and Berkman were granted an interview with Lenin. They went to the Kremlin and passed through a succession of locked doors. Lenin sat behind a huge desk, a map of the world covering the entire wall behind him. Emma saw a pair of slanting eyes. Lenin questioned them about the chance for revolution in the United States. He was sorry they had been deported. They would have been so much more useful to the cause in America. Emma asked why anarchists were being jailed. "Free speech is a bourgeois prejudice," Lenin said, "a soothing plaster for social ills. In the Workers' Republic economic well-being talks louder than speech, and its freedom is far more secure." This was like telling a blacksmith that horses are going out of fashion. Emma's whole career had been based on her being allowed to speak up. "In the present state of Russia," Lenin went on, "all prattle of free speech is merely food for the reaction trying to down Russia. Only bandits are guilty of that and they must be kept

under lock and key." When Emma mentioned other abuses she had
seen or heard of, Lenin told her she was suffering from bourgeois
sentimentality. Russia was igniting the world revolution and she was
concerned about a little bloodletting.

Emma was revolted by the Bolshevik claim that every form of
terror, including summary executions and the taking of hostages,
could be justified as a revolutionary necessity. At first she tried to
contribute to the new regime, but something always went wrong.
Plans to set up cafeterias in office buildings, to improve hospitals, to
supply warm meals to construction workers, were stuck in bureaucratic ruts.

Emma had arrived in Russia on January 19, 1920. She left on December 1, 1921, her dream shattered, her faith broken, her heart like
a stone. Her Russian experience ended her career as a militant. She
could no longer argue that there was a preferred alternative to
American society. Instead she wrote a book called *My Disillusion-
ment in Russia.*

She became a writer for capitalist publications like Herbert Bayard
Swopes' *World*, and the *American Mercury.* After leaving Russia she
came to London. Writers arranged a dinner where she could speak.
Among them was Rebecca West, who later recalled, in a previously
unpublished letter to S. N. Behrman, that Emma "was like a perfect
Helen Hokinson woman in appearance. She gave no sense of lively
intelligence or of any interest in intellectual things . . . after the
dinner she got up and made one of the worst speeches imaginable.
She had no gift of living phrase. All that she said about Russia was that
the wrong gang was on top and that they were not kind to people
who rebelled against them . . . She had happy recollections of the
days when she used to get thrown out of towns and was forbidden
to speak in halls and was persecuted by the police . . . She really
missed terribly not being under police surveillance. I misunderstood
this at once when she complained of being followed by the [London]
police. I did quite the wrong thing; I got an assurance that the police
were totally uninterested in her." At the age of sixty-four, Emma
returned to America for a triumphant lecture tour. She had mel-
lowed. For the first time, she had a popular cause. She could tell
Americans about the evils of Communist Russia. She had joined the
team.

The Goyization of Felix Frankfurter

By the time Felix Frankfurter came to America in 1894, nine years
after Emma Goldman, Ellis Island had replaced Castle Garden as the
immigrant depot. Born in 1882 in Vienna's Jewish ghetto, Frankfurter was a twelve-year-old steerage passenger aboard an immigrant tub called the *Marsala*. His family settled on the lower East
Side, where his father Leopold sold linens. In the summer he ped-
dled his wares from door to door in the suburbs. Felix went to P.S.
25 and City College. Something, a strong mother, the traditions of his
race, youthful insight, told him that social mobility depended on
learning. The immigrant mother is asked how old her children are.
"The doctor is four," she says, "and the lawyer is two and a half." A
college education to the immigrant of the 1890s was what the Homestead Act had been to the immigrant of the 1860s, a means of emancipation.

Felix was short in stature (five-foot-four) but rangy in ambition. He
had such command of his new language that he represented his City
College debating society in its annual prize debate, and graduated
third in his class. He did equally well at Harvard Law School. He was
hired by the firm of Hornblower, Byrne, Miller, and Potter, a hereto-
fore all-WASP bastion. One of the partners suggested that Frankfurter change his name. He was outraged. "My ancestors go back to
David," he said.

Henry L. Stimson had been appointed U.S. Attorney for the Southern District of New York. In 1906, Frankfurter took a pay cut to work
for Stimson. He remembered the aristocrats in his native Austria as
arbitrary and dissolute. Stimson, the American aristocrat, was the
enforcer of public morality. The rule of law was to him a means of
perfectibility.

And there came about the goyization of Felix Frankfurter. He
married the daughter of a Congregationalist minister, Marion A.
Denman, whose family had been in America since before the revolution. He formed close friendships with public-spirited members of
America's landed gentry, Franklin Roosevelt, Dean Acheson, Oliver
Wendell Holmes. He rode on Stimson's coattails. When Stimson ran
for governor of New York, Frankfurter was his assistant. When Stimson became Secretary of War, Frankfurter followed to Washington.
When Stimson left Washington, Frankfurter took a teaching job at

Harvard. The life of a gentleman scholar in the country's oldest university exercised a powerful attraction. It was another door to open, in a country where none seemed to be locked.

The president of Harvard, Abbott Lawrence Lowell, was the over-bred product of two sets of Brahmins. He had been a national vice president of the Immigration Restriction League since 1912. In 1923 he tried to institute a quota system for Jewish students. They were not the sort Harvard wanted. They did not go out for sports. They did not have the money to join clubs. They always had their noses in books. Lowell wanted gentlemen, not grinds. Frankfurter was put up for the committee on admissions, but his goyization was not yet complete. He exchanged some vitriolic letters with Lowell, and was not appointed.

On the afternoon of April 15, 1920, the paymaster of a shoe factory in South Braintree, Massachusetts, and his guard were robbed of their payroll and killed by two gunmen who escaped in a car. The police found the getaway car the next day in a garage. On May 5, they arrested the two men who came to get the car, Nicola Sacco, a shoe factory employee, and Bartolomeo Vanzetti, a Plymouth fish peddler. Neither man had an alibi for April 15. Both were notorious radicals and draft-dodgers. Both were Italian immigrants. The murders had come at the height of anti-red hysteria. Indicted in September, Sacco and Vanzetti were tried in May 1921 in Dedham, Massachusetts. Judge Webster Thayer volunteered for the case and asked for a jury of native sons. After a seven-week trial, the defendants were found guilty.

In 1925, there was a motion for a new trial, and Frankfurter's interest was aroused. He wrote an article in the *Atlantic Monthly* charging Judge Thayer with irregularities, which did not make him any more popular with the Harvard establishment. He expanded the article into a book, one immigrant defending two others, and turned over his royalties to the defense committee. It did no good. Thayer had pronounced the death sentence. Governor Alvin Fuller of Massachusetts was petitioned for clemency and appointed a commission to study the matter. Heading the commission was Abbott Lawrence Lowell, who could not be accused of having an open mind. John F. Moors, a Boston banker and Harvard Overseer, said that Lowell "was incapable of seeing that two wops could be right and the Yankee judiciary could be wrong." Lowell's dislike of Frankfurter, with whom he had clashed on the issue of the Jewish quota, was another factor. The practice of naming commissions made up of establishment figures with predictable opinions is enshrined in our system. The Lowell commission found that Sacco and Vanzetti had been properly convicted.

On August 22, 1927, Sacco and Vanzetti were put to death in Charlestown state prison. The headline in the *New York Times* the following morning read:

SACCO AND VANZETTI PUT TO DEATH
WALK TO DEATH CALMLY
SACCO CRIES "LONG LIVE ANARCHY"
VANZETTI INSISTS ON INNOCENCE
WARDEN CAN ONLY WHISPER
MUCH AFFECTED AS THE LONG-DELAYED EXECUTION
IS CARRIED OUT

I like the way the warden's hoarseness is given equal billing with the death sentence.

Judge Learned Hand saw Frankfurter on the day after the executions. "He was like a madman," he said, "he was really beside himself." His wife Marion helped edit Sacco and Vanzetti's letters. By this time she was under psychiatric care. She confided to her co-editor, Gardner Jackson, that she was under constant social pressure for having married a Jew. Her life was a constant struggle against the critics of her marriage.

Frankfurter's efforts to save the two anarchists did not damage his career. He had a gift for making friends, and one of his friends was Franklin Roosevelt, the American who best combined an aristocratic background with mass appeal. Roosevelt said of Frankfurter: "He has a brilliant mind but it clicks so fast it makes my head spin."

One day Roosevelt was speculating about future appointments with his Secretary of the Treasury, Henry J. Morgenthau. He said that Frankfurter would make a fine justice of the Supreme Court. "One of the troubles with Frankfurter is that he is overbrilliant," said Morgenthau. Clearly that was the wrong thing to be in government.

"I think I would have a terrible time getting him confirmed," Roosevelt said. Roosevelt already had two Jewish justices on the bench, Brandeis (the son of immigrants from Prague) and Cardozo. In 1938 Cardozo died, and Roosevelt sent Frankfurter's name to the Senate. A delegation of influential Jews begged Roosevelt not to appoint him. They thought it would stimulate anti-Semitism.

At the Senate Judiciary Committee hearings, right-wing zealots accused Frankfurter of radical sympathies because he belonged to the American Civil Liberties Union. Others argued that it was against the nation's best interests to put a foreign-born Jew on the high bench. Senator Pat McCarran of Nevada charged that Frankfurter was not a citizen because his father had fraudulently obtained his citizenship by filing his papers a year before he was eligible. Frankfurter had no trouble proving this charge to be false. McCarran asked him if he was a Marxist. Frankfurter replied: "Senator, I do not believe you have ever taken an oath to support the Constitution of the United States with fewer reservations than I have or would now, nor do I believe you are more attached to the theories and practices of Americanism than I am. I rest my answer on that statement." Frankfurter's nomination was unanimously confirmed by the Senate.

Senator McCarran's fears that Frankfurter would be a wild radical were unfounded. He disappointed those who expected him to be a leader of the liberal wing of the Roosevelt court. Frankfurter's opinions were influenced by his background. He was the immigrant who feels grateful to a country that has permitted him to reach an eminent position. He was thought of as a security risk. He would therefore prove his patriotism.

In Pennsylvania there was a law requiring children in public schools to salute the flag. The children of two Jehovah's Witnesses refused to comply. The case reached the Supreme Court in June 1940, and Frankfurter wrote the opinion. It was the first wartime civil liberties case. Frankfurter upheld the Pennsylvania law, and carried the rest of the court, with one dissenting vote. The state could compel schoolchildren to salute the flag even if it was a violation of their religious beliefs. Where was the absolutism of First Amendment guarantees that the court would later defend? Well, it was wartime, and America was a haven for persecuted Jews, and Frankfurter was himself a product of public schools, where he had learned love of country, and although it may have been bad law, to rule otherwise would have been to welsh on a debt of gratitude. This was the flag of the United States. Was it wrong for the states to teach children patriotism, particularly when America was the hope of the free world?

Liberals were shocked. The Supreme Court was associated in the public mind with the vindication of individuals. It was the last chance for the disadvantaged who had been mistreated by bigoted lower-court judges. It seemed as if Frankfurter was using the war to infringe on personal liberties. He was flooded with letters saying that as a Jew and an immigrant he ought to protect minorities. But it was precisely because he was a Jew and an immigrant that he had upheld the flag-salute state law. During a weekend at Hyde Park, Eleanor Roosevelt told Frankfurter that although she could not argue law with him, she felt that there was something wrong with an opinion that forced small children to salute the flag when such a ceremony was repugnant to their conscience. Frankfurter was crushed. He was only trying to be a good American.

In 1943, in another flag-salute case in West Virginia, the court reversed itself. The majority now said that uniformity of sentiment, even in wartime, cannot be produced by coercion. The lone dissenter was Felix Frankfurter, who argued that the Supreme Court did not have the power to forbid West Virginia to select the means by which to instill patriotism in its children. He was defending the right of state government to regulate civil rights, and limiting the court's function in the protection of those rights.

In 1951, the court, including Frankfurter, upheld the conviction of Communist leaders under the Smith Act, which made it illegal to conspire to advocate and teach the violent overthrow of government. Hugo Black and William O. Douglas dissented, protesting that First Amendment rights were being violated. But Frankfurter argued that not all free speech deserves the same degree of protection. Protecting advocates of violence was less important than protecting national security. Again, Frankfurter was a good American, one of whom Pat McCarran would approve.

To his credit, Frankfurter played a pivotal part in getting a unanimous court on the *Brown* v. *Board of Education* ruling in 1954, which outlawed school desegregation. The Supreme Court reversed its own doctrine (*Plessy* v. *Ferguson,* 1896) of separate but equal schools in the South. The nation would no longer condone by law a race-bound social system. But, one can ask, how could Frankfurter side with the right of states to regulate civil liberties in flag-salute cases, and against states' rights in the school desegregation decision? It was a matter of historical context. The court does not rule in a vacuum.

Frankfurter was on the bench for 23 years (he retired in 1962 and died in 1965), but he was not the leader that many had expected him to be. At Harvard, he was one of the most liberal thinkers of the New Deal. On the court, he was such a model of strict constitutional construction that even conservative Republican appointees voted against him. Compare his career with that of Hugo Black, whom Franklin Roosevelt named despite his former membership in the Ku Klux Klan, and who outgrew his youthful errors to become one of the most distinguished justices of this century. Frankfurter disappointed in several ways. He wanted too much to be liked and thought brilliant. He could never quite believe that he was there, on the high bench, the friend of great men, the confidant of a President. Justice Frank Murphy, who had once venerated him, later dismissed his scholarship as "elegant bunk." But Frankfurter could not have acted otherwise. He brought to the Supreme Court the mortgage of his immigrant background. He did not own himself outright.

Migrants and Feds (Contd.)

"In the early 1900s," Golda Meir told an interviewer, "to the Jews America was a kind of bank where you went to pick up the dollars scattered on the sidewalks and came back with your pockets full. We stayed in Pinsk until 1905, when the brutality of the czarist regime reached its height . . . Oh, we were so happy when my father wrote us to join him in America because in America things were good! In America I went to school, and lived there until I was almost twenty. Because . . . well, because in America I lost my terror of Pinsk, of Kiev. How can I explain the difference for me between America and Russia? Look, when we arrived, I was a little more than eight years old, my elder sister was seventeen, and my younger one four and a half. My father was working and belonged to the union. He was very proud of his union, and two months later, on Labor Day, he said to my mother, 'Today, there's a parade. If you all come to the corner of such and such a street, you'll see me marching with my union!' My mother took us along, and while we were waiting for the parade, along came the mounted police to clear a path for the marchers. But my little four-and-a-half-year-old sister couldn't know that, and when she saw the police on horseback, she began to tremble and cry 'The Cossacks, the Cossacks!' So, look, the America I knew is a place where men on horseback protect a parade of workers, the Russia I knew is a place where men on horseback massacre Jews and young Socialists."

To many Americans, these new immigrants from Russia like Golda Meir represented a threat. Under pressure from various lobbies, the federal government moved toward further restrictions. The anti-immigrant movement was an odd alliance of Boston Brahmins and organized labor (many of whose rank and file were themselves of recent vintage). Three Harvard graduates of the class of 1889, Robert De C. Ward, Prescott F. Hall, and Charles Warren, founded the Immigration Restriction League in 1894. Their dislike of new arrivals was deep and genuine. These social dregs would corrupt the natural paradise that was America. Many important men joined the league. As has already been noted, President Lowell of Harvard was a vice president. The popular novelist Owen Wister was a member. The league's most energetic ally in the Senate was Henry Cabot Lodge. Good men who believed in social justice were nonetheless prisoners of the prejudices of their time. Dr. Richard Cabot, a pioneer in health care for the poor, described his reaction to a patient at Massachusetts General Hospital: "I see not Abraham Cohen but a Jew; not the sharp clear outline of the unique sufferer, but the vague misty composite photograph of all the hundreds of Jews who in the past ten years have shuffled up . . . with bent back and deprecating eyes . . . I see a Jew — a nervous, complaining, whimpering Jew." For Henry Adams, descendant of two American Presidents, the word Jewish became a pejorative adjective meaning that love of money had replaced love of country. Anti-Semitism became a badge among nativist intellectuals. The sign "No Irish Need Apply" was replaced by "No Jews Allowed." Well-meaning men devoted themselves to saving America from ethnic deterioration.

Organized labor was the ally of these men. Immigration meant cheap labor. The unions had to protect jobs. They were all for raising the drawbridge after they had crossed the moat. In 1892 the Knights of Labor asked for the exclusion of immigrants who could not support themselves after one year's residence. Samuel Gompers, an Englishman of Dutch-Jewish stock, came to America when he was thirteen and joined the cigar makers' union. He organized the American Federation of Labor, and was its president from 1886 until his death in 1924. Gompers' position was simple: "Send 'em back," he said, because "cheap labor, ignorant labor, takes our jobs and cuts our wages."

By 1897, the restrictionists had a concrete proposal to offer Congress. It was to give adult immigrants a literacy test and to send back those who flunked it. The unions endorsed the proposal. Senator Lodge was the principal spokesman for the literacy test, which was passed by Congress three times, and was vetoed by three Presidents, Cleveland, Taft, and Wilson. The last time was 1917, when Wilson's veto was overruled. The literacy test became law, after a twenty-year battle in which the executive branch defended open immigration against the powerful alliance of restrictionists in Congress. The position of the Presidents was that a literacy test would not determine the potential worth of a citizen. The literacy test was the turning point. As Finley Peter Dunne's Mr. Dooley wrote in 1902: "'Tis time we put our back again' th' open dure an' keep out th' savage horde."

The federal government's general position was that immigration was a good thing, but that it should be controlled. To control it, it had to be placed under federal administration. In 1890 Castle Garden closed down, and for a while immigrants were processed at the Barge Office in Battery Park. Also in 1890, President Benjamin Harrison signed a bill authorizing the removal of an old navy arsenal from Ellis Island to protect mainlanders from possible explosions. A congressional committee picked Ellis Island as the new immigration station and appropriated $150,000 for the construction of a depot, which opened in 1892. Immigration was now under the direction of a federal commissioner. By 1906 federal officials were in complete charge. The point repeatedly made in newspaper articles inspired by immigration officials, however, was that the door should be kept open. Here is a headline from the *New York Times,* dated April 6, 1896:

DESIRABLE IMMIGRANTS
FIGURES SHOW NEW AMERICAN IMMIGRANTS ARE DESIRABLE
THERE HAS NOT BEEN A FLOOD OF HUNS AND VANDALS

Here is another headline, which has to do with a speech given by Robert Watchorn, the Commissioner of Immigration, on November 19, 1906.

IMMIGRATION IS HEALTH, SAYS ROBERT WATCHORN
COMMISSIONER TELLS AUDIENCE THE DOOR SHOULDN'T BE SHUT

And here is Watchorn again, on March 11, 1906:

IMMIGRATION RECORD WILL BE BROKEN THIS YEAR
YET COMMISSIONER WATCHORN SEES NO GROUNDS FOR ALARM
BETTER CLASS OF FOREIGNERS ARE COMING TO OUR SHORES

Watchorn attended union meetings to dispute their restrictionist stand. Here is a report in the *Times* on one of his chats:

—You are a carpenter?
—Yes.
—How long have you been in this country?
—26 years.

—What wages did you receive 26 years ago?

—2 1/2 dollars a day.

—What do you receive now?

—4 1/2 dollars a day.

—Has immigration hurt you then?

—I wasn't thinking about myself.

—You were thinking about something else about which you know nothing.

The first immigrant to use the facilities at Ellis Island, which gets its name from Samuel Ellis, a Manhattan butcher who bought the 27-acre island in colonial times and sold it to the state in 1808, was Miss Annie Moore of County Cork, Ireland, who was handed a ten-dollar gold piece. In that first year, 450,000 immigrants were processed. The central fact concerning Ellis Island is not that it kept immigrants out, but that more than 90 percent of the immigrants processed there were admitted. During the 62 years of its existence as a depot, between 1892 and 1954, it was the entrance gate for 12 million immigrants.

Even though only 10 percent were rejected, however, the immigrant's first American experience was steeped in the painful anxiety of competition for admittance. Taken by barge from the dock to Ellis Island, steerage passengers were tagged and assigned to groups of 30 (30 being the maximum number of names that would fit on each passenger-manifest sheet). After a long wait they were led into the enormous second-floor registry room, with vaulted ceilings and the same beige tiles as in Grand Central Station, where they nervously waited on wooden benches for their medical. The light of free America streamed in through tall side windows and the inspectors who could keep you out sat at high desks. Teams of doctors checked the immigrants' scalps and throats and teeth and eyes and hands. They opened high collars, looking for goiters. They removed hats and gloves, looking for ringworm. The "eye men" snapped back eyelids with a glove buttonhook, looking for trachoma, a form of conjunctivitis that was listed under a 1904 law as "loathsome and dangerous to public health." Trachoma was the source of more than half the medical detentions. Freaks from European circuses, dwarfs, Siamese twins, microcephalics, hydrocephalics, were allowed in for six months after paying a bond. Suspect immigrants were marked in chalk with an x and sent to a detention area for further examination. The terrible fear for all new arrivals was deportation. To have left everything, to be on the landing of the New World, and to have to go back — this was true failure. It was a brutal way to deal with people, and hundreds of immigrants killed themselves rather than be deported. One man spent five years in detention at Ellis Island. He arrived in August 1914 and was turned back for defective eyesight. But the war in Europe prevented his return. He worked as a tailor and barber (apparently he could see well enough to shave Ellis Island officials) and was sent back after the war.

Those who passed the physical went to the registry section and again waited on wooden benches for the examination that would determine admission. Huddled on the benches, the immigrants told each other, "Watch out, they'll trick you into saying the wrong thing." Everything depended on the right answer. There was a sort of Catch-22 involved. If you said you had been promised work, you could be excluded under the contract labor prohibition. If you said you had no promise of work, you could be excluded as likely to become a public charge. It was a fine line to tread, as in this dialogue between an immigrant and an inspector:

—What are you going to do in this country?
—I don't know. I am going to look for work.
—How much money have you?
—Twenty dollars.
—How long do you suppose twenty dollars will last?
—(hesitating): I have work.
—You have work? How do you know?
—My brother wrote me that he had a job for me.
—He did, did he? Who are you going to work for?
—I don't know.
—You don't know? Then how do you know you have a job?
—I don't know the name, it's the same place where my brother works.
—How much did they say they would pay you?
—Two dollars a day.

This man could be deported. His brother had solicited for him. Perhaps the inspector would let him through. Perhaps the immigrant would try to bribe him with his twenty dollars.

One of the first things the immigrant learned about America was the right of appeal. If he was detained, he was brought before a three-man board of inquiry. If the board recommended deportation, he could appeal to the Ellis Island Commissioner and the Commissioner of Immigration in Washington. The law of 1912, for instance, excluded "persons of constitutional psychopathic inferiority." An immigrant was brought before the Board of Inquiry under suspicion of such inferiority. The evidence was inconclusive. A member of the board said: "Anyway, I don't like the looks of the scoundrel and I move to exclude him as likely to become a public charge." There was an appeal, and the member of the board was disqualified.

After 1917, the immigrants had to pass the literacy test. They read printed test slips with 30 or 40 words in the language that they knew best. What bearing this had on their disposition to learn the language of the country they were entering is uncertain. Usually, the actual inspection process took about 45 minutes. But when there was a backlog, some immigrants had to stay at Ellis Island overnight, and were fed in a large dining room. Many of them had never seen white bread. They ate bananas with the peel on. Some would not eat tomatoes because they had been told that tomatoes were poisonous.

In its peak years, from 1905 to 1914, 10,121,940 immigrants passed through Ellis Island's "Golden Door." The war put a stop to immigration. In 1918 there were fewer than 30,000 immigrants. The island seemed almost deserted. Postwar feelings of isolationism led to immigration quotas. The island was closed down in 1954 and has now been reopened as a sort of museum. You can take a boat from the Battery and visit the place. A guide in a Forest Service uniform takes groups through the main building with its four spiked towers like Prussian helmets. I took my son and daughter, who were only mildly interested. It was too remote for them to have any feelings about it, although my thirteen-year-old son did point out to me that the one thing they did not have when immigrants were going through they have now: a suggestion box. In any case, we sat in the registry room and listened to the guide say: "I want you all to try and put yourselves in their position. You've come from the home country to seek a better life and you're kept here like cattle in a pen. The baggage room inspector has told you, 'Just put your stuff down there,' and you don't know whether you'll ever get it back. You come into a room and you see an inspector at a high desk who asks you questions. If he doesn't like your answer you're detained. If he mispronounces your name just be lucky it wasn't changed." I had no trouble putting myself in their position, but at the same time I reflected that Ellis Island was never meant to be a rose garden. These were minor inconveniences compared with the chance to start a new life. When we left, we were asked to fill out forms and to say what we thought should be done with Ellis Island. One of the men in our group wrote: "They should build something useful on it, like a brewery."

The End of Open Immigration

What a mixture came through Castle Garden and Ellis Island from the 1850s until 1921, when President Warren Harding signed the first quota law, what a *ragoût*, what an *olla podrida*, what a *kebab*, what a *gallimaufry*, what a *bollito misto*. Some of them didn't do badly. Joseph Bulova started a watch company. Ottmar Mergenthaler invented the linotype machine. Alexander Graham Bell gave us the telephone, and then spent twenty years developing a flock of six-nippled sheep on his estate in Nova Scotia, where he died in 1922, and where his tombstone says: "Died a Citizen of the United States." Leopold Damrosch founded the New York Symphony Society, which merged with the New York Philharmonic. Emile Berliner invented the shellac record. Adolph Zukor arrived in 1888 from Hungary with $40 sewn into the lining of his coat. Lewis Milestone, who made *All Quiet on the Western Front*, arrived from the Ukraine. Frank Capra, who made *It Happened One Night*, came from Palermo to work in the California orange groves. Andrew Carnegie came from Scotland at the age of thirteen, started as a bobbin boy in a cotton factory at $1.20 an hour, and ended up with $500 million. David Sarnoff came from Minsk at age nine, never went to high school, and became chairman of RCA. Seventeen-year-old Rocco Coresca found a basement on Hamilton Avenue in Brooklyn near the Ferry and put four chairs in. The sign outside said: "The best shine for ten cents." He put in mirrors and magazines, and slept on the premises. He promised himself that when he had saved $1000 he would go back to Italy and buy a farm. Instead he opened a second place near South Ferry. The urge to play Monopoly for real, to buy Park Place with a hotel on it, is hard to resist. This was in the early 1900s. A man came by the parlor one day and told Rocco he could make him an American for fifty cents and then his vote would be worth $2. It was an offer he could not refuse. By the time Rocco was nineteen he had saved $700 and wore a gold watch.

Immigrants were making an impact on American life, as entrepreneurs and en masse. Every four years the enviable fiction of the assimilated immigrant was set aside to deal with the reality of the ethnic vote. Give an Irishman a job, it used to be said, and he becomes a Republican. In more recent times, it's been Croatians for Nixon, Arriba con Barry y Bill, Druzina Za Svobodu Carter-Mondale, and Scandinavian-Americans for Ford and Dole. Thanks to the vote, ethnic enclaves affect foreign policy. Truman might not have been so quick to recognize Israel had not 1948 been an election year. He did so against the advice of his Secretary of State, George C. Marshall, who was so angry at this "transparent attempt to win the Jewish vote" that he told Truman he would vote against him. In 1944 Roosevelt asked Stalin not to publicize their agreement that the eastern third of Poland would go to Russia until after the American elections, so that he would not lose the Polish vote. By saying that Eastern European countries were not under the subjugation of Russia in his second pre-election debate, Ford may have handed the Balkan vote to Carter.

Why did they come? Relief from political oppression had been the main reason, but after the wave of refugees from the 1848 revolution had settled, that gave way to the promise of economic improvement. It was enough that at some point in the old country a member of the family had looked at the boiled cabbage steaming on his plate and said: "We can do better than this." Michael Pupin, arriving at Ellis Island from Yugoslavia at the turn of the century, sauntered forth into the streets of New York carrying his bags and wearing a red fez. A gang of youths who hung around the Battery harassing immigrants knocked the fez off his head. "My first victory on American soil," he recalled, "was won in New York when I fought for my right to wear the red fez."

A Lithuanian immigrant, Arrejas Vitkauskas, was startled to see when he landed on America's shores in the 1920s that *Collier's* magazine was taking the defense of the Trotskyist newspaper *The Militant*, which had been barred from the mails for "interfering with the morals of the Armed Forces." "We're glad to see the ACLU go to bat for *The Militant*," wrote *Collier's*, "and we hope *The Militant* (though we disagree absolutely with what we understand it habitually says) will win the fight." What kind of a crazy country was this, Arrejas Vitkauskas wondered, where you defended your enemy's right to express his views?

Leon Z. Surmelian came from Trebizond in Turkey to Kansas State College on a scholarship, speaking little English. He was one of those selected on the theory that young men from distant lands should have the opportunity of an American college education. Leon Z. Surmelian was given a student handbook and told to familiarize himself with the official football cheer, which went:

Jay rah, gee haw,
Jay hawk saw.
At 'em, eat 'em,
Raw, Raw, Raw.

Leon Z. Surmelian suffered intense culture shock.

Come to think of it, America is the only country in the world that exports culture shock. In the summer of 1976, a conference on North Sea oil was held in Stavanger, a town on the southwestern tip of Norway. Attending the conference was a living American artifact, the Chuck Wagon Gang from Odessa, Texas, which sits on top of the Permian basin, the richest deposit of oil in the mainland states. The Chuck Wagon Gang travels around the world serving up Texas-style barbecues to large crowds. They call themselves good-will ambassadors but actually they are exporters of cultural shock. They wear Stetsons, two-tone Western shirts with the Lone Star flag stitched on the right sleeve, Roy Rogers pipestem pants, and cobraskin cowboy boots. Five thousand Stavangerians were invited to their shindig. Outside the dome-shaped hall where the barbecue was held, a Chuck Wagon Gang member hollered, "Y'all come on in, heah? Eat 'em up!" Huge tables, laden with barbecued beef and chili beans, were flanked with bathtubs of ice and Lone Star beer. The Norwegians were baffled. Their ears hurt from the Willie Nelson records that echoed crazily through the dome. Their prim Lutheran palates found the beef too spicy. The beer was tasteless to their Nordic taste buds. Their deep sense of frugality was offended by the American display. They could not understand for the life of them why these freakily dressed, loud-voiced, permanently smiling mutants from the New World, however well-meaning, were creating a disturbance in their thousand-year-old fishing village. But most people do not have America come to them. They have to seek it out.

René Dubos, a research scientist at Rockefeller University, came from France as a twenty-three-year-old with a doctorate. "It was not an escape from Europe," he said. "I came without any precise plan, not with a job in view, not even with a student fellowship, simply as an old-fashioned immigrant in search of adventure." Dubos was drawn by the phrase "America, land of unlimited possibility." On his first night in America, in October 1924, in a small hotel in New Brunswick, New Jersey, one block from the Raritan River, he decided to take a walk, and headed for the river, as he would have done in a European town. He found that its banks were inaccessible to pedestrians. He watched the cars crossing the bridge from his hotel window. In Omaha, Nebraska, he had the same experience. The Missouri waterfront was occupied by highways, railroad yards, and industrial buildings. Why, he wondered, have Americans spoiled their waterfronts? In Europe, river banks were landscaped to enhance the charm of urban life. In America, they were reserved for commerce, they were not meant to be enjoyed. This first impression was the germ that made Dubos an environmentalist. He traveled west, and saw a sign in Spokane, Washington, that said WATCH SPOKANE GROW. He saw another sign in Seattle that said: SEATTLE GROWS WITHOUT BEING WATCHED. He began to understand America.

Among the experiences of the newly arrived, there is what might be called the immigrant gambit. The immigrant must make himself available to opportunity, no matter how outrageous the maneuver. Max Thorek, a Hungarian immigrant who became a well-known surgeon, needed a job to help put him through the University of Chicago. He played the violin. He thought of the university band. The conductor said: "What we need is the best snare drummer in Chicago." Thorek hated drums. Never in his life had he been near one. He heard his voice say: "Yes, I am the best snare drummer in Chicago." Luckily it was the end of the term, he was not asked to play, he had the summer to learn. He borrowed a snare drum and pounded his summer vacation away. His family was driven out of the house. The neighbors complained. In the fall, he auditioned. When he had finished, the conductor picked up the telephone and said: "President Harper, this fellow is a wonder. He's a find. He certainly does deserve full tuition. He has just snared Meyerbeer's 'Coronation March' as I have never heard it played in my life."

I once used the immigrant gambit myself, when I was working night rewrite for the late lamented *Herald Tribune*. One night when I was manning my rewrite desk and suffering from post-article tristesse, a call came in to the night city editor, a large and somnolent man named Jerry Katz (somnolent because he moonlighted on an afternoon paper). Holding the receiver in one hand, Jerry lifted his head and asked the three bored rewrite men: "Anybody here know anything about opera?" "I do," I immediately replied, "I'm a big opera buff." I had never been to an opera in my life. But my number one rule at the time was: "Anything to get out of the office."

It happened that two blocks away from the *Tribune,* where the

Metropolitan Opera was located before they built Lincoln Center, the baritone Leonard Warren was singing in *La Forza del Destino*. Our music critic, Jay Harrison, and the *New York Times* music critic, had left after the first act, as is the wont of that jaded and time-pressed species. But our man Harrison had the presence of mind to leave his wife behind to cover the rest of the performance. The call to Jerry Katz had come from the alert Mrs. Harrison, to inform him that Warren had collapsed on the stage while making his second-act exit. When I got there a couple of minutes later, the curtain had been lowered and Leonard Warren was dying on the stage, his head cradled in the arms of his weeping wife. Rudolf Bing announced the news to the audience. A priest arrived to administer the last rites. In the midst of this operatic drama about the forces of destiny a real death took place. A noted singer died in mid-aria, playing his death scene to his wife, his manager, and a full house. It was quite a story, and when I got back to the office to write it, I found that I had fifteen minutes to make the deadline for the Late City Edition. Forget the old saw about holding the presses, it's too expensive to hold the presses. But they did make up a new front page. And there was a copy boy standing next to my typewriter, snatching the takes out paragraph by paragraph and sprinting over to the copy desk with each take. And we did make the edition with a front-page story on March 5, 1960, that the *Times* did not have, which was rare in those days.

In May of 1961, I got a call from John Hay Whitney, who had become the owner of the *Herald Tribune*. Whitney knew next to nothing about the newspaper business, but he owned a stable of race horses and a number of fine paintings, so why not round out his possessions with a newspaper? By this time I was number two man in the Paris bureau. Whitney was calling me from New York. I had never received a direct communication from the boss, and I wondered what I could have done to deserve one now. I went over a list of possible misdeeds as I went to the phone. Whitney informed me that I had won the 1961 Pulitzer Prize for best local reporting under a deadline. The last *Tribune* Pulitzer had been won by Walter Lippmann for a distinguished body of work. Most Pulitzers represent at least a year of work, for a book, or a crusading series, or a sum of foreign reports. I had won a Pulitzer for half an hour's work. It was a tribute to writing fast. The prize had my name on it, but involved a platoon of people — the music critic's wife, the night city editor, the reporter (David Miller) who replaced me at the scene when I went back to the office to write, the copy editor, the night editor who changed the front page, the librarian in the morgue who brought me the clips on Warren — it wasn't something I could claim to have done single-handed. And, finally, it was an accident that the *Tribune* office was close enough to the Met so that I could get there in time. The only thing I could really congratulate myself on was the immigrant gambit — Boy, do I know about opera! As it turned out, mine was the last Pulitzer the *Trib* won before it folded in 1966. The plaque was unscrewed from the lobby wall and removed to parts unknown.

The Quota System

The equation was fairly simple: open immigration equaled nativist fears. In the Senate, Henry Cabot Lodge still brandished the Know-Nothing spear. In 1907 he became one of the nine members of the Federal Immigration Commission assigned to make an exhaustive study of the impact of immigration on the country. Exhaustive it was, taking up 41 volumes when it was published in 1911 as the Dillingham Report. The report was a compilation of prejudices, which distinguished between the productive immigrants of Northern stock and the undesirable immigrants from Eastern Europe and the Mediterranean. In the Dillingham Report were buried the seeds of the quota system favoring immigrants from Northern and Anglo-Saxon countries.

In 1916, the distinguished anthropologist Madison Grant wrote *The Passing of the Great Race,* which argued that the mongrelization of America could only lead to decline. The *New York Times,* however, continued to write stories about the new and improved breed of immigrant. "Ellis Island," began a story on June 20, 1920, "admitted into this country 10,527 aliens during the week that ended yesterday. Those who watch the flow of immigration into this port have agreed that a better class of immigrants are arriving than in the days prior to the war. A good-looking colleen who landed here yesterday from the White Star liner *Baltic* said to an inspector: it used to be true that most Irish girls came to be domestic servants. We are all stenographers now."

At about the same time that this article was written, Congress passed the first law regulating immigration by quota, but it was vetoed in Woodrow Wilson's last days in office. In 1921, Warren Harding, an Ohio Republican with little sympathy for the foreign-born, became President, and the quota bill passed. It was called the Johnson Act, which is ironic since another Johnson Act (Lyndon B.) put an end to the quota system in 1965. The Johnson Act of 1921 closed the open door. Immigrants could no longer come as they wished. They were admitted under a national quota that favored certain countries over others. The Johnson Act permitted the annual admission of 3 percent of the number of nationals who were in the country in 1910. It was designed as a temporary measure, but it was a turning point in that it introduced the principle of a cut-off number, which was 357,000.

Scheduled to expire on June 30, 1922, the Johnson Act was extended for two more years. America felt comfortable with the quota system. Madison Grant's book gave the sanction of academic scholarship to patently racist theories, which were picked up by the popular press. The House Committee on Immigration and Naturalization was looking for a way to make the Johnson Act permanent. It needed a biological argument for immigration control, and appointed Dr. Harry H. Laughlin as "expert eugenics agent." Laughlin's claim to fame was that he had advocated sterilization for the inmates of insane asylums. It came as no surprise when his report, submitted in 1922, suggested that "race is and should be one of the upper-most items in our list of standards." Recent immigrants from Southern and Eastern Europe, he wrote, "as a whole present a higher percentage of inborn socially inadequate qualities than do the older states." This was exactly what Congress wanted to hear, and lost no time enacting into law. A better bill to keep out undesirables was drafted, the Johnson-Reed Act, or National Origins Act. It was passed in 1924 by a vote of 308 to 58 in the House and 69 to 9 in the Senate, and signed by President Coolidge. Immigrant leaders had begged for an audience with Coolidge to ask him to veto the act, but he refused to see them. The annual quota would now be 2 percent of the number of nationals who were in the country in 1890, and the annual total of immigrants was cut from 357,000 to 164,667. The way they determined the number of nationals who were in America in 1890 was to go over the census schedules and draw up lists according to English or Scottish or German-sounding names. Of course many of those with long names from Eastern Europe and Greece and Russia had Anglicized and shortened their names, and they were listed as English or

Scottish. Thus the very basis of apportionment was biased. There was a transition phase from 1924 to 1929, when the quota system became permanent. It was now based on the national origins of the U.S. population in 1920, and the cut-off figure was 156,897.

As Emanuel Celler, one of the 58 members of the House who voted against the Act, later put it: "It was deliberately adopted to proscribe not only Southern and Eastern Europeans, but also Catholics and Jews. That is the unvarnished truth. I heard it stated time and time again on the floor of the House, and I have been battling ever since to wipe out that abomination. I called it that before and I call it that now with greater emphasis."

America is a country where it's not supposed to matter where you come from. But the quota law discriminated on the basis of accident of birth. Great Britain had a quota of more than 60,000 a year and used less than half. Poland had a quota of about 6000 and a huge backlog. Italy had a quota of 3845 and an even bigger backlog. The system had its amusing absurdities. The tiny Pyrenean enclave of Andorra had a population of 6500 and a quota of 100, while Spain, with a population of 28 million, had a quota of 250. The quota law is a good example of an ethnic establishment maintaining itself in power through the selection of a social theory that condemns other ethnic groups. Poles had to settle in the Chicago slums, and the social scientists drew the conclusion that Poles caused slums. Jews and Italians lived in wretched condition on the lower East Side, and the eugenics experts said *Voilà!* — they are wretched by nature. "Give me your tired, your poor, your huddled masses yearning to breathe free," wrote Emma Lazarus, to which John F. Kennedy added: "as long as they come from Northern Europe, are not too tired or too poor or slightly ill, never stole a loaf of bread, never joined any questionable organization, and can document their activities for the past two years."

Americanization

A by-product of restrictive quotas was the belief that the immigrant should become actively involved in the process of melting into the pot. In the days of open, easygoing immigration, it had been felt that assimilation would take care of itself. New York Jews coined Yiddish words to denote its varying degrees: deitschuks (assimilated German Jews), machers (men of affairs), alrightniks (smart climbers), lodgeniks (joiners), radikalke (emancipated women) and ototots (semi-assimilated men who compromised with tradition by wearing a short beard). In the spirit of that time was Bella Abzug's father, who went through Ellis Island, opened a butcher shop in Hell's Kitchen on Ninth Avenue and 39th Street, and called it the "Live and Let Live Meat Market." A Protestant minister on Long Island, who performed marriages for the Czech community, said, circa 1920: "Their weddings used to last three days, the most wonderful meals were served, and there was an abundance of everything. But the last time I married a couple we had lemonade, ice cream, and cake." The ethnic ties loosened, and the day came when home meant America and back there meant Italy, Germany, or Greece.

For some, they did not loosen fast enough. Along with the quota system, there were Americanization campaigns. The Daughters of the American Revolution printed a leaflet in fifteen languages that told immigrants the essentials: respect the Constitution, bank your salary, don't drop trash in the streets. Frances Kellor, an energetic lady who became head of the New York State Bureau of Industry and Immigration, founded Americanization schools where immigrants could lose their accents and their foreign ways.

But the true genius of Americanization was Henry Ford. He wanted to turn out Americans the way he turned out Model T's, on the assembly line. "I am more a manufacturer of men than of automobiles," he liked to say. In January 1914 he announced the five-dollar-a-day wage in his Highland Park plant, which was the world's largest and fastest assembly line. Thousands massed in front of the factory gates seeking work, which in many cases would double their salaries. Many of them were immigrants. They rioted in their rush to be hired, and hoses were turned on them.

The five-dollar-a-day wage was paid only to those immigrants who were willing to undergo the Ford process of Americanization. This meant attending the Ford English school. Ford believed that learning English would discourage the use of native tongues and hasten Americanization. The school had an enrollment of 2000 in classes of 25, which met twice a week for an hour and a half. The 58 nationalities represented at the plant were mixed in the classrooms. The 160 teachers were volunteers from the plant. Attendance was compulsory. If an immigrant refused to attend, a teacher carefully explained the school's advantages. If he continued to decline, he was laid off to give him time to think it over.

Ford had a Sociological Department, which sent inspectors with a car, a driver, and an interpreter to visit the workers' homes. The inspector questioned the worker about his marital life, his finances, whether he owned his own home, what the mortgage was, whether he was in debt, how much money he had saved, whether he had an insurance policy, how much money he sent back to the old country, and other pertinent data. The Sociological Department was an early version of Big Brotherism. It claimed, however, that it protected the worker from ethnic exploitation. On the basis of the statistics its inspectors compiled on blue and white forms, the Sociological Department drew up the worker's Americanization profile, judging him good, fair, or poor. Gambling was a poor habit, a savings account was a good habit. Living in a rooming-house was a poor habit, owning one's own home was a good habit. Ford thought that he was using the five-dollar wage to break down ethnic diversity. He did not realize that he was in some cases financing ethnic diversity. Some of the workers were saving money to buy passage back to their native land, or to bring over foreign relatives or a foreign wife. The Sociological Department investigated a group of 437 Armenians and was pleased to find that they were practicing the fine American habit of thrift. What the Sociological Department did not know was that the Armenians were saving money to establish clubs and organizations to keep their language and customs alive. Working at the plant, instead of making them lose their ethnic ties, reinforced them.

The strangest feature of the Ford school was the graduation ceremony. No writer of fiction, no chronicler of American incongruity, no Nathanael West, no Kurt Vonnegut, no William Gaddis, no John Cheever, could have invented anything more outrageous. Here it is described in the words of a Ford spokesman, in a document in the archives of the Henry Ford museum:

"Not long ago this school graduated over 500 men. Commencement exercises were held in the largest hall in the city. On the stage was represented an immigrant ship. In front of it was a huge melting pot. Down the gangplank came the members of the class dressed in their national garbs and carrying luggage such as they carried when they landed in this country. Down they poured into the Ford melting pot and disappeared. Then the teachers began to stir the contents of the pot with long ladles. Presently the pot began to boil over and out came the men dressed in their best American clothes and wearing American flags."

I have a photograph of that ceremony in front of me. A caldron as big as a house, inscribed FORD ENGLISH SCHOOL, in the center of the stage, is surrounded by graduates in business suits holding flags in their right hands. Some of them, standing behind the caldron, seem to be coming out of it. Behind them is a painted backdrop of a steamship. Above them is a sign that says E PLURIBUS UNUM. It's hard to see the faces, but some of them are swarthy and mustached. I see myself among them, having completed the process of my own Americanization. This doesn't mean I have to like baseball or "All in the Family," but it means that I speak English, pay my taxes, obey the law, and pledge allegiance to a system of government under which I live by choice. Perhaps I suffer from the immigrant's need to validate the country he has chosen. Perhaps I am too wary of filiopietism. I can do without the labored good cheer of ethnic parades, and without the ancient orders of Hibernians, Bretons, Bavarians, Moldavians, Ruthenians, and Bosnian Hergezovinans. I see myself stepping out of Henry Ford's caldron, but warily.

The point that Ford missed about the melting pot (the name of a 1908 drama by Israel Zangwill, which rapidly entered the language) is that in America we don't have complete assimilation and we don't have complete pluralism. We have the thing and its opposite coexisting. Since everyone is more or less recently uprooted, accommodation is always being negotiated. New groups want in, and that must be fought and bargained for. There are always new culprits of change. A nineteenth-century depression was the fault of the Irish, and the 1929 depression was the fault of the Jews.

Today's culprits are the illegal Mexicans and Caribbeans, conservatively estimated at six million. Nativist fears are revived as we see America deliberately moving from a white to a nonwhite society. The empire we wrested from Spain and Mexico is being reconquered. The Mexicans are occupying California and Texas, and the Cubans have got part of Florida. The old Hispanic Southwest is once again a state of fact. "They're not crossing the border," a retired admiral living in San Diego told me, "they're pushing it in front of them. We might as well take a strip going from San Diego to the Rio Grande and give it to them, and then build a wall like the Berlin wall on our side."

Alarm has grown over court rulings and government decisions that favor the "undocumented workers," as the illegals are called. A 1971

Supreme Court decision *(Graham* v. *Richardson)* ruled that a permanent resident could not be denied a particular benefit because of noncitizenship, without specifying whether the resident had to be here legally. This meant that illegal aliens could qualify for welfare. In 1974, the Supreme Court ruled unanimously *(Chan* v. *United States)* that the San Francisco public schools had to provide special language classes for non-English-speaking students. We are now getting multilingual programs that cost taxpayers millions. In San Francisco's "unified school district" forms are printed in English, Spanish, and Chinese. In April 1976, the Justice Department ruled that 513 political jurisdictions in 30 states must hold elections in more than one language to comply with 1975 amendments to the Voting Rights Act.

The doomsday boys, descendants of the Immigration Restriction League, warn of the day when massive illegal immigration will ruin our society. In a privately printed book called *The Immigration Bomb,* the following scenario was put forth: immigration will put such a strain on our resources that we will have a Bureau of Rationing with a huge bureaucracy. Household pets will be illegal because we won't be able to feed them. Permits of residency will be issued, designating areas of authorized residence. Golf courses, with their fertile acreage and huge water and fertilizer requirements, will fade into oblivion. Milk, eggs, poultry, and meat will become illegal; all food will by law come directly from the feed source instead of the less efficient by-products of the feed. Our main source of nourishment will be the soya bean. Visits to national parks will be by reservation only, with a waiting time of up to five years. And so on.

The sad truth is that we need the illegals. Who else is going to fill the low-paying, low-skilled, and low-status jobs that Americans shun? We should thank God that the border is porous and provides us with a lumpen proletariat at a time in our history when we are approaching zero population increase and when our own labor force is better educated and has higher expectations. Imagine the price rise to the consumer if goods now produced with alien labor were produced with American workers. Our food bills in particular would go up, and a number of small businesses that rely heavily on illegals would go bankrupt. In any case, a study done for the Massachusetts Institute of Technology shows that most Mexican illegals are in a shuttle pattern; they go home after about six months, only a small minority become permanent settlers.

While more and more unemployed Americans answering want ads

say: "Don't hire me, just sign the card to show the unemployment office I've been here," the illegals seem to be the only ones left who adhere to the Protestant work ethic and the old frontier values of self-reliance and personal hardiness. Who will make the better American, the college dropout who lives on unemployment benefits, or the Mexican who takes a job stripping paint at $1.35 an hour and goes to welding school at night? I continue to believe in this country's ability to absorb large numbers of new arrivals, and to carry out the mysterious process of their Americanization.

The latest incarnation of nativist fears, the syphilitic Frito Bandido, is in reality an "undocumented worker," who makes less and works harder, and whose quest for a better life is directed toward obtaining a *tarjeta verde* — a green card. So what if they form ethnic enclaves, listen to Spanish-language radio, read *La Opinión* and other Spanish-language dailies, and grow hot peppers in their back yards? They will have to learn English so they can talk to their children. It is natural for ethnic stereotypes to persist despite assimilation. There are still a hell of a lot of Greek cooks, Irish doormen, Italian masons, and Polish steelworkers. But Marcus Hansen is right to say that they were Americans before they landed. Somewhere between pluralism and assimilation lies the fulcrum of the American immigrant experience. My seven-year-old daughter Amber went to a birthday party in Great Neck, Long Island, in November 1976. She came home saying that she had learned a new game. It was called "Steal the Bagel."

The Egghead Immigration

The quota system worked. The flow of immigration subsided. The depression helped. In 1931, immigration fell below 100,000 for the first time since the Civil War. On August 18, 1932, there was this headline in the *New York Times:* ALIEN DEPARTURES EXCEEDED IMMIGRATION FOR THE FIRST TIME IN THE NATION'S HISTORY. That year, 35,576 aliens were admitted, but 103,295 left the country, and 32,-813 of those were deported. One side effect of the depression was an active policy of deportation. Immigrants were not wanted in hard times. They would merely add to the soup lines.

At the same time that the garden-variety immigrant was being turned away, something else was happening: European intellectuals and scientists, fleeing Nazi Germany, were finding refuge in the United States. This was a migration that was small in numbers but of great importance. The men whom Hitler banished guaranteed the fulfillment of America's destiny as a world power. They came bearing gifts, the foremost of which was the atom bomb. American history in the last forty years has been shaped by these men in more ways than we care to admit.

It was all thanks to Hitler, whose anti-Jewish policies robbed him of the men who might have made his victory possible. Hitler came to power in January 1933. That same year, Jewish professors by the hundreds were dismissed from German universities. By 1936, 1600 scholars had lost their jobs. Hitler said: "If the dismissal of Jewish scientists means the annihilation of contemporary German science, then we shall do without science for a few years."

As early as May 19, 1933, the Manchester *Guardian* published a full-page article listing 196 professors who had been dismissed between April 13 and May 4, which helped alert informed American opinion. Hitler's loss was America's gain. An Emergency Committee in Aid of Displaced German Scholars was formed. A panel of experts examined their credentials and, in some cases, rated them from A to D in scholarship, personality, adaptability, and teaching ability. Appointments and fellowships were found for them in universities. Foundations provided grants to subsidize their stay. A really remarkable effort was accomplished to make room for these displaced scholars. They were admitted on a nonquota basis as long as they had taught in Europe and could prove that they had a faculty appointment in America. Infirmities that would have disqualified the average immigrant were overlooked in their case. When Enrico Fermi's family arrived in 1939, an immigration doctor noticed that his seven-year-old daughter had an eye defect. A consular official whispered in the doctor's ear that Fermi was a Nobel Prize winner. The Fermis were waved through.

Taking physicists alone, about 100 reached America between 1933 and 1941, and among them were the men who gave America the atom bomb:

• Fleeing Mussolini's Italy, Enrico Fermi left Rome for New York. En route, he stopped off in Stockholm to pick up the Nobel Prize he had won "for his demonstration of the existence of new radioactive elements produced by neutron irradiation, and for his related discovery of nuclear reactions brought about by slow neutrons." Fermi was part of the group of physicists who built the first atomic pile, in 1942, in Chicago.

• Leo Szilard, a Budapest physicist teaching in Berlin, arrived in 1937. In 1934, Szilard had conceived the idea of a nuclear chain reaction producing a violent explosion and had taken out a patent on the process in favor of the British Admiralty. He became known as the Father of the Bomb, and worked with Fermi in Chicago on the first atomic pile.

• Edward Teller, a Budapest physicist teaching in Germany, came to America in 1935, worked with the Chicago group, and directed the Los Alamos scientific laboratory.

• Hans Bethe, a German physicist, arrived in 1935, and directed the theoretical physics division at Los Alamos. He won the Nobel Prize in 1967 for "his contributions to the theory of nuclear reaction, especially his discoveries concerning the energy production of stars."

• John von Neumann, a Budapest mathematician teaching in Hamburg, came to the Princeton Institute for Advanced Studies in 1930. He joined the Los Alamos team in 1943, and devised the first electronic computers to handle the formidable calculations involved in the nuclear program. He estimated that following the course of a thermonuclear reaction involved more than a billion arithmetical operations. The first two computers were called Johnniac (after his first name), and Maniac (mathematical and numerical integrator and calculator). In 1954, von Neumann was one of the five commissioners named to the Atomic Energy Commission. Admiral Lewis Strauss wrote: "The fact that he was a naturalized citizen caused some eyebrows to be raised in the joint congressional committee, but he was confirmed and quickly gained the respect of the Congress."

• Eugene Wigner, a Budapest physicist teaching in Berlin, arrived in 1930, because he thought of America as "a country on paper," and wanted to see how it really worked. He joined the Chicago group under Fermi and Szilard, which established the first self-sustaining nuclear chain reaction on December 2, 1942. Wigner won the Nobel Prize in 1963 "for his contributions to the theory of atomic nuclei and elementary particles, especially through the discovery and application of fundamental principles of symmetry."

• Stanislaw Ulam, a Polish mathematician who came here in 1936, joined the Los Alamos group, and is credited with inventing the H-bomb.

• And, of course, there was the greatest scientific figure of the century, Albert Einstein. He did not work on the bomb, but it was his formula for energy that demonstrated its potential destructive capacity, and it was his letter to Roosevelt that brought the bomb to the President's attention. When Hitler came to power, Einstein went to Belgium, surrendered his German passport, and asked that his citizenship be voided. His German bank account was confiscated, and his apartment and summer house were sealed. In 1933, Einstein came to Princeton, where he would live for twenty years. The Women's Patriotic Corporation tried to prevent his entry, claiming that he was a member of Communist organizations. "Never before," Einstein said, "have I experienced from the fair sex such energetic rejection of all advances." Pickets said, "Keep Einstein Out" and "Einstein Go Home." It was just one more example of the nativist reflex. The National Patriotic Council called Einstein a German Bolshevist and said that his theory of relativity was "of no scientific value or purpose, and is not understandable because there is nothing there to understand." "Wouldn't it be funny if they didn't let me in?" Einstein asked. "Why, the whole world would laugh at America."

On October 1, 1940, Einstein stood, with his daughter Margot, in federal district court in Trenton, in a vested suit, with several pens peeking from the handkerchief pocket, his spaniel eyes wide open, white hair curling over his shirt collar, his right hand raised, and he took the oath of allegiance. It was, he said, an important moment in his life. He was the symbol of the illustrious immigrant, of what America could gain by welcoming proscribed genius.

Men like Einstein and Szilard and hundreds of other highly qualified refugees from every art and every science were Hitler's gift to America. Here is Leo Szilard remembering his departure:

"Hitler came into office in January 1933, and I had no doubt what would happen. I lived in the faculty club of the Kaiser Wilhelm Institute in Berlin — Dahlem and I had my suitcases packed. By this I mean that I literally had two suitcases which were packed standing in my room; the key was in them, and all I had to do was turn the key and leave when things got too bad.

"I left Germany a few days after the Reichstag fire. How quickly things move you can see from this: I took a train from Berlin to Vienna on a certain date, close to the first of April 1933. The train was empty. The same train, on the next day, was overcrowded, was stopped at the frontier, and the people had to get out and everybody was interrogated by the Nazis. This just goes to show that if you want to succeed in this world you don't have to be much cleverer than other people, you just have to be one day earlier than most people. This is all that it takes."

Szilard arrived in New York with the idea for the bomb in his head. But getting the ear of Washington officialdom was another matter. The weapon that would end the war was available, but no one was interested. This is surely one of the most extraordinary episodes in American history: a handful of immigrant scientists peddling their idea for an atom bomb to a skeptical government. It became urgent for Szilard to make his case when he heard that on January 6, 1939, two German scientists, Otto Hahn and Fritz Strassmann, had discovered the fission of uranium, which broke into two parts upon absorbing a neutron. Szilard thought that the fission process would also emit neutrons, causing a chain reaction that could result in a violent explosion. He went to see Fermi with Isidor Rabi, a Columbia physics professor, and they asked him what he thought. "Well," said Fermi, "there is the *remote* possibility that neutrons may be emitted in the fission of uranium and then of course that a chain reaction can be made." "What do you mean by remote possibility?" Rabi asked. "Well, ten percent," Fermi said. Rabi said: "Ten percent is not a remote possibility if it means that we may die of it. If I have pneumonia and the doctor tells me that there is a remote possibility that I might die, and that it's ten percent, I get excited about it."

Szilard worried about what would happen if the Germans seized the uranium deposits in the Belgian Congo. In July, he and his fellow physicist Eugene Wigner decided to go and see Einstein, who was spending the summer on Long Island. Einstein knew the queen of Belgium and could warn her about the German danger. Einstein said he would write to a friend in the Belgian cabinet. Wigner then suggested that they should not write to a foreign government without first informing the State Department. Einstein sent a copy of his letter to the Belgian with a covering letter to the State Department. Thus, almost by accident, thanks to scientists who spoke broken English and knew nothing about the way America works, the possibility of nuclear warfare first came to the attention of the American government.

Szilard felt that not enough had been done. The letter to the State Department might gather dust for years. Through a friend, he got in touch with Dr. Alexander Sachs, a New Deal economic adviser. Sachs promised that if Einstein wrote Roosevelt, he would deliver the letter personally. Einstein said he would be glad to write the letter if Szilard would draft it. Szilard worried over how long the draft should be. How many words could he expect the President to read? How many words was the fission of uranium worth? He wrote a short draft and a long draft. Einstein chose the long draft, and sent it to Roosevelt on August 2, 1939.

"This new phenomenon," the letter said, "would also lead to the construction of bombs, and it is conceivable — though much less certain — that extremely powerful bombs of a new type may thus be constructed. A single bomb of this type, carried by boat or exploded in a port, might very well destroy the whole port together with some of the surrounding territory. However, such bombs might very well prove to be too heavy for transportation by air."

And so it was that the greatest scientific figure of his time and the greatest American statesman of his time united in giving birth to the age of nuclear destruction. The German Jewish immigrant and the American aristocrat were partners in bringing to the planet a change in the relation of man to the universe that would have a greater effect on human destiny than the theory of Copernicus or the law of gravity.

Perhaps we have here a model for several aspects of American identity: the combined contribution of the native and the immigrant; the implementation of policies for patriotic reasons that have unforeseen and potentially disastrous results; an effort made for the good of mankind which becomes a threat to mankind. We are betrayed by our good intentions. We intend to clear the land to make it habitable, and we end up plundering it past reclamation. We intend to save a distant people from a political system we disapprove of, and we end up selling out the people after having contributed with equal generosity to their standard of living and their destruction.

Einstein spent the rest of his life burdened with the guilt that he had helped launch the weapon that killed more than 130,000 men, women, and children in a few seconds. He later said: "I made one great mistake in my life — when I signed the letter to President Roosevelt recommending that atom bombs be made . . . but there was some justification — the danger that the Germans would make them."

Sachs did not deliver Einstein's letter until October. Roosevelt immediately appointed a committee to study the matter under the chairmanship of Lyman J. Briggs, director of the National Bureau of Standards. The committee met on October 21, 1939. Szilard and Fermi and Wigner explained that they wanted support to pursue their experiments. They said they needed $2000 to get started. The army representative, Col. K. R. Adamson, goes down in history as the man who said that research on atom bombs would be a waste of time. Adamson saw three impractical scientists who thought they could create a new explosive. If a new weapon was developed, he told them, it usually took two wars to find out whether it was any good. In any case, it was not weapons that won wars, it was the morale of the troops.

If that was the case, Wigner said, we should take another look at the army's budget, maybe it could be cut. Piqued, Adamson wheeled around, stared at Wigner, and said: "Well, as far as those two thousand dollars are concerned, you can have it." There wasn't much enthusiasm for the project, however. When Fermi gave a separate briefing to the navy, Ross Gunn, a Navy adviser, called Merle Tuve, a physicist at the Carnegie Institute and a friend of Fermi's, and asked suspiciously: "Who is this man Fermi? What kind of a man is he? Is he a Fascist or what?"

In April 1940, after some nudging from Roosevelt, the committee met again. It was now called the Advisory Committee on Uranium, and Szilard and Fermi were members. This raised a new problem. If the government made funds available on the recommendation of a committee two of whose members were aliens, there might be a congressional investigation. Research on nuclear fission stood still for another six months. Finally, in November 1940, Columbia University was given a contract to develop the Fermi-Szilard system. It was transferred to the University of Chicago in February 1942, and the work on the bomb continued under the code name Metallurgical Laboratory.

They worked under the stands of Stagg Field in a converted athletic building, and in December 1942 they released controlled atomic energy for the first time in history. After that, the work was placed under military authority, and diversified. The separation of Uranium 235 from Uranium 238 took place in Oak Ridge, Tennessee, while the bomb itself was built in Los Alamos, New Mexico. The supreme irony was that Szilard, Wigner, and Fermi, two Germans and one Italian who could not get their citizenship until their five-year residence period was up, were legally considered aliens. They were entrusted with the greatest secret of the war, but under the wartime regulations then in force, they could not cross a state line after 8 P.M., and when they went on a trip they needed the permission of the state attorney general.

In the spring of 1945, the war with Germany was over, but the atom bomb had not yet been tested. Szilard's motivation had been fear that the Germans would get it first. They never came close. It was later estimated that they might have had it by 1947. Now, he wondered what they were working for. He was concerned that if the bomb was used against Japan, an atomic arms race with Russia would start. He wrote a memo to Roosevelt, but Roosevelt died before he saw it, on April 12. Szilard went to see Truman, and was received by his appointment secretary Matt Connelly, who sent him to Spartanburg, South Carolina, to see James Byrnes, about to be named Truman's Secretary of State. The meeting between the Southern WASP and the Hungarian immigrant was not a success. Byrnes was convinced that there was no uranium in Russia, and that rattling the bomb would make the Russians more tractable. He shocked Szilard by saying: "Well, you come from Hungary — you would not want Russia to stay in Hungary indefinitely." Szilard was not worrying about Hungary; he was convinced that using the bomb would be a tragedy for all mankind. His visit to Spartanburg depressed him and left him thinking: "How much better off the world might have been had I been born in America and become influential in American politics, and had Byrnes been born in Hungary and studied physics. In all probability there would have been no atomic bomb, and no danger of an arms race between America and Russia."

Byrnes, in his autobiography, *All in One Lifetime,* remembers the meeting this way: "Szilard complained that he and some of his associates did not know enough about the policy of the government with regard to the use of the bomb. He felt that scientists, including himself, should discuss the matter with the Cabinet, which I did not feel desirable. His general demeanor and his desire to participate in policymaking made an unfavorable impression on me." What patrician distaste for the foreigner there lurks in that simple phrase "general demeanor."

In the meantime, Szilard's colleague Enrico Fermi had been named to a panel of four experts by the War Department. The other three were J. Robert Oppenheimer, director of the Los Alamos lab, Arthur H. Compton of the Metallurgical lab in Chicago, and Ernest O. Lawrence, director of the Berkeley Radiation lab. The panel was asked to comment on a proposal to explode the bomb in an unpopulated area before members of the United Nations. The panel was afraid the bomb might be a dud, or that if it went off the signs of destruction would not be dramatic enough. In their report on June 16, 1945, they concluded: "We can propose no technical demonstration likely to bring an end to the war. We can see no acceptable alternative to direct military use."

Fermi favored the use of the bomb, but Szilard continued to oppose it. He drafted a petition to Truman, asking him to refrain from using it, which he circulated among his fellow scientists on the Chicago project; he obtained 70 signatures. The petition was dated July 17, 1945, one day after the bomb was tested at Alamogordo, New Mexico. On August 6, the bomb was dropped on Hiroshima. It was no longer in the hands of scientists.

Szilard was overcome with guilt. He switched from physics to biology. He yearned to be part of a scientific breakthrough that was life-enhancing rather than destructive.

*   *   *

The scholar-migrants of the 1930s brought with them not only a device that guaranteed military supremacy, but something else that was perhaps equally important in terms of America's destiny: a technique of self-examination.

In 1933, psychoanalysis was banned from the Congress of Psychology in Leipzig as a "Jewish science." Freud, old and ill, had to leave his home at Berggasse 19 in Vienna with his daughter Anna, in 1938, and seek refuge in England, where he died a year later. Members of Freud's "inner circle," like Heinz Hartmann and Ernst Kris, arrived in an America where the master's teachings had not been widely accepted, and were soon busily engaged in putting Americans in touch with their neuroses. It is estimated that in the thirties between 100 and 200 psychoanalysts and between 30 and 50 psychologists came to America from Germany and Austria. Among them were Erik Erikson and Bruno Bettelheim, the child psychologist (Bettelheim arrived in 1939 after spending a year in a German concentration camp, and wrote a report called *Individual and Mass Behavior in Extreme Situations*, which General Eisenhower made required reading for members of the U.S. military government in Europe).

New York became the psychoanalytical capital of the world. Psychoanalysis today is considered a domestic American product, with far more influence than it could ever have gained in Europe. In psychoanalysis, we have the classic story of the immigrant who arrives unknown and undernourished, a penniless refugee, and who prospers through hard work, and begets children who are indistinguishable from their native-born neighbors.

The irony of all this is that Freud, who has been appropriated by Americans as an icon all their own, did not like or understand America, and foresaw a gloomy future for psychoanalysis there. Freud appreciated the dangers of American society far better than he did the dangers of his own, which eventually drove him into exile. He was a formal, nineteenth-century Austrian elitist, with a distrust of the common man and the power of the masses. American informality and the blurring of authority horrified him. The vigor and risk-taking of the American experiment escaped him. He saw the pressures toward group conformity, and not the degree of political freedom or the American habit of criticizing their own vulgarities. He distrusted the American passion for quick results. He thought American optimism and tolerance led to lack of judgment. He believed that the Old World was ruled by authority and the New World by dollars and there was no question which he preferred.

Freud would have been dead against the undertaking of the Chicago Psychoanalytic Institute — the indexing of all the references to America in his complete works. With one exception they are neutral or negative. After his first and last trip to America, in 1909, to lecture at Clark University in Worcester, Massachusetts, he said: "America is the most grandiose experiment the world has seen, but I am afraid it is not going to be a success." His response to the trip was a list of gripes. He blamed his colitis on American cooking. He had trouble understanding American English, and told an American patient that mumbling showed evidence of laxity in social relations. He remarked facetiously that blacks had been imported to America to rescue a mismanaged society. He complained about the worship of money. He spoke of "the unspeakable grimness of the American background."

How odd that the teachings of this man should have found such a fertile soil in the country he despised. Not so odd, really, for Freudian methods were peculiarly suited to the malfunctions of a society based on the premise that everyone can reach the top. The stress is such that people are bound to break down. Psychoanalysis addressed itself, among other things, to the discrepancy between the dream of success and the reality of failure in a supposedly egalitarian society. In structured Europe, you could blame your class origins, or going to the wrong school. In free-form America, there was no one to blame but oneself. The burden of failure was placed squarely on the individual. America was a country where anyone could be President (except naturalized citizens, of course). James R. Thompson, who was elected governor of Illinois in 1976, had this notation in his high-school yearbook: Jim Thompson, President of the United States, 1984–1992. Not only did he, while still in his teens, see himself as President, he gave himself two terms. But in the 35 years during which an American could conceivably be President, between the ages of thirty-five and seventy, there would be at most nine one-term Presidents, barring death in office. So many who wanted it, and only a handful who would get it, and the same was true in every field.

Psychoanalysis provided a reassuring explanation for failure. Your father was a brute, your mother didn't love you, your brothers and sisters broke your toys and called you names. The failure was not yours, it went back to your childhood, when it was already being secreted in forgotten incidents. The success of psychoanalysis in this country, its adoption by popular culture, and its extension to fields like marketing and advertising, is not so surprising, because it filled a need. A society as geared to individual self-appraisal as ours is ready to embrace any system of thought that provides an explanation. Americans are always measuring their net worth and book value, and psychoanalysis explains performance in terms of market trends rather than poor management.

Thomas Mann and Others

To America came not only Germany's greatest scientist, but Germany's greatest novelist, Thomas Mann, the author of *The Magic Mountain* and *Buddenbrooks,* who had won the Nobel Prize in 1929. Mann lived in exile after the Nazi takeover in 1933. The Nazis took away his citizenship, and President Beneš of Czechoslovakia gave him a passport. In 1938, Mann and his wife Katia moved to Princeton, where he was a visiting professor until 1940. Mann was sixty-three at the time; his life was behind him, his character had been formed. He tried to understand America, but he was not entirely successful. He mistrusted the masses, and admitted to "a wholehearted contempt for mediocrity. The mediocre know nothing of excellence and therefore lead an easy, stupid life." He tried to combine his patrician inclinations with faith in democracy, and wrote in a 1944 essay: "I don't primarily understand democracy as a claim for equality raised from below, but as kindness, justice, and sympathy from above. I don't consider it democratic if Mr. Smith or little Mr. Johnson slaps Beethoven on the back and calls out 'How are you, old man?' But when Beethoven sings: 'Seid umschlungen, Millionen, diesen Kuss de ganzen Welt!' *That* is democracy."

Mann good-naturedly met the demands Americans make on great men. He was invited to the homes of the rich, he dined with ambassadors, he lectured at the Library of Congress. He and his wife spent three days at the White House. Roosevelt mixed the cocktails — *that* was democracy. Roosevelt became Mann's idol, the representation of good, as Hitler was the representation of evil. In his historical novel, *Joseph the Provider,* the character of Joseph was modeled in part on Roosevelt.

Mann discovered the burden of celebrity. He helped a friend get a Guggenheim fellowship. He wrote three West Point cadets that he would be happy to see them after the Army-Princeton game. He politely refused to sponsor a committee to defend the rights of American telegraph boys. He was active in the German émigré movement, and made radio broadcasts to the German people. He traveled around the country giving lectures, to colleges, to Lions clubs, to veterans' organizations, to Hadassah, the Jewish women's group. His sons Klaus and Golo enlisted in the American army and fought against their native land.

The Manns were Einstein's neighbors, and saw him often. They tended to think of him as an idiot-savant. "His genius was very one-sided," Katia Mann wrote. "Really an enormously specialized talent."

In 1940, the Manns moved to California, and bought some property in Pacific Palisades, with a view overlooking Catalina Island. They were drawn by the climate, and by the massive migration of German artists and intellectuals to the Los Angeles area, which had become Berlin West. It seemed the natural place for Mann to be, along with Arnold Schönberg, Franz Werfel, Bruno Walter, Berthold Brecht, and many others. He saw more German writers than he had seen in Munich. The German émigré colony was a way for Mann to reconstruct the familiar in a foreign landscape, and to isolate himself from "the good-natured barbarians," as he referred to Americans in a 1943 letter to his son Klaus. In the same year, he wrote Bruno Walter that American faces were "curiously empty and amiably stereotyped." His love of tradition and classical culture made him uneasy in America. And yet he was a success in American terms. Each day the mail brought letters from admirers. His novel *Joseph in Egypt* was taken by the Book-of-the-Month Club.

Mann decided to become an American citizen. It was the only logical thing to do. The country had taken him in, and represented the hope of the free world. He had to pledge allegiance. He and Katia studied hard for their citizenship tests. "Not only did you have to be reasonably informed about the Constitution and the branches of government," she recalled in her book, *Unwritten Memories,* "but you also had to know something about the government and legislature of the individual states and cities, which was much more difficult. All in all, it was rather tricky . . . I had studied more than my husband, but he was clever and skillful enough to gloss over the points that weren't quite clear to him and to talk his way around the lady who was examining him."

The day came on Friday, June 23, 1944, and Mann remembered it in "The Story of a Novel" as a "memorable day . . . We rose very early and right after breakfast drove to the Federal Building in Los Angeles. There we were admitted into a crowded hall where an official was issuing instructions. The judge appeared, sat down on one of the chairs upon the platform, and made a little speech whose admirable form and kindly content surely reached into other hearts as well as mine. We rose to take the oath jointly and then went individually to another place to sign the citizenship papers. So we were now American citizens, and I am glad to think — but had best be brief in uttering this thought — that I became one under Roosevelt, in his America."

Mann presented the judge with a copy of *Buddenbrooks.* One of his witnesses was Max Horkheimer, a naturalized German sociologist of the Frankfurt School. When Horkheimer was asked under oath whether Thomas Mann would be a desirable citizen, he replied: "You bet!"

That summer, Mann campaigned for Roosevelt's re-election. He gave speeches at Democratic fund-raisers, and made no objection to being sandwiched between a Spanish magician and a lady ventriloquist. This was the carnival side of America, which he viewed with benign tolerance. In November, Mann voted in his first and last presidential election.

The following April, an afternoon newspaper brought Mann the news of Roosevelt's death. "We stood distracted," he wrote, "feeling that the world all around us was holding its breath." Mann heard of people who had opened bottles of champagne upon hearing the news of Roosevelt's death. "An era is ending," he wrote. "The America to which we came will no longer exist."

Mann became obsessed with the threat of fascism in America. He believed that Americans would never forgive Roosevelt for having defeated Germany instead of Russia. This was the European fallacy — judging America through the lesson of recent German history. He saw Eisenhower as another Hindenberg, a "respectable" forerunner of fascism. If Eisenhower was elected, he would be followed, Mann thought, by some American form of Hitler. The grim pattern would repeat itself — camps, loss of liberty, dictatorship. "Barbarism is descending upon us," he wrote, "a long night perhaps and a deep forgetting." He was shocked when Henry Wallace was forced to resign as Secretary of Commerce and was asked by his enemies to register as a foreign agent.

Soon, Mann was himself attacked by right-wing groups as a fellow-traveler and a Communist. Mingled with the letters from admirers now was anonymous hate mail. Feeling that Eisenhower would win the 1952 election and usher in a period of repression, Mann left America in June, and became convinced that if he ever returned his passport would be taken from him.

Mann spent fourteen years in America, but he always remained a conservative German patrician. Princeton did not rub off on him, nor did Southern California. He tried to understand America through the prism of his German experience, and made meaningless analogies. He had become an American citizen, but his commitment came from a sense of duty, not from the mind or the heart. His mind and his heart were always more comfortable in a neutral city like Zurich, which combined democracy with the European cultural tradition. It was in Zurich that he lived from 1952 until his death in 1955.

On the whole, however, it was amazing how quickly the scholar immigrants adjusted to American life, whether they taught in Ivy League colleges or lived in Hollywood. Language seemed the flimsiest of barriers, and the culture shock was quickly overcome. Theodor Adorno, the German social scientist teaching at Princeton, was surprised when a young lady asked him: "Are you an introvert or an extrovert?" He soon realized that the questionnaire is a form of American chitchat.

Adorno listed some of his discoveries:

• "In America, I was liberated from a certain naive belief in culture."

- "In America, democratic forms have penetrated the whole of life."
- "In America, I became acquainted with a potential for real generosity."

After the war, Adorno returned to Germany and taught at the University of Frankfurt. He was considered a theoretician of neo-Marxist revolution, like Marcuse, but he was not radical enough for some of his students, who heckled him in his classes. On one occasion they presented him with a red rubber teddy bear (Adorno was known as Teddy), and in 1969 girl students bared their breasts during his lectures to express the sexual liberation that was part of the "Frankfurt School" philosophy. One wonders whether Adorno regretted Princeton. Student harassment is believed to have been a contributing cause to his death.

Maurice Goldhaber, a refugee physicist, was enormously impressed when he was able to buy a vacuum tube for his nuclear research at the corner drugstore.

Marcel Breuer, the Hungarian Bauhaus architect who designed chrome-plated tubular furniture inspired by bicycle handlebars and tractor seats, marveled at the American instinct for efficiency. "I don't say 'know-how,'" he explained, "and I don't like the phrase. American efficiency goes deeper than 'know-how.' You see this quality in the smallest contractor. It's the way he plans every move; the way he orders materials; the way he stacks them and places them around the job. Americans have an instinct for building. Every housewife in America knows what a two-by-four is. European women don't know such things. Americans are efficient, Germans are systematic."

Rudolf Flesch came to America at the age of twenty-seven after studying for the Austrian bar, obtained a doctorate in library science from Columbia, and developed a workable statistical formula for testing the readability of English prose. Here is someone who learned the language in his late twenties and became a national authority on it. American writers who have read his books, such as *The Art of Plain Talk, The Art of Readable English,* and *The ABC of Style,* may not have realized that they were taking the advice of a foreigner concerning their native tongue.

Fernand Léger found an element of style in neon signs. "You were there talking to someone," he recalled, "and suddenly he became blue. Then the color disappeared and another came, and he became red, yellow. That kind of projected color is free, it is in space. I wanted to to do the same thing in my canvases."

In ways more or less subtle, the artist and scholar migrants became Americanized. Saul Steinberg, the Rumanian-born artist and cartoonist, arrived in 1942, and, to his total surprise, was drafted into the navy. "Perhaps they wanted an adventurer intellectual," he said. "They snatched me from the army and wanted to commission me. But a non-citizen could not be commissioned, so they made me a citizen and also an ensign. Right away sailors started saluting me. So I started saluting them."

The Refugee Question

America was richly rewarded for the way it welcomed the scholars and scientists of Europe. But when it came to the ordinary refugee, America did not show the same generous instincts. In 1935, the Nuremberg laws denied citizenship to Jews, who began leaving Germany in large numbers. On February 9, 1939, Senator Robert F. Wagner of New York and Representative Edith N. Rogers of Massachusetts introduced identical bills in both houses of Congress calling for the admission of 10,000 refugee children under the age of fourteen in each of the two years 1939 and 1940. Refugee organizations had offers from 5000 American families who had pledged to take a child. But when hearings were held, the nativist alliance of patriotic organizations once again showed its strength. The American Legion argued that there were already enough children in America. Mrs. Agnes Waters, who represented an organization of war widows, listed her impeccable WASP lineage and then said: "Let us not be maudlin in our sympathies, as charity begins at home." Mrs. James H. Houghteling, wife of the Commissioner of Immigration, told a friend at a Washington cocktail party that the trouble with the bill was that "10,000 children would all too soon grow up into 10,000 ugly adults." She seemed to be voicing a popular view. In 1939, 83 percent of those polled in a *Fortune* magazine quarterly survey were against relaxing the immigration quota. Nor was there a great deal of sympathy in Congress for the plight of Jewish children. There was still a residue of anti-Semitism from the Depression. Father Coughlin was at the height of his popularity. His radio audience was in the millions. Thanks to him, Irish Catholics could now join in the xenophobia that had once been directed against them. In 1938 and 1939 he was praising Hitler and blaming the war on the Jews. It was not until 1941 that his bishop silenced him.

Roosevelt did not get behind the bill because he did not want to antagonize Southern congressmen whose votes he would need for the defense appropriations soon to come. That was more important than Eleanor's humanitarian instincts. The Wagner-Roberts bill died in committee.

When government declined to take action, private initiative took over. Sponsored in part by Peggy Guggenheim and the Museum of Modern Art, the Emergency Rescue Committee was formed. In August 1940, it sent a delegate to France to rescue refugees. The delegate, a writer and teacher named Varian Fry, set up headquarters in Marseilles and managed to get about 1500 refugees out of France with forged passports and other less-than-legal methods before he was arrested and deported in August 1941. Fry was naïve enough at first to expect help from his own consulate, but the State Department cabled the U.S. consul in Marseilles: "This government cannot countenance the activities as reported of Mr. Fry and other persons in evading the laws of countries with which the United States maintains friendly relations."

It's hard to think of another country in the world where this kind of initiative could take place. In this case, charity did not begin at home, except in the sense that America could profit from importing European talent. A 1941 advertisement for the Emergency Rescue Committee said: "A gift of $350 will make possible the evacuation of one threatened man or woman." If the man was Chagall and the woman was Landowska, it was a bargain.

But there was also an aspect of genuine altruism. I have always been struck by private American concern over foreign disasters. We sometimes seem more receptive to the needs of distant people than to those in our own back yards. We are one vast rescue committee for the rest of the world, helping Italian flood victims, Guadeloupian volcano victims, Guatemalan earthquake victims, and sending wheat to our enemies when they suffer shortages. Perhaps this is the guilt tax we pay for being the richest country in the world, for being the 5.5 percent of the world's population that uses 33 percent of the world's raw materials, for having invented the modern idea of wealth, which is not based on the exploitation of poor countries but

on improved technology to increase production (our biggest export
to poor countries is not manufactured goods but grain). But I sometimes wonder: will the Italians help us when we have a flood, will the
Guatemalans send us medicine when we have an earthquake, will
the Russians ship us wheat when we have a shortage? In the meantime, mail your check today for the Bangladesh drought victims.

A Wartime Immigrant

Refugees who escaped from Europe and came to the United States
may have thought that their troubles were over, when in fact they
had only begun. Take Hans Natonek, a Czech writer who arrived in
New York in 1940, totally disoriented, with no web of useful connections, with nothing but a briefcase. A longshoreman on the pier,
seeing his hangdog look, told him: "You're okay here. You jest gotta
forget them bastards."

He found a hotel room, and instinctively reached for his passport, thinking that the clerk would want to see it. Then he
remembered that "in my new domicile nobody cares who I am,
from whence I come, nor where I am bound, so long as I can pay
my way." He almost regretted surveillance. It was a form of car-
ing. Here in this great new free country, no one cared, any more
than the sea cares about fish.

Natonek was a writer deprived of his principal resource, the language. "I feel my linguistic frustration as though it were a physical
deformity," he said. A Quaker lady at the National Refugee Service
told him: "I'm afraid you will have a hard time here. The American
public is not much interested in books and what readers there are
largely restrict themselves to the advertised best-sellers . . . Really,
you have little chance."

The manager of a neighborhood parking lot asked Natonek if he
wanted to wash cars. "I cannot become an American by pressing the
switch of gratitude," he reflected. He went to see his sponsor, an
immigrant art dealer named Philip Wobler, who told him: "I have
liquidated Europe completely and finally." Not all refugees felt this
way. Some were unable to adapt. They were caught between a society which did not want them and a society which they did not want.
Unable to liquidate Europe, they liquidated themselves. The Ger-

man writer Ernst Toller hanged himself in his hotel room in Manhattan in 1939. Carl Duncker, a founder of Gestalt psychology, was a suicide in 1940. The writer Stefan Zweig, after spending some time in America, was a suicide in Brazil in 1942.

Natonek wanted very badly to fit in. He joined a machine shop class. "Remember," the teacher said, "all things are possible to the man who understands the use of a screwdriver." He was given a degree that said: "This is to certify that the undersigned has successfully completed 225 hours of practical training in machine shop practice."

"What can I give to this country?" Natonek asked himself. "How can I blot out this guilt complex of indebtedness?" He felt that he was a substandard American: he was unable to "meet competition, arise refreshed from disappointment, and retain the semblance of outer confidence." He worked at understanding the society. Looking at the Chrysler Building, he thought: "In this country, the makers of cars build the national cathedrals."

With his machine shop degree, he found a job in a Long Island plant at 35 cents an hour, carrying parts from the loading platform to the elevators. His first paycheck was also his last. "Sorry," the boss said, "you're too slow. I've watched you. You don't have what it takes." He found a job in a medical lab, carrying corpses from the freezers to the dissecting tables. He was hired after assuring his employer that "I am incapable of shuddering."

At night, he kept a diary. Eventually, his command of English was good enough so that he could show fragments to an agent. One day, while hauling corpses, he learned that his book had been sold. America began to seem real. Someone had noticed him.

Postwar Immigration

After the war, the pattern of immigration was further restrictions on the one hand, with exceptions to the quota laws in response to emergencies on the other. The War Brides Act of December 28, 1945, led to some marriages that were not made in heaven. W. H. Auden, the naturalized English poet and professed homosexual, married Thomas Mann's daughter Erika so that she could join her father in California. The 1948 Displaced Persons Act allowed 400,000 homeless persons to come to America, but what looked like a magnanimous gesture had strings attached, since they were counted against the future quotas of their countries of origin. The practice began, whenever there was a foreign crisis, to admit refugees outside the quota. The 1953 Refugee Relief Act admitted about 200,000 persons, most of whom were fleeing Iron Curtain countries. In 1957, 32,000 Hungarian Freedom fighters were admitted. Most of them have done well. One of them, Laszlo Korbuly, an architect in South Bend, Indiana, says: "We are accepted and people have been kind and generous to us. But my cousin who went to Switzerland had a heck of a time and is still not accepted 100 percent. If he buys a new coat, everybody says, look at that refugee, he's not doing so bad in our country." In 1958 it was the turn of victims of an Azores earthquake and the Dutch who had been displaced from Indonesia. In 1962, several thousand Chinese who had escaped from Communist China were admitted. After 1962, thousands of anti-Castro Cubans were admitted. Each world crisis was met by a new exception to the immigration law.

At the same time, the Cold War fanned the old nativist fires. The Soviet Union exploded its first test atom bomb in 1949. How had they gotten it so fast? They must have been helped by spies. To the old argument that immigrants were an inferior human species could now be added the fear of subversion. Conservative congressmen worried that we would be swamped with Soviet agents, whereas in fact we were swamped with defectors. A comprehensive immigration act, tailored to the needs of the fifties, with its fear of reds and pinkos, was passed on June 27, 1952. It was called the McCarran-Walter bill, and it was passed by two thirds of the Senate after having been vetoed by President Truman. It kept the quota system, with its annual ceiling of 154,657. Its supporters said that it was not racist, because it let in a small number of Asiatics. There were now 21 Asian quota areas, each with a quota of 11, except for Japan (185) and China (105). Pat McCarran, the son of a poor Irish immigrant who had been elected to the Senate by the smallest constituency in that election year, said that it "does not contain one iota of racial or religious discrimination." Francis E. Walter said it was "the most liberal immigration law in history."

Not everyone agreed. The McCarran-Walter bill made it possible to refuse admission to immigrants or to have them deported for vague political reasons. It was a counter curtain to the Iron Curtain. Truman appointed a President's Commission to look into immigration laws, which recommended, in January 1953, that the McCarran-Walter Act be rewritten from start to finish. Speaking to the commission, Carl Friedrich, a professor of government at Harvard, said: "One of the most unfortunate things that we have done was the provision in the McCarran act by which aliens were barred from coming to this country because of membership in organizations objectionable for one reason or another to people in this country. You probably heard about the reaction in Italy where somebody got up in the Parliament and said he wished to introduce a law that the consulates in the U.S. be instructed that no one could be granted a visa to Italy from the U.S. who had belonged to the Ku Klux Klan or any other anti-democratic organization."

McCarran then pushed a special bill through Congress to allow the entry of 250 Basque shepherds, to tend the flocks of his constituents in Nevada, who could not have been admitted under the act he co-authored. Under the McCarran-Walter bill, which was law from 1952 to 1965, there were 31 classes of persons ineligible for visas, including all those, who, in the words of John Kenneth Galbraith, "couldn't pass a saliva test for political purity."

Those were the years of obsessive vigilance. A coalition of consular officials and congressional committees updated the Know-Nothing strategies of the previous century. In the early 1960s, the American consulate in London denied visas to the MacColl brothers, folk singers with left-wing associations, on the grounds that "some of their songs may have social significance — they may be about nuclear tests and fallout and the like." Secretary of State Dean Rusk finally ruled that the MacColl brothers were not a security threat.

In 1962, Professor Kaoru Yasui, dean of a Japanese law school and winner of the 1958 Lenin Peace Prize, was granted, thanks to the intervention of Robert F. Kennedy, a visa to speak at the Yale Law School, where he had been invited by the dean, Eugene V. Rostow. This seemingly harmless invitation led to a House Un-American Activities Committee investigation. Rusk had to testify on September 9, 1964, before a subcommittee chaired by Congressman Joe Pool of Texas. Rusk laboriously explained that the State Department's policy was free exchange rather than suppression of views. HUAC then subpoenaed three of Yasui's sponsors, in December 1964. They refused to testify in closed session, were cited for contempt of Congress, indicted, convicted, and given suspended sentences. On appeal their convictions were reversed. This is the kind of thing that went on in the McCarran Act years, when immigration was used as a weapon in the Cold War. The last laugh was had by the chiefs of five Indian tribes, who wrote Senator Hubert Humphrey that they were opposed to the McCarran Act, while sometimes wishing they had established a restrictive immigration law in 1492.

The McCarran Act was buried without regrets on October 3, 1965, when Lyndon B. Johnson signed Public Law 89–236. Before 1965, the bulk of immigration came from Western Europe. Today, it comes from the Third World, and this is its final phase. When the nations of Africa, Asia, and Latin America are able to offer their people a decent life, massive migration to this country will cease. But instead of holding our breath until that happens, let's look at the figures for legal immigration in fiscal 1975, which dramatize the change: Out of a total of 386,194 immigrants, there were 62,000 from Mexico, 31,000 from the Philippines, 28,000 from South Korea, 14,000 from India, 14,000 from the Dominican Republic, 12,000 from Hong Kong, 12,000 from Great Britain, 5000 from Germany, and 2000 from France. I see no reason why continuous outbreeding should not give us the advantages it has in the past. Our mongrelization keeps us ahead. Among American Nobel Prize winners, 41 percent are foreign-born.

Deporting a Beatle

The practice of using the Immigration Service for political ends has continued under the Johnson law. One example is the deportation proceeding against ex-Beatle John Lennon. Harassment of Lennon, who came to this country as the husband of the Japanese-American artist Yoko Ono, began shortly before the 1972 Republican convention. Senator Strom Thurmond of South Carolina informed the Justice Department that Lennon was planning to help a group of Yippies disrupt the convention. Thurmond wrote Attorney General John Mitchell on February 4, 1972, that action against Lennon could avoid "many headaches." Thurmond enclosed a memo from the Senate Internal Security Subcommittee stating that "a commune group" was preparing to go to California for the convention and that "a confidential source has learned that the activities of this group are being financed by John Lennon." Another memo said that the new left planned to use Lennon to promote rock festivals, the proceeds of which would be used for a "dump Nixon" program. The memo said: "If Lennon's visa is terminated, it would be a strategy counter-measure."

The Immigration and Naturalization Service was enlisted to carry out the "get Lennon" campaign. Deputy Attorney General Richard G. Kleindienst turned the Thurmond letter and the memos over to Raymond F. Farrell, then Immigration Commissioner, on February 14. Kleindienst asked if there was any basis for revoking Lennon's visa. It turned out that he had been convicted in 1968 in England after a small quantity of cannabis resin was found in his apartment.

Sol Marks, the New York District Director, said in a memo dated March 2, 1972, that he had been called by immigration in Washington and told to start deportation proceedings against Lennon. Marks said under oath during the deportation hearings: "I suspected that there were some people in high places who were terribly interested in getting Mr. Lennon out, but I never made inquiries about it."

Lennon fought the deportation order in the courts. In the meantime, his wife had several miscarriages. In October 1975, the U.S. Court of Appeals ruled that a marijuana conviction in England was insufficient grounds for deportation. Judge Irving R. Kaufman, chief judge of the Second Circuit, issued a warning that "the courts will not condone selective deportation based upon secret political grounds . . . If, in our 200 years of independence, we have in some measure realized our ideals, it is in large part because we have always found a place for those committed to the spirit of liberty and willing to help implement it. Lennon's four-year battle to remain in our country is testimony to his faith in the American dream."

It happens that Kaufman is the judge who sentenced Julius and Ethel Rosenberg to death in the 1950s. The sentence at that time was widely viewed as an example of Cold War–Korean war political hysteria. In his emotional sentencing speech, Kaufman managed to hold the Rosenbergs responsible for American casualties in the Korean war. He was, it was said, bowing to political pressure. Now, in the Lennon case, Judge Kaufman was coming to the rescue of a victim of political hysteria. I like to think that his decision was in partial atonement for the Rosenbergs, who, even if they were guilty, should have been given a lighter sentence.

The Immigration Service said it was suspending the deportation proceedings on humanitarian grounds, since Mrs. Lennon had finally given birth to a son, named Sean. On July 26, 1976, Lennon appeared before the immigration judge Ira Fildsteel. Why did Lennon want to live in this country? the judge asked. It was a good question, considering the harassment he had been through.

"This is the best place to bring up an Eurasian child," Lennon replied.

"I have to be satisfied that Mr. Lennon is not likely to become a public charge," Judge Fildsteel said. This was no doubt a tongue-in-cheek reference to the man whose foreign earnings helped make up the British balance-of-payments deficit several years running. Perhaps Mr. Lennon will now write a song called "Red, White, and Blue fields forever."

A Final Word on Nativism

Nativism lives on, not as an organized party, but as a private feeling of precedence. The immigrant is a favored target for pent-up hostilities. An unemployed native-born American blames his condition on employed immigrants. In May 1975, I saw a well-dressed young man with a blond mustache standing on the corner of Lexington Avenue and 70th Street with a dollar bill in each hand. He was waving his arms and shouting: "Why do they let those Orientals in? And then they wonder why there's no money! And the half-breeds and all the others! The next war is going to be right here!" I was having a key made by an Italian locksmith. "Fuckin' jerk," the locksmith said. A delivery boy was passing by with clothes in plastic envelopes over his shoulder and the locksmith called to him: "Hear that Jerry, he say you a millionaire — you got a million hair."

I was myself the recipient of a nativist communication after publishing an article on Cuba, in the *New York Times* magazine in November 1974, which won a Newspaper Guild Page One Award for best foreign reporting. I received this anonymous card: "Nice to see that a great writer like you can admire another great, Fidel Castrate, the Cuban cigar. It shows the intellectual ability you possess, your sensitivity, your erudition, your emotion, your stinking shit. Remarkable the many like you, Bernstein, Newman, Jane Fondle, Don Zutherland and assorted performing bears, all jews spicks niggers Cubanos wet-backs Africans Arabs and other fecal material dedicated to hating and destroying the U.S. You dogs want it both ways — the advantages and money of this country and the shithead warm feeling of being liberal and patronizing our ape brothers — wake up, it ain't so fashionable any more. Hope to see your name in the obituaries soon. Happy coronary."

Nativism is an outlet for our secret fears. It is in the literature and in films. In William Faulkner's *The Sound and the Fury,* Quentin Compson buys a bun for a small Italian girl and thinks to himself, "land of the kike home of the wop." It turns up in a remarkable film called *Legacy,* directed by Karen Arthur and written and acted by Joan Hotchkis. *Legacy* concerns the gradual breakdown of a Pasadena housewife, which culminates in a nativist tirade. She is alone in the dining room, setting the table for a black-tie dinner, and suddenly she explodes, externalizing her repressed anger against an imaginary enemy.

"My grandfather walked from Maine to California," she shouts. "It took him nine months — we were here first! Why don't the Irish go back to their mud huts and their Hail Marys? And the Jews — they want to win everything, they want to be first in everything. They've got a country of their own, why don't they go and live in it? We were here first, you dirty kikes!"

This is where the core of anger, whatever its real origin, can express itself. Being asked to share the country — why, it's unthinkable. It's like someone coming into your home and demanding to share the blanket on your bed. And so we dream of the past, of 1640, when the population was 25,000, of 1750, when it was one million, and the land was free and uncluttered. This kind of nostalgia is the American form of *Lebensraum.* And we continue to worry that immigration, unless restrained, will ruin our schools, aggravate unemployment, encourage subversion, and jeopardize presidential elections, the argument being that the foreign-born and their numerous offspring, supposing that all the ethnics vote alike, could swing the 275 electoral votes in the twelve big states, enough to carry the election.

A Metaphor for America

I see immigration as a metaphor for America. The way immigration works is the way America works. You start with an ideal, in this case the open door, and you find that reality interferes. The ideal cannot be lived up to. American history is the history of deteriorating ideals.

We start with an invitation to the world's dispossessed, and we end up with everybody pulling up the gangplank after they're aboard and shouting "Enough!" We pretend that something is noble and disinterested and humanitarian when in fact it is guided by self-interest. Today's immigration law gives priority to skills, which is a way of making immigration pay off. In the meantime, illegal immigration is tolerated, so that we can have a steady supply of unskilled wetbacks and Caribbeans to do the dirty jobs no one else wants to do and who won't ask for their rights because they're not supposed to be here. They are immediately ghettoized, since they don't have the legal proof of residence that would help absorb them into the general population. Employers love them because they're self-effacing, work off the books, and don't ask for raises. But they use schools and hospitals and welfare, just like everybody else. They cost the country an estimated $16 billion a year in unpaid taxes, plus welfare and other benefits, but somebody must think it's worth it. This way we have an unlimited supply of orange pickers and busboys, while third-world doctors and engineers come in on the quota. And it's all done in the name of the lady with the torch.

Immigration also demonstrates the corruption of the rule of law by partisan pressure and political interference. This too is the way America works. But the system also has the capacity to renew itself. Wound up with our sense of loss, like the yin and yang symbols, is a feeling of hope. Wrongs can be redressed. Laws can be changed. Pressures can be detected. There is the possibility of improvement. The system works on itself, just as Arnold Schwarzenegger, the Austrian-born Mr. Universe, works on his muscles, to correct its flaws.

Citizen Morgan

I came here in 1973 as a resident alien and got my "green card," the new model of which is actually blue, but they still call it the "green card." I have hated that word alien. It means foreign, different in nature, adverse, whereas I wanted to be not foreign, not different, and not adverse. The central aim of the immigrant is to join a society, not to be alienated from it. As the husband of an American citizen, I waited three years instead of five before I could apply for naturalization. I could have sidestepped the residence requirement by ask-

ing my congressman to pass a special bill on my behalf. This is traveling first class instead of steerage, and it is expensive. A Greek cousin
of mine, Charles Iossifoglu, paid about $5000 to get the Iossifoglu Bill
passed. In each session of Congress several thousands of these bills
are passed. In the 87th Congress, for instance, the 3500 private immigration bills made up about half of the total legislation. It is like
paying to cut ahead in line. In June 1976, a New Jersey congressman,
Henry Helstoski, a Democrat from East Rutherford, was indicted for
extorting $8735 from illegal Chilean and Argentine immigrants for
whom he had passed special bills. Helstoski was quite active in this
legislative specialty, having sponsored 168 immigration bills in his ten
years in the House. Chilean immigrants testifying before the grand
jury said the going rate was as high as $3000. Helstoski was defeated
in the November 1976 elections. I did not want a private bill. I think
the whole business stinks. Why should there be a shortcut for those
who can afford to hire a congressman to write them a bill? I went
through regular channels. In August 1976, with my residence requirement nearly up, I called the Manhattan office of the Immigration and Naturalization Service and said I wanted to become a citizen. I was told that I would be receiving some forms.

Each person applying for naturalization, the forms said, would
have to show his or her knowledge and understanding of the history,
principles, and form of government of the United States. There
would be no exception from this requirement. I would also be examined on my ability to read, write, and speak simple English. I would
be required to take the oath of allegiance. I was surprised by some
of the questions. Had I ever borne any hereditary title or belonged
to any order of nobility in any foreign state? Had I ever committed
adultery?

On December 23, a letter informed me that "your application has
been received and arrangements have been made to help you in the
next step towards naturalization." I was told to come to the eleventh
floor of the Immigration Building at 20 West Broadway at 2 P.M. on
January 11, with two witnesses who were U.S. citizens "who can
testify from personal knowledge and observation about your qualifi-
cations for naturalization during the past five years." On the Personal
Description Form, a line said: "If change of name is requested,
change to:" I wrote in: "Ted Morgan."

A couple of days before my appointment, my son Gabriel and I
were watching Jimmy Connors and Bjorn Borg in the finals of a
tennis tournament in Boca Raton, Florida. Tony Trabert, one of the

commentators, said: "I've played in a lot of countries, and this is the only country where the crowd roots for the other guy."

"But this country *is* the other guy," Gabriel said.

On January 11 at 2 P.M., I was on the eleventh floor of the Immigration Building with my wife Nancy and my sister-in-law Carol de Gramont. We waited on benches with other applicants, most of whom appeared to have originated west of Los Angeles or south of the Rio Grande. Each inspector had a cubicle, from which he emerged to call out the name of the person who was next. At one point an inspector came out and said to a colleague: "This is what exasperates me. I'm just waiting for an interpreter."

After a twenty-minute wait I was called into the office of a pleasant young man whose hair was swept from the back over his forehead and who wore tortoise-shell glasses. This was someone that I would see for half an hour of my life, but it was an essential half an hour. He could prevent me from becoming American.

As he went over my application, he noted that I had married my second wife, Nancy, in 1968. Then he noted that my son Gabriel had been born in 1962. Then he noted the form that I had signed saying that I had not committed adultery. "On the face of the record," he said, "you have committed adultery." The ripe smell of moral turpitude was in the air.

I was the drowning man who sees his life pass before him like a film clip on fast rewind. I saw an April morning in Paris, in 1961, one of those mornings that seem to be the work of a scenic designer. I was driving along the Right Bank *quais* with the top down, and at a red light I came up to another convertible, which was driven by a sad-faced American girl whom I knew slightly. Nancy was with her. I asked if either or both of them would like to have lunch with me. I was relieved that the sad-faced girl could not, and that Nancy could. After having worked as a secretary-researcher for the playwright S. N. Behrman for five years, Nancy had come to Paris to write poetry, and was living in a run-down hotel near Notre Dame, in a room so small that she had to write in bed. Two days later she moved into my apartment on the Ile Saint-Louis. Our agreement was renegotiated daily, for Nancy was a gypsy, and I was not myself the pipe-and-slippers type. We would have bet long odds against its lasting sixteen months, let alone sixteen years.

I was separated from my wife, who was in New York. In December 1961, I was sent to the Congo to cover the secession of Katanga and the United Nations military operation there. I was wounded in the fighting outside Elizabethville and came back to Paris with one cast from my neck to my waist and another cast on my left leg. There was not much of me that was not in a cast. I was bedridden, and what can one do in bed? We applied our ingenuity to finding ways to circumvent the casts, and we were so successful that in November 1962 Nancy gave birth to a son. My wife in New York, who in converting to Catholicism when she married me had become more Catholic than the Pope, would not give me a divorce.

By this time the *Herald Tribune* had given me the Rome bureau. I was in the right place to obtain an annulment. I hired a Vatican lawyer, and in the next two years I learned more than I wanted to know about ecclesiastical law. I was spurred on by the thought that if Lee Radziwill could get an annulment, why couldn't I? She must have had something I did not, because my application was turned down. I could not get unmarried, and I had a growing son by another woman. It was a predicament I was not sure the Immigration and Naturalization Department would appreciate.

In 1968 the good news came. My wife wanted to remarry, she was in fact in the same situation that Nancy and I had been in, and she agreed to a divorce. Nancy and I were married in Paris in the spring of 1968, and in 1969 Nancy had a daughter named Amber. I explained all this to the immigration inspector as best I could. Adultery, I argued, would have been sleeping with the wife I was separated from, not with the woman I was living with who was the mother of my child. The inspector mused. He put his head in his hands. He cleared his throat, and toyed with his pencil. Finally he nodded, and went on to the next question.

My literacy test consisted of writing "I am a writer" on the application form. I was then questioned on my knowledge of government and American history, a test which has, at least in New York, been reduced to the lowest common denominator.

This was on January 11. "Who is the President of the United States," the inspector asked?

"Jimmy Carter," I confidently replied, and then realizing that I had fallen into the most obvious of traps, lamely added: "As of January 20. Until then, it's Gerald Ford."

I was then asked about the Bill of Rights, and I recited half a dozen, after which I was asked what Lincoln was famous for. The final question, concerning the identity of the mayor of New York, ended the interview.

The general counsel, an alert young man with wavy hair, had a few more questions. "Would you bear arms against France?" he asked.

"France is a NATO ally," I said.

"What if it went Communist? Anything can happen."

"I'd ask to be sent to the Pacific front," I said.

"What if there was no Pacific front?"

"I'd volunteer for the ambulance corps."

This seemed to satisfy him. He then asked me whether I was prepared to renounce my title of count. "Gladly," I said.

"You're the second title I've had," he said. "I had a Bourbon princess once. Tell me, what does it get you?"

"A corner table at the Grenouille," I said.

And that was that, after paying a $25 fee. It was the bargain of the century.

On February 16, I was summoned to the United States Federal Courthouse on Foley Square, at 8:45 A.M., and I took my wife and children. I was one of a group of 168 aliens who were funneled into Room 506, a paneled courtroom with high windows where federal trials are heard. I took my seat, between a gentleman who was reading a Chinese newspaper and a lady chattering with a relative in Haitian pidgin French. Looking around the courtroom, where they sat in rows of ten, it appeared that few of my fellow aliens were of European descent. "My God," I whispered to my wife, "what are they letting into the country these days?" It was my first nativist reflex. Nancy advised me to adopt a more constructive attitude, befitting the occasion. I asked the gentleman on my right what the headlines were. He informed me that we were two days short of the Chinese New Year, which would be the Year of the Serpent, the most sacred Chinese symbol. He seemed to regard this as an auspicious beginning for citizenship.

Marvin Stang, a gravel-voiced and white-haired immigration lawyer, who wore an enameled flag in the lapel of his sky-blue suit, said: "May I have your attention please? We can only take you one row at a time. Hand over your letters and your green cards and you will be given two copies of a naturalization form which you will sign and hand over to the clerk."

When my turn came, I turned in my green card, and the crew-cut clerk looked up and said: "You're changing your name to Ted Morgan — that's quite a change." It certainly was, I replied. Five clerks sat at tables in the center of the courtroom, showed us where to sign our forms, and told us they would be mailed to us in ten days. I had studied cases where a change of name was denied. I had been told by my brother Pat that when he was naturalized some years ago, an Argentinean immigrant had asked to change his name. "What is your present name?" the judge asked. "Juan Lopez," the immigrant said. "And what do you want to change it to?" the judge asked. "Juan de Castillo Lopez," the immigrant said. "Request denied," the judge said. There was always the chance that my request would be denied. Some judges did not approve of immigrants discarding their ethnic origins by changing their names. I had prepared a little speech explaining my name-change, but when the clerk asked me to sign the naturalization forms with my new name, I realized that I would not need it.

Along with our naturalization certificates, we were given a *Welcome to the U.S.A. Citizenship* booklet, a *Documents from America's Past,* booklet and a four-page "Pledge of Allegiance to the Flag" brochure. I studied this material as my fellow aliens were processed, which took an hour and a half. How many of you know that the author of the pledge was Francis Bellamy, a Baptist minister from Mount Morris, New York, who was born in 1855 and died in 1931? The pledge was first used at the dedication of the Chicago World's Fair in 1892, the 400th anniversary of the official discovery of America, and has since been mumbled by generations of schoolchildren. On December 28, 1945, the 79th Congress voted Public Law 287, which made Mr. Bellamy's words the nation's official pledge. Ten years later, Representative Louis C. Rabaut of Michigan suggested that the words "under God" should be added to the pledge, which was done. Mr. Rabaut also proposed that the pledge should be set to music, and that was done by Irving Caesar, in march time. Mr. Caesar's composition was sung for the first time on Flag Day, June 14, 1955, on the floor of the House, by the "Singing Sergeants," the official Air Force choir.

The *Documents from America's Past* booklet listed reproductions of historic documents and artifacts available from the National Archives. Included in the selection were George Washington's Inaugural Address, a painting of the *Bon Homme Richard,* a book on polar exploration, and a Great Seal tie bar. I particularly liked the National Archives motto, which was featured over a drawing of an impressive Greek-temple-style columned building: "Sometimes research involves looking under rocks. Don't forget this one." I also liked some of the old posters that were offered for sale. They attested to changing times. A recruitment poster for the Naval Reserve showed a bobbed-haired girl in a sailor suit, saying: "Gee!! I wish I were a MAN,

I'd join the NAVY." A War Savings Stamps poster showed World War I double-wing fighter planes circling a huge bald eagle, with the caption KEEP HIM FREE. I reflected that the caption today would read KEEP HIM ALIVE and that America must be the only country in the world which has turned its national symbol into an endangered species. We would have been better off with the turkey, the bird that Benjamin Franklin recommended as a true American native, calling the eagle a bird of bad moral character who obtained his livelihood from the labor of others.

The *Welcome to the U.S.A. Citizenship* booklet listed "The Five Qualities of the Good Citizen," which I pondered as I waited for the ceremony.

1. *The Good Citizen cherishes democratic values and bases his actions on them.* That seemed fine for private behavior, but it could be a positive menace in corporate behavior. The "democratic value" of free enterprise capitalism was often a license to cheat and plunder, and dump waste matter into rivers. I cherish democratic values but I also cherish the regulation of big business, to keep the profit motive in line with the general good.

The Good Citizen is concerned with the general welfare of all people. Yes, I am, but the word welfare also reminds me of welfare cheats and the tens of thousands who have adopted the welfare life, which is a sort of permanent humiliation. It saps their self-respect. The red tape, the hours spent waiting in line and filling out forms, makes welfare an occupation. They have created a situation where it is time-consuming to be useless. In other countries the oppressed masses revolt. In America, they choose their oppression, having often come from distant lands to climb aboard the welfare wagon, and they are paid to remain submissive.

The Good Citizen is loyal to the principles of equality of opportunity. The corollary to equal opportunity is the disparity of wealth. As the old Portuguese saying has it: When shit turns into gold the poor will be born without assholes. The only way to win at the capitalist game is to accumulate capital. As Thorstein Veblen observed in 1899, capital in America is "the conventional basis of esteem." But most of us are salaried employees, not capitalists, and we never fully enjoy the fruits of the system. We can be wiped out by an illness in the family or a boss who doesn't like us. Family conditioning is another obstacle to equal opportunity. A rite of passage among the poor: going to the welfare office with your mother and standing in line to get your check. A rite of passage among the rich: being taken to Wall

Street by your father to have lunch with the family's trust officer.

2. *The Good Citizen practices democratic human relationships in the family, school, community, and the larger scene . . . He sincerely desires to help other persons.* Well, that's fine too, except that like everything else, helping other persons is complicated. There are so many examples in the newspaper of things not being what they seem that one's natural tendency to paranoia is reinforced. There is a nun who sits on the landing of a subway exit in Grand Central with a tin cup. I don't help her because I don't think she's a real nun, and I'm embarrassed to ask for proof that she is. I get appeals from charities, but I know that half the money I send will be pocketed by the fund-raiser. If I saw an elderly woman being mugged in the street, I like to think (still hearing the screams of Kitty Genovese) that I would come to her aid, but I can't be sure, my feet might not go in the direction I want them to. I'm relieved in a way that my capacity for gallantry has gone untested.

3. *The Good Citizen recognizes the social problems of the times and has the will and the abililty to work toward their solution . . . Problems of the United States in the place of world affairs; problems of the equitable use of resources; problems of family, school, community, and neighborhood living.* I'm all for that. Although here again, if you take the Vietnam war, what was the good citizen to do, join the Marines or burn his draft card? At the same time, I think that this is the only country in the world where a private person can have some influence on public issues. I have a friend who almost single-handedly prevented the Army Corps of Engineers from building a dam on the Delaware River, but she had to work at it full-time for several years. Most of us can't afford that kind of commitment. The rise of these grass-roots citizens groups, these ad hoc organizations formed to combat a specific local threat, is, I think, one of the important features of the seventies. They are the heirs of the war resisters of the sixties.

4. *The Good Citizen is aware of and takes responsibility for meeting basic human needs.* I really don't know what I can do about basic human needs. It takes a Billy Graham to love everybody. I try to do the best I can for my family, and I try not to exploit anybody. One of the reasons I like being a writer is that it's hard to exploit people: you have no employees, you use the language, which is available to everyone without charge, and you turn out your product with light equipment, a typewriter, a desk, a chair, and a ream of $2.48 bond.

5. *The Good Citizen possesses and uses knowledge, skills, and*

abilities necessary in a democratic society. What skills? America is the world capital of sharp practices. "It is good to be shifty in a new country," said Simon Suggs, the roguish hero of "Old Southwest" humor. Nixon developed the skills of lying and dishonesty to become President. Corporations teach us the skills of kickbacks, tax evasion, and fast-fraud franchises. In 1976, the business community showed us how to observe the Buy-Centennial. The art of survival in a democratic society means learning a number of negative abilities, such as sailing close to the wind, spending more than you make, promising what you can't deliver, and, if you are caught, hiring a smart lawyer who will get you off.

* * *

Almost everyone had been processed, and soon we'd be taking the oath, and, if I didn't like it here, this was my last chance to bow out. I could go to Russia and become a naturalized citizen there. The thought gave me the chills, although I was ready to concede three advantages to Communist society: it had no advertising agencies, psychoanalysts, or Hare Krishnas.

Marvin Stang's gravel voice interrupted my daydreaming with the announcement that "we're in the process of seeing that you all become citizens of the United States of America, the greatest democracy this world has ever seen. Your certificates will be mailed to you by the clerk of the court. That is all for the moment — I just want to congratulate you and hope that in the years to come you'll be healthy."

At 10:30 A.M., we were asked to rise, and Judge Charles H. Tenney, black-robed and bespectacled, entered the courtroom. Mr. Stang presented the motion for naturalization on behalf of the 168 of us, and asked that it be granted. The judge nodded. "Thirty of the petitioners have requested a change of name," Mr. Stang went on, "and I move that the request be granted." That was the reason the judge could not go into the reasons for name-changing. There were so many name-changers it had to be done on an assembly-line basis. "Three petitioners have been found eligible for a qualified oath by reason of religious training and belief," Mr. Stang continued (this applied to conscientious objectors, who declined to bear arms), "and I request a qualified oath for these petitioners. As for petitioner Sanche de Gramont, the petitioner has a title of nobility and I request that the title of nobility be renounced before the petitioner is committed to citizenship." I found his choice of words unfortunate. I was ready to be "committed" to a mental home if need be, but not to citizenship. I stood up and the judge asked: "Mr. Ted Morgan, do you renounce your title of count?" "Yes, I do, your honor," I replied, and that was that, de Gramont had become Morgan. I had been calling myself Morgan for three years, but this was the difference between living in sin and being married, I now had the sanction of the state.

We all rose and recited the Oath of Allegiance, and then, as new citizens, gave our pledge of allegiance to the flag. Judge Tenney gave a brief speech, reminding us that many officers of the court, including himself, were the sons and daughters of immigrants. He was pleased, he said, to be holding a proceeding so different from the usual trials held in his court. "This is no adversary proceeding," he said, "but comes from the desire to enjoy those rights peculiar to American citizens." This ceremony, he said, would have a great impact on all our lives. Our behavior would determine whether we were real or nominal Americans. We had all been created equal, but that did not mean we would remain equal. We would have to work at being citizens, by exercising our right to vote. And since we now had the right to a trial by jury, we would have the responsibility of serving as a juror in one of those trials. And since we had the right to freedom we would have the responsibility to defend it. "I congratulate you on this great step in your lives," Judge Tenney said.

And so it was that, forty-five days short of my forty-fifth birthday, I became an American citizen. In defiance of the actuarial tables, I hoped that I would live as long under the American flag as I had under the French. Since Foley Square is not far from Mott Street, we went to a Chinese restaurant for a celebration lunch. The fortune in my cookie said: "The best throw of the dice is to throw them away." In a literal sense, this message was a warning against gambling, but, to me, the best throw of the dice was what I had just thrown away: a former self.

There is a gravestone in Virginia's Shenandoah Valley that says: "Here lie the remains of John Lewis, who slew the Irish lord, settled in Augusta County, located the town of Staunton, and furnished five sons to fight the battles of the American Revolution." Not being able to claim any comparable achievements, I think I would want my gravestone to read: "Here lie the remains of Ted Morgan, who became an American."

PART THREE

THE WAY IT WORKS

Conrad the American

When Saul Bellow won the Nobel Prize for literature in 1976, he told an interviewer that as an undergraduate he had neglected his economics homework to read Joseph Conrad. "Perhaps Conrad appealed to me because he was like an American," Bellow said. "He was an uprooted Pole sailing exotic seas, speaking French and writing English with extraordinary power and beauty. Nothing could be more natural to me, the child of immigrants who grew up in one of Chicago's immigrant neighborhoods, than a Slav who was a British sea captain and knew his way around Marseilles and wrote an Oriental sort of English."

Jósef Theodor Konrad Korzeniowski was born in 1857, in unsettled times. Poland was under czarist rule. His father, Apollo Korzeniowski, was a failed rebel who personified his country's dilemma. He was arrested when Conrad was four, for advocating violence in a pamphlet, and was exiled to northern Russia, where his son joined him. Poland, for the boy growing up in Cracow after the death of his parents, was not a country but a psychological wound. Conrad left for France when he was seventeen. "I got into the train as a man gets into a dream," he said.

Conrad wanted to become a seaman. The need to go to sea was linked with the need to leave a landlocked country. It was not merely a form of youthful revolt against what cannot be changed. For Conrad, leaving the crumbling society of Poland was an act of self-preservation. He would later be criticized for deserting the dismembered body of Poland instead of working for its unity, for repudiating the principles for which his father had sacrificed his life, for exporting his talent, for discarding his mother tongue.

In Marseilles, Conrad was affected by a French law that prevented foreigners over twenty-one from serving in the merchant marine. It was because of this law that he signed on a British freighter and eventually went to live and write in England. Providence assumes strange shapes. It was just as well, for Conrad found French too perfectly "crystallized" to satisfy a temperament conscious of the haze that hangs over moral issues.

The merchant seaman is a displaced person. Conrad's books would create a literature of displaced persons, Kurtz, a Belgian in Africa, Rasumov, a Russian in Geneva, Nostromo, an Italian in South America, Jim, an Englishman in Malaya.

Conrad studied the language, and worked his way up from ordinary seaman to Master Mariner. "I have been quarrying my English out of a black night," he wrote, "working like a coal miner in his pit." The first English he heard was that of shipwrights and sailors. "Having unluckily no ear," he wrote, "my accentuation is uncertain." All his life, he spoke with a pronounced accent that dismayed his peers. John Galsworthy, who met him aboard ship while returning from Samoa, said that "he seemed to me strange on a British ship." Virginia Woolf saw him as "a foreigner, talking broken English." The first English he wrote was a reply to the ad of a London shipping agent.

For another Slavic writer who came late to the language, Vladimir Nabokov, writing English was "exceedingly painful, like learning anew to handle things after losing seven or eight fingers in an explosion." Nabokov considered himself "an American writer born in Russia and educated in England where I studied French literature before spending 15 years in Berlin."

Conrad's change of name had nothing to do with writing; it came earlier. As ships fly flags of convenience, Conrad took a name of convenience, a name that was chosen for him by his shipmates, even though ships' manifests still listed him as Konrad Korzeniowski. In his late twenties, he started asking some of his correspondents to direct their replies to J. Conrad. A few years later, he was signing some letters J. Conrad and others K. or J. Korzeniowski. When he began to live in London, he made the change to Conrad final, and he became a British subject in 1886, when he was twenty-nine.

Bored in London between ships, Conrad took up the pen one morning after breakfast, in 1889. "A sentiment akin to piety," he said, "prompted me to render in words assembled with conscientious care the memory of things far distant and of men who had lived." By then, Conrad had been at sea for fifteen years. He had worked on a steamer carrying coal to Constantinople, a wool clipper bound for Australia, and a shuttle freighter on the Congo River.

His first novel, *Almayer's Folly*, was published in 1895, and he would go on to write 26 more books and become known as the finest English novelist of the early twentieth century. But he continued to feel that "English . . . is still a foreign language to me, requiring an immense effort to handle." He deprecated his best work: "The Outcast is a heap of sand, the Nigger a splash of water, Jim a lump of clay." He had the displaced person's need for excellence. Doing something well becomes an inner homeland. Conrad's pride of craft as a seaman, the anchor of his existence, was transmitted to writing. "The attainment of proficiency," he wrote, "is a matter of vital concern."

There followed years of struggle, to win a public as a writer, and to find an identity in English society. The memory of Poland found its way into his work through the metaphor of desertion: Lord Jim's shameful secret is that he once deserted a ship crowded with pilgrims bound for Mecca. Success and honors came to Conrad in the last ten year of his life, but he continued to see himself as alienated. He believed that, like Kurtz in *Heart of Darkness*, he was "hollow at the core." He had, he said, "a private gnawing worm of my own." He would scribble his initials over and over again on the flyleaves of books as if to remind himself of who he was. He declined honorary degrees from the universities of Oxford, Edinburgh, Liverpool, and Durham, and in 1924 he turned down a knighthood. He was determined not to compromise his status as an outsider. His English friends found him evasive. How hard it was, said E. M. Forster, to enter "that severe little compartment that must, for want of a better word, be called his confidence."

Only a man as alienated as Conrad, a man who had to invent not only a style but an identity, could have imagined characters like Kurtz, the ivory trader who inhabits the heart of darkness. Kurtz is a learned man who instead of civilizing the natives has been made barbaric. Obsessed with ivory, he turns to human sacrifice to control the tribes. His house is surrounded by heads on stakes. He orders the natives to attack the company steamer that has come to fetch him. Deathly ill, he cries out his last words, a summary of his life: "The horror! The horror!" After which the company manager's boy pokes his head in the doorway of the steamer's dining room and announces: "Mistah Kurtz — he dead."

*   *   *

"E morto," said the Italian surgeon who opened the ambulance door. I thought he was talking about me. There were two of us stretched out in the ambulance. My feet were alongside the other man's head. At first, his hand clutched my left foot, but as we approached the United Nations hospital, I felt his grip relax. This was *my* Congo nightmare, in Katanga, in December 1961. The UN troops had surrounded the city of Elizabethville, which was held by Katangese gendarmes and white mercenaries. The press corps observed the fighting from under the arcades of the Leopold II Hotel. On December 15, I had been awakened by mortar fire which struck the hotel. Plaster shaken loose from the ceiling of my room fell on the bed. The post office was still functioning, and correspondents lined up before it opened to use the single Telex machine to file their copy. An English correspondent who had waited five hours to use it slammed his fist into it because it had broken down, but that did not help to start it up. The UN, equipped with SAAB fighter-bombers, gave the press corps a demonstration of pinpoint bombing, destroying the post office with rockets. There was no way we could get our stories out, except by leaving Elizabethville.

On December 18, the mercenaries and the black gendarmes, who had been roaring around town in jeeps armed with 75mm. recoilless rifles, were no longer in evidence. I spotted two Swedish "bathtubs" (long, oval-shaped armored cars), the first sign that UN troops were moving into the center of the city. The UN contingent reminded me of the jokes that used to be made about a United Europe: the cooks would be English, the police would be German, and so on. Swedes, who had not fought a war in 300 years, were the combat troops, and the medical team was Italian.

At 10.30 A.M. in front of the Leopold II, a car was about to leave for Northern Rhodesia, about an hour's drive in normal circumstances. The car, a four-door right-hand-drive Vauxhall, belonged to John Nugent of *Newsweek,* who had loaned it to Jim Biddulph of the Rhodesian Broadcasting Corporation. Jim had a 1 P.M. radio connection in Kitwe, just the other side of the border. Sitting on Jim's left was Jean-Claude Favre, a Swiss member of Katanga's Economic Affairs Ministry, who was leaving Elizabethville and traveling light, with a shoe box as his only luggage. I was later told that the shoe box was filled with pound notes in large denominations. I should have chosen my traveling companions more carefully, but I wanted to file my story and beat my competition, the resourceful Dave Halberstam of the *New York Times*. I grabbed my portable typewriter and climbed into the back seat, which was loaded with tape recorders, suitcases, and a 20-gallon can of gasoline. A swarm of bees had affixed itself to the rear left window, and, despite the heat, we closed the other windows.

There were three ways out of Elizabethville to Northern Rhodesia. One went by the Union Minière buildings and another passed Camp Massart, but there was still fighting in both those places. We chose the third way, over a dirt road through an African township. We were outside the city limits, driving about fifteen miles an hour, when we approached a deserted railroad crossing that was littered with bicycles and debris. Bicycles with no people was not a healthy sign.

The debris made it necessary for us to proceed on the left side of the road. We were moving slowly toward the crossing when a burst of machine-gun fire came from the bush on the left, shattering the left front window. Several bullets struck Jean-Claude Favre, who was on Jim Biddulph's left, and a bullet grazed Biddulph's head. In a reflex action, Jim's foot went down on the accelerator, and the big sedan lurched ahead. A few yards farther, a bazooka shell fired at close range struck the column between the two doors, making a hole the size of a grapefruit, and shattering the windshield and the remaining windows.

I was in the back seat, reading Robert Graves' *I, Claudius*, when the firing began. I put my head between my knees and my hands over the back of my neck. I felt shell fragments tear into my back and my left knee. I did not have the slightest idea how badly hit I was. I put my hand inside my shirt front, thinking that the shell fragments had gone right through and expecting to feel blood.

Jim Biddulph opened the door on his side and fell out. His head reminded me of the Sherwin Williams ad where a can of red paint is being poured over a globe, with the caption "Covers the Earth." Favre could not move and remained hunched over in the front seat, clutching his shoe box and moaning. I pushed my door open and fell in the dirt next to Jim. We did not know who had fired at us. I was sure that someone was going to come out of the bush and finish us off. What a way to end, I thought, in a dirt road in Katanga.

"I have wrestled with death," says Marlow, the narrator in *Heart of Darkness*. "It is the most unexciting contest you can imagine. It takes place in an impalpable grayness, with nothing underfoot, with nothing around, without spectators, without clamor, without glory, without the great desire of victory, without the great fear of defeat, in a sickly atmosphere of tepid skepticism, without much belief in your own right, and still less in that of your adversary. If such is the form of ultimate wisdom, then life is a greater riddle than some of us think it to be." I wish I could have written that, although at that point life was not a riddle but an absurdity.

Jim and I lay in the road, yelling *"au secours!"* and "help!" and "unarmed," and "journalists," and "goddammshitassfuck." After about two minutes, a squad of Swedish soldiers came out of the bush and circled us. They were holding the railway crossing, and had mistaken us, in our unmarked car, for mercenaries . . . unless, as someone later theorized, they had been tipped off that Favre and his shoe box were in the car. When Favre saw the soldiers, he moaned, "Help me and I'll help you. I have something for you."

The Swedes called for two ambulances, which took us to the UN hospital at the Elizabethville airport, about a fifteen-minute drive. Biddulph was in one ambulance and I was in the other with Favre, who, as the Italian surgeon pointed out when we got there, was dead on arrival. The shoe box somehow disappeared.

Captain Surgeon Chipolat, a tall man with a bony, Punchinello-like face and dark intelligent eyes, had been operating nonstop for 48 hours. Casualties were high, and 150 United Nations wounded had been brought in, of whom he had lost two. Biddulph and I joined the assembly line. Jim had several shell fragments under his scalp which could not be removed, and his left arm was paralyzed. To this day, he wears a metal plate in his head. About a dozen shell fragments had dug into my shoulder and fractured my collarbone. Chipolat removed those he could find, as well as three fragments in my knee-cap. A plaster cast was wrapped around my torso and my left leg. But Chipolat sewed up my knee without removing several threads from my torn trouser-leg which had stuck to the wound. The knee became infected, and I had to be operated on again, this time in London. No matter, he was a fine surgeon and a fine man, and he saved many lives. We were taken from the operating table to the improvised infirmary for the wounded, which included Gurkha, Irish, and Swedish soldiers. The Swedes were the only ones who received packages from home, crammed with chocolate, cigarettes, sausage, and Swedish delicacies like smoked remindeer meat. They never shared any of this loot with the other soldiers. To this day, I can admit to no special fondness for Swedes. High UN officials, including Brigadier R. A. S. Raja and Brian Urquart, came to our bedside and assured us that the incident had been a tragic mistake. After five days in the infirmary, with nights made sleepless by the cries of the wounded, I was offered a ride to Leopoldville aboard the private DC–6 of the UN commander, General Sean McKeown. In Leopoldville, the American embassy, advised by my newspaper, arranged to have me put on a Sabena flight to London. My own embassy, the French, did not get involved in any way.

The incident at the UN roadblock left me with a strong sense of my own impermanence. I had known that I would die someday, known it as an impersonal fact, but I had not believed it. Now I believed it. I saw the rest of my life in the form of a reprieve. The line between life and death had depended on a seating arrangement. If I had sat up front with Biddulph, instead of in back with the luggage, I would have caught the machine-gun fire. If that had happened, I asked myself, what would I have died for? For a story, for a headline, for something people throw away after reading it.

Well, yes, trivial enough, but at the same time I would have died in the exercise of my profession, which was in the scheme of things. There was nothing shameful in it; nothing devoutly to be wished for, either. The *Herald Tribune* had taken good care of me. They had been concerned. They had gone to considerable trouble and expense. They had put me in a private room in St. George's Hospital in London, and they had kept me on salary during the months of my convalescence. They had not, however, agreed to pay their share of the destroyed *Newsweek* Vauxhall, a rented car whose owner was asking for $1500. My newspaper's accountant wrote *Newsweek* that "the Herald Tribune will only pay its share of the mileage to the point of destruction for the time our correspondent shared the vehicle with you." That was about two miles, or $1.50 plus tip in a New York taxi. Drunken colleagues, their pockets filled with quarters, called me in my London hospital room from the pay phone in the Artists and Writers Club, next to the *Trib* building. It was only natural, you may say, but my own people, the French, had not bothered to investigate my mishap. It was the American consul, Lewis Hoffacker, who came to see me in the UN hospital, not the French. In Katanga, I was ignored by the French and taken care of by the Americans. The form my gratitude took was a small kernel of allegiance, toward my newspaper, and by extension, toward the country in which it was published. I think it was in Katanga that I decided

I was an American, although another fifteen years elapsed before I took the necessary steps to become one.

The Transformation

I feel that Ted Morgan and Sanche de Gramont are two different persons. Much more than my name has changed. De Gramont was concerned with proprieties. He kissed women's hands. At dinner parties he made polite conversation, first with the woman on his left, then with the woman on his right. There were rules to be observed. Morgan, at a dinner party, became so absorbed in telling someone across the table what a porcine opportunist Pat Moynihan was (just look at that face, the bloated forum of a hundred dishonorable compromises) that he forgot to take the finger bowl off his plate and dumped a large helping of peach melba into it.

De Gramont was an elitist, conscious of family background. Morgan admired people who had come up from nothing, simple citizens who became great by no other means than the energy of their own character, self-made elitists like Bernard Berenson, the Latvian immigrant who grew up in Boston and made himself the world authority on Florentine painting. Berenson spent most of his adult life in his famous villa outside Florence, I Tatti, the curator of his private museum. "I have been in Italy for sixty years," he wrote, "and am not a bit of an Italian . . . Nationality means identifying oneself with the entire *past* of a people, its political and social history, its great men in all fields, its myths, and its present position. That did happen to me in the twelve years of my boyhood and youth that I passed in Boston, and I still feel that America is my only country and Boston my only home."

When one of his American friends said something offensive about the French, de Gramont felt obliged to defend his countrymen. Morgan realized that he had settled into his new identity one night at the home of his friends Ann and Herman Roiphe, where one of the guests was a lady novelist catapulted to prominence by the candor of her sexual scenes. The mascot of this courtesan of letters was a thin bearded youth whom she held on an invisible leash. The conversation turned to nudism, and our hostess said that she had been to the French nudist colony in the Ile du Levant once, and that the nudists were extremely doctrinaire: they had all kinds of regulations, there was no touching of any kind. "That's the frogs for you," the lady novelist's consort said. A remark like that would have started de Gramont's adrenalin flowing, but Morgan was impassive. "God, that's so froggy," the consort went on. "The French are despicable. They allow their dogs in the best restaurants. You go to a three-star restaurant and it's full of smelly dogs." I was amused that the consort was complaining about dogs when he was so evidently his mistress' pet, heeling on demand. But I did not come to the defense of the French. It was no longer my quarrel. I was pleased that nothing about me had tipped the consort off to my origins. It was like passing for white in a group of red-necks.

De Gramont was a male chauvinist. He would rather have swum the East River than washed a dish. He was, after all, the grandson of a man who had refused to let his wife breast-feed her children because it would interfere with his social schedule. De Gramont had once written an article entitled "How to Train an American Wife," in which he explained how he had taught his wife to clean lettuce by drying each leaf individually with a towel.

Morgan was responsive to the arguments of the women's movement. He felt that women were equal, if not superior to men. He wanted more women in government, and business, and the professions, and in the Sanitation Department. He wanted them to be paid as much money as men. He promised his wife that he would abandon all seigniorial pretensions and do his share of the housework. Morgan made the bed and did the shopping, although he hated supermarkets. They were the last enclaves of social conditioning, where female anarchy reigned.

Morgan liked to get the shopping done fast, but such was not the goal of many women shoppers, whose carts blocked the aisles as they stared dreamily at the shelves. Shopping for them seemed to fulfill some emotional need. Morgan was irate at the women who stood in the express line (eight items or less) with both decks of their shopping cart heavily laden. Remonstrances (Madam, I wonder if you realize . . .) went unheeded. Then there were the absent-minded ones, who took their place in line, but abandoned their carts to hunt down some forgotten item. And the ones with a half-pint of cottage cheese and one green pepper who wrote out a check that had to be approved by the manager. Once Morgan was in line behind a woman who had a can of something which said on the back of the label that if the label was returned she would get ten cents off the price of the next can purchased. She tore the label off and demanded her ten cents off, a gesture of such bold illogic that the cashier was rendered speechless. Morgan felt like the dreamer in John Cheever's "The Death of Justine," who pushes his cart through a supermarket where all the labels have been removed, while his fellow shoppers deliberate gravely over mysterious containers, about the contents of which nothing is known. It is possible to draw up the personality profile of a woman by the way she behaves in a supermarket. It is one of the ways in which she reveals her true self, like her handwriting or the position she sleeps in. Another type that made Morgan's teeth gnash was the well-meaning busybody who hunted down the manager and said: "Joe, you're out of Softweve."

De Gramont was a French father, strict and unyielding. Children had to be in bed at the appointed hour, rooms had to be kept neat, television was forbidden. Morgan was a permissive father, who let his children stay up in messy rooms and watch the tube. Morgan allowed his fourteen-year-old son to grow a marijuana plant in his room. He rationalized this by saying that it was a good way to get him interested in botany. His son paid far more attention to his plant than to his school work, lovingly spraying its every leaf and tendril with an atomizer, and inviting his school friends up to gaze at this wonder of urban gardening. Morgan sometimes came home to find his son and several of his friends smoking pot, and when they offered him a drag, he took it. De Gramont would never have allowed marijuana in the house. He would have punished his son had he caught him smoking it. Morgan's strategy was that if he banned it, it would be smoked in any case, secretly. It was better to keep it in the open, and to talk about it, and to know what was going on. The transaction was: you can smoke pot, as long as you do it infrequently, as long as your grades don't drop, and as long as I know about it. The stories his son brought home concerning the drug scene in his private school in the East Seventies (angel dust and acid) made Morgan feel that his policy of containment was paying off.

De Gramont had not been completely committed to his writing. He was easily distracted. He devoted himself with equal interest to the pleasures of the flesh. He wrote books for the wrong reasons. He had written a book on the Niger River because he wanted to take his wife on a trip across the Sahara and into black Africa. The book was secondary to the trip. It should have been the other way around. Morgan was obsessively concerned with his work. It was the one way he had of confirming his new identity. He was pleased when an editor told him that his writing had improved. De Gramont had a penchant for the polished phrase. Morgan was moving in the direction of a "no frills" style, soundly engineered, but economical. When he won a prize for an article and heard his name called and stood up to receive it, he knew that Ted Morgan existed. Striving for excellence was his inner homeland. Since assuming his name in 1973, Morgan had worked harder and accomplished more than de Gramont had in fifteen years of writing. Morgan had caught the American virus for achievement. He knew it was a chestnut, but he wanted to be the immigrant who makes good. He wanted it as badly as Sergeant York wanted that piece of bottom land.

A Song of America

There is a land mass between New York and Los Angeles. It is known as America. I sing of America, one nation, indistinguishable, with appliances and accessories for all.

Split Logs, not Atoms.
PIG Means Pride, Integrity, and Grit.
God Said It! I Believe It! And That Settles It!
You'll Get My Gun When You Pry It from My Cold Dead Fingers.
Did the Coyotes Get Your Deer?
In God We Trusted, In Kansas We Busted.
Navy Divers Do It Deeper.
Honk if You Love Mozart.
Virginia Is for Living Lovers.
We Brake for Garage Sales.
OUR GREATEST ASSET—YOUR GOOD WILL.

Home of the Chickahominy Indians.

> *For 25,000 years*
> *Before the white man came,*
> *Indians were running this country.*
> *No taxes, no debts, no phones,*
> *No jailhouses, courthouses, cathouses,*
> *No nuthouses, no banks.*
> *WOMEN DID ALL THE WORK!*
> *White man thought he could improve*
> *Upon a system like that.*

"We'll have more on the soybean situation after this message."

Serviceman's outlet — repossessed mobile homes.

U-PIC CUKES.

Sleep in Comfort, Texas, between Alice, Texas, and Louise, Texas.

Mike's Dineraunt — Easy On, Easy Off.

The Above and Beyond Police Officers Association of Savannah, Georgia, Welcomes You-All.

PRIVATE PROPERTY KEEP OUT — THIS MEANS YOU!

> Oh give me a big silver dollar
> To slap on the bar with a bang.
> A bill that is creased
> May do in the East
> But we want *our* money to *clang!*

Bob Chanler had a passion for the names of the states of America. He used to say that such names as Ohio, Alabama, Oklahoma, Wyoming and so forth, were beautiful words. Often while sitting in his huge chair, or even at the dining room table, his great voice would suddenly bellow out over the noisy conversation, O H I O, O H I O, *he would shout over and over again, or* U T A H, U T A H.

Fight Truth Decay South of the Border — Pedro.

He had the ring, he had the flat, she felt his chin, and that was that.

WE TRIM OUR BEEF, NOT OUR CUSTOMERS.

"There's an old adage in the meat business — you sell it or you smell it. But back to the WNCT Farm Hour."

"The slack pine is the only pine that grows in water. Spanish moss is not a parasite, it's an air-feeding plant that can grow on dead trees and does not harm the trees. The black gum tree is covered with a lichen called Old Man's Beard."

"Here's a tip on how to keep your Christmas tree fresh."

The state song of Idaho is: Here We Have Idaho.

The easternmost point of America is West Quoddy Head.

> *Engine engine number nine*
> *Going down Chicago line,*
> *If the train goes off the track*
> *Do you want your money back?*

The Eye of Providence in a Radiant Triangle.

SQUEEZE A FRUIT FOR ANITA BRYANT.

I was working in a grocery store.
The manager kept after me.
I took off my apron and handed it to him and said "Here, you can do
this better than I can."
He said he'd complain to the union.
I said, "The phone is on the wall."

"Montana, land of the shining mountains, last of the big-time splendors, casts 20 votes for a great American, Ronald Reagan."

FREE LUNCH R.I.P.

"Buy motorcycles made in America by Americans. Why buy a motorcycle made by a bunch of people we defeated in the war? A bunch of people we wiped out at Hiroshima?"

"The walls of Hemingway's house were built of Baltimore blocks. These were used as ballast for ships bringing ice to Key West."

"When we were kids in North Carolina our mother gave us kerosene as a cure-all, a spoonful with sugar. We ate red clay — it was real good. We ate it by the spoonful. When we came North she really insisted on it, but she couldn't find any. She ate laundry starch, she said it had the same texture."

"We just can't pick 'em up too fresh," said the man who sells lacquered buffalo chips from Catalina island at $30 each.

SEALTEST HEAVENLY HASH — MMMMM GOOD.

"Bread was then not sliced or wrapped. Children and maids waited with baskets to take home loaves hot from the oven."

The people of the South, animated by the spirit of 1776, to preserve their rights, withdrew from the federal compact in 1861. The North resorted to coercion. During the war there were 2254 engagements; in 1882 of those at least a regiment took part. Number of men enlisted: Confederate armies, 800,000; federal armies, 2,859,132. Losses from all causes: Confederate, 437,000; Federal, 485,216.

General Sherman was Atlanta's first urban renewal expert.

"I don't like to make waves. You waste a lot of hull speed making waves."

The Driskill, Host to Famous Americans since 1866. Luncheon and Socializing Parlor.

Pull 'er up a tad, please, mister.

The group of children in Kansas City's Loose Park were wearing T-shirts that said: Recreation With a Purpose.

Back in New York:
Would you fight if they attacked Texas?
I'd cheer.
What if they attacked New York?
Where in New York?
The Bronx.
I'd be delighted.
The West Side.
I wouldn't even fight for the West Side. I'd start fighting when they got a block away, when they got to 71st Street. I'd fight for my block association. That's the extent of my loyalty.
What about the domino theory? If 71st Street goes, 70th Street will go too.
It didn't work in Vietnam, why should it work here? I'll man the barricades at 70th Street.

(The preceding dialogue is not an attempt to show the absurdity of isolationism but an illustration of Morton Grodzin's theory in *The Loyal and the Disloyal* that in a democracy, loyalty to the nation is a pyramid of individual loyalties to groups and idea-systems that satisfy life-needs).

* * *

I want to get all of America down but I can't, all I can offer is a cut-rate tour. De Tocqueville is looking over my shoulder and saying, why bother, I've said it all, and behind him there are a thousand others. I've been waking up in a cold sweat in the early morning hours and shouting "This is impossible." This is going to be a book of fragments, of overlooked corners and found objects like the pieces of driftwood that Santa Barbara housewives turn into lamps. I can't possibly come close, there's too much to be said, too much to grasp, it would take twenty lifetimes. But I feel this is the right country for me. Not only that, compared to the rest of the world, it works.

America and the World

Ignazio Silone tells the story of a mysterious impresario who visits a small Abruzzi village and slowly, without anyone knowing how, accumulates all the wealth. The impresario's prosperity reminds the villagers of the success stories of Italian emigrants to America. "The peasants have to cross the sea to find America," the villagers said, "but this robber has found it here." "America," some other villagers replied, "America is far away and doesn't even look like this." At this point, the impresario came on the scene and told them: "America is everywhere. It's everywhere, you just have to know how to look for it."

When I say that today America is everywhere, I don't mean that blue jeans are sold on the black market in Moscow and that rock music is popular in Prague and that copies of *Playboy* are smuggled at great cost into Saudi Arabia and that the French are having problems with Franglais. I mean that America, not China, is the country of the permanent revolution and the vanguard for the rest of the world. America did what China under Mao could not; it brought down its own "gang of the four" (Nixon, Haldeman, Erlichman, and Mitchell). This was a revolution without revolutionaries, done with due process, with reporters taking the place of bomb-throwers. This is something so phenomenal that people don't grasp its significance: built into this country's framework is the possibility of permanent revolution. America is the incubator where the wild schemes are hatched. It offers the example of people successfully demonstrating for their rights. As Brian Moore said, "the Catholic protests in Northern Ireland began in Selma, Alabama."

Percy Qoboza, thirty-nine year-old editor of *The World*, South Africa's principal black newspaper, and author of the column "Percy's Pitch," was radicalized when he went to Harvard as a Niemann Fellow in 1975. "At first I found it hard to adjust to the fact that I was living in a free society," he said. "When I went to Harvard Square for a meal, I was tempted to look in the window of a place, to see if there were any blacks inside, before going in. The experience forced me to look at myself, and I was surprised to find that I was an Uncle Tom. When I went back to South Africa, I was unable to accept things that had seemed quite normal before." In October 1977 the South African government closed down *The World* and jailed Qoboza.

The parallel between the situation in South Africa and America's civil rights movement was made explicit by Andrew Young when he visited Johannesburg in May 1976. "With all the obvious differences of time and place," he told 200 South African business leaders, most of them white, "I have myself lived through some experiences that could have some meaning for you." Young, of course, had been an aide of Martin Luther King, Jr., and had lived through the boycotts and the marches. To see a black American civil rights leader addressing a group of white businessmen, most of whom were sympathizers with, if nor architects of, apartheid, was a historical incongruity that brought to mind La Pasionaria addressing an audience of Falangists, or Solzhenitsyn lecturing to the plenary congress of the Communist party. Before his speech was over, more than one of his listeners must have wondered by what aberration their government had opened its gates to this Trojan-American horse. The originality of his message lay in its appeal for the abolition of ideology. Guns had not been his weapon, but the boycott, which affected business interests. This was the American way: "People will vote their interest, not their ideology." Like Selma businessmen, South Africans had no choice but "to work it out or fight it out, and I hope you work it out."

The message spread to the Eastern bloc. In the fifties, the sorcerer's apprentices in the CIA goaded dissident Hungarians into revolution, with false promises of assistance and predictable results. In the seventies, as part of détente, the Soviet Union signed the Helsinki agreement, with its provision for human rights. Today, with-

out interference from the CIA, but with our own civil rights movement as an example to follow, there is a flourishing human rights
movement in the Soviet Union. For Jimmy Carter to receive a Soviet
dissident at the White House strikes me as an improvement over
inciting Hungarians to revolt.

This is one world in the sense that certain things cannot be stopped
at the border. We couldn't stop clouds emitted by a Chinese nuclear
bomb test held on September 26, 1976, from dropping fallout on the
Northeastern United States in heavy October rains, and causing
Pennsylvania cows to give radioactive milk. Nor can the Eastern bloc
completely keep from its people some of the strange happenings in
this country, such as school desegregation, the appointment of blacks
to cabinet posts, and the relentless public airing of our scandals.
"When I return from Eastern Europe with its censored news," John
Cheever says, "it is weeks before I can comprehend the astonishment
and naiveté with which the *New York Times* reports that venerable
judges, esteemed doctors and Princes of the Church accept bribes,
fornicate, and spit on the floor."

As Louis Simpson describes "A Visitor from Russia,"

> In Russia, he said, a poet is important,
> "Like one of your own senators."
> If two poets meet one evening,
> Next day what they said is all
> Over Moscow.
>
> It was different here, I told him.
> A poet can say anything,
> It has no effect
> We don't have those great evenings
> In Moscow
> Or the long nights in Siberia.

I'm not talking about the 10,000 political and religious prisoners
(according to Amnesty) who in their despair pretend to escape so
they can be shot by their guards, or who swallow nails and thermom-
eters and chess pieces and ground glass in attempts at self-mutilation.
I'm not talking about the dissidents like the mathematician Leonid
Plyusch, whose one letter of protest earned him five years in a mental
hospital, the Cuckoo's Nest Soviet style. I'm talking about the average Russian, the one who accepts the system, the one who reads
Pravda and gets drunk on Saturday night, and the withering of his

spirit, and the cant he has to stuff his mind with. When the great Cuban runner Juantorena won the 800 meters at the Montreal Olympics in 1976, he said: "I dedicate this to our leader Fidel Castro. As any revolutionary, I worked in the sugar fields and helped the economy of our country, and I would do it again. During the race, I didn't think of anything except winning the gold medal for Cuba, my country." My mind wandered back to the Munich Olympics, when I had seen two black American runners give the black power salute as they received their medals. I preferred their proud and public dissidence to Juantorena's canned patriotism. There are always one or two Eastern-bloc athletes who defect during the Olympics, because America is everywhere.

The Russians don't realize that when they let American rock groups perform in the Soviet Union while they continue to jam Radio Free Europe (a feeble propaganda effort which convinces no one), they have got things ass-backward. Rock music is the true American form of agit-prop, a subversive force that has blown the minds of thousands of young Russians. When the Nitty Gritty Dirt Band from Aspen, Colorado, became the first American rock band to tour Russia in May 1977, their 100-decibel rock brought their young audiences to a frenzy they had never experienced by attending indoctrination lectures. The musicians were amazed at the reaction, and at the teen-age girls who showed up wearing T-shirts that read, in English, "Friendship U.S.A."

America is everywhere because it was finally able to turn its back on Europe. It fulfilled the prophecy in Emerson's famous Phi Beta Kappa address at Harvard: "Our day of dependence, our long apprenticeship to the learning of other lands, draws to a close. Events, actions, arise, that must be sung, that will sing themselves." Henry James' nineteenth-century reverence for England (he felt he needed an accumulation of history and custom, absent from the texture of American life, to form a fund of suggestion for his work), is outdated. So is T. S. Eliot's rejection of his American upbringing and his Unitarian faith (the good man subordinating his selfish desires to the good of church and community) in favor of "a new imagined order . . . based on royalism, classicism, and Anglo-Catholicism." So is the corollary of uncritical admiration of Europe, the chip-on-the-shoulder attitude of the Yankee Puritan in Europe-Babylon. We should maintain a healthy irreverence toward Europe. I like the tone of the college student I heard last summer talking about his year in Switzerland. "I met a guy who told me he was from the North of Switzerland," he said. "I said, there's no North of Switzerland, it's like saying you're from the North of Connecticut. What about the mountain passes, he said? We were studying advanced wood shaving. One time an instructor sneezed. He went Achi. I said, back home we go Achoo. And we started discussing what was right, Achi or Achoo."

The other attitude today is Europe as a museum, a reminder of what we have lost, a collection of pretty landscapes and quaint customs which it does the soul good to visit once in a while. This is the way James Dickey sees Europe, and I'm willing to listen, because I admire James Dickey, not only as a poet, but because he has lived two lives. He was a college football star and went to war in a bomber crew, and then he settled down as an advertising copywriter, working on the Coca-Cola account for McCann Erickson, where he was known as Jingle Jim. But the clock was running, as they say in football games, and he quit to write poetry at the age of thirty-eight, when most would-be lyric poets have either died of consumption or abandoned all hope. Here is what he has to say about Europe: "What we'll end up with if the world gets increasingly Americanized is life in a gigantic Rexall's. Of course you can go into Rexall's and get a lot of things you need. You can also get a lot of things you don't need, but might be interested in having. There are a lot of diversified products in Rexall's but Rexall's is Rexall's.

"It's not the same as going to a bullfight or going to a folk dance in Sicily or going into the Uffizi museum in Florence. When an American goes to Europe, he doesn't go there to get just another version of America. He wants difference. You see fields of tulips in Holland. You never saw anything like that in your life. You see cliffs down on the Amalfi Drive, you see people in an Italian village. The guys having a drink together: Why, by God, they fall into each other's arms — and they just saw each other last night; they were probably drunk together last night. You don't see Americans doing that. Americans are pushing each other away all the time, even the men and the women."

Well, that's fine, if you can accept countries that cannot and will not get off dead center. Above all, history has taught Europe a sense of limitations. They know what cannot be done because it has been tried before, what is not worth doing, what is pointless and has been proved wrong, they are smothered in obstructionism. European countries are played out. They've lived through their growing pains and their maturity and now they are enjoying the golden years of retirement. Their chiefs of state are museum curators, in charge of old masters that need a little cleaning and retouching from time to time. America, by comparison, is still an unquarried block of rough marble.

My God, look at England, with its anachronistic religious war in Northern Ireland and its decaying upper classes; the grandsons of the empire-makers have turned innkeepers in order to pay the taxes on their historic estates. England, with its stultifying monarchy (visit courts and monarchies as you would visit a zoo, Jefferson advised) — here is an extract from the points of protocol during Queen Elizabeth's 1976 visit to America: "Shaking hands: in large crowds, the Queen and the Duke of Edinburgh usually do not shake hands. When being introduced, wait until they have extended their hands before extending yours. Bowing or curtsying: The Queen does not expect Americans to curtsy or bow, especially in an informal situation. You may, however, merely bow your head slightly when being introduced. If you wish to curtsy, it should be a short, quick bob. Men should simply bow their heads." Well, it's mighty big of Her Majesty not to expect Americans to curtsy and bow (she should curtsy to us for keeping the sceptered isle afloat through two world wars), but I feel sorry for a country that has this pair of useless puppets as role models. "Sometimes I wish we could hear of a country that's out of kings," Huck Finn said to Nigger Jim. In the third quarter of the twentieth century, an overriding concern with protocol and tradition is a sign of stagnation. Prince Philip is so hemmed in by tradition that he was unable to have removed from Buckingham Palace the bagpiper that serenades his breakfast. Queen Elizabeth is so tradition-bound that she rode to her coronation in an eighteenth-century carriage. Tradition in this sense is a web of archaic restrictions, bad habits like the five-times-a-day tea break, and insurance companies that don't investigate your claims, but investigate your lineage.

At least England has a working parliamentary government, but what to think of a country like Greece, where the shipping magnates dictate to the government? "So you want to tax our foreign assets," the shipping magnates said, "in that case Greece will no longer have one of the world's largest merchant fleets." And their foreign assets were not taxed. Even the most advanced European nations are in some way deadening and retrograde. Ah, the beauty of Switzerland, and the efficiency: the phones work, the mails work, they understand business, they wouldn't even exist if it weren't for the banks, it's a democracy, they have proud traditions of freedom. Much to my surprise, I learned that one thing they forgot in their democracy was habeas corpus. Swiss authorities can hold you indefinitely in what they call "investigatory custody." A Spanish banker named Munoz, whose bank failed in 1965, was held for nine years, setting a record. Aside from that, the Swiss are on the same scale as their country, small-minded, penny-pinching, and ever-conscious of boundaries that must not be crossed. It's a nation of kindergarten teachers, busy listing do's and dont's on the blackboard.

And what about Scandinavia, the Socialist paradise? One of my best friends, a writer named Michael Wolfert, was living in New York with his Swedish wife, Sieme. She hated it. She worked herself up into such a state that she was afraid to go out in the street. She finally convinced him that they should go live in Sweden. "It's going to be great," he told me. "They have cradle-to-grave welfare, every citizen is taken care of, Sieme can register at Lund University — that's on the Swedish Riviera — and she'll be paid for going to school. That's the way they do it over there, they pay you for going to school. And I'll get some kind of job, and we'll drink aquavit and eat smoked reindeer meat." Six months later Michael wrote me: "Life here is full of small minds and small discouragements . . . I quit my job as carwasher because the conditions were bad and the pay was bad and I got the cancer fear from the chemicals. It took two weeks to find another job — as a packer in a warehouse, an absolutely mind-numbing job. The carwashing was a million times better — if only there had been some air to breathe and you didn't have to swallow so much acid and photogen. The warehouse is a sad place full of racists and mental cripples. There is never any possibility of being free here. There is no one who walks around looking free. You see the deliberation and the planning in every step."

Granted the tulip fields and the Amalfi cliffs and the bullfighting and the changing of the guard and the edelweiss and the Norwegian fjords and all the other collector's items, there is something numbing and constricted about Europe. Europe became irrelevant during my lifetime. One has to come to America to get a sense of life's possibilities. I like to go back to Europe once in a while to eat the good food and drink the good wine and drive through the "old master" landscapes, and it does my heart good, it brings me serenity, but I no more want to live in Europe than I want to be a peasant in a Brueghel painting. I'd rather be a half-sketched figure on the unfinished canvas of America. We are after all not so far removed from the days when Boston Harbor, in the words of Carlyle, was "black with unexpected tea." D. H. Lawrence, who fled the shopkeeper's mentality of his own country, understood this, and what he had to say fifty years ago in "The Spirit of Place" is still worth hearing: "Somewhere deep in every American heart lies a rebellion against the old parenthood of Europe. Yet no American feels he has completely escaped its mastery. America has never been easy, and is not easy today. Americans have always been at a certain tension. Their liberty is a thing of sheer will . . . The real American day hasn't begun yet. Or at least not yet sunrise. So far it has been the false dawn. That is, in the progressive American consciousness there has been the one dominant desire, to do away with the old thing . . . But underneath, and contrary to this open ideal, the first hints and revelations of IT, IT, the American whole soul."

Lawrence did not live to see America escape Europe's mastery. America had to bail out Europe in two world wars before escaping its mastery. Then America found its own touchstones and talismans. Then America saw that it no longer needed Europe because it had assimilated Europe through the open pores of its immigration policies and the purchasing power of its museums. I wish Lawrence were alive today to see that there is no IT, no single version of the American whole soul, but a THEM, a plural, perhaps making a pattern like a forest seen from high altitude.

I stumble upon the American whole soul in out-of-the-way places. In the Brandywine Museum in Pennsylvania I came across a painting by N. C. Wyeth, the father of Andrew Wyeth. N. C. Wyeth was a magazine illustrator known for his painstaking research. For instance, he read Nicolay and Hay's ten-volume history of Lincoln before attempting a panel for the Boston Federal Reserve Bank. The painting I saw in the Brandywine Museum, occupying an entire wall, is called: "In a Dream I Meet General Washington." It is a painting that makes the mythical past homey and familiar. Instead of seeing Washington the face on the quarter, we see Washington as one of us, as he must have been, trying to buy food from the good people of New Jersey, who preferred selling it to the British and getting paid in sterling instead of Continentals. Wyeth stands on a scaffolding, brushes in hand, with his back to the viewer, and Washington, leading his troops through a field, with hills and woods and puffs of smoke and fallen soldiers in the background, stops for a moment in midbattle and leans from his horse to chat with the artist, across the centuries. I would call this a great work of American surrealism if it were not so utterly convincing.

Better one Wyeth than ten imitators of the Paris school. Better a neon sign than a bust in the manner of Rodin. Better a General Electric frost-free refrigerator than a Louis XIV chair. Why this breast-beating because we don't revere antiques, because we don't pass on wormy bureaus to our children? I want no family furniture, no cherished bric-a-brac, no heirlooms, no chairs and tables worn smooth by the accumulated rubbing of generations. America has given us the discardo culture. It is the only country rich enough to be able to afford to throw away its tangible past. We are what we discard, or rather, we were what we discarded, for the discardo culture affirms our independence from objects. If we want to collect something, it's no more foolish to collect early Coca-Cola machines, old Wurlitzers, or period Iron City Beer cans (a 1935 example of which is worth $400 on today's market). The discardo culture is anti-keepsake and anti-clutter. I wish there were more things we could throw away, like clothing once it's been worn. My son, when he was four, made me a throwaway tie for Christmas, a paper tie with a design that I was supposed to wear once and throw away. It was one of the nicest presents I ever received. In Europe, as Daniel Boorstin pointed out, it takes a revolution for a building to be torn down. Why wait for rampaging mobs to destroy the Bastille when you can hire a contractor? Americans don't build monuments to be demolished by future insurrections, they put up housing with built-in obsolescence. Thus, America's relics are not destroyed to deny the past but to improve on it.

Having dealt with Europe and the Eastern bloc, let me now give the Third World, where I spent a number of years, its due. Most of these countries, recently emerged from colonialism, are still in their infancy, and their problems are those of infant survival. It's impossible for Americans to imagine that there are countries which cannot feed themselves. That is why the Peace Corps was valuable, not only in terms of the assistance given, but in terms of the education received by the volunteers. They gained a first-hand experience of human misery. The United Nations ambassador from Upper Volta, one of the poorest countries in the world, once said to me: "How can Americans understand a country with a per capita income of $100 a year, when they spend that for a night out?"

When I was traveling through West Africa in 1972, I stayed in villages where you could not buy an egg. You would go to the market and there would be nothing to buy except cassava root. What if an American shopper was faced with an empty supermarket and a manager who said: "We're out of everything." There were nights in West Africa when, after a meal of manioc or rice, I dreamed of supermarkets. There were times when I saw Nigerian villages that made urban ghettos like Brownsville and the South Bronx seem like desirable neighborhoods. We are complacent about what we have because our imagination cannot grasp what it is not to have it. To me, a supermarket is a miraculous place. I remember the covered market in Ouagadougou, with the vultures perched on its pillars, and the children in rags who followed me for blocks until I dropped my cigar stub, and who fought over it in the gutter.

The Third World is a school for hopelessness. Just as we take abundance for granted, we think personal freedom thrives in all climates. I was in the Fiji Islands in the spring of 1976 with Malcolm Forbes, the owner of *Forbes* magazine, who was inspecting an island he had bought. Forbes' secretary, Mary-Ann Danner, was talking to the wife of the man who managed the copra plantation, a New Zealander, who said: "I've been wanting to send my sons to school in New Zealand, but the Fijians won't allow it, they say, we've got schools. I can't even leave the country for medical help. The Fijians say — we've got doctors."

"It seems incredible that they won't let you do what you want," Mary-Ann Danner said.

It does to you, Mary-Ann, but these are the conditions prevailing on four fifths of the planet. Americans think democracy is the rule, when it is the exception. As Jorge Luis Borges told Bill Buckley, "I think that in 100 years Argentina may be ready for democracy." It's the same all over the Third World; even when the standard of living rises, there is misery and institutionalized corruption and disregard for the rule of law. In Mexico, 65 years after the Mexican revolution, four million peasants are still without land and five million others can barely feed their families, and the Ministry of Agrarian Reform is a corrupt and confusing bureaucracy. The one thing they know how to do is double their population every thirty years and send the surplus across the Rio Grande. In Brazil, they rely on torture and death squads to keep law and order, while Chile's right-wing regimentation is nicely balanced by Cuba's left-wing regimentation.

I lived in Morocco for four years, and while the country was beautiful, the government of King Hassan II was corrupt and arbitrary. The king's brother, Moulay Hassan, was the man foreign businessmen had to pay off if they wanted a deal to go through. A small example of the arbitrariness was the problem a friend of mine had when he bought a piece of land in Tangier and wanted to build on it. His permit to build was turned down without a reason. He later learned that his projected house would have blocked the view that Princess Lala Fatima Zora, one of the king's aunts, had of the dog cemetery, where one of her best-loved poodles was buried.

I recently got together with two writer friends who had lived in Morocco, William Burroughs and John Hopkins, and we were talking about what it was like there, and wondering about another writer, Paul Bowles, who still lives in Tangier and shows no inclination to depart. "Paul wrote me," Burroughs said, "that he was parked by the side of the road in his car drinking a cup of coffee and smoking a cigarette when he was arrested as a spy. I wrote him back — you could be sitting by the side of the road and drinking coffee in this country and you would not be arrested as a spy. It would not happen in this country."

John Hopkins told about a Spanish painter named Bravo who had been arrested as a spy because he had a telescope in his house. He also told about Driss, a young Moroccan who had come to the United States to go to forestry school and who had returned to Morocco as one of the few persons qualified in his field. But when he tried to get a job there was so much resentment over his American education that he left Morocco in disgust. That is another thing about the Third World — these countries have a way of alienating their best people.

The curious thing about Burroughs is that his work, from *Naked Lunch* to the book he is now working on, *Cities of the Red Night*, has been an indictment of American society. And yet, after years of wandering, he came back to America in 1973 and now says: "I like this country more and more." Burroughs for years was an outcast, his books were banned and he was thought of as some sort of evil genius. Since he was completely candid about his drug addiction, his name was on the customs suspect list in the United States and Great Britain. It usually took him at least an hour to get through customs. Once, arriving in England, the customs official gave him a hard look and asked: "Why have you come to this country, Mr. Burroughs?" "For the food and the climate," Burroughs replied. In 1959, when *Naked Lunch* was published in Paris by Olympia Press, it was banned in the United States as a dirty book. I was in Paris that summer, and a publisher friend asked me to bring him back a copy. I concealed the book in the battery compartment of my Zenith portable radio, where a customs inspector found it. "What are you doing with this?" he asked, holding the book between two fingers as though it might contaminate him?

"I'm a writer," I said, "and I need it for my work."

"Where do you work," the inspector asked, "the Kansas City whorehouse?" He confiscated my copy of *Naked Lunch.*

Today, Burroughs is a part of the literary establishment and frequently reads from his work on college campuses. He has given a reading in Washington attended by members of both houses of Congress, and he recently read in that citadel of pious thinking, the University of Notre Dame. Burroughs is an example of America reaching out and assimilating its dissidents and outsiders.

America's dissidents are not committed to mental hospitals and sent into exile; they thrive and prosper and buy a house in Nantucket and take flyers in the commodities market. Allen Ginsberg, the salmon in the river of American poetry, who swims upstream to spawn, has incorporated himself for tax purposes.

My first reaction, that of the grateful immigrant, is to say: "Don't pick on America — I'll throw you to Merle Haggard":

> If you don't love it leave it
> Let the song that I'm singin' be a warnin',
> When you're runnin' down our country hoss,
> You're walking on the fightin' side of me.

My second reaction, that of the acclimated citizen, is to say: "You're missing the point, Merle. One of the reasons I like this country is that I can run it down to my heart's content without being sent to a cold dark place."

Only in America

Contemporary America is impossible to satirize because no one can imagine anything more far-fetched than what is actually happening. When Summit County Prosecutor Stephen M. Gabalac was discussing the possibility that the 1973 all-American soapbox derby was rigged, he said: "It's like learning that the Ivory Snow girl was making blue movies." Well, the Ivory Snow girl, Marilyn Chambers, *was* making blue movies like *Behind the Green Door,* and the soapbox derby *was* rigged.

If you wanted to satirize higher education, you could write a skit about a course in garbage. It would be true. At the University of

Arizona, William Rathje teaches "Garbage Archeology," or "Garbology." Funded by foundation grants, and inoculated against tetanus and diphtheria, Rathje and his students pick through Tucson garbage cans for the same reason other archeologists dig for Aztec potsherds, to learn about the culture ("they must be nice people," I heard someone in my building once say, "they have such nice garbage"). Not surprisingly, their main discovery was that conspicuous waste knows no class boundaries. Mexican-Americans throw away food with the same abandon as their more prosperous Anglo neighbors. Rathje and his field workers found entire cooked steaks, bags of marshmallows, and tons of cole slaw that were dumped by school cafeterias. They estimated that Tucson's 300,000 citizens were throwing away enough food each year to feed 13,000 people. This is just another aspect of the discardo culture. Or as Bo Diddley put it in one of his songs, "Man, that's the biggest load of rubbish I've ever heard."

If you were trying to imagine the most outrageous plot for a spy novel, it would have to be doctoring the weather to cripple an enemy. But that is exactly what the CIA did to Cuba, according to a former Pentagon think-tank researcher named Lowell Ponte. The spooks seeded clouds in wind currents that carry rain to Cuba, Ponte said, to cause an artificial drought and ruin the sugar crop. This was in 1972, when Castro swore he would bring in ten million tons of sugar or resign. The CIA decided that if he didn't meet his goal the country would be demoralized. In fact, the sugar harvest did fall short and Castro did offer to resign, but mass demonstrations were held asking him to stay. Lowell Ponte, who worked for one of those outfits whose names are like cloud cover, the International Research and Technology Corporation, said the CIA was routinely attempting to "destabilize" the weather in various areas of the world. This was done so that America's food surplus could be used as a political weapon, the way the Arabs have been using oil. It's interesting to note that the same euphemism, destabilization, is used for overthrowing governments. Maybe the 1977 California drought was a Soviet reprisal for the way we have been messing around with their weather. In any case, now that sunshine and rain are no longer Acts of God, Mr. Ponte suggests international controls for weather tampering.

If you wanted to write a situation comedy involving a teacher, you could not be more far-fetched than to imagine a distinguished, white-haired professor who goes to a precinct in East Harlem to teach diplomatic history to New York City policemen, and who talks to them in Citizen's Band jargon. And yet that is exactly what a friend of mine does as part of a City College program. Twice a week he goes up to the 25th Precinct and greets his blue-uniformed students with these words: "Clap me ten, bro." Having thus gained their attention, he asks: "Got your ears on, Smoky Bears?" and throws himself into his lecture on America and the idea of Manifest Destiny from 1815 to 1830. When the hour is up, he says: "Ten-four, Smokeys, see you on the bounce."

Teaching in the precincts, he found, was a two-way street. He was also learning a few things. One day, he was leaving the precinct in the bitter cold of a February morning, after an 8 A.M. class, when one of his students, a big Irish desk sergeant to whom he had given a good grade, said: "Hey teach, you ain't goin' out there alone, are you?" "Have you got any better suggestions?" he asked. "We'll give you a ride in the squad car to the DMZ," the desk sergeant said. As they drove down Lenox Avenue, my friend, making idle chitchat, said: "I didn't realize there would be so many people out at this hour of the morning." "Didn't you know," the cop driving the squad car said, "that heroin is thirteen dollars an ounce cheaper north of One hundred tenth street?" My friend replied that he had not seen that bit of financial information published in the *Wall Street Journal.* He opined that it must be fairly risky for white customers to come to this part of the city with substantial amounts of cash. "We pick up the bodies every morning," the cop said.

Rarely does a day go by without my seeing or hearing something that strikes me as peculiar to these shores, and I shake my head and say "Only in America." Americans fail to realize that to the rest of the world they are as strange as creatures from another planet. Perhaps this is what is meant by American civilization: an accumulation of peculiarities. I see it everywhere around me, in small things. Last summer, Nancy and I visited our seven-year-old daughter Amber at Camp Snipatuit, near Marion, Massachusetts. "When we go on hikes," Amber said, "we're allowed to chew gum but we're not allowed to blow bubbles because they put insect spray on our faces and they don't want us to get it into our mouths." Only in America. Switching channels one night just before the 1976 presidential elections, I watched the Socialist Labor Party candidate expend his allotted half hour of public television time by explaining that capitalism was in the last gasps of expiration. The system was bankrupt, he said, with 20 million people on welfare, with the unions in collusion with the corporations, with the unemployed and the underemployed, and with a tiny group of power brokers who secretly ran the country. I switched to another channel where a young man who had won $164,000 on Break the Bank was telling the announcer that he would spend part of the money to take his girl friend to Bermuda. America is multi-channeled; most other countries have but one, often state-owned.

I have started keeping an "Only in America" file, with "Only in America" categories, such as Forms of Success, Second Acts, and Native Dangers. One of my favorite forms of success is the look-alike success. Here is a guy who by virtue of an anatomical accident is propelled into fame and wealth. Did France hold look-alike contests for Charles de Gaulle? No, the French felt that one was enough. Did Nikita Khrushchev invite his look-alike to his inaugural? Did Winston Churchill's look-alike get anything out of it except the holy terror of being killed when he was used as a decoy during World War II? And here we have Walter Hanna, a forty-eight-year-old financial consultant from Wisconsin who won the Carter double contest at the Hollywood Palladium, and who now has acquired an agent determined to make him a millionaire. Hanna is taking elocution lessons to develop a Georgia drawl, while pondering offers from talk shows, advertising agencies, book publishers, and nightclubs. Fuzzy on issues? Not Walter Hanna. He's ready to make a pile on his resemblance to the President . . . but with good taste.

The Second Act category refers to F. Scott Fitzgerald's statement that there are no second acts in American lives. How wrong he was. America is a culture medium for second acts, twists of fate, odd reversals, and the promise of the beatitudes: the last will be first. In America, at least I like to think so, one never reaches the exhaustion of possibilities. A headline like the following signifies the fusion of American myth with American reality: FORMER CONVICT, 36, SWORN IN AS JUDGE IN CALIFORNIA. It happens that Bob Young stole a credit card when he was nineteen and went to jail for twenty months. He was then a member in good standing of a Los Angeles motorcycle gang called the Galloping Gooses. Upon his release from jail, he was arrested again with other gang members on charges of attempted murder and assault with a deadly weapon, but the charges against him were dismissed. Young quit the gang, went to college, and applied to eleven law schools before he found one that would take him. Admitted to the state bar in 1972, he worked on the public defender's staff in Loomis, California. When the local judge retired,

Young ran for the office in November 1976 and won 52 percent of the vote. "I know this sounds cliché," Young said, "but I think this is the only country where a person like myself could come up from where I've been and be what I am now." It's also the only country where a man who always wanted to play college football finally realized his dream at the age of forty-three. Mal Dixon of Englewood, New Jersey, had a heart murmur as a boy that kept him from sports, and his family could not send him to college. In 1973, he enrolled at Fairleigh Dickinson University as a freshman and made the varsity football team. The coach had him playing as a defensive back and an offensive end. Dixon was forty-seven when he hung up his cleats, probably the oldest collegiate football player in history.

Second Acts; sharp turns on the road of life — they're commonplace here. A Yale classmate of mine, Hendon Chubb, was indentured to the family underwriting business for seventeen years. Having served his time, he put his Brooks Brothers three-piece suits in mothballs, let his hair grow to his shoulders, got himself some beads and embroidered denim suits, and hitchhiked to Esalen with his fifteen-year-old daughter. He had lived his last forty years first, and now he was living through his adolescence, thumbing across the country like a runaway teen-ager and going to massage workshops and learning about "pathways to sensuality." Hendon is now finishing a Ph.D. in clinical psychology, and will soon embark upon young adulthood. Another Yale classmate, Ben Hopkins, taught law for twenty years, then grew a beard (by now gray), and began conducting workshops in Transcendental Meditation. I went to see him in Honolulu, and met several of his friends. The conversation turned to what everyone was "into." "I'm into hatha yoga," one person said. "I'm into tantric exercises," another said. My turn came. "Er, I'm into prose writing," I said, a disclosure which cast a pall on those assembled.

In Europe you can treat people like shit; you can be rude to them if they come from a different social background because you can be sure they will never extricate themselves from the mire. They will remain what they are, the objects of your snub. In America there are so many surprising reversals that it makes sense to be nice to people. As James Bryce said, equality does not lead to bad manners but to improved manners. The office boy may someday be board chairman. Jack Brebbia, whom I knew as a waiter on Cape Cod, and who in those days showed little inclination to advance himself, became a Washington lawyer and an early backer of Jimmy Carter and called me when he was in New York for the 1976 Democratic convention to tell me that he was running the Virginia delegation. And look at the careers of Jody Powell and Hamilton Jordan; up from nowhere. Jody Powell was thrown out of the Air Force Academy for cheating on a history exam. You never can tell. Whoever you kick on the ladder on your way up is going to kick you back when he reaches your rung. In Europe there isn't even a ladder.

My Native Dangers file lists peculiarly American causes of illness and deaths. Thomas Gilsenan and his wife Ann both died of heart attacks right after eating Thanksgiving dinner with their six children. Holidays can be dangerous. Good news can kill you, and there are people who collapse upon hearing that they have won $1000 for life in a lottery. So, of course, can bad news, and there are people who lose the will to live when they are told they have cancer. Inside each one of us, there is a stock market ticker tape that overreacts to the news. We never know where the danger may be coming from. A family in Ohio became violently ill after eating at an outdoor barbecue. There was nothing wrong with the food. Investigators were baffled until one of the victims mentioned that they had grilled the steaks on an old refrigerator shelf. The shelf was cadmium-plated. The cadmium had melted and stuck to the steaks and poisoned them all. Only in America.

Let me conclude my Native Dangers list on a personal note. On Sunday, March 13, 1977, my wife, my two children, and I were returning from a weekend in Kent, Connecticut, driving south on Route 7. It was raining hard, and I was driving too fast, because I am compulsively punctual and I wanted to be back in the city before 2 P.M., when some friends were coming by to pick us up and take us to a Sunday off-Broadway matinee. Outside New Milford, I hit a water-filled depression in the road and I lost traction. The car planed over the water, swerved into the other lane, hit the side of an oncoming van, made a 360-degree turn, and landed in a ditch, back end first. I looked at my wife beside me and my children in the back seat. None of them had a scratch. It was truly miraculous.

The van had tipped over on its side and slid 25 or 30 feet to a stop. Inside the van were a man and his wife and nine children, their own and the children of neighbors, one an infant in her mother's arms, who were returning from a church service. None of them was hurt either. The inside of the van was upholstered with carpeting, which had cushioned the shock. I was limp with relief. In my mind I could hear ambulance sirens and see stretchers carrying off small bodies.

I had endangered the lives of those whose safety was entrusted to me. Danger had not come from an outside force but from their own father. And then there were all those other children. If I had been the driver of the van I would have been foaming at the mouth. Instead, when I ran from my car to the van, he wanted to know if we were all right. "The Lord was with us," he said. There was not a trace of anger. Within minutes, the conversation turned to more practical matters. The driver of the van worked for the local Ford-Mercury dealer. My car was a Mercury. He could arrange to have it towed to the shop, where my bashed-in front end could be fixed. What had been a near tragedy had shifted to the neutral terrain of business. As we drove to the station in a squad car to make our statements, we discussed what it would cost, and whether my frame was bent, and we exchanged insurance information. The whole incident became a comedy of the absurd when the tow truck arrived. In bright yellow lettering on the beam of the crane was the tow company slogan: WE MEET BY ACCIDENT. Only in America.

P.S. The man I had "met by accident" ended up selling me a new car and taking my wreck as a trade-in.

Lists

Americans are keepers of lists. Only in America could a *Book of Lists* be published. The list is a way to maintain orderly hierarchies in an overcompetitive society. As the weather forecast tells us whether we should spend our weekend indoors or out, the list-maker keeps us from social and economic uncertainty by giving us the identities of the ten best-dressed women, the top 100 corporations, the ten biggest box-office draws, the ten best-sellers, and the ten most active stocks for the day. Thanks to the list-makers, we know where we are. Lists made by private individuals about their own concerns are also social indicators, and as an example, I would like to offer the contents of my first wife's 1961 Christmas stocking list, which she kept and left to me as part of our divorce settlement. If this list is found a thousand years from now by an archeologist sifting the debris of our civilization for clues, it may give him as much information as the discovery of linear B tablets provided to specialists on ancient Greece.

1. Chanel no. 5 perfume, small, with directions in box for opening stopper.

2. Thick gold-banded heart-shaped pin from Raymond Yard, jeweler in New York (Tiffany rival).

3. Tutti-Frutti Surprise Ball, "the toy you destroy to enjoy — unwrap — find hidden toys!" Painted with face of girl with black fuzzy crepe-paper hair.

4. Tuck'n'Grip, home and travel clothes line with detergent caps. No clothes pin needed. Light blue line in a plastic box.

5. Leathersmith of London Ltd., small red leather engagement book with "Merry Christmas to Marga from Mother, 1961," written inside.

6. A tiny gray woolly mouse with Christmas greeting attached saying Sis and Tom Thumb (Sis and Tom Thumb are the two rats in the cottage in Far Hills. Mummy refuses to set traps for them, in fact she leaves food out for them).

7. A red and white doll sock with Chapstick for lips and Chaphans for hands.

8. Fluffipuff, pale green powder puff, "imported French Swansdown."

9. White rubber gloves for washing clothes and dishes.

10. A bottle and can opener with a large heart-shaped opening in a black and red leather case.

11. A small red leather manicure case "made in Western Germany."

12. A small red plastic sewing kit.

13. A small stuffed baby deer from Walt Disney Productions, with a Merry Christmas card that says "love from Bambi."

14. While-U-Sleep beauty gloves. Wear them through the night after applying your favorite lotion or cream. Extra large size.

15. A light blue small leather key-tote case. "Snap it open — snap it shut."

16. A "Sight-Savers" dispenser, a box of silicone-treated eyeglass tissues.

17. A white band to go around neck and hold eyeglasses.

18. A small white doll in a small white snowsuit, made in Japan.

19. Two tiny scented angels with pale blue satin dresses and gold wings.

20. A small sleeping doll in pink and white pajamas, with a bell on her nightcap, made in Japan.

21. A white garter belt.

22. A purple and white satin case with three pairs of nylon stockings inside.

23. A small woolly stuffed owl with a "Merry Christmas from Mother" card and the Mother Goose verse:

> A wise old owl
> Lived in an oak;
> The more he saw
> The less he spoke;
> The less he spoke
> The more he heard.
> Why can't we all be
> Like that old bird?"

Here is another list I like: the ten most useless inventions, a back-handed tribute to American ingenuity, compiled from the records of the patent office (a friend of mine calls this tribute to things that don't work "the essence of American liberalism"):

1. Goggles for chickens to keep them from getting their eyes pecked.

2. A rocking chair with a bellows in its base to help rock it.

3. A locket with an anticorrosive lining to carry chewing gum.

4. A bullet that goes around corners.

5. A bicycle seat with a cavity to allow comfortable clearance for the sexual organs of the male rider.

6. A method for preserving the dead in a block of transparent glass.

7. A hose attachment for nursing mothers.

8. A device for producing dimples.

9. An alarm clock that wakes you up by rubbing your face with corks.

10. A humane rat-trap which allows the rat to return to its hole.

By contrast, here are *Ten Useful American Devices:*

1. *The Dollar:* Take a look at a dollar bill, richer in symbolism than purchasing power. See the eye of providence in the radiant triangle, the eagle with a ribbon in its beak that says E Pluribus Unum, the portrait of the founder of our country, see the scrollwork and fancy engraving, the treasury seal, the federal reserve seal, the code letters indicating the reserve bank of its provenance, and the promise that it is legal tender for all debts public and private (I was once shown how to fold the bill when handing it to a hotel bellboy so that the

phrase read "gal tender and private"). The dollar is more than currency, it is a historical document.

Like so many of our *objets usuels,* which we take for granted without knowing their origins, the dollar in its present green and anemic form is of recent vintage. So many components of our lifestyle have come into being in the last 75 years or so — among them the mass-produced car, the interstate highway, the telephone, television, talking movies, nuclear energy, and computers — that a case can be made for calling America the only twentieth-century nation that is the only nation whose civilization is the result of twentieth-century technology. America hovers between the countries whose historical accretions hold them back, like Europe and Russia (Soviet Communism being the modern form of the Byzantine doctrine of making people perfect at the expense of freedom), and the countries of the Third World, still carrying the albatross of their colonial past. America is the present.

Even though it is said that Americans were the first people in the Christian world to use paper money (which was common in pagan China a thousand years ago), the dollar as we know it did not come into being until November 1914, when the Federal Reserve Bank went into operation, and Congress delegated to it the right to coin money. "In order to furnish suitable notes for circulation as Federal Reserve notes," said the Federal Reserve Act, "the Comptroller of the Currency shall, under the direction of the Secretary of the Treasury, cause plates and dies to be engraved in the best manner to guard against counterfeits and fraudulent alterations, and shall have printed therefrom and numbered such quantities of such notes of the denominations of $5, $10, $20, $50, $100, as may be required to supply the Federal Reserve banks." Thus was born the modern dollar, although its pedigree goes back to the Middle Ages.

Whence the dollar? The Count of Schlick, a man of substance who lived in the Thal (or valley) of St. Joachim in Bohemia, had a silver mine on his land and operated a private mint where he struck coins that were widely sought because of their uniformity. The first one, in 1486, was called the Guldengroschen, and later issues were the Schlickenthalers and the Joachimthalers. These coins, roughly the same size as an American silver dollar, were used far and wide and became known as thalers. In Italy it was the tallero, and in the English-speaking world it became the doler, dolor, dollor, and dollar. By the time Shakespeare was writing, dollar was a commonly used English word. Spain in its imperial age issued an imitation of the thaler which was known as the Spanish dollar. It circulated in both Americas. The American colonies also used wampum as the Indians did — shells were legal tender in Massachusetts in 1641, and Virginia made tobacco legal tender in 1642. The link between tobacco and money was so ingrained that New Jersey, which was not a tobacco-growing state, printed notes that carried a tobacco leaf, with the warning: To Counterfeit is Death.

Barter and wampum were abandoned when the colonies discovered paper money. The Massachusetts Bay Colony led the way with the first of many worthless issues, in 1690. In Puritan New England, the printing press turned out to have other uses than the publication of Bibles. In 1729, Ben Franklin, that legendary advocate of thrift, published "A Modest Enquiry into the Nature and Necessity of a Paper Currency," an argument for increasing the paper money supply. Printing money went on with abandon, to the point that the English Parliament banned its use, which became one of the less publicized causes of tension between England and the colonies.

The War of Independence was won with paper money. The Continental Congress, between June 1775 and November 1779, printed 42 issues with a total face value of more than $241 million. By 1779 a Continental dollar was worth three cents. The phrase "not worth a Continental" entered the language and a nation owed its birth to fiscal irresponsibility.

The founding fathers, horrified by this flood of worthless paper, forbade the states and the national government to issue paper notes, and restricted the right of coinage to Congress. But what should the currency be called? In those days, the colonies used all sorts of coins, including British pounds, Spanish dollars, and French guineas. Jefferson referred to the Spanish dollar as "a known coin and the most familiar of all to the minds of the people." On August 8, 1786, an Act of Congress established the dollar as the new unit of American coinage, throwing off the troublesome system of pounds, shillings, and farthings, which was a reminder of the colonial past.

Whence the dollar sign? On Spanish dollars, there was the abbreviation P.S. after the amount. The colonists, who used both English pounds and Spanish dollars, grew accustomed to placing the abbreviation before the amount, as they did with the sign for pounds. The P.S. Spanish dollar sign was gradually streamlined into the $. A letter written in 1792 by Robert Morris, the financier of the revolution, contains the earliest known pen-made dollar sign, with only one stroke through the S.

Alexander Hamilton founded a central bank, of which Jefferson was deeply suspicious, saying: "I have ever been the enemy of banks . . . Shall we build an altar to the old paper money of the revolution, which ruined individuals but saved the republic, and burn on that all the bank charters present and future, and their notes with them? For these are the ruin of both republic and individuals." The central bank did not have its charter renewed when Madison succeeded Jefferson in 1809, and state banks proliferated. A second central bank was chartered in 1816, but Andrew Jackson, speaking for the little man and states' rights, vetoed a bill renewing its charter in 1832. Now that the banks are among our most powerful institutions, and play a crucial part in the financing of city government, it is curious to look back to the days when their right to exist hung in the balance, and there were pro-bank forces and con-bank forces, and The Bank was an issue in presidential elections.

Paper notes, despite constitutional prohibition, turned up in wartime, first in the War of 1812 and then during the Civil War. Just as the Continental saved the colonial insurgents, the greenback saved the Union. Secretary of the Treasury Salmon Portland Chase, whose portrait graces the $5000 bill, floated $356 million worth of greenbacks. After the war, the greenback remained in use, and the nation's financial system stumbled along from panic to panic, until important banks failed in the Great Panic of 1907. Theodore Roosevelt appointed a commission, which recommended a central bank, and in 1913 the Federal Reserve was born. How surprising it is that the great period of this country's settlement and growth was achieved with makeshift currencies and state banks and no central banking authority. The dollar, long subject to the vagaries of wars and state manipulation, finally became respectable. Let us now kneel in worship before the Almighty Dollar, the one thing no American can be without, the measure of human worth, the maker of friends and influencer of people, the overthrower of regimes, the opener of doors, the diploma of status, the basic unit of energy in the American power plant. As Barbara Hutton once put it, "Money alone can't bring you happiness, but money alone has not brought me unhappiness." Or, as the saying goes, it's no disgrace to be poor, but it sure is inconvenient.

2. *The Interstate:* A generation is reaching adulthood that never knew what life was like without the Interstate. They don't remember

the days when the best roads were two-lane blacktops with soft shoulders. If you could do 300 miles a day, you were doing well. Today, the cloverleaf is our national flower, and environmentalists throw up their arms in dismay: the face of America is latticed with highways, neighborhoods are sliced to death, the sick inner city is layered with concrete bandages, the environment is defiled by the interstate subculture.

I like the interstate. It confers freedom from geography upon the average car-owning American. It makes the whole country easily available. Walt Whitman: "I inhale great draughts of space, the East and the West are mine, and the North and the South are mine." Kansans can ski in Colorado. Indianans can sail on the Great Lakes. Florida lettuce arrives unwilted in New York. The interstate has made all of America a back yard. It is a plum for the rootless. I wonder if there could have been a counterculture without it, with the hippies living in their VW vans and moving from scene to scene, crossing the country to attend a rock festival. *Zen & the Art of Motorcycle Maintenance* is a byproduct of the interstate; Robert Pirsig stuck to the back roads to avoid the interstate, which is pointless unless there is an interstate to avoid. Pirsig traveled back roads because he had the option, just as environmentalists who object to the interstate have the option to ride bicycles, or to walk.

"William Penn's father never rode in a vehicle until he came to this continent," one such purist told me. "It was that Quaker thing — 'God gave me legs to walk,' he said." "But that's just the point," I said, "in America he gave in. The scale of America demands vehicles. This isn't just a country, it's half a hemisphere. And that, to me, is where the rubber meets the road."

The interstate is responsible for the drop in the highway death rate. In 1956, there were 6.28 deaths per 100 million miles traveled, which had dropped to 3.57 deaths by 1974. Which brings us to the real surprise, the interstate's recent birth. The first eight-mile stretch (not counting pieces of state turnpike which later became part of the network) was opened to traffic outside Topeka, Kansas, on November 14, 1956, a year after Jack Kerouac's *On the Road* was published. It was built with funds from the Federal Aid Highway Act of 1956, which paid ninety cents on the dollar, and has thus far shelled out $62 billion for 38,000 miles of connective asphalt.

The question we should be asking is not "Do we want the interstate," which is purely academic, but "Why did it take so long to get it?" The answer is that the vehicle creates the highway. There was no point in the government putting money into roads until two things happened. The first thing was the accidental discovery by Charles Goodyear in 1839 that when he dropped a mixture of rubber and sulphur on a hot stove the rubber became strong and resilient. He named the process after the Roman god of fire. Before vulcanization, rubber melted in the summer and froze in the winter. After vulcanization, it could be used to make tires, first for bicycles, then for cars, and the best surface for a rubber tire was the smooth concrete highway. The second thing that happened was that Henry Ford put the Model T on the market in 1908 and sold so many of them that he dropped the price as volume increased. By 1925 he was selling the Runabout for $250. Faced with the rubber tire and the mass-produced car, the government started thinking about road improvement.

Early interest in roads, aside from postal routes, had been killed by the railroad. The Age of the Rail lasted from 1829, when the steam locomotive was imported from England, to 1910, when Henry Ford put up the 60-acre Highland Park plant to mass-produce the Model T. For eighty years Americans sang the song of rolling stock rather than the song of the open road. The West was settled by rail, with tens of thousands of immigrants carried in windowless boxcars that derisive trainmen called Zulu cars. Americans had the same passion for trains that they now have for cars. Today those vanished or vanishing names, like great dynasties overthrown, have an archaic ring: the Boston & Lowell, the Newcastle & Frenchtown, the Philadelphia & Columbia, the St. Paul, Minnesota & Manitoba. We have gone from railroad geography to interstate geography. The open road is a symbol of freedom. Rail travel is bound by a fixed itinerary, a timetable, fellow passengers, and a conductor. It does not provide the satisfaction of getting into a car when you feel like it and going where you want.

In July 1977, my wife and I spent six days on the interstate, embarking on the Jersey side of the George Washington Bridge and disembarking in San Francisco. I was a purist, I wanted to complete the journey without leaving the interstate, I wanted to eat, drink, and sleep on it, but Nancy said she felt as if she were in a tube that went from coast to coast and it gave her claustrophobia. So each day we got off the interstate for an hour or so and made a side trip to the real world. The rest of the time we were part of the interstate subculture, with its own life-style and pecularities. Unbeknownst to the nation at large, the interstate has become the 51st state — the state of mobility. It is self-sustaining, has its own economy and culture, and every-thing a person might need, from a hospital to be born in to a funeral parlor to die in. You could live all your life without getting off the interstate, continually on the move to avoid state and local taxes, a turnpike refugee.

Traveling the interstate is what they call a "learning experience." Road signs are the interstate mass media. Truckers are the perma-nent residents and taxpayers: THIS VEHICLE PAYS $6700 A YEAR IN ROAD USE TAXES. There is also an interstate language, known as CB jive, and, for a newcomer, the language barrier can be overcome with the help of a Citizen's Band-English phrase book, which can be purchased in selected service areas:

> Super skate is dropping the hammer = the sports car is speeding.
> That cotton-picker just cut me off = euphemism for motherfucker.
> A Tijuani taxi is going after an 18-wheeler = a police car with roof lights is following a tractor-trailer.
> There's a Harvey Wallbanger holding on to your mud flaps = there's a reckless driver right behind you.
> Watch for the Smokey in the plain brown wrapper = watch for the unmarked police car.
> Truck 'em easy, pal = have a good trip.

Critics complain that there is a gray sameness to the interstate — not so, there is great variety. All through Pennsylvania, both banks of the road are lined with vinca, pink and white flowers that look like clover, so that crossing the state is like going through a 500-mile field of flowers. One picks up odd bits of infor-mation and local history. In the middle of the Pennsylvania Ap-palachians, there is a town called Jersey Shore. In Lancaster, Pennsylvania, they are manufacturing a watch that measures pulse as well as time. It is an American compulsion to want to know not only the time but the state of one's health at every mo-ment of the day. In Meadville, on one of our side trips, we learned from a local resident that President McKinley had been expelled from Allegheny College for putting a cow in the belfry. Americans, know your country! Every town has a history, not of Gothic churches and coronations, but of settlement and industry, and men and women who rose on merit.

On another side trip, we saw that reports of Lake Erie's death are exaggerated, if one is to judge by the number of bait shops that sell "lake shiners," and by the number of restaurants that offer "all you can eat" perch dinners. The turnpike from Ohio to Indiana is called "the Main Street of the Midwest." In Indiana you can buy gas at the Ernie Pyle Service Area, sleep in the World's Largest Lodging Chain (Best Western), and fix your car at Little America, the world's largest service station (50 pumps).

On the interstate, the idea is that if you can make it rhyme you can make it sell: head shed (a Pennsylvania barber shop), meal real (an Ohio restaurant), sleep cheap (an Indiana motel), keen cuisine (a Wyoming diner), and sin bin (a California motel lounge) are a few examples.

A learning experience, I said. Although we did not cross Michigan, I learned of the secessionist movement in the Upper Peninsula, a piece of land separated from the rest of the state by lakes Michigan and Huron. Its only land border is with Wisconsin, to which by reason of geography it naturally belongs. But when Michigan lost out on the Toledo strip, which went to Ohio in the 1830s, the federal government gave it the Upper Peninsula as a consolation prize. The people of the Upper Peninsula feel like orphans, neglected by the state government in Lansing. Many maps of Michigan show the state without the Upper Peninsula. In downstate Michigan, they don't tell Polish jokes, they tell Upper Peninsula jokes: Why do all the roads in the Upper Peninsula have deep ditches on either side? So Upper Peninsula folk can swing their arms when they're walking.

Some fed-up citizens of the Upper Peninsula have started a movement to make their area the 51st state. They want to call it State Superior (lake Superior bathes the northern shore of the peninsula) or Hiawatha State. They are taking their case to court and will argue that the Upper Peninsula belonged to the Indians and the federal government had no right to cede it as part of a tradeoff. If they are rebuffed in the courts, they are thinking of seceding to Canada. They point out that they are closer to Winnipeg than to Lansing. Remember Passport to Pimlico? Here it is in the flesh.

At the Illinois-Iowa border, we sat on a wooden dock at sunset, on the Iowa bank of the Mississippi, and ate Chinese take-out food washed down with Green Hungary wine. Motorboats sped down the river pulling water skiers and sending out waves that made the dock bob. Behind us a freight train pulled up with its long line of cars, Union Pacific, Santa Fe, Minneapolis piggy-back, and behind the train rose a wooden tavern called Sneaky Pete's. The darkening blue sky, the pleasure boats, the couple fishing off the tip of the dock, the freight train, and the tavern, the first one we had found that served Coors on draft (not normally found east of the Mississippi), gave us the feel of a waterway that was there to be employed and enjoyed, while the river's breadth and sweep gave us a sense of the country's scale.

In Iowa, we passed the town of What Cheer, and the town of Leclaire, the home of Buffalo Bill, where a red clapboard museum stands in the shade of a green tree five times its size. We passed West Branch, where Herbert Hoover was born and is buried. We discovered the solidarity of the license plate:

"Hey, you from New York? We're from upstate."
"Hey, it was fierce yesterday. One hundred and two where we were. They say we're getting thunderstorms today, cool things off."
"We're heading for Yellowstone. Probably be bumper to bumper. Have a nice day."

You have to be in the heart and heat of Iowa for two New Yorkers to take such casual notice of each other.

Utah: Along the steep drop into Salt Lake City, there is a sign that says: Runaway Trucks, Left Lane . . . this is part of the American genius, the will to organize catastrophe.

Wyoming:

THESE COLORS NEVER RUN.
ONLY LOVE BEATS MILK.

Laramie: "Come on in, let's talk hay machinery."

Nevada: In Nevada, I made my first citizen's arrest. I arrested my wife for throwing an apple juice can out the window and I collected the $100 fine which was posted on the highway, which I kept.

California: People are generous here. They invite you to their homes and give directions ungrudgingly. But, more than that, American generosity is self-possessed, while European generosity is often ingratiating, one feels there is something behind it, that something will be asked in return. Europe has nations of headwaiters, like the French, but Americans are rarely ingratiating, except at the corporate level and on the New York literary scene.

In Mammoth Lakes, California, on our last side trip, we spent the night with an old friend, Bob Kaiser, at 7000 feet in the high sierras, about 20 miles southeast of Yosemite National Park. Bob had invited friends for dinner, and was preparing a roast for the oven. Unfamiliar with the latest in oven technology, I fiddled with the dials and inadvertently set it on Clean. The oven would not turn on until its two-hour cleaning cycle was over. Every improvement has its disadvantage, and the disadvantage of a self-cleaning oven is that you cannot interrupt its cleaning cycle if you want to use it. The roast could not be eaten raw. Bob's next-door neighbors, whom he hardly knew, were out for the day, but had left their front door open, as he did himself (he also left his car keys under the front seat), so he carried the roast next door and cooked it in their oven. To a New Yorker, so many unlocked doors seemed like courting disaster, or, at best, a relic of a bygone America, but in Mammoth Lakes the open-door policy is still in practice, and without being maudlin about it, it would not be farfetched to talk of community relations based on mutual trust. Perhaps Mammoth Lakes is in a time warp, out of step with the rest of America, or perhaps there are many such communities, unadvertised because bad news has a lock on the headlines.

3. *Fast Food:* I know this is heresy, but I would like to say a few words in defense of Fast Food. Most people prefer Slow Food, but who wants a seven-course banquet every day? One of my gluttonous French great-uncles was once meeting a lady for lunch at the Hotel de Paris in Monte Carlo. The lady pointed out that his fly was open. "You're luckier than I am," he said, "I haven't seen it for six years." When I was living in Rome in the sixties, I gorged myself with pasta and cheese, took naps in the afternoon, gained twenty pounds, spent more time digesting than working, and generally deteriorated. The Italians are drowning in a sea of pasta. Their decline has much to do with their eating habits. The hand that painted the *Mona Lisa* was not the hand of a spaghetti twirler.

Fast Food informs us that food is not an end in itself, it is fuel. Fast Food establishments are filling stations, and if the attendant doesn't keep you waiting and the fuel doesn't clog your carburetor, what more do you want? I also like the sameness of fast food places, which offer uniformity in a chaotic world. When you are traveling, they are little islands of predictability. In New York, I particularly like Chock Full o'Nuts, for the world's best whole-wheat donut, for the menu, secure in its red-roofed plastic house, and for the sullen black waitresses, their names clipped to their brown dresses like medals won on the field of battle, whose manner is a reminder that you are not there to enjoy yourself but to fuel up. They always serve you in turn — it takes a ghetto-bred black waitress to know unerringly Who's Next. Among national chains, I'm partial to McDonald's. Colonel

Sanders is hit or miss — I had some marvelous fried chicken in Durham, North Carolina, and some inedible glock in Washington, D.C. But going through the Golden Arches is a standardized and ritualized transaction, a form of religious experience. You know what to ask for, and you know what it will look like and taste like, and exactly what will be said, from the request for a Big Mac to the final "Have a good day." I also like the way they designed the cups for French fries, so that it looks as if you're getting a heaping spillover portion, whereas in fact each customer gets an identical amount.

While I am on the subject of food, let me say that I find American cuisine much maligned. The best of it is still to be found in private homes rather than restaurants. New York, which has restaurants specializing in dishes from every region of China, is not so well represented when it comes to American regional cooking. You can eat a 100-year-old egg or shark's fin soup, but where can you get Chesapeake Bay terrapin? And so it goes down the list of ethnic menus. You can find boeuf en daube or wiener schnitzel or Hungarian goulash far more readily than you can a good gumbo or properly prepared fried chicken.

There is a great American cuisine, based not on fancy sauces but on matchless and fresh ingredients. The best trout dish is not the pretentious and flavor-disguising "truite amandine," but the trout that is fried in butter five minutes after it has been caught.

TEN MATCHLESS AMERICAN THINGS TO EAT AND DRINK
1. Virginia ham (superior to jambon de Bayonne).
2. Maple Syrup.
3. Jack Daniels sour mash whiskey (better than many cognacs as an after-dinner drink).
4. Soft-shell crabs.
5. Florida pompano, perhaps the best saltwater fish in the world (avoid sauces — a dab of butter, a pinch of paprika and lemon pepper, and under the broiler).
6. Bay scallops, so delicate they can be eaten raw.
7. Sweet corn, the Indian's greatest gift to the white man.
8. Grain-fed U.S.D.A. prime beef, finely marbled, and far superior to grass-fed Scotch beef and improperly aged French beef.
9. The Idaho potato, the best in the world, worth presenting in a Tiffany case.
10. California wines, the finest of which, in recent international blind tastings, have consistently won out over their French counterparts.

4. *The Snapshot:* Technology is the great equalizer. The spirit of democracy is contained in machines. The manufacture of interchangeable parts was America's Great Leap Forward. The machine turned out identical parts in great numbers, which the eye and hand cannot do. The automobile was invented in Europe but the car is American. The penny press made available to everyone the same level of information. That's why we call it the mass media. Television permits no class distinctions; its appeal is to the lowest common denominator. The phonograph made music plebeian. It was miraculous, a machine that sang, and it was all done with a needle and diaphragm, and a flat shellac disk that was stamped out like Chiclets.

Thanks to Edison, every man became a music lover. Thanks to George Eastman, every man became a recorder of events. Photography was not invented by an American (Joseph Nicéphore Niepce took the first photograph in 1826) but it was "democratized" by the Rochester bank clerk George Eastman. Before Eastman, photographers were rare birds. With the wet-plate collodion process, you needed an assistant, and a portable darkroom if you wanted to go out of doors. To take a photograph required formidable skill, unlimited patience, and expensive equipment. Eastman produced gelatin dry plates, and mounted the photographic carrier on rolls of paper instead of glass. "You press the button and we do the rest" — the slogan of the century. Anyone could do it, it was no longer for experts, and photography went from high art to the snapshot, with transparent film, daylight loading, the one-dollar Brownie, and, more recently, the camera of instant gratification, the Polaroid.

Here is an early Kodak ad that says it all.

Jack: Do you think baby will be quiet long enough to take her picture, Mama?

Mama: The Kodak will catch her whether she moves or not: it is "quick as a wink."

Americans take 6.4 billion snapshots a year. They are leaving a pictorial record of themselves unmatched by any previous civilization. They have outdone the sum total of Egyptian friezes, Hellenic statuary, Roman mosaics, and European portrait painting, because they have done away with the privileged recorder, the commissioned artist. Thanks to George Eastman, there are as many recorders of events as there are cameras sold. What Lascaux gave us from the walls of its caves we will give the Martians with our snapshot albums.

Taking snapshots may be the primary American form of self-expression. The Great American Bore wants you to look at a trayload of slides. Life is a series of "picture opportunities." There is no important difference between the amateur photographer and the news photographer. They are interchangeable. News photography is the only category in the Pulitzer Prizes that can be won by an amateur, and has been, three times. Most news photographs *are* snapshots, and show the famous in familiar guises. Who is that woman walking her daughter to school? Why, it's Rosalynn Carter. Who's the Big Mamma with the C.B. radio? Why, it's Betty Ford. Who is that tall man in the chef's hat broiling steaks on an outdoor barbecue? Why, it's Lyndon Johnson. Who are those two people with their arms around each other on the beach? Why, it's Jack and Jackie Kennedy. Snapshots inform us that the humble and the great have identical pastimes . . . and suffer identical fates. The man walking on the beach is shot while riding in a car . . . a snapshot. An issue of *Life* contains the snapshots of Americans killed in Vietnam in one week. It is hard to imagine those self-confident faces coming home in coffins, but every snapshot is a reminder of mortality, since by the time we see it we are older than when it was taken.

Snapshots are a way of measuring our estrangement from ourselves, says Michael Lesy, the historian who uses photographs as primary sources in books like *Wisconsin Death Trip* and *Real Life*. He calls this "visual anthropology." He discovers what the society is about by studying the moments it chooses to record. Lesy is working on a compilation of family snapshots called *Diary of a Gesture*. He goes from door to door collecting snapshots and saying: "I'm a scholar. I'm doing a book on how people take pictures of their lives with snapshots . . . I can read pictures the way some people can read palms."

5. *The Shopping Center:* Nothing is more powerful than an idea whose time has come. The Eastern bloc has Marxism, and Americans have shopping-center theory. The more complicated of the two, I can assure you, is shopping-center theory. The simple act of attracting customers to patronize your center requires more planning and strategy than any Communist five-year plan. Shopping centers, like the interstate and partly because of the interstate, are a development of the last quarter century. There are roughly 17,000 of them in the United States, and they haven't really caught on anywhere else.

In the strict hierarchy determined by the Urban Land Institute, there are A or regional centers with a full-line department store selling major appliances, B or community centers with a junior department store, and C or neighborhood centers with a supermarket. Shopping-center theory has a language of its own. The two terms which spring most often to the lips of shopping center experts are GLA (gross leasable area) and ROI (return on investment). The large store is called the anchor store. The ideal situation is an anchor tenant at each end of the mall, which is called anchoring the mall, with the customers bouncing back and forth between the two anchors and hitting the smaller stores in between. The basic "store layout grids" are T, L, U, Triangle, Dumbbell, and Double Dumbbell. The spaces in the parking lots are called stalls and painting the lines is called striping the lot. The recommended stall size is nine by twenty, but when a center opens, each stall is striped a foot wider than necessary to give the illusion of easy parking and make the place seem more crowded than it is. Engineering studies determine whether the parking lot should have right angle parking, which fits more cars, or angle parking, which is recommended for a smoother flow of traffic. Late-model shopping centers also have bicycle stands, responding to the trend in physical fitness, and wheelchair ramps, responding less to compassion for the disabled than to market studies showing that they too have money to spend.

Major tenants want the best positions, closest to the cars. This is called tenant hierarchy. Shopping centers want the right kind of tenant, balancing profit with attractiveness. Pawn shops and army surplus stores they don't want. This is called tenant mix. Here are some of the problems that the shopping center entrepreneur must deal with: Proximity to a major intersection. Degrees of complexity of access. Zoning, site orientation, site conditions, water and vegetation patterns, site utilities, site restrictions, site economics. Vandal-resistant materials. Entrance doors that can take a lot of punishment. Washrooms with disposal facilities for paper towels and sanitary napkins, the alternative being closed drains. All of our society's failings must be anticipated by shopping center theorists, not to change them, but to stay in business in spite of them.

The shopping center could not exist without a modest but indispensable invention: the shopping cart, which made the noble idea of self-service convenient. In primitive times before the shopping cart, shoppers carried baskets under their arms. Along came Sylvan N. Goldman of Oklahoma City, who operated the Standard Supermarket. He introduced the shopping cart on June 4, 1937. At first there was customer resistance. Offended women told him, "I've pushed my last baby buggy." Goldman had to hire people to push carts through the aisles of his supermarket so customers would get the idea. Soon, the shopping cart went national, and Goldman's company was turning out more than a million a year. Goldman collected a royalty on every shopping cart in the country until his patents ran out. He is one of those obscure entrepreneurs who quietly rang up millions with a single, simple idea. Stores found that if they increased the size of the basket, the customers bought more. The American consumer abhors a vacuum.

Shopping center theory includes studies on the duration of the weekly shopping excursion (average, 1.75 hours) and the reasons for customer fatigue. Can any positive side to customer fatigue be found? Yes, it can lead to an impulse snack. Since it leads to impulse snacks, should the shopping center have a gourmet fair, where Taco Queen and Burger King reign? There are pros and cons. The gourmet fair creates an interesting atmosphere and generates high rents, but it's noisy and smelly and hard to keep clean. There is a reason for everything in shopping center theory, which stems, like Marxism, from a deterministic view of economic man.

What should the center do about socially motivated browsers who congregate there on Friday afternoons? Should benches be provided? If they are, old people will spend the day there. The answer is to provide uncomfortable benches, with slat seats or without backrests. Customer fatigue is caused by mothers dragging their children around. The answer is to provide a playground, a parking lot for children.

Basically, a shopping center is nothing but a collection of stores and a parking lot, but it presents itself as an asset to the community. To prove its community-mindedness, it provides a community room in an area that is normally hard to lease. A by-product of the community room is that it helps build shopper traffic. Doing the right thing is also profitable. But the community room creates a whole new set of problems. The shopping center manager soon discovers that the world is full of worthy causes. Protest groups may want to meet there. Charitable organizations may spill out of the community room and solicit in the stores. There may be a cooking demonstration using a range with a brand name that the anchor store does not carry, thereby incurring its wrath. But every problem is worth solving, because shopping centers are attractive investments. The failure rate among them has been minute. The shopping center of the future will eliminate the parking lot. Ordering will be done over closed-circuit television. All orders will be computerized, which will mean no cash, no cashiers, no robberies, no vandals, and no customer fatigue. Even though the GLA may shrink, the ROI is sure to increase.

6. *Chewing Gum:* This may be one of the archetypal American inventions (among others, there was the wave in the bobby pin, to make it stick): it was invented by accident, it is essentially superfluous, and it is marketed as a product that is not only pleasurable but beneficial. It made a great American out of Thomas Adams, a Jersey City inventor who was trying to find a substitute for rubber. He imported from Central America the gum of the sapodilla tree, but it was not resistant enough. One day in 1869, Adams saw a little girl in a drugstore buying paraffin chewing wax, a popular item in those days, America having been a nation of ruminants long before Juicy Fruit. There occurred in Adams what might be called the "Eureka!" moment, comparable to the apple knocking Newton on the head. Adams went home, and with his son Horatio, rolled the Central American chicle into bite-sized balls, packaged it, and sold it through drugstores, unflavored. The next steps in these American real-life myths, after the Eureka moment, are improvement, expansion, and mergers. Licorice and peppermint were the first flavors added, and a Cleveland pharmacist added pepsin as an aid to digestion. The balls gave way to convenient sticks, machine-cut and sprinkled with sugar.

The Wrigley Building, for a time the highest in Chicago, was the house that chewing gum built. It wasn't enough that it gave your jaws a workout, it had to be doing you some good too. "Keeps teeth clean, breath sweet," said the Wrigley's ads. "Aids appetite and digestion." Chewing gum became one of America's most popular bad habits. By 1915, it was being exported as far as Australia. Today, Americans spend $300 million a year on gum. My daughter comes home from school singing: "Does the chewing gum lose its flavor on the bedpost overnight?"

We are told that chewing gum helps schoolchildren concentrate, relieves the tensions of soldiers and the boredom of factory workers, and keeps athletes calm. What would the World Series be without it? It brightens the day and relieves temporary deafness on airplanes. It is the American panacea, more than a candy, obtainable without a prescription, harmless and cheap, and mysteriously satisfying. Its disposal is a test of the ability of Americans to get along with each other. Its steady use has, according to the Spanish writer Julio Camba, altered the American face. "Little by little," Camba writes, "chewing will create a typical American physiognomy, in which the jaw will predominate. If in the future there ever exists a typical

American, with clearly marked characteristics, as there is today a typical Englishman, a typical Frenchman, or a typical Spaniard, the Americans will be able to say that they formed him by chewing away millions of dollars in gum. This country will acquire cohesion by gum-power."

7. *The Zipper:* The modest zipper has its share in the sexual revolution. Before the zipper, sex was cumbersome and required planning. The logistics were sometimes insoluble. It was mainly an indoor activity. The zipper freed sex from its confinement. To the zipper we are obligated for back-seat-of-the-car sex, lunch-hour affairs, golf course sex at women's colleges (what at Vassar was called the 19th hole), sex on a Greyhound bus, and a number of other interesting variations. Before the zipper, women were formidably protected against their inclinations. They had to think twice, not about romance, but about whether they wanted to go to the time and trouble of unfastening all those hooks and stays. More time was spent in dressing and undressing than in bed. In the emancipation of women, the zipper should rank right up there with the Equal Rights Amendment.

We all owe a debt of gratitude to Colonel Lewis Walker, a corporation lawyer from Meadville, Pennsylvania (as there were Kentucky Colonels, there were Pennsylvania Colonels). Colonel Walker did not invent the zipper, but he believed in it with the fervor of an early Christian. Thrown more than once to the lions of insolvency, his faith was never shaken.

The saga of the zipper begins in 1893, when a Chicago inventor named Whitcomb L. Judson took out a patent for a slide fastener which he called "the clasp locker and unlocker for shoes." This device still used the method of hooks-and-eyes, which were closed by a slider running over them. Colonel Walker saw unlimited possibilities in a fastener that would do away with buttons and laces. The zipper was an *American* idea; it saved time and it was luminously simple. He raised the capital to manufacture the first zippers, and wore them on his shoes, the herald of a zippered age. But the early models either stuck or popped open, and salesmen left in their wake hordes of dissatisfied customers, particularly after the zipper was used in women's corsets.

Colonel Walker hired a Westinghouse engineer called Gideon Sundback, who developed "Hookless no. 2," the zipper as we know it, identical thin plates that interlocked when the fastener was pulled. In 1913, Colonel Walker founded the Hookless Fastener Company, with his two sons as salesmen. But there was consumer resistance. The zipper was too newfangled to appeal to people mourning the passage of the horse, and those who had tried the earlier models bad-mouthed the product.

America's entry into World War I saved the zipper. War, certain historians maintain, is the midwife of progress. When the American Expeditionary Force went "over there," its men were equipped with zippered money belts. The zipper came into its own as a modest item of Government Issue.

After 1918, the zipper was used mainly in tobacco pouches. In 1923, Bertram C. Work, the president of B. F. Goodrich, came into the office with a zippered tobacco pouch in one hand and a pair of snap-button galoshes in the other. It was one of those "Eureka!" moments. Work also coined the term zipper, which he registered as a trade-mark. The zipper caught on. It spread from galoshes to children's wear. Mothers loved it because there were no more buttons to sew. It eventually found a secure place in women's dresses, and in the fly of men's trousers. Meadville became the zipper capital of the world. By 1924, Colonel Walker had five plants and 300 employees. He remained president until his death in 1938.

Alfred E. Carlisle, a retired Hookless Fastener engineer whom I met in Meadville, told me that when he was first employed by Colonel Walker as a young man, his father said: "When you go to work, don't tell your boss 'I have nothing to do,' tell him 'I have an idea I think might work.'" Applying this piece of advice, Carlisle retired from the firm with 52 patents to his credit. I learned from him that since a patent can only be held for 17 years, companies delay the final approval as long as possible. This is why one so often sees the mention "patent pending." If they could keep it pending forever, they would.

Colonel Walker, tall and grown stout with advancing years, retained the missionary spirit until his death. He truly believed that with the zipper he had improved humanity. He stood at the junction of salesmanship and evangelism. Indeed, his first factory was grafted onto a building that had previously contained a Unitarian college. He always came to company picnics and delivered the same speech, talking through his dentures: "This great hookless family," he would intone to the gathered herd of employees, "this vast enterprise. Your contribution to humanity has been . . ." and then his dentures would slip and the rest of his message was lost to posterity.

In World War II, drafted once again, the zipper was used in 123 different ways, from instrument covers to jungle hammocks. Today, it is featured in astronaut suits. The zipper is more than practical, it is Utopian, as Aldous Huxley saw by giving it a prominent place in his *Brave New World.* The zipper was an improvement of man over nature. If human beings were zippered, the savings in gynecological and surgical costs would be truly wondrous.

8. *The Census:* This is the only country in the world that in the year of its founding set in motion a process of statistical profile. The founding fathers wrote it into the Constitution that we should enumerate ourselves every ten years. The first article of the Constitution specifies that "the actual enumeration shall be made within three years after the first meeting of the Congress of the United States, and within every subsequent term of ten years, in such a manner as they shall by law direct."

From its modest initial goal of enumeration, the Census Bureau gradually broadened its prerogative to the point of becoming a benign Big Brother. It knows all about us. It tracks every move we make and every dollar we spend. What we won't tell it, it imputes. Anyone with the courage to plod through language that seems deliberately arcane will learn that the census has methods for "imputing" missing responses. They will assign to a sample person the information obtained from another sample person with similar demographic and economic characteristics. Say, a carpenter won't tell you what he's making. They impute the salary of another carpenter in the same age group. This is called the "hot deck" imputation. It is alarming to consider that the statistical profile of this great nation may be distorted by "hot deck" imputations.

The Census Bureau is the nation's foremost fact-finding mill, churning out data by the ton. The ground it covers is vast, as these random titles show: Consumer Buying Indicators, Market Absorption of Apartments, Green Coffee Inventories, Fuels and Electric Energy used by Industry Groups, and Cotton Ginnings by County. But buried in these myriad publications are the keys to understanding ourselves.

On February 1, 1977, the estimated population of the United States, including Armed Forces overseas, was 216,123,000. This population is growing by 125,000 a month, 101,000 of which represents a net gain of births over deaths, while the other 24,000 is made up of immigrants.

The sex ratio remains uneven. There are 95.2 men for every hundred women. In the over-65 group, there are 69 men for every hundred women. Ergo, there are a lot of lonely old women.

One out of three married persons between the ages of 25 and 35 will end their first marriage in divorce. Ergo, first marriages are becoming testing grounds rather than commitments.

The proportion of women between the ages of 20 and 24 who do not marry rose from 28 percent in 1960 to 43 percent in 1976. Ergo, women are becoming pilgrims in search of the self.

The birth rate continues to drop. Ergo, we will have to rely more heavily on immigration for population increase.

The census uses terms like in-migration and out-migration to tell us simple truths. People are moving south and west and out of cities. Today, five cities in the Southwest are among the nation's top ten, while Washington, D.C., and Cleveland no longer rank. Florida is first of the in-migration states, while New York leads the out-migration states. Every census report is accompanied by a description of the statistical methods used. A report on population estimates in New York state used the "Regression" method. I can think of no better term to characterize the present situation of New York, one of the two states that had a net loss of population between 1970 and 1975 (the other was Rhode Island).

The census reminds us that the poor are always with us. In 1975, 25,877,000 Americans were on the wrong side of the poverty line, that is, they made $5500 or less in a family of four, $3506 in a family of two, and $2724 for a single. This amounts to 12.3 percent of the population, and it is a shocking statistic. With prices what they are, I would personally classify as poor anyone making less than $25,000, but that is another story. The census tells us that statistical poverty ends at $5501, and the census is the highest authority in these matters.

The single most important statistic that the Census Bureau has to offer is this: 52 percent of American families have incomes between $10,000 and $25,000. If you forget everything else, this is the one fact that must be remembered about this country. The middle class has an absolute majority. It is flanked by 7.9 million families (14.1%) with incomes above $25,000, and 6.8 million families (12%) with incomes below $5000. This is what Mrs. Virginia L. McLeary, the lady from Luling, Texas, was saying when she sent a pie to Khrushchev during his American tour in 1960. The pie was mistaken for a bomb, but in fact it was an edible census report on family income. It had a lot of filling between a thin upper crust and a thin lower crust.

America operates according to Newton's third law of motion: every action has an equal and opposite reaction. A sailing ship is driven forward by the counteraction of two forces, the action of the wind on the sail, and the counteraction of the water on the keel. If a ship is well ballasted, it's hard to overturn. The middle class is a huge body of reasonably content and self-concerned people who provide the ballast for the American ship of state. What the Census Bureau is telling us is that there will be no revolution here.

9. *Disasters:* Americans worry about disasters to externalize their capacity for doom. No other people has so many disasters on its collective mind. In Guatemala, earthquakes happen; in America they are anticipated, forecast, prepared for, written about, and discussed on talk shows. All of us have free-floating anxieties that we need to make concrete. In a single day the average American is confronted with the many shapes of doom, both natural and man-made. He can worry about the Palmdale Bubble, the drought, the Continental Drift, the New Ice Age, the Sonic Boom, the ozone layer, nuclear waste, cancer, multiple sclerosis, muscular dystrophy, heart disease, mental illness, cystic fibrosis, nephritis, hepatitis, cerebral palsy, leukemia, venereal disease, tennis elbow, and many others. Like our bodies, our anxieties are overnourished. We are regularly given lists of the ten biggest killers. "Four million Americans," says a sign on a bus, "don't know they have an incurable disease. Find out about diabetes and count yourself in."

I am going to make a fortune starting a Disaster-of-the-Month club. Each month, members will receive, at a nominal cost, the full documentation of one disaster, along with a "what to do" kit — i.e., what to do in case of a fire, what to do in case of an earthquake, what to do in case a flying saucer lands in your back yard. All members will receive a news letter with disaster highlights from around the world, written by experts in the field, and including disaster bulletins about new dangers. BULLETIN: "Fifty percent of false teeth worn in the United States today are made of porcelain containing depleted uranium that delivers alpha and beta radiation to mouth tissues. According to *Nucleonics Week,* 20 million Americans are walking around with radioactive smiles." Charter members will receive, as a bonus disaster item, a recording of Orson Welles' Martian broadcast. It is a measure of America's predilection for disaster that thousands of listeners took the broadcast seriously and barricaded themselves in their homes, while some reported seeing Martians. Anything with "American disaster" in it is bound to be a hit, as was a hamburger joint in London called "The Great American Disaster."

In 1976, I was assigned to write the lead article for the *New York Times* magazine's bicentennial issue. The central idea was The Good

Life on the San Andreas Fault. This struck me as an apt metaphor for the American condition, which is a mixture of great blessings and great fears. The fault is the big crack in the ground that runs from the Mexican border to north of San Francisco. We know that at more or less regular intervals the crack opens and swallows those who live on its edge. It is the price they pay for the Good Life. In every fairy tale there is a bad witch, and disasters are our bad witch. They also help us focus our fears. It is probably healthier to worry about the earthquake than to go through the day with an unfocused fear.

10. *Home:* A nineteenth-century English traveler to America wrote that "attachment to locality is scarcely known; and shifting from place to place, a thousand miles at a stretch, with a view to bettering the condition, seems to be an ordinary occurrence. There is, in fact, an immense internal migration." Well, that hasn't changed, every day is still moving day. The population remains unsettled, and the average American family changes its home every three or four years. Why not? Where else can you travel thousands of miles without showing papers? But while full attention has been paid to American rootlessness, it is only one side of the coin, the other side being attachment to home. Every American wants to be a homeowner, to confirm his image of self-sufficiency. Owning a home is the practical application of Emerson's goal of Each Man a State. When you own a home and the land it's on, you own a tiny piece of the country. It's something that can't be taken away from you (the corollary to this being foreclosure of mortgage).

In no other country has the government done so much to help its citizens buy single-family homes. The mystique of home ownership has been translated into housing policies which are on every elected official's list of sacred cows, like Mom and the Fourth of July. As Herbert Hoover told a national housing conference in 1931, no immortal ballads have ever been written about apartments. Home ownership has been encouraged through mortgage-finance reforms, the GI bill, and tax subsidies. The federal government is currently spending $7 billion a year to make it easier for people to buy homes.

Homes, judging by the two file drawers full of entries in the 42d Street branch of the New York Public Library, must be the most important word in the American language. Here is an illustrative sample: home almanac, home amusements, home appliances, home aquariums, home book of money-saving formulas, home brokers, home of the brave, home-brewed beer, home cooking, home care, home carpentry, home for Christmas, home decoration, home defense, home for the blind, home economics, home for fallen and friendless girls, home fires burning, home front, home furnishings, home-grown, home guard, home gymnastics for well and sick, home help, home life, home for the homeless, home is the hunter, home improvement, home for incurables, home indemnity, home industry, home insurance, homemade pickles, home market, home mechanics, home missions, home mortgage, home needlework, home office, home for orphans, home de proue *(sic)*, home radio, home on the range, home relief, home run, homespun, homestead, home stretch, home study, home sweet home, home topics, hometown, home truth, home veterinarian's handbook, home weaving, and homework. Without the word home, the language would be impoverished.

The American home is both a symbol of security and something that can be quickly disposed of. "In the United States," de Tocqueville wrote, "a man builds a house in which to spend his old age, and he sells it before the roof is on." The American is walking a tightrope between the two poles of rootlessness and staying put. Hence the expression, home on the range, which reconciles the two and expresses the will to make your home wherever you are, to carry the idea of home around with you, and to find an ideal place, where seldom is heard a discouraging word. The American home is not a building, it's an idea, it's feeling comfortable wherever you are. Remember the old saying, a Frenchman walks into a place as if he owns it, an American walks into a place as if he doesn't care who owns it. Look at the shacks of rural workers photographed by Walker Evans in *Let Us Now Praise Famous Men.* They were homes, even though those people had nothing, because they were life-sustaining. Look at migrant workers. They are not migrants because they are naturally restless; their restlessness has been forced upon them by the circumstances of their employment. Robert Coles tells us that the children of migrant workers are passionately attached to a few things that are theirs, a comb, a rabbit's foot, a scarf, a mirror. In those modest objects, there is the idea of home. In America the rich become sedentary, they buy roots, or they commute between properties. The poor carry their homes with them.

The idea of the home sustains America. It is a fortress against ambiguity and disorder. We know that the state cannot help us, that the solutions to our problems are in ourselves. The home is the place where we can focus our love, find relief from abstraction, and develop the ethics of kinship. It is the place where all emotions can be satisfied. It is the secure environment where we can drop our guard and be ourselves, the one place where we can walk around with our blemishes showing. It is an intense, half-closed universe protected from the indignities of the outside world, where the admiration of children is an element of dignity in the life of the parents. This is the way it's supposed to work, of course, and nothing works the way it should, and we have children who run away from their parents and parents who run away from their children, but I think that the idea of the home and the way it *should* work is one of the most powerful ideas in American life.

Ten American Stereotypes

Stereotypes change with the times. Harriet Martineau, who came to America in 1834, promised a friend that she would bring back a living American stereotype, a six-foot, tobacco-squirting judge, lank as a flail, with a solemn face and a dogmatic manner, who hated blacks and pitied foreigners. Among nineteenth-century stereotypes, there was "the lady who can be vulgar with safety," and "the young man who pushes his way." One of today's stereotypes might be the affluent proletarian with the unisex ponytail, wearing a Goodwill work shirt, boots, and bib overalls, who sits in the lotus position and closes his eyes when he listens to Jethro Tull. Here are my ten all-time favorite American stereotypes:

1. The only white man the natives trust.

2. The kid who lies about his age to join the Marines.

3. The fellow with the dream job. One example: "After prohibition, I was hired by Seagrams to go from bar to bar in the Broadway area ordering their product. Boy, what a job — I lasted three months."

4. The used car salesman who was voted most likely to succeed in the high school year book.

5. The quiet kid next door, who helped the neighbors rake the leaves, and was an Eagle Scout and an altar boy, and got good grades, and had a paper route, and who kills his parents and his two sisters with a shotgun.

6. The dotty millionaire who's terrified of germs.

7. The stage mother who makes her pigeon-toed daughter take tap-dancing lessons.

8. The company president who has no small talk and lunches on cottage cheese at his desk.

9. The writer who finds his inspiration in lonely sand dunes and worries about selling out.

10. The Rockfeller heir who worked his way through Yale by waiting on table.

Dictionary of Accepted Ideas

This is an American version of Gustave Flaubert's "Dictionnaire des Idées Reçues." Flaubert began collecting his material at the age of nine, when he copied down the inane remarks of a lady who was visiting his father. His list of "ready-made" phrases which conventional thought swaddles in respectability was found among his papers after his death, and was published as an annex to his posthumous novel, *Bouvard et Pécuchet*. Accepted ideas are part of the cultural swill of every era. They spring fully formed from the lips, such, as, in Flaubert's time:

America: Will conquer the earth.

Modern Man: Has become a machine.

They add up to a body of assumption that helps to define a society. We are what we mindlessly repeat. Here is a start on a "Dictionary of Accepted Ideas for 20th-Century America." Readers are invited to make further contributions.

America: Has never started a war, but has sent thousands of soldiers to fight on foreign soil so that others could be free.

The Businessman: The great American middleman who meshes the economic gears of the nation.

Death: Not an end, but a beginning.

The Farmer: Always tan and lean, he never refuses a helping hand to a stranger.

The Father: Buys baseball gloves for his son, goes to see his daughter in the school play, talks about how he walked five miles to school when he was young, and complains about lights left on in the basement.

The Hometown: No matter how far you have gone, in distance or achievement, you always remember it fondly.

The Irishman: Quick to flare and quick to forgive, he carries his homeland with him wherever he goes.

The Leader: The sparkplug of every community, he knows the loneliness of leadership.

Man: Should like the feel of leather and the smell of new hay in a field; should feel at home with guns and have a way with dogs and children.

The Mother: She only cries at night.

The Mother-in-Law: No artist ever painted her.

Mountains: No man can tame one.

Nickel: A nickel earned is of far more value than a dollar found.

Railroads: What has happened to the steam engine, with its familiar whistle?

The Rancher: Eats buckwheat cakes for breakfast and goes to town on Saturday night.

Steel: Only the test of fire makes fine steel.

Teachers: They believe they have the greatest job of all.

Teen-agers: They should be listened to because they are tomorrow's adults.

Truckdrivers: They will stop ten tons of wheeled steel to let a twelve-ounce kitten cross the road. They are always threatening to give up the road and live a normal life.

The Veteran: Likes the sound of a bugle playing "Taps," and keeps his Good Conduct Medal in his keepsake box.

Woman: Should like spring gardens, sunsets, kittens, and small things made of porcelain.

The Wife: Can't balance the checkbook, but is the mainstay of the family.

Ten American Traits

Americans, perhaps more than any other people on earth, have a need for assurances about their identity. But in no country on earth is national character so resistant to definition. Where are the signs of behavior and tradition that might help tell them who they are? Each of the following American traits has its opposite. The thing and its opposite coexist in our society. Perhaps this is a clue to understanding the national character. It won't sit still for its portrait. The society is in such a state of flux that its significant traits must be seen in terms of paired opposites.

1. *Puritanism:* I come from a Catholic Mediterranean country, and Puritanism escapes me. Are we really living in the "land of the

pilgrims' pride"? Those generations of clergymen who banned theater and lawn bowling, and who installed pillories in town squares,
what were they all about? Those "chosen" and intolerant people,
who preached the strenuous life, and saw America as a setting for
redemption, and claimed to have fixed "the maladjusted mechanism
of man," what strange Christian heresy were they pushing?

To come to grips with the Puritan legacy, I consulted my friend
Trumbull Higgins. Trumbull is one of those Americans with two last
names, like Hamilton Fish, Caskie Stinett, Calvin Coolidge, and Rutherford B. Hayes. I gather that it is a special mark of distinction to
have two last names; it is the next best thing to having a title, it sets
you apart from the folk with common Christian names. Trumbull,
who is a historian, comes from a long line of stern-faced and thin-
lipped Puritans. On his mother's side, there was the Rev. Benjamin
Trumbull, who upbraided Connecticut legislators after they had
passed a divorce law on grounds of "inveterate hatred," for encouraging "vice to walk with a bare face and a stretched-out neck."
On his father's side there was a Higgins who came to America to join
the New Harmony colony founded by Robert Owen and was massa-
cred by the Indians. Trumbull's father, an architect, was fond of
saying: soft words don't butter the parsnips.

Trumbull, believes that all of America can be explained by the
Puritan legacy. "It's the key that opens all the locks," he says. So,
without further introduction, let me turn the floor over to Chairman
Higgins.

"The term, as you know, comes from pure in heart. To these
people, the Church of England was not sufficiently pure in its Christian faith. Their doctrine was based on an all-powerful and all-know-
ing God who was aware in advance of who was going to be let into
heaven. They set up a small group of the elect who would be recognized by their pure behavior, who would live a life of breathless
purity, or, as it might more accurately be put, of breathless hypocrisy.
The abiding sin of Puritanism is hypocrisy, because people can't live
up to the standards they impose on themselves. That's why contemporary Puritans go to Jewish psychiatrists, since they can't go to
Catholic priests.

"The Puritans banished purgatory, because the smallest sin could
not be compensated by any amount of virtue. That is why MacArthur
could write a pacifist constitution for Japan and advocate nuclear
weapons in Korea. It was the two sides of the Puritan coin; you must

have either perfect peace or complete hell. That's why when General Sherman said that war is hell, he meant that war *should* be hell, it should not be fought according to the Aquinan doctrine of the just war. The Senate committee that met on MacArthur's recall said that the concept of limited war was immoral, unchristian, and un-American. This of course is Puritanism in action.

"With Puritanism, every man was a priest. The distinction between the profane and the sacred was abolished. Every home was a church. Puritan churches weren't called churches, they were called meeting-places. Puritans believed that the bishops were just as evil as the king, that hierarchy was sinful, that authority was suspect, that each man entered into his own Covenant with God. Our political democracy stems from there. It is an expression of the hatred of the state and the loathing of authority that is implicit in Puritanism. It is the transition from religious individualism to political individualism, the idea of government by consent. But by setting this insane high standard of every man a priest, and by doing away with purgatory, politicians must offer the kingdom of heaven on election eve, and this is known as the campaign promise. Nixon had to engage in unspeakable hypocrisy to live up to the standard, so that Puritanism gave us Watergate.

"Puritanism permeates every aspect of American life. The elect should become prosperous, there was nothing reprehensible in shrewd trade, so that slowly Good became Goods. Begging was sinful because it was unproductive. Poverty was not a virtue. If you lacked property you were by definition bad and should be punished. The Republican party still feels this way. Who said that the business of America is business — *Calvin* Coolidge. This is the essence of the Puritan approach. The corporation is the perfect model of Calvinism, based on a covenant, a contract, and limited liability.

"Full employment is never an issue to a Puritan. You're always employed in the business of being virtuous and if you don't have a job it's because you're sinful and deserve to be punished. That was the key to the quarrel between the banks and New York City. The bankers, as custodians of the Puritan ethic, did not want to lend money to a city full of unemployed poor.

"This crazy system does make sense if you look at it through the Puritan lens. America was a country built by the Puritans for the Puritans. Look at the double-hang window. They wanted a tight fit so as not to let Nature in. The Puritan house is either heated or air-conditioned, because Nature is always suspect. The Puritan wants to control everything, including room temperature. Look at the whitewashed churches with the steeples knocked off, for obvious reasons; look at the banishment of stained-glass windows because that was color and color was Nature and Nature was sinful; look at the straight-backed pews. Straight is a good Puritan word. That's why so many American cities are built on the gridiron pattern; straight streets are better than curved streets resembling the design of nature. Tom Sawyer was the epitome of Puritanism, whitewashing the fence, whereas Huck Finn, representing nature, wasn't going to get involved in any Puritan activity.

"The Puritan attitude toward sex was to have lots of children in the interest of productivity. Jimmy Carter, the twice-born Christian, sits on his front porch with his wife and four children to show the American people that he is sexually productive.

"Immigrants were Calvinized, a process similar to vulcanization; their inner psyches were pulled out of their bodies at tremendous temperatures. The Italians have finally been Calvinized, no small feat, and even the Mafia is laundering its money. Puritanism is founded on laundering money, it's the corporate form of cleanliness. The reason Negroes played such an important part in this country is that they were the only ones who couldn't be Calvinized, so they were left alone to play jazz and dance and wear bright colors, they didn't have to be literate in order to read the Bible. So you see, Puritanism is the great synthesizer, the thing that links everything together. Today's society in many ways seems to contradict the Puritan ethic of productive work and careful thrift, but remember, a society that's been raised this way doesn't cease to be this way by rebelling against it. In today's young people I see neo-Puritanism. They feel guilty about comfort; the box spring and the turkey dinner are not for them, they'd rather sleep on a mattress on the floor and eat ghastly vegetarian meals. The Puritan mansion has many rooms, with a lock on every door."

The reverse of Puritanism is the permissive society, the narcissism of the seventies, the "get in touch with your feelings" movement, and the sexual revolution. What would the Puritan fathers have thought of lesbian ministers, high school teachers marching in Gay Liberation parades, and group sex explained as an attempt to act out standard American values and realize the ideal of marital stability. One of the women interviewed in Masters and Johnson's *The Pleasure Bond* found a constitutional basis for swinging. "I think this had a philosophical basis for me," she said. "I want to be as happy and as able to pursue happiness in this world as I can . . . I don't want any restrictions inside of me; I want to be able to go out and pursue happiness."

2. *Altruism:* In its basic definition, an unselfish interest in the welfare of others. Americans really are generous and helpful. The reverse is urban selfishness, what Edward Abbey, the Arizona maverick and hater of cities, calls "the air poisonous with hatred," the rudeness of city-dwellers, the taxi drivers at Kennedy who charge a foreigner $50 for a $10 ride, the fights over a parking space. When you have space and abundance, as you have in most of this country, you have altruism, and when you have the urban jungle, you have Darwinian survival.

I signed up for a summer course at Harvard and the registrar wrote: We want to do everything we can to make your stay with us productive and comfortable. All right, it's on a form and it may be meaningless. But I don't think so. I think Americans cultivate the habit of helpfulness. Whether it springs pristine from the heart or is a cultivated art, is it any less real? Whatever people say and do often enough becomes true. If you want to pray, Pascal said, first get on your knees.

I am staggered by this statistic: in 1975, Americans donated a record $26.88 billion to charity. That is more than the gross national product of many countries, and it's what we give away. I know there are tax incentives for gifts, but again, there is a habit of giving. And beyond the habit, just as there is impulse buying, there is impulse giving — look at the responses to hard-luck stories on television, the checks that pour in for the family of eight burned out of their home or for the little Guatemalan boy who needs open-heart surgery in Texas. We are a nation of givers. What other country would make voluntary contributions, above and beyond taxes, to its Treasury? In 1974, the Treasury received from private citizens $418,000 to help pay off the national debt. (I am advised by a reader of this passage that American generosity is a form of guilt tax for being the richest country in the world. But I know other rich countries, like France, that pay no guilt tax at all).

Where else but America could you have a group like the Gleaners, college kids in the midwest who work the rows of corn on big farms, picking up what the combines miss, sell the corn, and donate the proceeds to agencies like CARE that feed the world's poor? The Gleaners originated in Illinois's Eureka College (Ronald Reagan's alma mater) and have spread to half a dozen campuses. They mobilize at harvest time and follow the reapers with gunnysacks, which they fill with the 5 percent of the crop that the big machines miss. They take advantage of the wastefulness of mechanized agriculture. Hundreds of thousands of bushels are left to rot in the fields. With corn at $3 a bushel, the Gleaners are in business. The farmers lend them bins to store the corn and trucks to drive it to the elevators. It's voluntary, it's practical, and it works.

If you would do good, Samuel Butler said, begin to do so in minute particulars. Here are two minute examples of American altruism which I find more interesting than statistics on lend-lease. Let's call them a story of two Beverlys.

When Beverly Sills sang in Iowa, the president of the university gave a party for her, and among the guests were the women who had prepared the food. One of the women had made toffee nut candy, but Beverly was dieting. "God, if only I could eat it," she said. The woman asked when she was going off her diet. "On my birthday I treat myself," Beverly said. "I allow myself to eat anything. I buy peanut clusters and just get disgusting." The woman asked when her birthday was and Beverly told her it was May 25. On May 24 there arrived at her home a tiny box with one piece of toffee nut candy and a note that said "Happy Birthday."

An English journalist I know named Beverley Nichols came to America in the twenties and visited J. P. Morgan (the son of J. Pierpont Morgan) in New York. Nichols was in the library browsing among treasures, when he saw a lock of hair under a glass case bound with a piece of ribbon and a label that said: "A lock of the hair of Keats. Given to Shelley by Keats' friend." J. P. caught him staring at it and said, "Like to hold it for a minute?" He produced a key, opened the case, and handed the lock of hair to Nichols. Then he said, "Give it to me for a moment." He extracted a single hair from the lock, a long curly one, put it on a piece of paper, dropped a spot of sealing wax at one end, and wrote: "Keats; hair. From a lock in my collection. J. P. Morgan."

"That's the last hair from that lock that I'll give away," Morgan told Nichols. "If we remove any more I won't have a lock, I'll have a bald patch."

3. *Anti-intellectualism:* The founding fathers were intellectuals, and whatever anti-intellectualism they expressed was in terms of the pastoral ideal. Jefferson saw the true American as a farmer ("Those who labor in the earth are the chosen people of God"), and was

always ready to side with rural simplicity against urban sophistica-
tion. "State a moral case," he wrote, "to a ploughman and a professor.
The former will decide it as well, and often better than the latter,
because he has not been led astray by artificial rules." The unspoiled
American man in the unspoiled American landscape could be
counted upon to make sound moral judgments. When America burst
the bounds of the thirteen states, a less idyllic and more pragmatic
frontier tradition of anti-intellectualism sprang up, pitting against
one another two sets of values, the founder against the settler, the
striped-pants boys against the man in buckskins, the sedentary
against the nomadic, the man of thought against the man of action,
the rule of law against the rule of the gun, book learning against
hard-earned experience, precedent against improvisation, the specu-
lative mind against the clearer of forests, philosophy against sound
common sense, refinement against ruggedness, eloquence against
cussing, the dude against the cowpuncher. It was a regional antagonism of West against East and it was a generational antagonism
between the early- and late-settled parts of America.

These antagonisms became political weapons. The 1828 presidential election was seen as a contest between . . .

> John Quincy Adams who can write
> And Andrew Jackson who can fight.

Jacksonian populism promoted the anti-intellectual set of values.
Davy Crockett, who could "whip his weight in wildcats," served
three terms in Congress and boasted that "I have never read a page
in a law book in all my life." The Jacksonian conviction that any
citizen can fill a government post (the office makes the man) was in
direct opposition to the notion that the ship of state had to be piloted
by exceptional men (the man makes the office).

It was natural for the clearers of forests to have no use for art. Art
was sissy. Fifty years ago, a man in a Midwestern town was barred
from society because at a house party a book of poetry was found in
his room. A Yale man who became a museum curator in another
Midwestern city was shunned by gentlemen who were sure that the
curator of an art museum must be effeminate. He finally won their
confidence because he was an excellent steeplechase rider. Athletic
ability compensated for intellectual leanings. The frontier attitude to
culture is still with us, as when Toots Shor, standing in the lobby
during the first intermission of Maurice Evans' *Hamlet*, said: "I'm the
only sonofabitch here who doesn't know how this goddamn thing is

gonna come out." This kind of anti-intellectual posturing is always good for a laugh, and was lamented by Ezra Pound:

> The thought of what America
> The thought of what America
> The thought of what America would be like
> If the classics had a wide circulation . . .
> Oh well! It troubles my sleep.

There were rare presidents who could reconcile the two sets of values, like Teddy Roosevelt. He was a Harvard man who wore eyeglasses on the end of a black silk cord, but he was also a big game hunter, an outdoor man who knew the West and could handle a horse. Adlai Stevenson, on the other hand, put off many voters because he was too articulate, too witty, too much of an egghead. When Stevenson was nominated, the nation's intellectuals became a special-interest group. Humboldt "thought that if Adlai could beat Ike in the November elections, culture would come into its own in Washington," writes Saul Bellow in *Humboldt's Gift.* "If Stevenson is in, we're in, Charlie. Stevenson reads my poems . . . Stevenson carries my ballads with him on the campaign trail. Intellectuals are coming up in this country." But Stevenson did not, like Teddy Roosevelt, have a macho side to make his brilliance palatable. The voice of populism in New York, the *Daily News,* called him Adelaide and said he delivered his speeches in a fruity voice. Eisenhower, the mail-order candidate, won the election and catered to the anti-intellectual mood of the country. His lips moved when he read Zane Grey novels. In a 1954 speech, he defined an intellectual as "a man who takes more words than are necessary to tell more than he knows." By this time, thanks to Joe McCarthy, intellectuals had become an oppressed minority. The intellectual was not only an elitist, but, as Hiss had shown, he was a subversive, not to be trusted, alienated from the real values of the land.

Like Teddy Roosevelt, John Kennedy was able to straddle the issue. He was himself an author *(Why England Slept),* but he was also a man of action (PT 109). He was athletic (touch football at Hyannis), but he did not look upon artists and intellectuals as irrelevant. He invited Robert Frost to read at his inauguration, he gave a dinner for Nobel laureates in the spring of 1962, and, a month before he died, at a Convocation Address at Amherst College, he said: "I look forward to an America which will not be afraid of grace and beauty."

After Kennedy, the frontier set of values asserted itself in the

deliberately homespun and vulgar style of Lyndon Johnson, a man
of the people (albeit a wealthy one) who was damned if he was going
to change just because he was squatting in the White House. I had
a sneaking admiration for the Johnson style. I was on the rebound
from French culture, which worships intellectual achievement the
way Americans worship success. The French term for intellectual
achievement was *bouton de mandarin,* named for the little button
on the top of a Chinese mandarin's hat which identified him as a
person of high rank. After living in a society in which the purpose of
life was to serve as the subject of discourse, and seeing at close hand
the stifling pomposity of a leader like Charles de Gaulle (who had
won his mandarin's button by writing memoirs in a pedantic and
classical style), Lyndon Johnson's breezy vulgarity was tonic. You had
to hand it to him for imposing the frontier style on the nation's
capital. What a relief, after the *ancien régime* protocol of Gaullism,
to hear that Johnson had received Abba Eban with the words, "Mr.
Ambassador, Ah'm sittin' here scratchin' my ass and thinkin' about
Is-ra-el." Without the Vietnam war, Johnson would have been an
endearing President. The editor of a women's magazine told me this
story: Twenty editors were invited to the White House for lunch.
Johnson arrived two hours late and shook hands all around. A waiter
brought him two bourbon old-fashioneds on a silver tray; he downed
them in two gulps. The conversation turned to childbirth. "Ah was
a big baby," Johnson said. "Ah ripped my poor mama so bad when
Ah came out it cost sixteen hundred dollars to sew her up again."
After the lunch, Johnson insisted on taking the editors on a tour of
the White House. He pushed open a door, revealing Lady Bird in bed
with the flu, her hair in curlers. Concealing her astonishment and
displeasure, Lady Bird gave a brave little wave of the hand, smiled,
and said, "Hi, everybody." Johnson beamed and told the trailing
editors: "That little lady right there had twenty miscarriages, but she
never gave up." I found the Davy Crockett side of Johnson refresh-
ing, although perhaps what he was really saying was: when you have
power, you don't need dignity. "Beware of the man," wrote Edgar
Lee Masters, "who rises to power from one suspender."

The reverse of anti-intellectualism is reverence for eggheads, and
even Johnson had a few around. Today the Brain Trust reigns and
one of the main functions of Eastern universities is to hatch presidential advisers. The scholar has a mandate to articulate the problems of
society, at the cabinet level, in the *New York Review of Books,* and
on the Op-ed page of the *New York Times.* Henry Kissinger's mete-

oric rise may represent the apogee of the intellectual in American history. For the first time we had the intellectual as superstar, in constant orbit, dating starlets, trading quips with chiefs of state, leaking tidbits to favored reporters. He was not merely a powerful man, he was well-liked, he shot up in the popularity polls, in spite of the fact that he looked like an itinerant peddler and sounded like somebody trying to tell an ethnic joke.

Perhaps the days of sneering at eggheads are over. Life has become too complicated to do without them. In 1954, when Charles E. Wilson was Secretary of Defense, he was asked why the Pentagon did not subsidize more pure research. "I am not much interested as a military project in why potatoes turn brown when they are fried," "Engine Charlie" said. He had come to government via the business community, which today is at the mercy of its research and development teams. The scholar and the scientist are in charge of our future. Ma Bell employs 1500 Ph.D.s. "How many Englishmen understand, or want to understand," wrote Sir Charles Snow in 1962, "that during the past twenty years the United States has done something like 80 per cent of the science and scholarship of the entire Western world?"

With more and more eggheads being injected into the system, we get situations like the following: A man in Los Alamos, New Mexico, was arrested for speeding. Brought before a judge, he argued that a thunderstorm had struck in the area just before his arrest, and that this had ionized the air and affected the speed radar unit. The judge said the argument made sense. Static electricity in the air, he acknowledged, could bend the radar beam and result in a false reading. The judge found the defendant not guilty. Both men were theoretical physicists at Los Alamos Scientific Laboratory. "Only in Los Alamos," said the physicist who served part-time as a municipal judge, "could a defendant use a principle of advanced physics in his defense and have a judge understand what he's saying." This may be the shape of things to come, when the doctoral candidates outnumber the rest of us.

4. *Provincialism:* George Washington was a provincial. He never saw Europe. He never left the country to which his paternity is attributed. The French sculptor Houdon had to come to Mount Vernon in 1785 to model his bust. Thomas Jefferson was a provincial. He warned American youth against the pitfalls of Europe. The results of travel, far from the benign influences of their native ground, would be incalculably harmful, he wrote, and would include acquiring a fondness for European dissipation, fascination with the privileges of

European aristocrats, abhorrence with the equality in their own country, consorting with whores, learning to consider fidelity to the marriage bed pointless, and growing to speak and write their native tongue as foreigners. The evils that Jefferson saw in a trip abroad were such as to make the most seasoned travel agent look for another line of work. The reverse of provincialism is cosmopolitanism, and in contrast to Washington and Jefferson we have the expatriate Benjamin Franklin, envoy to the court of Louis XVI, at ease in Paris society, and author of flattering notes in French to ladies he admired.

Since World War II, when America lost its innocence for good, passports have been required for travel abroad. I was surprised to learn that only 14 million Americans hold passports. The great majority of Americans never leave the continental United States, emulating Washington rather than Franklin. I'm not sure that provincialism is the right word in a country where the distances are so great. As a German visitor wrote: "In America they will ask you on your arrival in New York: 'I suppose you will take in Yellowstone Park and California?' As though a man traveling from London to Berlin were asked whether he would not include in his journey an excursion to Leningrad and Egypt." Americans have plenty of elbow room, and if they want a change of scenery, they can find it at home. In addition, they can find approximations of America all over the world, they can go to the Holiday Inn in Marrakesh and rent a car from Hertz in Geneva. This is probably what most American travelers want, a worldwide excrescence of the interstate subculture. Leaving America means abandoning the safety of a large land mass where the same language is spoken from coast to coast and where you do not get stopped at a border every 500 miles. Americans are provincial in the sense that they are always comparing the way foreigners do things with the way they do things. They have an unlimited capacity for being shocked by the natives. In Nice airport once I heard an indignant American tourist tell a fellow traveler that she and her husband had visited the Nice outdoor market, where they had seen rabbits being sold with the fur still on their legs. To the French housewife, this was no more than proof that the rabbit was freshly killed. To the American tourist, it was evidence of cruel behavior toward our furry friends. "They wouldn't allow that at home," she said. Nor would they allow faulty plumbing, food that gives you the trots, driving on the left side of the road, unrefrigerated soft drinks, and countless other tribulations that the American abroad must face. The wives of American professors on sabbatical leave in France suffer from culture shock. They can't believe how rude everyone is, their infants break out with diaper rash, they are lost without their brand names and friendly neighbors.

Another form of provincialism is indifference to the outside world. During the Vietnam war, a *Redbook* poll found that four out of ten mothers with sons in Vietnam did not know where it was. They had not taken the trouble to locate that part of the world from which their offspring might not return. Nor had many of the sons. I remember being at the Saigon airport in 1965, when the first massive airlifts of American troops arrived. One of them, walking from the plane to the truck that would take him to his base, turned to a reporter and asked: "Hey, Mac, what's the name of this island?"

We overlook how few Americans travel abroad, because expatriates are so much in evidence. It turns out that we did not need the Marines to colonize the world. In every corner of the globe there are American enclaves, hippie communities in Nepal, construction workers in Saudi Arabia, oil crews in Nigeria, acolytes in Indian ashrams, retirement communities in Mexico, and coupon-clippers in Riviera villas. When I went to the Fiji Islands, I thought, this is one place where there won't be any Americans. I was wrong. In Suva, the capital, we ran into an escapee from the SCLS (Southern California Life-Style), who was doing PR work for the Fijian government. He said he had to go as far as Fiji to escape the smog.

5. *The Success Cult:* New Guinea tribes have the Cargo Cult, in which the jet plane is incorporated into their system of deities, and we have the Success Cult, which sometimes seems equally baffling. The reverse of the Success Cult is a romantic fascination with failure.

I am told that the insistence on material success goes back to the Puritan clergy's argument that it was the mark of the "visible saint." The Success Cult has religious origins: it has its breviary, its clergy, and its faithful. And what else is there to believe in a classless society in which a man can rise whatever his origins? Society did not hold you back, only your own limitations held you back. Success was the natural goal in a competitive society, the triumph of unfettered individualism.

Our friend Alexis, the man with the X-ray vision, may have been the first to see that a nation of ambitious grabbers, all after the brass ring, was anxiety-producing. Why this restlessness in the midst of prosperity, he wondered, why this melancholy in the midst of abundance, why this disgust with life in the midst of easy circumstances? Alexis had seen in the Old World poor and ignorant people who seemed happy, while in the New, "I saw the freest and most enlightened men placed in the happiest circumstances which the world affords; it seemed to me as if a cloud habitually hung upon their brow, and I thought them serious, and almost sad, even in their pleasures."

But that was not a cloud, Alexis, it was the hard-won halo of success. No one ever said that success led to serenity. If you want serenity, try transcendental meditation. Those who enter the Success Marathon have to keep running, and looking over their shoulders to see if they are being overtaken. The Success Cult was not meant to produce peace of mind, but an interesting life, as in the ancient Chinese curse: may you have an interesting life.

Somewhere along the way, success got a bad name. Some of the best minds of the nineteenth century developed a counter-cult, which was to get off the treadmill and cultivate the inner man. "Have we no culture, no refinement," asked Thoreau, "but skill only to . . . acquire a little worldly wealth, or fame, or liberty, and make a false show with it, as if we were all husk and shell, with no tender and living kernel to us?" It was William James, in a 1906 letter to H. G. Wells, who found the killing term, when he decried "the moral flabbiness born of the exclusive worship of the Bitch-Goddess Success. That — with the squalid cash interpretation put on the word success — is our national disease."

Success got a bad name because it was appropriated by a special-interest group, the business community, and was used as an argument against government interference. In that golden age before the personal income tax, when corporations unencumbered by federal regulations plundered the public domain and exploited labor, their justification was the Success Cult. Success was the driving wheel of industry, the spur of progress, the essential American aim. Carnegie, Rockefeller, and other industrial barons had started from scratch. The idea was that anybody could do it if he learned a few simple rules. In 1907, John D. Rockefeller said of his employees, "I see in each of them infinite possibilities. They have but to master the knack of economy, thrift, honesty, and perseverance, and success is theirs."

Endless volumes of self-help literature spread the gospel, from McGuffey's reader to Bruce Barton's articles, such as "What to do if you want to sit at the Boss's desk." Each year, Horatio Alger awards were given out (and still are), accompanied by articles headlined IT STILL HAPPENS IN AMERICA. No mention was made of the thousands to whom it did not happen. The myth propagated by business interests was that success had less to do with business acumen than with character development. Since this was available to everyone, the merit of success was self-evident. It required no explanation, and failure permitted no excuse.

Thus, when the Federal Trade Commission was established, it was attacked on the grounds that it was trying to push inefficient businessmen on the ladder to success. It was jamming the gears of a system that rewarded the deserving.

Big business was brought to heel by Teddy Roosevelt and by the New Deal, but the negative image of the Success Cult persisted, and we have Harry S. Truman addressing his colleagues in the Senate in December 1937 in the style of a soapbox orator:

"We worship money instead of honor. A billionaire in our estimation, is much greater in the eyes of the people than the public servants who work for the public interest. It makes no difference if the billionaire rode to wealth on the sweat of little children and the blood of underpaid labor. We do not recognize that the Carnegie Libraries are steeped in the blood of the Homestead steel workers, but they are. We do not remember that the Rockefeller Foundation is founded on the dead miners of the Colorado Fuel Company. We worship Mammon."

In a backhanded way, Truman is responding to Thoreau's argument that there is a divorce between wealth and culture. The way the American Success Cult works is that it *converts* money into culture. Once wealth has been obtained, culture is pursued with equal passion. Medieval French cloisters are transplanted to bluffs on the Hudson. Scottish castles are shipped stone by stone to California. Great libraries are built to contain the purchases of magnates turned collectors. Cities compete for orchestra conductors. The industrial barons gave the artist more patronage than the Medici and Hapsburg courts combined. There is considerable merit to the assumption that a better material life leads to a thriving culture. Mammon and the Muses go hand in hand.

But for the individual, the idea of success needs to be rehabilitated and secularized, that is, freed from the "cult" definition of wealth. Success is more important than wealth, it is the measure of one's personal worth. It should not be a dirty little secret, something you have to step over someone to obtain, or the result of dishonorable strategies, but the respect of one's peers, the consecration of excellence, the satisfaction of doing something well. For the academic it's tenure, for the playwright it's Broadway, for the surgeon it's a low mortality rate, for the trial lawyer it's winning a case, for the actor it's curtain calls, for the reporter it's an exclusive, for the politician it's getting re-elected, for the civil servant it's promotion. Those Americans who are denied success are the ones who find no meaning in their work.

The success ethic also helps to buttress the democratic system. Take politics: "Winning is everything," say the Olympic runner and the politician. They are both running, one for the tape and the other for office. With the possibility of winning, ideology is abolished. It doesn't matter whether you're in the left lane or the right lane, but whether you finish in the money. Jack Kennedy was a close friend of Joe McCarthy until he got the presidential bug. Then he had to abandon his friends and his views in exchange for the "which way is the mob headed, I'm its leader" mentality. As Harry Truman said of Jack Kennedy: "He had his ear so close to the ground it was full of grasshoppers." Presidential candidates must abandon ideology to build a "broad consensus." Carter's absence of ideology was such that one of his speech-writers, who quit during the campaign, told him: "I'm not sure what you believe in, besides yourself." The speech-writer was upset because Carter insisted on tailoring his speeches to suit his audiences. He would reel off a litany of heroes, for instance, including half a dozen of his favorite Presidents, and in front of black audiences he would add Martin Luther King. But in front of white audiences, King was dropped. Well, Carter was a politician, not an evangelist. It would be naïve to think that he would act otherwise, since winning is everything.

If you want to win, there can be no loyalty to principle, and Ronald Reagan was willing to run on a ticket with his ideological opposite to gain a tactical advantage at the 1976 Republican Convention. The revolutionaries of the sixties become the candidates of the seventies. Tom Hayden and Bobbie Seale put their rhetoric in mothballs and learned the art of the campaign promise. Talk about co-opting! This system could co-opt the Loch Ness monster. The possibility of success helps push radicals toward a middle ground. It promotes consensus politics. To move away from that consensus, as George McGovern and Barry Goldwater know, is to run the Olympic mile in army boots.

Success also gives the classless society its credibility. Gunnar Myrdal pointed out 30 years ago that the belief in the success creed is shared by rich and poor. The rich believe in it in order to hang on to their advantages and the poor believe in it because it seems a better paved road to upward mobility than the class struggle. Americans prefer the slogan "deal me in" to the slogan "soak the rich." All they ask is to be dealt a fair hand (and who knows what that is with so many wild cards). How can you have a class struggle when the rich and the poor keep the same faith?

Modern dissenters from the Success Cult, heirs of Thoreau and William James, thin the ranks of the affluent. Timothy Leary taught at Harvard and surrounded himself with wealthy disciples. To tune in and drop out, you must be solvent. The assumption that a better material life leads to a better spiritual life, which horrified Thoreau, is borne out by his heirs. Material wealth provides options, as the guru-shoppers and psyche-builders know. The pretty blond Buddhist with the Vuitton luggage and the first-class ticket on Air India is on her way to Madras for six months of self-denial in a cave.

I asked a writer friend of mine what his son did. He looked grieved. "That's like asking your host how many times a week he sleeps with his wife," he said. "He graduated from high school and went to college for two months before deciding he wanted nothing to do with bourgeois values. Since then he's been doing odd jobs and resting in between. He picked potatoes for a while but quit because the farmer was using chemicals. There is always some ecological principle that keeps him from being gainfully employed. I call him Saint Francis of Assisi because he won't let me kill mosquitoes in my own house. All life is sacred, you see."

"How does he spend his days?" I asked.

"That's a very good question, as Richard Nixon used to say," my friend replied.

What about those who fall from grace? In our gladiator society, the losers are fed to the lions, but they fascinate us nonetheless. We love stories about the demise of the famous. The "Whatever Happened To" column is an American chronicle of failure. We derive immense satisfaction from reading that Veronica Lake is working as a cocktail waitress, that Rita Hayworth is drying out in a clinic for alcoholics, that Joe Louis ended up broke and is working as a greeter in Las Vegas, and that Marilyn Monroe went off the deep end and killed herself. Such items remind us of the perils of success — when you fly too close to the sun your wings melt.

The self-destructive artist becomes a cult figure. Scott Fitzgerald was worshiped by a generation of college students, who imitated his self-indulgence but not his art. In a society of abundance, the wasting of gifts seems somehow fitting. We reserve a special place of honor for those artists who ended badly, in poverty like Edgar Allan Poe, or suicides like John Berryman, Sylvia Plath, and Anne Sexton. They become tragic figures, cut down by the pitiless harvesters of American reality. We worship them posthumously, as casualties of the Success Cult.

The paradox is that in a society that worships success the best-known character in twentieth-century American theater is the prototypical failure, Willy Loman. Willy is the sap who believed all the self-help guff. Just master two or three simple rules and you will join the managerial elite. You don't have to be brilliant, the right personality is enough. "It's not what you say, it's how you say it." Then why isn't he rich and famous? The whole system has blown up in his face. Willy Loman is the victim of a Darwinian success ethic. There are the fit and the unfit, and they owe each other nothing.

6. *Exploitation*, of which the reverse is conservation, as the following story illustrates: In Jeddah, my friend Michael Palmer, who is a partner in a Saudi-Arabian investment company, was talking with the American contractor of a road-building project. "What are we gonna do about this goddamn congestion in Jeddah harbor when we unload our caterpillars?" the contractor asked. "Hey, there's that stream we went swimming in. We could put the cats in LSTs and float them up that stream." Michael, one of whose only pleasures in the austere desert kingdom is snorkeling in the stream on weekends, said: "I hope you don't disturb the fish." The contractor's face turned the color of Red Sea coral. "What are you, one of these goddamn ecology freaks," he shouted. "Christ, they wouldn't let us build the Alaska pipeline because we kept the elks from fucking." "I thought he was going to hit me," Michael said.

Tempers flare in the collision between two equally enshrined and equally legitimate American traditions: the pastoral bias and the exploitation economy. Ingenuity for the improvement of mankind against protection of the environment. Businessmen, who once thought of themselves as the stewards of economic and social order, are now seen as polluters and plunderers. Some of our most cherished beliefs are in the defendant's dock. The idea was that private groups would make decisions that were good not only for them but for society. But Adam Smith's invisible hand went arthritic, and all these great ideas, like private ownership of capital, profit, free enterprise, efficiency, and technology, ended up ruining the environment, impoverishing the human spirit, fostering worldwide corruption, and contributing to international instability.

The businessman fights back. The contractor is not going to let Michael deprive him of his solution, just to save a few fish. The businessman will tell you that conservation is a luxury for the rich that the poor pay for. To manufacture a detergent in a pollution-free plant, you raise the price to the consumer. You stop throwing your waste in the stream, which benefits the rich people who have homes there and the fishermen. The poor who buy the detergent will be subsidizing the ecology. The argument has been going on for more than a century. "If a man walk in the woods for love of them half of each day," Thoreau wrote, "he is in danger of being regarded as a loafer; but if he spends the whole day as a speculator, shearing off those woods and making the earth bald before her time, he is esteemed an industrious and enterprising citizen. As if a town had no interest in its woods but to cut them down."

But it wasn't just shearing woods, it was solving problems that permitted the settlement of the rest of the country. In 1830, John B. Jervis was asked to build the Mohawk and Hudson Railroad from Albany to Schenectady, at a time when the steam locomotive had just been imported from England and no one in America knew how to build a roadbed, what to use for ties and rails, or what weight the locomotive could pull. Jervis, operating by trial and error, used a gravel roadbed, timber ties, and rails of wood with iron capping. He tried his system out in 1831 and found that the locomotive bounced on the straight and wore away the rails in curves, losing its traction. He came up with a four-wheel swivel truck that could go around curves and didn't bounce.

Congress solved the problem of how to get the railroads to lay more track by giving them free land, as much as forty miles on either side of the track. The Northern Pacific Railroad alone got 40 million acres, a tract almost as big as North Dakota. The century of problem-solving was also the century of wasteful exploitation of resources. No one then believed that resources were exhaustible. The role of government was to help business exhaust the inexhaustible. Under such conditions, it is a wonder that Congress established government forest reserves. It is an even greater wonder that in 1864, in the midst of the Civil War, Abraham Lincoln gave Yosemite to California for "public use, resort, and recreation." This was a great moment in American history, the first time that federal land was given for a nonutilitarian purpose. The peculiar idea of preserving rather than plundering the natural paradise entered into law, and by the time the National Park Service was established in 1916, there were already 14 national parks in existence.

Somehow the problem-solvers and the conservationists are always at loggerheads. Thomas Edison's first electric light bulb used a carbonized sewing thread as the filament, but it burned out after a short time. A team of problem-solvers was put to work to come up with a bulb that would burn brightly for a long time at low cost. Dr. William D. Coolidge tried tungsten, which has the highest melting point of any metal. The problem was how to thread tungsten. Coolidge's team at the General Electric lab in 1911 was called "the ductile tungsten group." They finally obtained ductile tungsten, which by 1914 was used in 85 percent of all light bulbs. There were other problems. The tungsten filament gave off gases which blackened the wall of the bulb. The problem-solvers found that if you surrounded the filament with nitrogen the bulb did not blacken, but there was heat loss. If you coiled the filament, however, you made up for the heat loss. With inert gas and a coiled filament, you had a bulb that lasted 300 hours. By bringing electric lighting into every home, Coolidge and his "ductile tungsten group" might be called one of the precursors of the energy crisis. Today's problem-solvers offer nuclear energy as an alternative to oil, and this is probably the single issue that conservationists are most upset about.

Somehow things go wrong. The problem-solver goes too far in his pursuit of the useful. It is the mentality that insists that it is always better to act than to leave well enough alone. It crosses over into politics. Robert McNamara, when he was Secretary of Defense, is supposed to have said: "Castro's assassination is the only productive way of dealing with Cuba."

The American way seems to be an oscillation between extremes. When the problem-solvers run amok, there is a slight correction. Today government tries to regulate the exploitation of resources without alienating the business community. There is fierce lobbying by a coalition of industry and labor against any legislation that threatens jobs or plant sites, and by environmental groups against any further plunder. Government can go either way. In October 1976 a federal judge in Virginia fined the Allied Chemical Corporation a record $13,375,000 for dumping tons of Kepone, an ant poison, into the James River, where it killed the shad and the oysters. But in the House, a federal land-use bill providing financial incentives for states preserving their land in its natural state was killed in committee.

Small battles are being fought at every level. Should a $200 million pulp mill be built on farmland along the Connecticut River in Walpole, New Hampshire? It would have created jobs and boosted the tax base, but 690 were for it and 899 against. Should 73 acres of undeveloped land be turned into an industrial park in Fairfax County, Virginia? This is historic country, where George Washington worked as a surveyor. He later invested in real estate, buying farmland in the Ohio valley and on New York's Mohawk River, and tripling his money in three years. That's quite a precedent, but the Fairfax Board of Supervisors voted against the industrial park. Should the Reserve Mining Company in Silver Bay, Minnesota, be prevented from dumping 67,000 tons a day of taconite tailings into Lake Superior (taconite in iron-rich pellets is used to feed blast furnaces)? The issue has been in the courts for years, and when it is decided it will be a landmark case in environmental law. Should the timber industry be permitted "even-aged cutting?" They say it's good for the trees. Environmentalists call it clear-cutting and say it's a cause of erosion and silting of streams. In 1976 a federal judge banned clear-cutting in Monongahela, West Virginia. These small battles add up to the most important issue of our time. The accommodation between the problem-solvers and the save-the-land groups goes on in every state. Problem-solving is contested today, it's not gospel anymore, it's not like the good old days of one-dimensional moral issues, when the invention of the milk-fat tester was hailed as the only thing that kept dairymen honest. The exploiters can no longer offer salvation, although they are trying in a multitude of ways, from the square tomato to grain-driven gasoline. The environmentalists, meanwhile, are defending a morally impregnable cause. What person in his right mind is against clean water and clean air? And what laissez-faire fanatic would argue that a plant has the right to pollute a river? The environmentalists have become our society's true crusaders. They really believe that they can flip over industrial civilization, like flipping over a record that's been played so long on one side its grooves are worn, and come up with a society that is based on the nonacquisitive search for knowledge of self and nature. They are going against the sacrosanct tradition of using up natural resources to improve the standard of living and keep the economy going. They also reinforce the American sense of place against rootlessness. People who care enough about a particular place to keep it the way it is form militant groups that go out loaded for bear, the bears in this case being big business or the corps of engineers or the real estate developers. And sometimes they bring back the bearskin.

The latest reading on the oscillometer is that the environmentalists sometimes overstate their case with doomsday predictions. Barry Commoner predicted the death of Lake Erie, which still supports a thriving fishing industry. They have added to our inventory of fears with mercury poisoning from fish and depletion of the ozone layer, which may be pure hogwash. The pendulum is swinging, and ten years after Rachel Carson's *Silent Spring*, Dr. Norman E. Borlaug, who won the Nobel peace prize for his work on new strains of wheat, had a few kind words to say about DDT, before a Congressional committee, in October 1971: "The pollution of the environment is the result of every human activity as well as the whims of nature. It is a tragic error to believe that agricultural chemicals are a prime factor in the deterioration of our environment. The indiscriminate cancellation, suspension, or outright banning of such pesticides as DDT is a game of dominos we will live to regret . . . I have dedicated myself to finding better methods of feeding the world's starving populations. Without DDT and other important agricultural chemicals, our goals are simply unattainable. Perhaps more than any other single factor in the world today, DDT has a unique contribution to make to the relief of human suffering."

This is an ongoing discourse, in which neither side should be given the final word. It may be that Dr. Borlaug misrepresented the dangers of DDT, which is said to destroy the life chain by which plants, animals and people survive, and which leads to the development of strains of pests that are immune to it. I belong to Friends of the Earth, and I hope that we can save both the world's starving populations and the Hawaiian nene bird. What really worries me about environmentalists is not their goals, but the way they are translated in bureaucratic terms. In California, perhaps the state most actively concerned with such issues, I have heard Governor Jerry Brown's conservation policies referred to as "humanist fascism." When the coastal commission tells you the size your windows must be to conserve energy, and when the Forest Service harasses an elderly lady in order to buy her land, which is adjacent to a National Forest, we are getting perilously close to Big-Brotherism. Environmentalists reply that the option is doomsday, but when I travel through this country I get no sense of its approach. There is so much open and unpolluted land that the population could double and we would still enjoy one of the lowest densities on the planet.

7. *Perfectibility:* Americans have a modest ambition. They all want

to be perfect. The reverse of perfectibility is what might be called the fallibility neurosis, of which more later. Our desire for perfection can be measured by the shelves of how-to literature. We have a naïve faith in prescriptions. We actually believe that we can learn how to be better spouses, better lovers, better parents, and better all-around human beings. We can improve our tennis game by attending a tennis clinic. We can attain inner peace by buying a mantra for $75 from the maharishi. We can conquer obesity by having our jaws wired. We can prolong our lives by jogging. I can hear the elevator operator in the department store of America: Ninth floor, Self-Improvement, Everybody Out. Our leader shows the way. Jimmy Carter is a demon for perfectibility. It's not enough that he's running the country, he listens to classical music during office hours, and took a crash course in art so that he would know something about the paintings in the White House, and mastered speed reading, which allows him to read 1200 words a minute, and finish three books a night. I expect to hear any day that he is learning to fly his own plane like King Hussein of Jordan, in order to pilot *Air Force One.*

My wife and I recently met the parents of a five-year-old girl; they had attended an eight-week course in PET (Parent Effectiveness Training), which is designed to make you a better parent. "I went reluctantly," the father said, "but I realized it was helping." "It is designed to build up self-esteem in the child," the mother explained. "You are taught Active Listening, and asking 'I' questions rather than 'You' questions. For instance, I won't say to my daughter, 'Stay off this floor, you filthy child,' I'll say, 'I just waxed this floor, dear, and I don't want anyone to walk over it.' " "Liza wanted to be a boy," the mother went on, "I couldn't get her to wear a dress. PET taught me that the way she dressed was her business."

We were in a friend's back yard in New Jersey and Liza fell out of a hammock and came over to her mother, crying. I could almost hear the sound of file cards being shuffled as the PET mother searched her mind for the correct response. "Are you hurt, dear?" she asked. Emphasizing the obvious must be a favorite PET technique. Liza kissed her mother on the cheek. The mother put her hand to her cheek, reached into her purse for a tissue, and wiped her cheek. No amount of PET could change the fact that physical demonstrations of affection made her uncomfortable. I saw in this incident the flaw to all self-improvement techniques. There is a point beyond which you cannot defy nature. If you are flat-footed and have poor coordination, you will never be a tennis star. If you are extremely high-strung, saying a mantra will not soothe your nerves. We are, to a certain extent, stuck with ourselves. "Nature makes fifty poor melons for one that is good," Emerson wrote . . . "and she scatters nations of naked Indians and nations of clothed Christians, with two or three good heads among them. Nature works very hard, and only hits the white once in a million throws."

On the other hand, we have hard evidence of perfectibility. Performances are being improved all over the lot. Our life expectancy has taken a big jump, 81 years for women and 71.8 for men. Our death rate is less than our birth rate. Statistically, we are tending toward zero mortality. Children are taller, healthier, and better-looking than their parents. The performance of athletes is a measure of perfectibility. It wasn't so long ago that the four-minute mile was an unattainable dream. I have no doubt that Jimmy Connors could beat Bill Tilden in straight sets and that Mark Spitz could outswim Johnny Weissmuller. There are simple rules of diet and exercise that can help us all. We can improve the shell, but can we improve the kernel?

Some people may be confused by conflicting doctrines of perfectibility. Women, for instance, can choose between Women's Lib and Total Woman. They can greet their husbands with a meat cleaver or a flimsy negligee. They can go the route of total emancipation or total submission. Either way, the end result is supposed to be a Better Woman.

Brainwashed as we are by the perfectibility propagandists, we have become distrustful of our true and fallible selves. We suffer from a fallibility neurosis. Take the "average idealized" family of four on television commercials. It lives in a temperate climate, where all major credit cards are acceptable, and within reach of a scheduled airline. It buys its gas at a station where the attendant is delighted to clean your windshield, and its children play ball and ride bikes when they are not eating breakfast cereals. But this average idealized family suffers from a wide array of disorders — headaches, nerves, upset stomach, acid indigestion, and nagging backache. They are in terrible pain, they have transparent sinuses, and hammers in their heads. But wait, relief is at hand, within seconds of taking the right spray or cream or tablet. We are artificially threatened, and then swamped with remedies. The average idealized family beams with happiness because it has been restored to perfectibility. We have been convinced that we should not be satisfied with the way we are engineered, and we are willing to listen to anyone who confirms our suspicions. Confirming our suspicions is a billion-dollar-a-year business. Gerard B. Lambert is a great American; he introduced halitosis. So fight bad breath, and fight sinus headache three ways, and if that doesn't work, send your sinuses to Arizona.

8. *Fraud and Moral Accounting:* During basketball practice, my son points to a fellow player and says: "He fouled me." The coach shouts: "What if the ref didn't see it?" Throughout America, the prevailing moral code seems to be: WHAT IF THE REF DIDN'T SEE IT? Or, as Raquel Welch said in a *Playboy* interview: "fucking people over has become the national pastime."

There is a tradition of fraud in this country, which probably goes back to cheating the Indians. In the Puritan ethic, sharp trading was a virtue. When Captain Frederick Marryat came here in 1837 to write his *Diary in America,* he was amused "by a reply given me by an American in office here. I asked him how much his office was worth, and his answer was $600 besides *stealings."*

For the alert immigrant who sold his vote to the political club, fraud was an avenue of upward mobility. As George Washington Plunkett of Tammany Hall put it: "I seen my opportunities and I took 'em." That too is in the American grain. There is no point in rehashing the history of fraud, the railroad scandals, the land scandals, the public officials taking kickbacks, President Warren Harding disgraced by his Secretary of the Interior Albert Fall, who turned government oil reserves over to private oil companies in exchange for $400,000 . . . it's all par for the course. It's no accident that baseball, the national pastime, is the only game with built-in theft. The player is encouraged to take advantage of an unexpected opportunity and "steal" a base. One might argue that deviousness is built into many sports, but only baseball has the word "steal" in its rule book.

Widespread fraud is a part of the democratic system. The lack of controls is an invitation to fraud. The system requires that citizens monitor themselves. Most of them do. But there is always a newsworthy minority that is figuring out ways to beat the system. In America there is always a loophole, and we are a nation of loophole experts. The examples come from above. Mort Sahl had Richard Nixon reading the Constitution and looking for loopholes.

It's all so easy. Take the Palestinian students who helped finance their political movement by filing more than $5 million in phony insurance claims. They took out multiple policies for the same car, since the insurance companies didn't check with one another. They found out how easily the insurance companies paid off. They bought new cars, sent them to the Middle East, where they were sold for twice their purchase price, and reported them stolen, collecting on the multiple claims. Above all, in order not to use their distinctive Arab names, they learned how easy it is to obtain a false ID. Anyone can go through birth registers, find someone who died in infancy and whose date of birth matches his, obtain a copy of the birth certificate, and assume that dead infant's identity. A Federal Advisory Committee on False Identification has estimated that false IDs are costing the country $20 billion a year in tax fraud, welfare fraud, credit card fraud, and bad check fraud. The Palestinian insurance caper is a drop in the bucket. And yet, if we have to choose between stopping fraud and corseting the country in regulations, what to do? The advisory committee ruled out the establishment of a national card of identity, which is the way the French and other overregulated nations keep tabs on their subjects.

Fraud applies traditional American virtues, such as ingenuity, know-how, hard work, and stick-to-it-iveness to the promotion of illegal gain. Take the 1975 grain scandals, which led to 57 indictments. The variety of techniques employed, from the farmer to the shipper, was a tribute to the problem-solving ability discussed earlier. The farmer sprayed his grain with water to increase its weight, adulterated the grain by adding mercury-treated seed supplies, and rigged the protein-content analysis, which ups the grade and means a big difference in price. Countering these measures, the wholesalers used rigged moisture meters to weigh the grain. It was fraud against fraud, and may the best thief win. The federal grading system allows for a small percentage of foreign matter. No. 3 corn, for instance, can contain 4 percent broken kernels and foreign matter. This tolerance makes the grain-elevator blender a specialist much in demand. He mixes in as many rice hulls and other debris as he thinks he can get past the inspector. If he somehow miscalculates, the inspector, who works for a private firm under contract to the Department of Agriculture, can be persuaded to look the other way. In New Orleans, the focus of the 1975 investigation, the ships bound for India and Asia were short-loaded by 3 percent, on the assumption that Third-World weighing equipment was too broken-down to detect the difference. This was no two-bit operation, it was done systematically under orders from grain company executives trying to improve the quarterly statements to their stockholders. This is where the performance ethic gets you. Philip H. McCaull, a director of Cook Industries, the world's third largest grain exporter, went to jail for three months for conspiring to short-load grain shipments in New Orleans. He had received large bonuses from his company based on his splendid performance, which was due in part to stealing from his Third World customers.

I am constantly amazed at the inventiveness of fraud in this country, at the misapplied ingenuity. Thieves are always finding new twists. In the last five years, for instance, arson-for-profit has become big business, accounting for $2 billion in insurance losses each year. Bank robberies are small potatoes compared to the money to be made by arson, which has become a highly specialized and highly organized profession. There are dignified brokers who read the *Wall Street Journal,* looking for unprofitable properties, and who act as the middlemen between the businessmen and the master torches, who tend to be experts with doctorates in chemistry or military experience in demolition. In one case, the owners of the Dixie Bakery in Louisville, Kentucky, were going out of business, and contracted to have their plant burned down. The contract arsonist's big problem was how to make the sprinkler system inoperative in a way that no insurance inspector could detect. He built a wooden collar around the main pipe, and filled it with dry ice, which froze the water in the pipe. A burning cigarette ignited a matchbook, which in turn lit a gasoline-soaked rag fuse leading to gasoline in plastic bags hung inside cardboard drums. The evidence of tampering with the sprinkler system melted during the fire. Agatha Christie could have conceived of no scheme more ingenious.

Well, this is the way it goes, and we get our role models for fraud from our most respected citizens, from the President on down. If it were fiction it would seem implausible. It's the world upside down when our highest law enforcement official, the attorney general, goes to jail; when other law enforcers such as FBI and CIA agents are indicted for criminal offenses, when bank presidents rob banks and postmasters rob post offices. No wonder the spirit of fraud filters down to the average man. Fraud is democratic, it cuts across class lines. Here is my quarterly statement on fraud cases, which includes some familiar names:

• The presidents of two New Jersey Banks, the bank of Bloomfield and the State Bank of Springfield, were indicted for siphoning off $4 million to finance loan-sharking operations. The chairman of the Northwestern Bank in Winston-Salem, North Carolina, convicted of misapplying $257,000 in the bank funds, argued in his defense that he had done no worse than the resigned budget director, Bert Lance.

- Atlantic City Postmaster Gordon F. Lawson, a veteran of 20 years with the P.O., was arrested in June 1977 for masterminding a $1 million dollar robbery in the main post office there. He gave the building's master key to his confederates, who drilled through the vaults and got away with a million in cash and bonds, and enough stamps to start a mail-order business.

- FBI agents in important positions were investigated for misappropriating bureau funds and taking kickbacks from companies that sold them equipment. An FBI supervisor was indicted on charges that agents working under him had allegedly opened mail and tapped telephones.

- General Motors substituted Chevrolet engines in 100,000 Oldsmobiles.

- Marlborough Gallery head Frank Lloyd was indicted for forging his New York gallery stock books.

- Joseph Monserrat, a member of the New York City Board of Education, was indicted for serving as a consultant to an audiovisual company that did business with city schools.

- Two Massachusetts state senators were convicted of shaking down a contractor for $40,000.

- Henry Kearns, when he was head of the Import-Export Bank, persuaded a Japanese trading conglomerate to whom he had granted 37 loan guarantees to purchase his stock in a Thai paper company above its market value.

- Lockheed designated at least $22 million in bribes and payoffs to stimulate foreign sales.

- The Good Humor Company was fined $85,000 for forging records to cover up high bacteria counts in its ice cream.

- In New York, a research scientist painted the mice to fake the results of his experiments.

- A New York internist was sentenced to a year in jail for defrauding the government by submitting false Medicaid invoices. The total Medicaid fraud was put at $300 million a year and was said to involve more than 12,000 physicians. A New Jersey surgeon removed warts and billed for cancerous tumors. A dentist treated prostate conditions. There are so many loopholes in the Medicaid program that it's an invitation to steal. In addition, Medicaid mills are paying thousands to mobsters in an updated version of the old protection racket.

- There are just as many loopholes in collecting unemployment insurance, which is known among the young as "loophole heaven."

The new life-style is to work for a year and stay on vacation for a year. For many young Americans, avoiding work has become the purpose of life. Since the 1975 recession, it has been possible to collect for as long as 65 weeks, and there's little or no monitoring; a close relative can pick up your check. In Michigan, a convict was found to be collecting unemployment checks that his brother was picking up. Unemployment statistics are thrown out of kilter by this new class of the voluntarily unemployed, and by those who continue to collect unemployment insurance while holding a job. There are currently about five million persons collecting jobless benefits. A lot of them are being subsidized by taxpayers to work every other year. Unemployment joke: will the last person out of Seattle please turn off the lights?

• The U.S. Military Mission in Iran, suspected of misuse of funds, destroyed its financial records prior to an investigation.

• Employees of the Internal Revenue Service in Pittsburgh were investigated for taking bribes from Gulf Oil.

• Representative Otto Passman was investigated for using his influence to obtain lucrative shipping contracts for friends.

• New York State Supreme Court Justice Irving H. Saypol, 25 years on the bench, a model of judicial decorum, and previously the prosecutor in the Rosenberg case, was indicted for bribery and perjury.

• In New York, 31 meat inspectors were indicted for taking bribes from meat packers to overlook sanitary violations. In Boston, meat inspectors admitted taking bribes to allow meat packers to substitute cheap cuts for prime in shipments to army posts.

• The elevator repair men from the New York City housing authority made phony overtime claims and cheated the city out of more than a million dollars.

Pervasive fraud is the American malaise. Too many people who are given positions of public trust, whether they be doctors or FBI men or congressmen or meat inspectors, seem to regard it as a license to steal. It seems as if the thumb is always on the scale, and that everyone who can is switching chuck for ground sirloin.

The other side of this is moral accounting. Our passion for uncovering fraud is equal to our passion for fraud. We have made a mythic figure of the investigator. In this country, people cheat, but they get caught. All the examples of fraud previously listed were made public because those involved were found out. Medicaid doctors go to jail. Congressmen are reprimanded by the

House Ethics Committee. Judges who have spent a lifetime sentencing others get a taste of prison themselves. The most interesting thing about Watergate was the process by which it was uncovered. The rest of the world was stunned by the way this scandal was aired before the nation. In other countries, washing dirty linen in public is the cardinal sin. In America, we hold televised congressional hearings so that everyone can be told how the linen got dirty in the first place. We have learned, thanks to the uncovering of fraud, not to trust authority figures, from the President on down. We have learned that whatever fraud we can imagine, no matter how outrageous, is conceivable: the President enriching himself in office; the Secretary of State taking bribes from a foreign power; a Supreme Court judge being paid off by a big corporation to give a dissenting opinion in a land-use case; Billy Graham an FBI informant. We have been taught by what we read in the papers that there is nothing that can't be fixed. But by the same token, we know that our watchdogs will uncover these scandals.

The Vietnam war may have been the tragedy of the century for America, based on the ill-conceived notion that America should become embroiled in other nations' affairs, defend democracy in areas of the world where the word has no meaning, and win a land war in Asia. Well, it's over now, the deserters are having their discharges upgraded and many are returning from Canada, and America forgets easily. But we aren't being allowed to forget. Moral accounting demands that scars should not heal. We can look forward to more books to lengthen the already existing shelf on how, why, and where we went wrong. The urge to lay blame is as unrelenting as the war itself. The people in the peace movement want to be proved right retroactively. We must do penance for our sins.

9. *Good Sportsmanship,* the reverse of which is Dirty Tricks. Coming from a European culture, it's always struck me here how political candidates who are bent on doing each other in can maintain a façade of smiling friendliness. They are political enemies but they embrace like best friends. They will do almost anything to each other to win the election, but they are all smiles and warm remarks when they meet. Three Democratic candidates, Jimmy Carter, Scoop Jackson, and Mo Udall, are on the same platform, joking and smiling, and each one knows that his chance for victory depends on the demise of the others. They may hate each others' guts, but the American way demands that they pretend to be amicable opponents in a game. To

be a sore loser is counterproductive. Muskie did himself irreparable harm by rising to the bait of spurious allegations about his wife and weeping with rage in public. The successful candidate must pretend that it's all good clean fun and that nothing gets under his skin. This is the unwritten law of the campaign, and it demands deep reserves of discipline.

I covered a legislative election in central France in the sixties, in a town called Brive-la-Gaillarde. I was observed having lunch with the Socialist candidate by the press secretary of the Gaullist candidate. The Gaullist candidate would not see me because I had broken bread with his opponent. Suspicion reigned. One had to take sides. It was inconceivable that one could talk to both candidates and write a fair story. I don't think you could get two French presidential candidates to share the same platform. Their mutual distrust would darken the air. Another thing I like in American elections is the loser's message to the winner. It's hard to be a loser because the media rubs your face in it. "How do you feel about losing, President Ford, after having come so close?" "And what about you, Mrs. Ford, do you feel at all emotional about it?" Good God, man, does the Queen Mother squat? But, although he may be overwhelmed with bitterness, the loser calls his opponent to wish him the best.

Good Sportsmanship is one of the demands we make on our public figures. They are not allowed to display anger or malice in public. It's amazing to me what reporters ask of a candidate. This is probably the justification of a long campaign, and of primaries. If a candidate can take the national press over an extended period of time without cracking, he can take anything. In the 1976 campaign, there was a reporter who asked Jimmy Carter whether he was capable of self-deprecating humor. Mo Udall, the reporter noted, had kidded himself for his part in organizing the postal service. Carter said that if he'd had anything to do with the postal service, he'd kid about it too. But the question had been meant seriously, as if a self-deprecating sense of humor really were a criteria for the White House. The incident made me think back to General de Gaulle's stage-managed press conferences, several of which I had covered in the sixties. Favored reporters were asked ahead of time by the general's press secretary to ask this or that question. Curtains would part, he would emerge, the prearranged questions would be asked, and the general would nod as if the questions did not surprise him. The general would deliver a speech he had learned by rote, in which he grouped the questions by topic. He would then retire, and the solemn farce would end. I imagined myself asking de Gaulle whether he had a self-deprecating sense of humor. Such irreverence would have been considered lese majesty.

Good Sportsmanship is a part of the American sense of fairness, and it's always a pleasure to see fairness win the day. For me, the best moment of the 1976 Republican convention in Kansas City came during the debate on whether Ronald Reagan should be allowed to announce his running mate before the nomination. A blond delegate from Georgia said that she had arrived at the convention uncommitted, but that in Georgia they played checkers, and before they started a game they decided whether they were going to play that you had to jump or you didn't have to jump, and if you decided you had to jump you might get to a point in the game where you didn't want to jump, but you jumped just the same, because those were the rules and you didn't change the rules in the middle of the game. Well, she felt that Reagan was trying to change the rules in the middle of the game. It might be a good idea to announce your running mate before the nomination, so the delegates could vote for a ticket instead of a man, but in 1980, not now. This appeal to fairness was heard.

Changing the rules to win is the other side of Good Sportsmanship. The Department of Dirty Tricks entered domestic government via the intelligence community. The age of innocence ended in the United States when the OSS was set up as a World War II espionage outfit. Espionage is a game in which dirty tricks replace rules. The British were masters of deceit and the Americans caught on fast. After the war, when the CIA was chartered, secrecy and dirty tricks were enshrined as legitimate methods of operation. Its activities largely escaped the usual watchdogs. It scored an impressive series of successes with such techniques as political assassinations and the manipulation of foreign political parties.

The CIA made dirty tricks respectable. Almost anything could be justified on grounds of national security. Watergate was simply CIA techniques coming home to roost. Since you could win an election in a foreign country by using espionage techniques, why not use those techniques to win an election at home, and why not use some experienced CIA operatives, like Howard Hunt and the Miami Cubans, to carry out the operation? It had worked in Tehran and Guatemala City, why couldn't it work in Washington, D.C.? The Plumbers were merely a domestic spin-off of the CIA agent working abroad. Interference in national elections was one of the CIA's main areas of expertise.

10. *Individualism,* the reverse of which is the Passion for Associations. Individualism is the social ideology for the pursuit of happiness. We believe that we are individually entitled to happiness. This lifetime warranty for the parts and labor of happiness is written into the Constitution. I don't think that in other countries the average man has such high expectations. Our sense of entitlement is reinforced by history. We *deserve* to be happy because we are the people who mastered a continent. The next step was self-mastery. The success of Eastern philosophies and the human potential movement can be attributed to our conscious effort to keep pursuing happiness after it was no longer available in geographical terms.

The idea of a man acting alone operates a powerful seduction. At its best it is a noble affirmation against the crassness of groups. In his essay on self-reliance, in which there occurs the celebrated phrase "A foolish consistency is the hobgoblin of little minds," Emerson writes that "society everywhere is in conspiracy against the manhood of every one of its members." The private impulse is sacred, but requires discipline rather than self-indulgence. "Instead of the gong for dinner," writes Emerson, "let us hear a whistle from a Spartan fife." The fulfilled individual must march to that Spartan fife.

The American experience gave birth to a literature of self-reliance. The bards of self-reliance told us that we could trust no one but ourselves. "Wherever a man goes," Thoreau said, "men will pursue and paw him with their dirty institutions." Noninterference was seen as an absolute virtue. Government was a necessary evil. Nowhere in the world has the very idea of government been under such constant scrutiny, by the very men who govern, by the finest writers, by the deepest thinkers. Individualism was the prize worth keeping above all others. It "gives character to the aggregate," wrote Walt Whitman.

We continue to believe in the myth of the man who does it alone. Kissinger in that famous interview saw himself as the lone cowboy, defeating the bad guys and saving the town, whereas he had the whole State Department behind him and was totally dependent on staff work. But oh, to have done it alone, like the millionaire brother in *Death of a Salesman:* "When I was seventeen, I walked into the jungle. And when I was twenty-one, I walked out, and by God, I was rich."

The individual against the system is another seductive theme in the literature of self-reliance. An individual with one share of stock can cause a giant corporation to justify its policies to its stockholders. He can make the corporation spend a great deal of time and money to get the proxies it needs, and to defend itself through institutional advertising. He can initiate a class action suit. The individual who bucks the system is a folk hero, like Mrs. Klussman, who in the 1940s organized a successful drive to save the San Francisco cable cars, or like Dr. A. J. Haagen-Smit, the Cal Tech biochemist who was the first man to prove that smog was chemically created in the atmosphere, and who fought the car companies for years over the effectiveness of antipollution devices, and won.

Alas, in our industrial society, these are isolated cases. The sad truth is that the creed of individualism has been stolen from the individual and made to serve the interests of big business. Corporations are the most tireless promoters of self-reliance and noninterference. Unbridled individualism becomes a permit to plunder. The evils of big government are served up to justify price-fixing and disregard for the environment.

In the spring of 1976, I attended a dinner given by Malcolm Forbes in his home in Far Hills, New Jersey, in honor of the nation's motorcycle press. Forbes, in addition to running the magazine that bears his name and being involved in some spectacular real estate ventures, owns the largest motorcycle dealership in New Jersey. He is a motorcycle nut, and has had several serious accidents while pursuing this activity in remote places.

The motorcycle industry was being criticized by environmentalists for its emission standards. Forbes told the gathered motorcycle writers: "The problems of emission standards and noise pollution could cost us out of the motorcycle business. We've got to play up the motorcycle as one of the last vestiges of individual freedom. We're like the old hedgehog pilots." There it was in a nutshell. The creed of self-reliance being used to protect a business interest from government regulation.

There followed a discussion about the wearing of helmets. Helmets saved lives and were a great thing, but some people didn't want to wear them, and they were bad for business. Was it constitutional to protect people from themselves and tell them they had to wear helmets? Was that not an infringement on individual rights? Some states had repealed the helmet law. Forbes felt it was grossly unfair for the federal government to tell the states,

"If you don't pass a helmet law we'll withold your highway funds." Again, the creed of self-reliance was used in defense of the motorcycle business.

I listened with a sympathetic ear, for I have always thought of individualism as a form of personal endeavor. I had chosen a profession where I could be self-employed, where no boss gave me orders. If I wanted to stay in bed for a week, I could. If I wanted to listen to the Spartan fife and work on weekends, I could. I did what I wanted to do, and I liked to think that I depended on no one. I burned my bridges as if I would never have to cross water again. So I tended to agree; I wanted the right not to wear a motorcycle helmet, even if it kills me.

But I also knew that excessive individualism becomes a form of nihilism. It leads to alienation. It can conceal a desperate desire for recognition, while making that recognition impossible because one insists on turning one's back on the world. Political assassination is the extreme form that the creed of individualism takes. The man alone who is obsessed with doing something important, the man who is going to change history single-handedly, the man who is going to leave his mark without outside assistance, ends up shooting a President. The political assassin represents the creed of self-reliance run amok.

That is, if you believe that Oswald acted alone. If you prefer to believe a conspiracy theory, then the political assassin is the extreme example of the American passion for association. According to Trumbull Higgins, my consultant on Puritanism, the passion for association is something else we can thank the pilgrims for. They formed a voluntary association of like-minded persons who made a covenant with God, at a time when British subjects had to profess the same faith as their king, and attend services or face punishment. When they reached these shores, they banded together, not   only   to worship, but to survive. The Vermonters in Vermontville, Michigan, associated to kill a bear that had been carrying off pigs.

The true fact of the frontier is that while it exalted the man who acted alone, you could get very little done without help from your neighbor. A letter quoted by Frederick Jackson Turner, from a frontier settler to his friend back East, nicely sums up this dual attitude: "It is a universal rule here to help one another, each one keeping an eye single to his own business."

The tendency to band together is a self-defense mechanism. After that, it becomes something else. The society nudges one into associational activity. Voluntary service becomes a way of making one's place in the community. It's a form of tithing. Belonging to the Heart Fund and the PTA is time-consuming but it also extends the ego, it's a merging of self with something larger. In most cases, the individual alone is powerless. The tradition of civil disobedience is individualistic. Why should a citizen "for a moment, or in the least degree, resign his conscience to the legislator," asked Thoreau. But to become a movement, civil disobedience depends on numbers. What is one abolitionist, or one suffragette, or one war resister, or one member of the Clamshell Alliance?

Causes aside, most people need to submerge themselves in groups. Listen to company men introducing themselves at a convention. "I'm Xerox," "I'm General Mills." They have checked their identities in the corporation lobby. I sometimes think that my brother George may be happier than I am because he is part of something he believes in, even if it is iced tea mix. But that's in a narrow sense, in a larger sense he believes in the corporation, he believes that it makes a useful product and keeps a lot of people employed and contributes to social stability. The pension plan is good, the medical plan is good, and if you get to be a vice president they will give you a car and change it every two years. They will, in short, take care of you. They will take an interest in your family. When George's eight-year-old daughter Nina suggested a new product called "Grade A Dad" cherry soda, she received a letter from the Office of the President of Thomas J. Lipton, Inc. "I have personally reviewed your suggestion," the letter said. "As you know, the key to the continued strength of the free enterprise system is ideas that produce profits for companies like Lipton Tea, profits that enable us to hire people like your father . . . We liked your idea and we researched it to determine if we should sell it as a Lipton product . . . there is one problem . . . Because of the upward spiral of the cost of sugar, we would have to price 'Grade A Dad' at about $1.00 a quart . . . But keep up the good work, and I will be glad to consider any other ideas you have for potential money-making products for Lipton." To me, that letter is an example of the length people go to in this country to maintain the strength of associative ties.

This is a useful national habit. Whenever two or more Americans have a common problem, they form a Committee of Concerned Citizens. It's still on the same level as the frontiersmen who banded together to kill the bear that was stealing the pigs, except that today the bear is a highway scheduled to go through your back yard or a methadone clinic next door or a chemical plant dumping waste in the lake where you fish and swim and get your drinking water.

I wonder if there is a single American who does not belong to some association, to the Rotary, or the "Y," or the public library, or the church choir, or the alumni association, or the Republican party: land of the workshop, home of the affiliated. I once thought I had found one, a hermit who lived in an abandoned silver mine in the wilderness area of Idaho's Salmon River. But he told me he belonged to the National Association of Hermits. I enjoy hearing about oddball groups, like the Philadelphia Mummers, the New Year's Shooters, the Nerveless Nocks (polesitters), the American Begonia Society, the Star Trek Associates, the Lesbian Mothers' National Defense Fund, the National Association to Aid Fat Americans, and the Society for the Preservation of Barbershop Quartet Signing.

There seem to be national cycles of collective and individual action. The sixties was a decade of mass action against the draft and the war and for civil rights and women. The *New York Review of Books* was a sixties organ, because it articulated the demands of the protest movements. The seventies is a decade for individual self-fulfillment and the quest for personal happiness, and the seventies organ is *People* magazine, which focuses on individuals and tells their little narcissistic fables of success and happiness.

Like everything else in this land, the passion for association has its dark side, and freaky people can find one another by joining the Nazi party or the Ku Klux Klan or the Hell's Angels. Aberrant behavior has its collective outlets. The First Amendment guarantees "the right of the people peaceably to assemble." In rare cases, limits have been set by state law. There are churches in Tennessee whose parishioners fondle poisonous snakes. They occasionally die as a result of snake bites incurred during religious services. Tennessee state law banned snake handling in churches. A court of appeals ruled that it had no right to do this under the First Amendment. The Tennessee Supreme Court reversed that ruling in September 1975, arguing that Tennessee "has the right to guard against the unnecessary creation of widows and orphans." The United States Supreme Court has let that judgment stand.

The truly original outcome of the American split between individualism and association is the fusion of the two, what might be called "collective individualism." As Gertrude Stein put it, "Americans act as if they all go together one by one and so any one is not leading."

Everybody on Stage

Rennie Davis made the transition from the protest movements of the sixties to the Eastern self-fulfillment movements of the seventies by joining the guru Maharaj ji, the fifteen-year-old boy sage who gathered his followers in the Houston Astrodome in October 1973 for a week-long celebration, during which, it was rumored, his testicles dropped. When Rennie Davis was organizing the Astrodome occasion, he tried to recruit his former Chicago Seven co-defendant, Abbie Hoffman. "I'll join," said Abbie, "if you put me on stage."

Everybody wants to be on stage. The compulsion is stronger than belief in the cause. The cause is the means to the end of being on stage. What do Abbie Hoffman and Pat Moynihan have in common? They will sacrifice any principle in order to be on stage. Moynihan is a Democratic senator who once worked for Nixon. He used one job to lay the foundations of another. He prepared his campaign for the Senate by taking positions as United Nations ambassador that were calculated to please the New York electorate. What does such a man believe in? He believes in being on stage.

Eldridge Cleaver was one of the founders of the Black Panther party. After the Oakland shootout, he jumped bail, left the country, and wound up in Algeria, where he set up an International Black Panther party. When I went to see him there in 1970, his uniformed goons stood me against the wall and took mug shots, full face and profile. Cleaver had borrowed his methods of operation from the Oakland police he knew so well. He soon realized what a mistake he had made by going into exile. Two blacks in New York were looking at Cleaver's photograph in his Black Panther uniform on the cover of the *New York Times* magazine. One said to the other: "There he is, all dressed up to go to his job at the post office." America has no Finland Station. Its exiled revolutionaries are flushed down the toilet of history. The country goes on to other things. It's amazing how fast a person can move from the "In the Spotlight" column to the "Whatever Became Of" column. Cleaver began to negotiate for his return, and it's better not to look too closely at the deal he made. In any case, he came back, announced that he was no longer a revolutionary, and that he had found God. He was taken up by a fundamentalist Christian group as its star convert. I saw him on television in Indiana, backed by a choir of surpliced maidens, and explaining how the lord had come to him in jail (outside visiting hours) and given him grace.

The Christian group put his children in their private school and helped finance a $100,000 home for Cleaver in Los Altos. When I expressed reservations about Cleaver's conversion to the poet Allen Ginsberg, he said: "Haven't you ever had a religious experience?" I said that although I had not yet been blessed with one, I didn't put it down, I merely admired Cleaver's timing. On stage, Eldridge Cleaver.

Back in 1968, I was invited to a fancy dinner in Paris given by Thierry Van Zuylen, whose sister had married Guy de Rothschild, the head of the French bank of the same name. The Van Zuylens lived on the Avenue Foch, in a paneled apartment that had roughly the same acreage as the Gare du Nord, hung with Mirós and Mattas and Aubusson tapestries. It was a stylish assemblage of period and modern. One of the guests was Bob Silvers, the pudgy editor of the *New York Review of Books,* who, by dint of importing the opinions of English dons, had acquired an Oxbridge accent. We sat down to eat lobster thermidor served by footmen in gold-edged plates, but Silvers could not sit still. Every five minutes he hopped from the table and went into the study to call Memphis, Tennessee. It developed that Martin Luther King's funeral was taking place, and Silvers felt personally involved. He had to have a step-by-step, minute-by-minute account, and jumped like a self-important jackrabbit every time the phone rang. This was the essence of radical chic. To be invited to dinner at the Van Zuylens, with the usual mix of money and titles, and to be terribly concerned about Martin Luther King's funeral. On stage, Bob Silvers.

More recently, in the fall of 1976, I was in Los Angeles on a magazine assignment. It was Sunday afternoon, and I went to see a friend who was expecting company. I looked out the window and saw Jerry Rubin coming up the driveway, pushing a wheelchair. Inside the wheelchair was the Vietnam veteran who had spoken at the Democratic convention, Ron Kovic. Jerry Rubin was to me the prototype of the man without convictions looking for a stage, and now he had latched on to Ron Kovic, whom I thought of as a sincere, dedicated guy. And who had better credentials for speaking out on Vietnam? Kovic had just written a book, and he was pleased with its reception. People were asking for his autograph. A week ago, he said, he had been in the kitchen of his home in Long Island, and his mother had answered the phone and said in a hushed voice: "Ron, it's Eugene McCarthy." Ron went to the phone. McCarthy wanted Ron as his vice-presidential candidate. Ron said he would think it over. Now

Ron was being taken up by the professional media manipulators like Jerry Rubin. Ron was thinking of making Jerry his campaign manager. Jerry Rubin pushing Ron Kovic's wheelchair was, I thought, the ultimate image of the American compulsion for being on stage.

I use the word stage advisedly, for in this country political life and show business are interchangeable. It is hard to take seriously people whose main interest is in giving a performance. This was brought home to me when I attended the 20th anniversary of the *National Review*, in November 1975, as a guest of Bill Buckley's literary agent. Among the distinguished guests were Barry Goldwater, Pat Moynihan (sitting next to Leonard Garment, his colleague in the Nixon White House), and Ronald Reagan, a former actor then running for the country's highest office, and the only candidate with prematurely red hair. Reagan was an actor turned politician, and Bill Buckley was a political commentator turned television performer. Both were driven by the compulsion to be on stage.

The dinner was an exercise in nostalgia, recalling memories of better days. The consensus was that the country was going down the drain. Buckley and the other aristocrats of arrested development bristled with Cold War rhetoric. The Cold War was the only period of recent history in which they felt comfortable. Buckley castigated our leaders for dealing with the Russians and quoted Alexander Solzhenitsyn. Although his mind was closed to contemporary thought, Buckley had an unlimited fund of outrage, like someone who could still get angry at the Germans for using mustard gas in World War I. I spotted Clare Booth Luce, chic in white satin, who had flown in from Hawaii for the occasion, and remembered something she had once written about Mussolini, which applied to the present occasion, that he was like a kiwi bird, which flew backward because it did not want to see where it was going, it only wanted to see where it had been. As for Ronald Reagan, his mind, like his familiar celluloid face, was blank. He positioned himself as an anti-intellectual, a regular guy, who was slightly suspicious of this fellow Buckley who used long words. Buckley had come to see him in California, he said, and he was using this German word, and his California friends came up to him and said, "What is it with this Zeitgeist?" and Reagan had asked Buckley to please use plain English. The whole evening was pathetic, and several good conservatives at my table wondered as it broke up whether Buckley's secret aim was to help the cause to self-destruct. But what could one expect of people whose true cause was being on stage? They were bound to keep everything on a frivolous level. Buckley had never left Yale. He was a terminal sophomore. His buffoonery robbed the conservative cause of whatever seriousness it might have had.

When the worlds of politics and show business are interchangeable, potentially dangerous political figures can be rendered harmless by being turned into media personalities. In January 1977, Ralph Nader co-hosted the "Saturday Night" variety show, and did a comedy routine. On stage everybody! We don't have to worry about radicals, because as soon as they become well known we give them one-liners to deliver on comedy shows. As Marcuse said, the system has a great capacity for absorbing its enemies.

At the same time that political figures become showbiz personalities, actors become social activists. They endorse candidates, or put money into their favorite cause, like Robert Redford saving Utah, or Marlon Brando with his miniature eco-system in Tahiti. Our tendency is to confuse celebrity with authority. Frank Sinatra and John Wayne tell us how to vote. Warren Beatty tells us what to think about the First Amendment. A dress designer has something to say about defense spending. These are our oracles, not because they know anything, but because they have high visibility. Instead of listening to one another, we watch the canned chatter of celebrities on talk shows.

"There's a certain attraction that politicians and show-business people have for each other," said Jeff Wald, Helen Reddy's husband. "They are a kind of American royalty and each group holds the other in awe." Political candidates court actors for their endorsement. Every candidate must have his star, and almost any star could become a candidate. If Robert Redford wanted to run for the Senate, he could throw darts at the map of America and pick his seat. Ronald Reagan had John Wayne and Jimmy Stewart in his camp. Sarge Shriver co-opted the Camelot repertory company. Nixon got Sammy Davis, Jr., by promising to appoint him to a presidential commission. Since the new campaign law went into effect, limiting individual contributions to $1000, rock groups have come into their own as power brokers. Who else can fill a stadium and raise $100,000 in a single night? This is exactly what Gregg Allman did for Jimmy Carter. The pols and the stars are locked in such a sweaty embrace it's impossible to tell them apart. Here is Jimmy Carter accepting the nomination at the Democratic convention: "We have an America that, in Bob Dylan's phrase, is busy being born, not busy dying."

Candidates don't quote Jefferson and Franklin anymore, they quote Bob Dylan.

Celebrities really are America's royalty. Telly Savalas was invited to the white tie state dinner for Queen Elizabeth at the White House. Peter Falk turned down an invitation to meet Emperor Hirohito of Japan, where *Columbo* is rated number one. Where else could an actor stand up an emperor? I turned on my car radio in Palm Springs, California, and this is what I heard: "Temperature in the low desert ranging from 40 at night to 85 during the day. In the mountains 26 to 61 degrees. That's the weather for today, folks. Do you like onions? Frank Sinatra does. Yesterday he had a hamburger at the Tamarisk Golf Club and they didn't have Maui onions, so he phoned the island of Maui and two bushels are being delivered to his Cathedral City hacienda in time for dinner tonight." We are told about the unimportant occurrences in Frank Sinatra's life, just as British subjects are told in the daily court calendar what the queen is up to. The item also serves to sustain Sinatra's celebrity by disclosing the extravagance of his demands. He is behaving like a star.

E. M. Forster wanted, "not an aristocracy of power, based upon rank and influence, but an aristocracy of the sensitive, the considerate, and the plucky." Our aristocracy of celebrities is a far cry from that, it is based on fame without greatness, the Big Name who is not a Big Man. If a nation perpetuates what it rewards, then we are perpetuating mediocrity in all its forms. Perhaps a democratic society has a low tolerance for greatness. The great man is undemocratic, he imposes his will on the masses. We don't want real royalty, we want tinsel royalty, who abdicate when their series is dropped. We are tending toward the true democracy of fame predicted by Andy Warhol, when each and every one of us will be famous for fifteen minutes.

Coolers

Erik Erikson has explored the idea of an American identity. Americans feel on common ground without having to behave alike. We are the sum of our disparities, and yet we are linked, we form a community. There are areas of voluntary mass behavior, some of which I would call coolers, that is, thermostatic devices that keep the society from boiling over. In the parlance of the con man, the cooler is the plant in the audience who volunteers for the shell game and wins, thereby drawing the suckers. The cooler is what makes people go along and remain under control. I once wrote a story on the Tombs prison in New York. The brutal guard had been replaced by the prison psychologist, who used massive doses of Thorazine to keep difficult inmates under control. He was not there to help the inmates, but to make the prison population tractable. He was a cooler. Every society has its coolers, going back to the bread and circuses of the Romans. They are mass experiences that unite the nation, give us an outlet for our gripes, and help us define ourselves as Americans. Without coolers, it can be argued, democracy would short-circuit.

Professional football is a cooler. Every American has the inalienable right to see two professional football games in their entirety on Sunday afternoon. This is part of our cultural inventory. It is not limited to a class or an ethnic group or an age group or a gender or a region. It represents the whole of America. Television has brought bread and circuses to the entire nation, in the form of beer and football. The staggering number of Americans who saw the Superbowl in 1977 was 75 million. One third of the nation stayed home to watch the Minnesota Vikings play the Oakland Raiders, and the crime rate dropped. This is not merely a sporting event, it's a therapeutic ritual.

Something in the American psyche responds to football, a sport which has not developed a following anywhere else in the world. Football is the perfect game for a technological society. It is highly organized. It combines violence with complicated strategy, and it is based on territorial incursion. It is a war game.

In the fall of 1976 I went to see the Jets play the Baltimore Colts. Each player was a highly specialized machine. There was a player whose only job was to center the ball for the point after touchdown. There were kicking machines, running machines, passing machines, blocking machines, and, in the case of Joe Namath, a lying-down-before-he-is-tackled machine. The machines are faceless, they are used sparingly, so that they remain in good working order, and they are oiled with six-figure salaries.

The machines are deployed in complicated patterns. The game is played by alternating committee meetings called huddles with brief spurts of violence. You forget that you are watching human beings, because they don't act like human beings except when they are hurt and their helmet is removed and they are lying on the field with a doctor hovering over them and you can see their faces. So what you have is this lumbering machinery moving down the field until it meets this other lumbering machinery. Namath's right arm was worth $440,000 a year, and when the tacklers converged on him he lay down like a trapped porcupine to protect that expensive and noninterchangeable part.

The connection between war and football was made in a rather interesting manner in "A Mad Fight Song for William S. Carpenter," by the poet James Wright. Carpenter, the celebrated "lonesome end" on the West Point football team, called for his own troops to be napalmed rather than have them surrender when he was an officer in Vietnam. It goes in part like this:

> At the edges of Southeast Asia this afternoon
> The quarterbacks and the lines are beginning to fall,
> A spring snow,
> And terrified young men
> Quick on their feet
> Lob one another's skulls across
> Wings of strange birds that are burning
> Themselves alive.

Apparently there is some historical basis for this, since football is said to go back (via rugby) to English soldiers who used the skulls of their fallen enemy in a kicking match.

The combination of violence and teamwork appeals mightily to the American public, which finds in the Sunday ritual an inoffensive way to vent its own hostilities. The high salaries of football players are justified in that they act out for us in a way that is sanctioned by the rules of the game forms of behavior which in any other context would have to be defined as simple or aggravated assault.

Another cooler is the comic strip. Even more Americans than watch the Superbowl read comic strips — 110 million. The comic strip not only amuses, it reassures. It tells us where we are and what the country is up to. It supports average American mores and beliefs. If a nation wanted to devise an effective form of high-saturation propaganda, it could do no better than the comic strip. The family unity of *Blondie,* the upward mobility of *Jiggs,* the struggle against adversity of *Little Orphan Annie,* the busybody common sense of *Mary Worth,* and the children's world of *Peanuts,* are familiar features of our human landscape.

As public attitudes change, the comic strip changes. When I was a boy, I liked Joe Palooka, who was incorruptible but naïvely stupid. He was the kind of good man America was supposed to produce, the man that Jefferson believed would make the right moral decision even though he was dumb. He curiously combined the profession of boxer with pacifist convictions, but when the war came he enlisted as a private (not knowing enough to get a commission). Joe Palooka was a monument to America's lost innocence. He needed his street-wise manager Knobby Walsh and his friend Jerry Leemy to save him from the corrupt world.

As life became more complicated, so did comic strips, and we have Pogo tackling the issues of the day, Howland Owl trying to make an atom bomb, and Albert the Alligator on trial for eating a puppy dog. We have *Peanuts,* whose small characters talk in psychiatric jargon. All this is a long way from Joe Palooka. The comic strip keeps up with the times. It continues to be a symposium on national attitudes. It is part of our cultural feedback.

If an anthropologist was to apply to American society the methods used to study primitive tribes, he might draw some interesting conclusions from the practice of roasting, which is a kind of verbal cannibalism. A dinner is given during which the guests of honor are insulted by their friends. This qualifies as a cooler because it has, again thanks to television, become available to the masses, and because it has spread from show business to politics. Roasting is an egalitarian ritual, a way of saying, "you've got the job but you're no better than we are," a reminder to elected officials that they serve by consent of the governed. One of the triumphs of the common man in a democracy is that he has the right to insult his leaders, and roasting is the institutionalization of that right.

Roasting has long been connected with the Friars Club, a group of entertainers who devised the testimonial where you are chopped up by your friends. This might be called negative endearment. The more you admire someone, the more well done the roast.

At a roast for Frank Sinatra, the Sinatra persona, carefully nurtured over three decades of media manipulation, was enshrined in remarks such as these:

"If your zipper could only talk."

"Don't just sit there, Frank, enjoy yourself — hit somebody."

"Invitations were extended to this dinner in an unusual fashion. A guy drove up in a cement truck and asked me for my shoe size."

"Frank thinks of the press as a family. How often have I heard him say, get rid of these mothers."

"Everything Sinatra touches turns to gold. I'm afraid to go to the toilet with him."

Roasting proves that no one is above insult. The New York press corps roasts the mayor, and the Washington press corps roasts the President, although perhaps the loftier the figure the more muted the insult. At a recent roasting in New York, the comic Pat Henry squinted and said, "Someone was looking for Mayor Beame and he was told, hey there he is pacing up and down nervously underneath a table." And Don Rickles told Governor Hugh Carey: "It's good to see you're here. You're Irish. We need the Irish . . . for parades." Pretty tame, but the idea is there, and what in other countries would seem a shocking lack of decorum is in the United States one of the ways we keep in touch with our elected officials.

The most important cooler of all is the media, which brings us daily evidence that wrongs can be righted, that official secrets can be revealed, and that no issue is too sacred to be aired. It is one of our peculiar maladies to agonize over the things we do best, and we worry whether the media is destroying privacy, whether it is abusing its right to know, or, conversely, whether it has abdicated its adversary role and become an echo chamber for the powers that be. Anyone who has lived abroad and gained some firsthand knowledge of the press in other parts of the world knows how fortunate we are. The American press is the best in the world, and the most powerful. It really delivers the goods. Its abuses are the price one pays for the way it works.

Free expression is the greatest of coolers. Blowing off steam keeps the kettle from exploding. The price we pay is a lack of restraint. One line of print can destroy a member of the Cabinet. The press has not changed since Dickens, in *Martin Chuzzlewit,* had a newsboy for the "New York *Sewer"* crying, "here's the *Sewer's* exclusive account of a flagrant act of dishonesty committed by the Secretary of State when he was eight years old, now communicated at great expense by his own nurse."

Earl Butz had to resign as Secretary of Agriculture in October 1976, because he made the mistake of talking off the cuff in front of former White House lawyer John W. Dean III. Butz, on a plane with Dean and entertainer Pat Boone during the campaign, remarked that the reason more blacks were not rallying to the Republican banner was because "coloreds" only wanted three things, "tight pussy, loose shoes, and a warm place to shit." This was locker-room talk, best left unsaid, but also best left unreported. Dean, covering the campaign for *Rolling Stone,* quoted the remark without attribution, and *New Times* in a separate article attributed it. That was the end for Butz, who should have known better than to say anything he did not want repeated in front of the "King Rat" of Nixon advisers.

Actually what Dean did was carry to its logical conclusion one of the media's basic assumptions: that our public figures should be totally accessible. A reporter for *Time* magazine spends the day with Jimmy Carter and reports what he ate for lunch and what he said to his wife over dinner. We take this for granted, but it is part of a complicated transaction. The media disseminates an image of the President as an ordinary man. He is one of us, he wears an open-necked shirt and has pork chops and mashed potatos for dinner. Such cozy scenes almost make us forget that he is the world's most powerful man. The media's role is also to make an unknown candidate instantly familiar. Cooked in the microwave oven of the media, Jimmy Carter took the Democratic party away from the bosses, with their tight hierarchies and their years of faithful service and their slow rise through the ranks. His meteoric rise was made possible by media exposure, such as the *Time* magazine cover that made him look like John Kennedy. The media presides over the making of myths and the breaking of taboos. Jimmy Carter's victory was the making of the myth of the little man coming out of nowhere, and the breaking of the taboo that a Southerner could not be President. The South had been on probation since the Civil War, breeding toads like George Wallace in the swamp of its isolation, and here was Carter, in the kind of wand-waving magic that America admires, pulling the South back into the mainstream.

On a less exalted level, the media is a creator and destroyer of fads. The guru Maharaj ji rented the Houston Astrodome in October 1973 in the hope of obtaining some media attention. He succeeded. The overweight Oriental teen-ager was devoured by the cannibal media and never heard from again. What was being hailed as a new religion turned out to be a minor media event. For the unwary, the media is the kiss of death.

The media, and here I mean television, acts as a pacifier. It soothes and reassures by making all issues seem trivial. Everything on television is brought to the viewer with equal urgency, a football game, a war, an election campaign, or a soap commercial. Everything is reduced to talk show chitchat. Ex-premier Cao Ky of South Vietnam, who is now running a liquor store in California, was asked by the host of a Midwest panel show: "We still have a minute left. Could you tell us what went wrong?" The premise of television is that anything that does not lend itself to capsuled pronouncements cannot be worth discussing.

Nowhere is the relationship between the community and the media so close as in a small town newspaper, where the editor knows most of the people he is writing about. An old friend of mine, Bob Kaiser, recently took over the weekly Lakes District *Review* in Mammoth Lakes, California, a town of 2000 in the high sierras. Bob, a prize-winning correspondent for *Time* and *Look*, and the author of four books, found himself returning to his cub reporter days, and covering firemen's picnics and county supervisor's meetings as he put out the paper single-handedly.

Bob's baptism of fire came when he covered the Little League All-Star game, pitting the Mammoth Mets against the June Lake Loopers, who won six to nothing. Like any good sportswriter, Bob reported runs, hits, and errors. He wrote that the starting pitcher for the Mammoth Mets had a little trouble finding home plate in the first inning, and that the Mets center fielder had "watched a long fly to dead center fall to the grass — with apparent disinterest — while three runs crossed the plate."

Well, you would have thought from the resultant outcry that Bob was Bluebeard making a comeback. One page of the sixteen-page weekly was devoted to letters from parents and concerned citizens protesting Bob's slurs on Mammoth's finest. "I was appalled at the inhumane treatment of individual children," wrote Merveen Rogers, "and I must stress these individuals are children aged 8 thru 12, not major-league all-stars. To point out errors on the part of individual children is not only demoralizing but humiliating."

"I see that you are now picking on 10 and 12-year-old boys," wrote Jan Gilman. "What I would like to know is, where was the Lakes District Review when they won all those games to reach the league title? Instead, you show up at a game they lost, so you can belittle and degrade them." Another concerned parent wrote that he would like to hit Bob Kaiser in the chops with a Little League bat. Bob wrote an apology. "I wanted to report the game just as if I were Don Merry of the L.A. *Times* writing about the Dodgers," he said, "but I went too far. This is some profession, newspapering. Lawyers visit their mistakes in jail. Doctors bury theirs. But editors publish theirs for everyone to read."

Trivial, perhaps, but it gives some idea of the community forum that a small-town newspaper becomes, and of the personal involvement of its readers. If I had to choose between the newspaper as oracle, selecting what is important for its readers and telling them what to think, and the newspaper as a kind of printed town hall meeting, where anyone can have his say, and the pronouncements of statesmen are no more sacred than those of your next-door neighbor, I would choose the latter. I have no trouble understanding Bob Kaiser when he tells me he gets ten times as much satisfaction putting out the Lakes District *Review* as he did working for *Time*.

It is in the righting of wrongs that the media prove their worth, not merely in exposing corruption and injustice, but in validating our institutions, in showing that justice is obtainable and that exposure leads to reform. The media help maintain what Jefferson said was the distinctive mark of an American, "that in cases of commotion he enlists under no man's banner, enquires for no man's name, but repairs to the standard of the law."

Watergate is the best example, but there are hundreds of others. One that I like, because it is a textbook illustration of how America works, is the case of Peter Reilly, a youth convicted of killing his mother in Connecticut and sentenced in 1974 to six to sixteen years. An article by Joan Barthel appeared in *New Times,* suggesting that Reilly's confession had been coerced. Arthur Miller, who lives in the area, got interested in the case, and hired an investigator. In the meantime (passion for association), a Peter Reilly Defense Committee was formed. Miller took his findings to the *New York Times,* which listened more carefully than if he had been John Doe (the uses of celebrity). It appeared that the prosecutor had suppressed evidence (winning is everything). The prosecutor is animated by the same impulse as the investigative reporter, who wants the story at all costs, while the prosecutor wants to convict at all costs, without regard to the merit of the defendant's case. The state police, which had obtained the confession, also wanted the conviction upheld, to protect its reputation. The combined efforts of the *Times* and Mr. Miller led to release and a new trial for Peter Reilly. As Mr. Miller put it, "this case shows that if people don't simply accept what's handed down from above, and if they don't surrender to despair, then they can change things, they can get justice." In this case, a collaboration between a private citizen of some note and a leading newspaper led to judicial action. Without the original Barthel article, and the nationwide attention focused on the case by the front-page treatment in the *Times,* Reilly's conviction would have stood.

The Basic Thing

When Nancy and I came back to America in September 1973 after a twelve-year absence, our son Gabriel was eleven and our daughter Amber was four. They had American passports, but had grown up in Europe and Morocco. Amber had been born in Morocco and spoke Arabic by the time she was two. Gabriel had been born in Rome, and had grown up speaking fluent Italian, indistinguishable from the other bambini who rode bicycles around the Piazza Navona. When we settled in New York, Gabriel had never seen snow or television. In Morocco, our previous domicile, television programming consisted mostly of the king making speeches in Arabic. Political life was nonexistent, except for the annual attempt to assassinate the king, after which the country subsided into its customary apathy. The newspapers were court calendars with headlines.

Gabriel discovered America, absorbing it through his pores. Watergate was much in the news at that time, and through television, politics became one of Gabriel's preoccupations. In Morocco, he had not bothered to learn the name of the king. Here, a certain degree of knowledge became unavoidable. One day, he asked me: "What is a right-wing militant? I've got a hunch, but I'm not sure. Is it an airplane part?" I decided to question him on current events. "What is Watergate?" I asked. "The President bugged certain desks and the people got mad," he said. "One of his operators, Dean, double-crossed him, and the Watergate tapes were conversations that he had and the committee is trying to get hold of them." "What is impeachment?" I asked. "It's when you show the whole country how rotten and dumb the President is and he's removed and another President is put in his place." "Do you think Nixon should be impeached?" I asked. "Yes, Nixon is horrible and so will the President after him be and so will the President after him." "Who is the new Vice President?" I asked. "Gerald Ford," he said, pronouncing Gerald with a hard g, as in gold. "He looks very innocent."

In his own way, without instruction from parents or teachers, Gabriel had come to grips with the basic thing, the amazing thing, the thing we take for granted but should sometimes pause to consider, because, like sex in marriage, when you have it it's not that important, but when you don't have it it becomes crucial. I am talking about the consent of the governed.

As an advertisement for Henry Steele Commager's *The Empire of*

Reason puts it: "While Europeans talked about the Enlightenment, these men (the founding fathers) made it happen." The original American impulse was breaking away from Europe. With no divine-right king and no feudal past, what did "these men" have to build on? It was like being given a game and told to make up the rules. The exceptional novelty of the situation should be kept in mind. They took some untested ideas that were floating around in Europe and applied them to the practice of government.

The consent of the governed was expressed in the first words of the Constitution: "We the People." This was the great innovation. It meant that to hold power in this country you must win the allegiance of the majority, and to do that you must prove that you grasp their concerns. Both parties must base their appeal on the same assumption — their candidate understands best the needs of the voters. Voters support a candidate who is in some way like them. The consent of the governed is the game's first rule, and an assumption soon learned. Nina, my eight-year-old niece, ran for president of her class. She had a campaign manager who helped prepare her speech and she brought a tape recorder to the classroom to play "The Stars and Stripes Forever" as background music. "I can't promise you buildings and freeways," Nina said, "but I know a president has to have a sense of responsibility and I can promise you that." She came home that evening and told her parents: "I think I'm going to win. The other candidates are two boys and another girl. There are more girls than boys in the class and nobody likes the other girl." She did win, and after her first day in office she came home and said: "I'm not sure I like being president — everyone wants something from you."

Between Nina and Jimmy Carter there is a difference of degree but not of kind. He probably feels the same way. He too keeps in mind the aspirations of the governed. It was reassuring to hear him on the radio in March 1977, jawing with ordinary citizens about their concerns, and discussing Amy's school with eleven-year-old Michelle Stanley of North Benton, Ohio. To forget that his power depends on the consent of the governed is disastrous for a President. This was Richard Nixon's oversight. It was not that he was guilty of this or that offense, but that, as Gabriel understood, he had broken the pact of consent and "the people got mad."

There was something else. Gabriel loved to wander around supermarkets, those warehouses of abundance, after living in a country where for most people there was never enough. He bought a box of chocolate chip cookies. He was incensed because the photograph of the cookies on the box had twice as many chocolate chips as the cookies themselves. Clipping a box top, Gabriel sent away for "Instant Life Sea Monkeys in Crystal Form." I warned him that sending away for things was like putting a message in a bottle and throwing it into the sea, but the Sea Monkeys arrived. "Things are organized pretty good here," Gabriel said, a statement which could be interpreted as meaning that he was exercising his right to life, liberty, and the pursuit of happiness.

That promissory note which each American holds by virtue of the Declaration of Independence was an improvement over John Locke's life, liberty, and the security of property. Americans could substitute happiness for the security of property because in America there was unlimited land, "land enough," as Jefferson said, "for our descendants to the thousandth and ten thousandth generation."

The right to life, liberty, and the pursuit of happiness was not a frivolous promise. Although it has been ridiculed as vaporous and utopian, it was seriously meant. It was intended as a basic assumption that every American should share. It was not arguable, even though at the very moment it was drafted it was already being violated through the ownership of slaves. In the drafting of the Declaration there is a great moment when Benjamin Franklin changes the phrasing from "we hold these truths to be sacred and undeniable" to "We hold these truths to be self-evident." Not only was Franklin setting a concrete American tone, once removed from European rhetoric, but in those two words he summed up the peculiar American brand of pragmatic idealism. These truths were not to be qualified, they were self-evident, there was nothing more to be said about them.

In practice, these truths have to be constantly redefined. It is quite a program to promise people life, liberty, and the pursuit of happiness, even if we know that by happiness Jefferson did not mean unrestrained behavior but doing the right thing. How far can liberty go before it collides with someone else's liberty? This is what laws are supposed to tell us, but somehow there are always gray areas, like tracts of unsurveyed land.

When Bennett Masel, a reporter for the *Yipster Times*, spit on Senator Henry M. Jackson in March of 1976 in Madison, Wisconsin, was he exercising his inalienable right to liberty and his constitutional right to withhold respect from a political candidate? He was arrested and charged with assaulting a member of Congress. Judge James E. Doyle sentenced him to fifteen days in jail. Spitting, said the judge, was not a constitutional right. This was "a spontaneous act by a pretentious and graceless young man . . . an ignoble small performance. A small performance deserves a small penalty."

The limits of liberty and the limits of the pursuit of happiness will continue to be tested in the courts. The system was not designed, as Justice Brandeis said, "to avoid friction but, by means of the inevitable friction incident to the distribution of the governmental powers among the three departments, to save the people from autocracy." Friction is part of the system.

So here we have a system of government that was created without the emblems and stigmata of the Old World — no crown, no miter, no basalt castles, the barest of pasts, and no imperial requirements — America was its own colony. With a continent to settle it would never know the yearning for empire. Montesquieu had written that it was impossible to create a republic except in a small territory. America had done it on a vast scale. It was the dream realized, but in so doing the great flaw was also born. The great flaw was to think that what was being done in America could serve all mankind.

It was one thing to believe in the nobility of one's cause, as when Jefferson wrote John Adams: "Old Europe will have to lean on our shoulders and hobble along by our side under the monkish trammels of priests and kings as best she can. What a colossus shall we be when the southern continent comes up to our mark!"

It was quite another thing to believe that the American experience could be passed on to others, as when Patrick Henry wrote that America had "lighted the candle for all the world." Self-satisfaction among the founding fathers took the form of seeing America as an example for humanity. Benjamin Rush: "I was acting for the benefit of the whole world." Benjamin Franklin: "Our cause is the cause of all mankind." The confusion of American interests with humanity's interests is our original sin. Why is it that when we land a man on the moon that man first plants the American flag and then says that he is taking "one giant leap for mankind"? I have yet to see what benefits mankind has derived from the American moon shot.

Our insistence that the American model had a universal application finally came to roost with a vengeance, in Vietnam. There were three assumptions involved in the escalation: our system is the best; it is not only the best for us but for others; we must interfere in the affairs of other nations to prove to them that our system is the best. In this way the spreader of universal ideas became embroiled in a land war in Asia which was a denial of the very ideas it wanted to spread. In this way the self-appointed guardian of international peace became munitions merchant to the world, selling 100 billion dollars' worth of weapons a year to 136 countries. In this way, American blood was spilled in the misguided exporting of the American creed. When I went to Vietnam in 1965, in the year of the big buildup, I saw that it did not take long for American soldiers to realize that the whole thing was a mistake, that they were no more fighting for democracy than an ant fights for democracy. They retreated into professionalism, into the old American problem-solving categories. Most of them didn't ask themselves why they were there, they just tried to do a job. The reality of the situation had not been presented to them. They had to discover it for themselves. Joseph Maxwell Cleland, who lost an arm and two legs, discovered that "there was no way to beat the political fact that we were foreign and they were out of the soil."

I hope Vietnam taught us to mistrust our sense of mission. We developed a unique system of government, and then we tried to force it down other people's throats. I hope we know now that the American way is not an export item. Countries at different stages of development in different parts of the world need our economic help, not our political advice. In 1977, Daniel Bell wrote an article called "The End of American Exceptionalism," in which he argued that the era of manifest destiny was over. We have not been better or more moral or happier than others, and we should stop giving the world lessons. I would amend that to say that American exceptionalism has been corrupted by its sense of mission. America is exceptional insofar as it accepts its uniqueness without trying to change the world. America is exceptional because the experiment is still going on, nothing is finished here, there is still a "men working" sign next to the manhole.

Today, our manifest destiny is to solve our domestic problems, not to send troops to Zaire or land the Marines in Eritrea. Let the striped-pants boys handle foreign policy, and let us get our priorities straight. The basic assumptions shared by Americans are the consent of the governed and the promises in the Declaration of Independence. People want what they have been promised. But the Declaration of Independence is a farce for the 20 percent of the population who missed the upward-mobility escalator. They are not in revolt against the system, they are waiting for their turn. It's fairly simple when you get it, as Grace Paley wrote: "We've had as good times as this country gives — cars, renting in Jersey summers, TV the minute it first came out, everything grand for the kitchen. I have no complaints worth troubling the manager about."

Process and Paradox

Process in the dictionary definition is something going on; a natural phenomenon marked by gradual changes that lead toward a particular result. America is pure process, it is an open-ended system, like the comic strip and the soap opera which continue next week or tomorrow, like the open road, like an open-ended future: what I'm going to do next, I think. We are a people in transit, propelled by the hi-test fuel of innovation. We are able to adapt, we are not the prisoners of a closed system. We are not frozen in fixed positions. We have an unlimited capacity for conversion. America, said F. Scott Fitzgerald, is a willingness of the heart.

America grew amid a series of contradictions. In America there was more freedom than in Europe, but there was also a slavery unknown in Europe. The apostles of freedom and equality were unable to transmit those benefits to blacks. In America there was an earthly paradise, but there was also a machine technology working against the dream of pastoral fulfillment. In America there was the rule of law but there were also groups of "regulators" who took the law into their own hands and created organized lawlessness. Walt Whitman summed up American history when he wrote:

> Do I contradict myself?
> Very well I contradict myself.
> (I am large, I contain multitudes).

Within this context, the process may be seen as the tension between the two poles of the contradiction. The process in the contradiction between freedom and slavery is the area between those two poles where the contradiction can be resolved. America is a long list of contradictions that are in the process of being resolved, between freedom and authority, between the puritan and the hedonist, between the native and the immigrant, between the pragmatist and the idealist, between nature and technology, between abundance and poverty, between friendliness and brutality . . . one could go on down the page.

The society itself was dualistic, with one set of rules for whites and another for blacks, with an industrial North and an agrarian South, with its national emblem holding arrows in one claw and an olive branch in the other. It was natural for Americans to accept the contradictions in their own natures. Henry Adams called himself a conservative anarchist. Felix Frankfurter called himself a believing unbeliever. Jimmy Carter has been dubbed a conservative populist. He is described as both aloof and accessible, thereby embodying another national contradiction.

It is part of being American to live at the heart of a contradiction. We are an unfinished society because we are still picking our way through a rock garden of unresolved contradictions. What should we do, for instance, about the locomotive in the garden, or, in more contemporary terms, the nuclear plant on the beach? Should we strip-mine, should we extend the redwood national park, should we dam the Middle Fork of the Salmon River, should we ban plutonium reactors, should we build the Alaska pipeline, should we save our endangered species? Jimmy Carter's decisions on energy and conservation are made against a philosophical backdrop going back to Jefferson: how can our institutions guarantee our ideal landscape? How does the pastoral dream fit in with the restless striving of Americans? Today, we are still trying to reach a balance between the plunder of the land and its safekeeping. Try to tell an unemployed logger than you are saving the redwoods for the weekend enjoyment of his family. Try to tell a California community on an earthquake fault that you are building a nuclear plant next door to provide it with cheaper electricity.

Everywhere one goes in America one sees a society defined by its contradictions. Things are never what they seem. A law designed to regulate a profession in the public interest is in reality drafted to protect the regulated profession. I saw this in Texas, where the State Board of Morticians is composed entirely of funeral directors. The law governing the profession was written by funeral directors for funeral directors, to restrict competition. Obstructions were set up to impede the granting of new licenses. State law prohibited cremation within 48 hours after death, but required that bodies be embalmed within 24 hours. One could, I suppose, embalm and then cremate. I'm sure that every state in America is riddled with self-serving statutes of this sort.

In California, I found the American Civil Liberties Union defending the Ku Klux Klan. Now, the ACLU is usually thought of as a bunch of bleeding hearts. I was once working on an assignment in a New York City police station, and I heard one cop say to the other: "Did you see where the ACLU filed a class action suit on behalf of the dog that's been going to high school to learn how to sniff marijuana, claiming that its constitutional rights were violated?" This is the customary image the ACLU projects. But in February 1977, the San Diego chapter filed a suit seeking $775,-000 in damages for ten Marine Klansmen who had been transferred to other bases after terrorizing black enlisted men at the Camp Pendleton training base. The ACLU argued that their constitutional rights had been violated. "However repugnant the Klan and its white racism may be," an ACLU lawyer explained, "it exists legally and its members are entitled to the same protection of their civil liberties as any other persons. The Bill of Rights is the ACLU's only client." It might have been pertinent to ask why the Bill of Rights should protect an organization dedicated to preventing minorities from enjoying their rights, but this is the kind of contradiction the American system thrives on.

Our very expectations are contradictory. We want to eat and stay thin, commit adultery and have a happy home life, put down roots and move on. Ladybird Johnson's father owned a store in Karnack, Texas, and on the front of that store there was a sign that said: T. J. Taylor, Dealer in Everything. That is what Americans are, dealers in everything.

The only way to rise above the contradictions is to join the opposites, and no one can do this better than the advertising men. They will tell you anything so long as it promotes the image of overnight self-improvement. They will tell you about "city-minded fashions for country-minded women." They will describe a trip to the edge of a Brazilian waterfall as "thrilling, yet perfectly safe." Advertising is have-your-cake-and-eat-it-land. The product itself is less important than the image it conveys in the land of sweeps-as-it-cleans, melts-in-your-mouth, takes-the-worry-out, tans-doesn't-burn, try-it-you'll-like-it, aren't-you-glad-you-did, you-deserve-a-break. No wonder Harry S. Truman thought BBD&O stood for Bull, Baloney, Deceit, and Obfuscation.

The connection between advertising and politics has been enshrined in presidential elections. Malcolm D. McDougall, who was Gerald Ford's "creative director" (he also handled Salada Tea and A & W Root Beer), had to keep reminding himself that "the product was the candidate, after all, not a piece of soap." It didn't really matter, since you sell a candidate just like a piece of soap, except in the last days of the campaign, when in desperation, McDougall considered seeding the clouds on election day over half a dozen heavily

Democratic cities. But basically it's the same technique. The primary is the testing of a new product in a regional market, for shelf life and consumer appeal. Primaries are expensive, and Raggedy Ann disposable diapers cost Scott Paper $12 million before the product was dropped. If the product and the candidate don't catch on, they don't go national.

One new product in 50, and one new candidate in 50, has what it takes to go national. Can he do the job? Will he meet consumer resistance? The outsider going against an established product with an entrenched market position (also known as the incumbent) is a long shot. Bristol Myers spent $11 million with Resolve, trying to break Alka-Seltzer's hold on the hangover market. Once in a blue moon, and this is the American dream come true, a product or a candidate comes out of nowhere and wins. Jimmy Carter was like Mop and Glo, which came on the scene in '72 and swept all opponents aside to become number one in the floor-care market.

The product and the candidate are interchangeable. Here is Marvin Sloves, president of Scali, McCabe and Sloves, making a presentation to J. C. Penney: "We're only interested in one thing, selling your product. We want to know your product better than you know yourselves. We want to study your market in depth, with all its parameters. Your problems are our problems. We understand Mrs. Middle Majority Consumer, the one with two and a half kids." Just substitute the word "candidate" for the word "product."

Misleading advertising, however, is more severely regulated than misleading campaign promises. Campbell soup put colorless glass marbles in its minestrone to make the diced vegetables rise to the surface, a device which provoked the disapproval of the FTC. But the path to the White House is littered with broken campaign promises. Ed McCabe, the creative director at Scali, McCabe and Sloves, once showed me what might happen to the Declaration of Independence if it were submitted to the same regulations as advertising. Here are some of his comments, added to the margins of the text:

Life, liberty, and the pursuit of happiness: this is an implied guarantee. Copy must state that we don't guarantee it.

The History of the present King of Great Britain: need a signed release.

He has refused his Assent to Laws: disparaging! Do we have adequate research to back up?

And so on. McCabe's point being that if we submitted politicians to the same scrutiny as the advertising business, they too would fall under FTC bans. McCabe believes that false campaign promises and false ad promises are counterproductive. "The moment of truth comes," he says, "when they put that stuff on their teeth and no one comes up and licks their ear."

And so, in copywriting conferences and speechwriting conferences, the creative teams keep searching for a better way.

—"What about this, B.J. — take a bath in the dark tonight and let the water make love to your skin?"

—"Christ, Norman, that's ridiculous. Who takes baths in the dark?"

—"How's this, B.J. — the cat with the appetite alarm?"

—"Christ, Norman, it's like chewing cotton. Why don't you write it in Esperanto?"

—"What about this, B.J. — only Lark cigarettes have the gas-trap filter?"

—"Christ, Norman, that sounds like my son wrote it."

Image is everything, which is why IBM, a company that does not sell products to the individual consumer (with the exception of type-writers) maintains a multimillion-dollar advertising budget. IBM is to other products as the statesman is to the politician, and it spends money to convey the statesman image. A friend of mine who works on the IBM account told me that "everybody resents them because they've got 85 percent of the market, so they spend money to im-prove their image. They just want to be shown as warm and human. They run a free school in Bedford Stuyvesant to teach data process-ing to the disadvantaged. They came up with a typewriter for the Navajo Indians, who have an 88-character alphabet, and donated them to the reservations. It's obvious PR, but you don't see the Bureau of Indian Affairs doing it."

The eighteenth-century controversy persists: was America a mis-take? Read Robert Lowell in "Endecott and the Red Cross:" "I'm not a bird-watcher or an Indian, Mr. Morton. I don't see the point of this outpost of England."

Then read Thomas Wolfe: "I think the true discovery of Amer-ica is before us. I think the true fulfillment of our spirit, of our people, of our mighty and immortal land, is yet to come. I think the true discovery of our own democracy is still before us. And I think that all these things are as certain as the morning, as inevi-table as noon."

Sharing the Power

A block association can keep a McDonald's from going up. An ad hoc citizen's group can keep the Army Corps of Engineers from building a dam. A union can make you walk through garbage-littered streets and close the school your children attend. It is proper and fitting to worry about the military-industrial complex and the labor-management complex. These concentrations of power exist, but they should not blind us to the extent to which power is shared.

There are broadly-based galaxies of power, crisscrossing and overlapping one another. Your draft board has the power to send your son to war. A smart doctor has the power to keep him home. The Supreme Court has the power to make your child take a bus to attend a school miles from his home. A community has the power to establish a private school for those who oppose busing. A lobbyist has the power to change the phrasing of a bill so that his aerospace company will benefit from it. A newspaper has the power to put his maneuvers on the front page. A fund-raiser has the power to finance an election campaign. Voters have the power to see to it that there is no return on that investment. A regulatory agency has the power to prevent us from using artificial sweeteners. A consumer-business alliance has the power to get that ruling changed. Universities have power, movie stars have power, multinationals have power, Ralph Nader has power, the Mafia has power, athletes have power, television anchormen have power, Gray Panthers have power, the Junior League has power, the Porcellian Club has power, the PEN club has power, the Metropolitan Museum has power, the National Rifle Association has power, garden clubs have power, churches have power, Hugh Hefner has power, editorial writers have power, banks have power, the Sierra Club has power, the B'nai B'rith has power, the NAACP has power, the Chicanos have power, the Navajos have power, the gays have power, the citrus growers have power, the Hare Krishnas have power, veterans have power, vegetarians have power, Quakers have power, anyone who belongs to any organization has his modicum of power, and if all else fails, the man with a gun has power.

Obviously, money buys power, and national politics is not open to paupers. But if power increased in direct proportion to wealth, Nelson Rockefeller would be President, Henry Ford would be Vice President, and Malcolm Forbes would be governor of New Jersey (a more outgoing presser of flesh and kisser of babies you will not meet, and yet he failed in his bid). The power structure in this country is far too complex to lend itself to a single-cause explanation. Power isn't only the way men are made, but the way they are unmade. The demise of Wayne Hays for keeping his mistress on the payroll illustrates the power of public morality, as does the failure of Howard Baker to win the vice-presidential nomination because his wife was a reformed alcoholic. Our public figures must be above reproach, not because of any inherent requirement of virtue in the political structure, but because if they have anything to hide it is likely to be discovered and they will become liabilities to the ticket. This too is a form of power. Teddy Kennedy, in spite of his personal appeal and his membership in America's best-loved dynasty, will never be President because of Chappaquidick. We are strict with our public figures, particularly in matters sexual. I suspect that if you subtracted Manhattan, Cambridge, Los Angeles, and San Francisco, the sexual map of America would look like Anita Bryant.

The thing that strikes me about the connection between wealth and power is the number of wealthy persons who demonstrate a total lack of interest in public life. They flee to Europe to avoid power. They want no part of it. They think it is undignified. I call them the disenfranchised rich. They are the ones with a real distaste for their country. They stew over things, rant and rail, and move abroad. They would rather jump off the Golden Gate Bridge than use their money for a political purpose.

I happened upon a gathering of the disenfranchised rich at a dinner on Park Avenue in 1976. I got my bearings during drinks when I heard a woman say: "She's one of those people who think that elevator men should have names." At dinner, I had the good fortune to be seated next to a woman who had a castle in Normandy and apartments in Paris and London. "I've got so many homes it's hard to give them equal time," she said. She bred race horses, and came back to America each year to attend the Kentucky Derby and gauge the extent of national deterioration. "It's getting worse and worse and it's not going to get any better," she said. "I went to the Club the other day — the Knickerbocker if you must know — and I had my coat on — and . . ." she paused to let the magnitude of the information she was about to convey sink in . . . "there was no one to take my coat. There were various persons standing about and when I finally said, *but I would like someone to take my coat,* I was directed to the ladies' room downstairs. So you see, it's hopeless."

After dinner, I found myself sitting next to a tiny, pale, black-eyed woman from Louisiana who had married an Italian count with a papal title purchased at great expense through a Vatican lobbyist. I told her my son was in the Lenox School. "I see a lot of black children coming out of there," she said ominously. She then launched into an extraordinary diatribe: "These filthy black rats raping white women. I'm for emasculating them all. They're the cause of all the trouble. It's no use giving them schooling because they can't learn." I listened politely. I was surprised. It had been some time since I had last heard her arguments.

Another woman joined the conversation, a flaming liberal by comparison, who said: "They should be given a chance. They're in the same position as other immigrant groups like the Irish."

"Well, of course," said the lady from Louisiana, "the Kennedys were shanty Irish, they were nobodies."

"All the blacks want are the same chances other people get," the second lady persisted.

"They should be killed when they commit crimes," said the lady from Louisiana. "In New Orleans you see them everywhere."

Across the room, a ruddy-faced, white-haired man was saying: "that Patty Hearst, that bitch, that little turd."

The lady from Louisiana's mouth fell open. "Did you hear what that man said? Did you hear that four-letter word? If he were in my home I would ask him to leave. But then, he wouldn't get into my home."

The peculiar Southern mixture of courtliness and viciousness had been demonstrated once again. I felt sorry for these people who spent most of their time abroad, who had not the slightest understanding of their own country, and whom wealth had fossilized.

Absorption and Accommodation

Everett Dirksen said he was a man of fixed and unbending principle, the first of which was to be flexible at all times. It's all right in this country to change one's mind. It is not seen as a betrayal of principle. This is the healthy side of pragmatism. In Europe, people are frozen in their attitudes. If a European political figure suffers an ideological conversion, he has to write a book of 500 wool-gathering pages to explain why.

During the Senate nuclear test-ban treaty hearings in 1963, Edward Teller appeared as a witness to oppose the treaty. Senator Frank Church read some of Teller's past statements, which were inconsistent with his present position. "How do you explain that?" Church asked.

"It's easy, Senator," Teller replied. "I have changed my mind." America is a country where you can change your mind without being visited by the seven deadly plagues.

Nothing is fixed — the Constitution is changed through amendment, the laws are changed, programs go into reverse, habits of a century are discarded, people's minds are turned around, attitudes come full circle. As Erik Erikson notes, the WASPs who looked down on Mediterranean immigrants for the way they let their children run wild were, in later years, the first to adopt the new permissiveness counseled by child psychologists.

How quickly the old taboos lose their power. Catholics need not apply was laid to rest by Kennedy in 1960. Southerners need not apply was killed by Carter in 1976. The need-not-apply theme was skillfully used by Carter's media people, who positioned their man as the outsider. One of Carter's TV spots showed a hand knocking on a door and a voice saying: "The people behind that door are the people who run things, and they don't want you in there." Now Carter, the barefoot boy from Georgia, is the man behind the door. How swift these reversals are.

Look at civil rights. I remember in 1964 going to see Malcolm X at the St. Theresa Hotel in Harlem. He took out his wallet and showed me a small plastic card like a credit card. On it was the Bill of Rights. He had underlined the part about the right to bear arms. He was convinced that armed struggle was the only way for the black minority to win its rights. I remember going to see Eldridge Cleaver in Algiers in 1970, all dressed up in his International Panther uniform. He told me he was never returning to the United States, because, as he put it, "I can't relate" to the Justice Department. He spoke of Third World revolutions that would eventually ignite a black uprising in America. Six years later he was back in his native state of California, saying that black radicalism had become irrelevant, because the goals of the civil rights movement had been met. Indeed, the pendulum had swung the other way, with the government telling universities that they must hire professors because they belong to a minority group, and with two blacks in Washington challenging the constitutionality of a police literacy test they flunked on the grounds that a higher percentage of blacks than whites failed. Beverley Johnson, the first black model to make the cover of *Vogue* and charge more than $100 an hour for commercial work, is as much a black symbol of the seventies as Eldridge Cleaver and Huey Newton were of the sixties. Cleaver became redundant in less than a decade.

The astonishing American digestive tract has an unlimited capacity for absorption. It absorbed the Vietnam war, the protest movement, the hippies, the dropouts, the communes, the women's movement, the black radicals, the Symbionese Army and other related groups, the Yippies, the Chicago Seven, and all the turbulence and collective hysteria of the sixties. It is now in the process of absorbing Eastern disciplines, tantric exercises, assertiveness training, relaxation responses, and the whole Sears, Roebuck catalogue of sensitivity training. In the meantime, we are all waiting for WHAT'S NEXT. Things change so fast that historians, who used to study the meaning of centuries (eighteenth-century France, nineteenth-century England), now scrutinize America decade by decade: what were the sixties about? Are the seventies a return to the fifties?

There is room in America for the whole spectrum of life-styles. If you take the generation that came of age in the sixties, some of them are still groping, tunneling inward in a trough of hope, experimentation, apathy, and self-analysis, tentatively circling the void of their old commitments. They have chosen the inner voyage. But some of those undergraduates who were screaming Marxist slogans and disrupting the campuses are now public servants. It turns out that the guerrilla tactics of the sixties were a training ground for the establishment. John Froines, one of the Chicago Seven, is the official who supervises industrial health regulations in Vermont. Paul Soglin, who in 1967 organized a protest against Dow Chemical at the University of Wisconsin, is now mayor of Madison. These are the little ironies of American life. One year you are clubbed by the forces of law and order, and the next year you are responsible for the police budget. Soglin was elected in 1972, thanks to the amendment allowing eighteen-year-olds to vote. His conversion came with the belief that the system could be changed from within, but the system is also bound to change him. Outflanked by his own kind, he almost lost his bid for re-election when another radical ran against him.

This is what is known as accommodation. It involves a respect for procedure and an appreciation of limits. It involves the swing of the pendulum. Something goes too far and there is a slight correction. When civil rights threaten to become an infringement on individual rights, a slight correction comes from the Supreme Court, which rules that because a suburb is predominantly white it does not necessarily have to alter its racial composition. Why should Arlington Heights allow Chicago developers to build low-rent subsidized housing there? Arlington Heights refused, sticking to its traditional zoning policy, and the Supreme Court ruled that there was no discriminatory purpose in that.

The habit of accommodation oils the gears of government, and helps the system avoid coercion. Carter allows some water projects to go through so that he can ban others. Legislation to mint aluminum pennies died in 1974 because the vending machine lobby objected that the new pennies would jam their machines. The 1.5 million pennies experimentally run off were melted down. When the FDA announced that it was banning saccharin, there was a hue and cry: how can they allow a proven killer like cigarettes to be sold on the open market and then ban saccharin, which so far has been shown harmful only when administered to rats in massive doses. There ensued an accommodation among the people who wanted it, the companies who made it, and the government agency and consumer groups who wanted to ban it. Saccharin would be banned in prepared food and beverages, where the unsuspecting consumer might not know it was an ingredient, but it would be sold as an over-the-counter drug in containers warning that it could cause cancer.

Congress is our forum of accommodation. It is the place where give-and-take assumes a higher meaning. There is a certain way to operate within the bounds of accommodation that congressmen know. A senator who wants to kill a missile program but isn't sure he has the votes in committee asks for a vulnerability study that he knows will delay the program until the next session.

I read the *Congressional Record* as a textbook in the art of accommodation. It provides me with moments of unadulterated delight. As an example, let me quote extracts from the debate on tax deductions for art. Prior to 1969, artists could take a deduction on the market value of a donated painting. After the 1969 bill, they could only deduct the value of the paint and the canvas and the brushes. In 1976, the Senate passed an amendment restoring the deduction, but on September 9, 1976, a joint House-Senate conference killed the amendment.

This was one of the few issues upon which Barry Goldwater and Hubert Humphrey agreed. They both favored restoring the deduction. "It is not generally known," Goldwater said, "but I engage in art and sell a little of my own once in a while . . . I have called the attention of my colleagues to an unusual thing that happened just about two weeks ago, or it might have been three. One of America's most talented artists, a boy of Mexican extraction named Ted De Grazia — he and I went to school together, and he has become one of the most popular artists in the West. When he found out that he could not take any benefits from taxation at all by deduction of expenses, and so forth, he took about 200 of his paintings out in the desert, piled them up, and burned them . . . If we did not have the people of wealth and the companies of wealth to buy good paintings and good works of art to give, the young children would never know what a work of art resembled; or, even more important, they would not be able to understand, say, the Renaissance period, which is most difficult for a person born in Arizona to understand. They can understand the Alamo and Davy Crockett a lot better . . ."

"Most artists I have met," Hubert Humphrey said, "are poorer than church mice and wander around in sandals, not because of a life-style but because they have not much more . . . Rembrandt is dead. Picasso is gone. The folks I know out my way who are artists are poorer than some of the folks who are trying to farm on dry land . . . I ran the art program for the government back in the WPA days. I was manager of the music project and of the arts project. May I say that they did a lot of good for this country, and the government of the United States paid for it."

Despite these impassioned pleas from two of the Senate's finest orators, the majority view, here expressed by Senator Russell Long, was that deductions should not be restored. ". . . There was one fine lady," Senator Long said, "a member of the Driscoll family who lived in Philadelphia. She joined a Catholic order as a nun. She had a lot of income coming to her. So some members of Congress said it was not fair to make that lady pay taxes on income when she had taken a vow of poverty and dedicated everything she had to the Lord. So we then had a dedicated member of Congress fight for a bill to relieve the burden of his constituent, who had taken this vow of poverty, and say she would not have to pay a tax on that income which she had dedicated to our Merciful Maker. Then we go down the road a few years and then we find that 23 percent of the millionaires are paying no tax. They are taking advantage of a law that we passed for that nun who had dedicated everything she had for charity. So, Mr. President, here we get started with the same kind of thing all over again, not in the name of religion this time, but in the name of art . . ."

Change and Progress

Robert Penn Warren's grandfather, a Southern gentleman who was born in 1838 and fought in the Civil War, said he hated modern technology, but admitted that "they have got two things that make life worthwhile — flyscreens and painless dentistry."

I suppose one could object to the flyscreen on the grounds that it spoils the view, but the benefits outweight the inconvenience. Each improvement brings with it a new set of problems, and we tend to focus on the problems rather than remember what we had before. We complain about the decibel level of subways and the carbon dioxide emitted by buses, and we forget that in the days of the horse-drawn streetcar there were 150,000 horses dumping two million pounds of manure a day in the streets of New York. The city looked and smelled like a huge dirty stable. Today we worry about microwaves blinding the editors of newspapers who work on the computerized consoles, or asbestos poisoning, or radioactivity. Seventy years ago, workers polishing safes were blinded by metal grindings, iron puddlers were overcome by smoke, miners were poisoned by coal gas, and train brakemen fell off the icy roofs of railroad cars. As technology becomes more refined, so do its perils.

It was not so long ago that railroads ran through cities, and grade-crossing deaths were a serious urban problem. DEATH ON THE TRACK was a familiar headline. Chicago had 330 grade-crossing deaths in a single year, which led to the construction of overpasses. We forget what life was like only a few generations ago, when landlords had absolute right of eviction over tenants, when bad plumbing and leaking sewer gas made cities pestilential, when employers could hire and fire at will ("I can hire one half of the working class to kill the other half," Jay Gould said), when nine-year-olds stood on boxes to work the spindles in textile mills, and their parents were paid $1 to release the company of claims in case of injury.

We forget that in New York at the turn of the century, milk was as a matter of routine diluted, grocers sold bogus butter made from casein and water, and marble dust was added to sugar, starch paste to catsup, and alum to flour. Distilleries kept cows and fed them mash, and the cows produced "swill milk." Heroin was sold over the counter as a cough medicine. Cocaine wine was advertised as a sedative allaying nervous fright. Winslow's Baby Syrup was liberally laced with opium.

I am talking about recent times, 100 years ago or less. Too many people died unnecessarily. A yellow fever epidemic in Memphis in 1878 took 5150 lives. Most American surgeons ignored Joseph Lister's antiseptic research, which involved protecting open wounds from germs. President Garfield would probably have survived Guiteau's bullet in 1881 had the most elementary antiseptic principles been followed. He died of secondary infection, after surgeons probed for the bullet with dirty fingers. Another form of death was lynching, a popular leisure activity in the rural South. According to the Chicago *Tribune,* 3337 blacks were lynched between 1882 and 1903. They were not always lynched for attempted rape or suspected crimes. On February 22, 1898, a black man named F. B. Baker was lynched in Lake City, South Carolina, for accepting the office of postmaster. In 99 percent of the cases no arrests were made.

I don't think I can be accused of Pollyannaism if I say that things have improved. I feel no nostalgia for the past. I have no desire to go back to horse-drawn streetcars and telephones that hummed with static and child labor and lynch mobs. I am not sensitive to the poetry of times when icemen delivered 75-pound slabs of ice and you never saw an orange in the winter north of Florida. I think a case can be made for progress. We get sidetracked, and mired in long and costly mistakes, but there always seem to be some good guys to keep things from slipping into depravity. A middle road of decent behavior is part of the American landscape, and whoever strays too far from its path is going to be in trouble.

The case for progress is based on the obvious. We live longer and we have more money. In 1776, the average life expectancy was 34. In today's terms, that is half a life. In 1900, it was 47, in 1940, it was 63, and, today, a baby born in 1976 can expect to live to 72.4 years. As for the statistical years by which my wife will outlive me, I have left them to her in my will. The average family income has doubled, in dollars corrected for inflation, from $6861 in 1929 to $13,622 in 1974. Many of us have more discretionary income. We can afford the bare necessities, like a week in January in St. Croix.

The American genius has been to make life more convenient for the vast majority of people, freeing them from material concerns. "Lan's sakes," cried the family as Aunt Polly emerged from the kitchen bearing steaming platters of food. But early stoves were penal rockpiles upon which the housewife, sentenced to hard labor for life, expended her vigor and health. The criticism of Americans as materialistic reminds me of the war in *Gulliver's Travels* between the little Indians and the big Indians over what end of the egg to eat for breakfast. Only people who have reached a certain standard of living can be freed from obsession with material things. Spiritual development is possible once material demands have been met. The human-potential movement is the by-product of a rich society. Indian gurus who flock here because of a dwindling domestic clientele will be among the first to tell you this. One must have known affluence to go beyond it. The children of the affluent, inoculated against materialism, are free to eat brown rice, wear saffron robes, and find themselves.

A case for progress can also be made in terms of clean government. Newspaper headlines remind us daily of finagling in high places. Cabinet members resign and senators are investigated because of their connections with private corporations. Candidates divest themselves of their stock portfolios. Their money must be laundered before they can take office. We tend to forget that the founding fathers did not have such scruples. Many members of Congress furthered legislation that coincided with their private interests. Robert Morris, Samuel Wharton, and Benjamin Franklin were stockholders in land companies that made fortunes, thanks to the laws they helped pass. Opportunity wore down the righteousness of early Americans. The bearers of Puritan standards abandoned them in the stampede for wealth. The Ohio Company contract passed by Congress in July 1787, which gave speculators the right to buy options on millions of acres of government land, was secured by bribing a number of members of Congress, and the fellow who did the bribing was William Duer, the Secretary of the Board of Treasury. When we worry about morality in office today, we should remember that graft was the norm when there was a whole continent out there waiting to be grabbed.

We should also remember that the Supreme Court was not always the model of rectitude we see today. There was a time when the rulings of the high court shielded the privileges of industrial wealth. The judges appointed themselves the protectors of business against the Sherman Antitrust Act, which had been passed in 1890. In an 1894 railroad strike, the Sherman Antitrust Act was used against a union, to enjoin it from conspiracy in restraint of commerce. But, in 1895, to save the sugar monopoly from conviction under the same act, the court found that the refining of sugar was outside commerce and was thus not liable to regulation by the Interstate Commerce Commission. In 1898 the court ruled that under the Fourteenth Amendment a person had the right to enter into whatever agreement he chose to and work as many hours as he wanted, thus finding unconstitutional a New York statute limiting the work day. In 1895, when the first federal income tax law was passed, the Supreme Court ruled it was unconstitutional by a 5-to-4 vote. It was a direct tax, said the court, whereas according to the Constitution, taxes had to be apportioned among the states on the basis of their population. In his dissent, Justice Oliver Wendell Holmes argued that the majority had a right to embody its opinions into law. But the federal income tax had to wait.

There would have been no muckrakers had there not been muck to rake: millions of acres of public land given to the railroads, the Standard Oil deals, the robber barons, the manipulation of stocks on Wall Street, the corruption of legislators and judges, and the broad-gauge graft of Warren Harding's Ohio gang. Abuses illustrated the need for regulation. The American system had the ability to repair itself. The National Child Labor Committee was form in 1904, and child labor was outlawed. Lynchings were prosecuted. The Narcotics Drug Act of 1905 banned opium and its derivatives. As a result of the Embalmed Beef scandal in the Spanish American War, the first Pure Food and Drug Act was enacted in 1905. Regulation was not preventive, it came as a response to ample evidence that when people were left to themselves, they did not, as Jefferson had hoped, make moral decisions. In 1902 Teddy Roosevelt revived the moribund Sherman antitrust law and used it against the Northern Securities Company, a holding concern set up by J. P. Morgan to control railroads in the West. Morgan was shocked and told his friends that Roosevelt was not a gentleman. The Northern Securities Company was dissolved. President Taft continued in the same vein, securing 43 antitrust indictments during his administration.

The thread here is not merely the new forms that graft and injustice take, but America's capacity to reform itself within the limits of due process. Take the case of the rottenest egg the American eagle ever laid, the black problem. Here too, patient progress has been made. Here too, we should remember that blacks were made legally inferior in the 1896 *Plessy* v. *Ferguson* decision, condoning "separate but equal" facilities. As Senator "Pitchfork" Ben Tillman of South Carolina said at the time, "we have done our best" to disenfranchise the Negro. "We have scratched our heads to find out how we could eliminate the last one of them. We stuffed ballot boxes. We shot them. We are not ashamed of it." Three quarters of a century later, one of Senator Tillman's neighbors, Governor Jimmy Carter of Georgia, won 95 percent of the black vote, which gave him the necessary margin to capture the presidency. As posters for the Voter Education Project said: "The hand that once picked cotton now can pick a President." In 1960, there were one million blacks registered to vote in the eleven states of the deep South — there are now about four million.

The milestones of progress are there for everyone to see:

• In 1931, the Scottsboro case established that blacks could not be excluded from juries.

• In 1948, President Truman signed the executive order ending segregation in the armed forces: "There shall be equality of treatment and opportunity for all persons in the Armed Services without regard to race, color, religion, or national origin."

• In 1954, *Brown* v. *Board of Education* (in Topeka, Kansas) barred segregation in public schools. At that time, one third of this country's school enrollment was segregated by law. The Supreme Court reversed itself on its 1896 "separate but equal" ruling.

• In 1965, the Voting Rights Act ended voter qualification tests, immediately adding one million blacks to the nation's voting rolls.

In 1960, there were about 50 elected black officials, today there are about 2000. In 1967, Carl Stokes in Cleveland and Richard Hatcher in Gary became the first blacks to govern major American cities. Today there are 152 black mayors, 40 of them in cities with white majorities, cities like Detroit, Los Angeles, Newark, and Washington, D.C. When Maynard Jackson, Jr., became mayor of Atlanta in 1974, he described himself as "the youngest, fattest, blackest mayor in America." He lost no time appointing a personal friend and college classmate as Atlanta's first black police commissioner, proving by this demonstration of cronyism that he was in the mainstream of the American political tradition. Texas Congresswoman Barbara Jordan, whom Jimmy Carter tried to tap for a cabinet post (she held out for Attorney General), was asked by Barbara Walters whether she could have done as well had she been white. "When I'm realistic," Barbara Jordan replied, "I realize that my success has been due to my being black and turning it to my advantage." Southern white politicians known in former days for their outspoken racist views are today courting the black electorate. Dick Gregory, jailed in Mississippi during the civil rights movement of the sixties, was made an honorary colonel of that state in January 1976 by its governor, Cliff Finch, and was invited to the Inaugural Ball. Similar gains have been made in education. Today, there are nearly a million blacks in the nation's colleges, compared with 274,000 ten years ago. Blacks, who represent 11.4% of the overall population, make up 10 percent of all college students. The army was once a stronghold of de facto racism. Today, there is a black Secretary of the Army, and the commander of what is often cited as the finest American division (the 82d Airborne) is black.

Black income, too, has grown in relation to white income, although it still lags badly — it was 37 percent of white income in 1939, 54 percent in 1960, 64 percent in 1970, and it dropped slightly to 62 percent in 1974, when the white median family income was $13,356 and the black median family income was $8265. But there is the same disparity of wealth among blacks as among whites. Super-rich blacks, like Mohammed Ali and Alex Haley, can serve as role models. Alex Haley, although his account of how he traced his origins through West African *griots* is pure fantasy (anyone who has been to West Africa knows that the *griots* are mercenaries of the spoken word, who will tell you anything you want to hear once money has changed hands), will be remembered as an important figure in the development of a black American identity. He achieved what James Joyce set out to do in *Ulysses*, "to forge in the smithy of my soul the uncreated conscience of my race." Haley reclaimed for all American blacks a past which they had been told was shameful, and gave it dignity. The self-perpetuating dilemma of racism, as de Tocqueville saw, was that "memories of slavery disgrace the race, and race perpetuates memories of slavery." Thanks to Haley, blacks could now take pride in their shackled past. The slave ships became their *Mayflower*.

In the same vein, we have in recent years seen the evolution of the word nigger from a common to a proscribed form of designation. When I was growing up in Washington, D.C., during the war years, a supermarket manager would summon his delivery boy with the words, "Nigger, get over here." There was no slur intended, it was force of habit. It didn't even mean you were a bigot. Nigger was simply the word that came most naturally to white lips in three quarters of the United States. As William Styron said in his eulogy for James Jones in May 1977: "Take the word nigger, which I often heard you use in conversation with a certain casual and disarming precision that was almost breathtaking. You were the only man I ever knew upon whose lips that word had no connotation of ugliness or animosity but instead was uttered with a kind of large, innocent, open sense of fraternity, and I often wondered at this, at how it could be, until I realized that in that word, or at least in the way you spoke it, there were profound echoes of your great predecessors Sherwood Anderson and Dreiser and above all, Mark Twain — whose peculiarly border sensibility, part southern, part midwestern, but achingly American, you inherited in full measure."

Well, notwithstanding Nigger Jim, the ingrained habit has lost ground. Today, the word nigger strikes the ear as out of place, as if a person was using an archaic expression. And in the same month that Styron fondly recalled his friend's disarming way with the word nigger, the only black man in the Maine legislature got a bill passed aimed at removing the word from place names in his state.

"No one in this body has been brought up under that name and still carries the scar of that name," said Representative Gerald E. Talbot. The bill was passed unanimously in the state Senate, but in the House there were 26 votes against it, on the part of traditionalists who wanted to maintain names like Nigger Brook and Nigger Hill, arguing that they were no different from such names as Squaw Mountain or Frenchman Bay. Talbot's effort could be added to the long list of recent victories in favor of his race.

Blacks themselves, however, are not so sanguine about the progress they have made. They are like mountain climbers who, thinking they have reached the top, find that it is only another ridge. They feel that they have advanced from being hated to being ignored. The new racism, they say, is that of "nobodyness." To survive, blacks feel they must achieve a state of healthy cultural paranoia. They must cope while remaining suspicious. The prevailing attitude is one of "two-ness." They have gained some acceptance but still don't feel they really belong. Some of them think integration is a farce. Using the rhetoric of black power to make a de facto situation seem like their choice, they talk about whitelisting us.

Dr. Carlton Goodlett, one-time doctor to the Black Panthers, publisher of the San Francisco *Sun Reporter,* and one of the most lucid black spokesmen, feels that the black dilemma still exists: "Blacks buy the American dream hook, line and sinker," he said, "there is no one more American — but they're not allowed to join. The nature of the black experience — 22 percent unemployment, 48 percent of teen-agers unemployed or with police records, 60 percent drug abuse, is so sordid and so hopeless that it has nothing to do with the American dream. Blacks aren't interested in guru trips and Eastern philosophies, they aren't interested in saving the redwoods and strip-mining in Death Valley, they're too busy surviving. Blacks see the women's movement as a white maneuver to take the heat off civil rights. Eighty percent of the blacks who have broken into the media are women, so that whitey can deal with two areas of protest at the same time."

Dr. Goodlett sees the future as the coexistence of two separate communities. He points out that the 25 largest cities in the United States each have black populations of more than 100,000. One third of the total black population lives in these 25 cities. The tendency, he says, is for whites to yield their decaying cities to the blacks. "It's going to get to the point where black separatism is a fact," he says. "Blacks are urban, they don't want to move to the country, it reminds them too much of the plantations they came from. They are city-dwellers. Figure it out, there are 200 working days a year, two hours to commute, that's 400 hours, or ten 40-hour weeks. It's going to be urban black America against rural white America."

I hope Dr. Goodlet is wrong about the two separate communities. The answer, now that blacks have equal legal rights and an equal chance at college, is clearly that they must win an equal slice of the economic pie, they must achieve economic integration. The most important color in America is not black or white, but green. The July 1977 New York City blackout was a proof of this. Looting, the black ghetto-dweller's only way of enjoying the equivalent of discretionary income, did not break down according to racial lines. Poor blacks stole from merchant blacks, and white cops did not feel that a black teen-ager's life was the proper price tag on a color television set.

From race, let us move to gender, and the only minority group that is also a majority group, since there are more women than men. Here again, it's useful to remember what things were like when we look at the current situation of women. In a 1926 Chesterfields ad in *Life* magazine, a man and a woman are in adjoining deck chairs, aboard an ocean liner. The man is smoking and the woman is saying: "Not at all — the aroma is delightful." The ad does not dare go further than suggest that a woman might like the smell of cigarette smoke.

It was thanks to the women's movement that I learned the meaning of collective responsibility. In 1971, while spending a month in New York, my wife and I decided to attend a "rape speak-out" in a West Side church. This turned out to be an emotion-charged assembly during which a number of women recounted their experiences with rapists. Several, in defiance of the law of averages, had multiple incidents to relate, which they did with a wealth of detail. I was one of three men in the audience, and as story followed story of men doing violence to women, I began to feel distinctly uncomfortable. I had nothing to feel guilty about, never having taken by force something which, in the course of courtship, was willingly given. But I was receiving hostile vibrations in this roomful of angry women. I was guilty by gender. As case histories unfolded, of rape in an elevator, rape in a laundry room, rape in an alley, and rape in one's apartment, heads turned to glare at me, and I began to have intimations of what a lynch mob is like.

When one woman, who held a black belt in karate, demonstrated how she had dealt a potential rapist a kick to the groin, I instinctively crossed my legs. And when another woman suggested that the penalty for rape should be castration, I seized my wife's hand for the comfort of one woman who did not want me gelded. It seemed to me that the issue of rape was being used to ventilate a general hatred of men, and that a form of aberrant behavior was being made to serve as a model for male-female relationships. At the same time my consciousness was raised, for I saw women taking their destinies into their own hands, and refusing to submit to any form of male dominance. I saw the emergence, for the first time in history, of the truly independent woman. The women at the rape speak-out were, I thought, a strident but necessary vanguard, whose attitudes, thankfully diluted, would filter down to their more conventional sisters.

That they had filtered down became clear six years later, when I read about the two MIT juniors who had graded the sexual performances of 36 male students and published their findings, names included, in the campus weekly *thursday*. The two investigative reporters, Roxanne Ritchie and Susan Gilbert, had wanted to turn the tables on the word-of-mouth rating system men use for women. At the same time, their "Consumer Guide to MIT Men" could be seen as the vindication of the women at the rape speak-out. In this case, women were the aggressors and men were the victims, by having their bedroom behavior made public. They were rated no star for "a turkey," one star for "recommended in emergencies only," two stars for "mediocre but maybe worth trying," three stars for "a good lay," and four stars for "a must fuck."

Each of the 36 men was described in embarrassing detail. "If you want to be treated like a piece of cold meat, try this one," was the verdict on a no-star rating, while a four-star earned this encomium: "Close your eyes and waves crash, mountains erupt, and flowers bloom. He has a very large gorgeous cock."

The article caused quite a flap. The president of MIT condemned it, the Student Activity Board censured the campus weekly, the Committee on Discipline placed the two co-eds on probation, and 200 students signed a protest petition. But, like the women at the rape speak-out, Roxanne Ritchie and Susan Gilbert were campaigning for the one form of equality that the ERA will not provide: sexual equality. It seems obvious that women should be equal under the law, but how can we legislate sexual equality? It strikes me as a healthy sign that this last bastion of masculine privilege is being stormed, and I would be happy to do my bit and accept the verdict of Roxanne Ritchie and Susan Gilbert, who, when last heard from, were about to start a magazine called "Rate Your Mate."

Things that Scare Me

When I look at this country, I see a society so varied and complex that it defies explanation. I also see a society that is attempting, through trial and error, to give each man a decent life. This is where the mistakes are being made, and this is where the solutions will be found. But every solution brings with it a fresh set of problems. When solar heat becomes practical, a man will sue his neighbor for throwing a shadow across his roof. It's amazing how fast a novelty can become a racket. There is nothing like a new field, which no one knows anything about, to attract the unscrupulous. Already, consumer complaints from people who were sold solar-powered heaters that didn't work, or who were promised rebate money from the federal government, are being filed in Florida and other states.

The capacity for mischief in this country is as great as the will for reform, and I see things that scare me. The use of federal agencies for political purposes scares me. It was Nixon who perfected the computer-selected tax audit for political dissenters. In the South, black civil rights leaders are still being audited with a thoroughness that cannot be haphazard. One black state senator from Alabama has been audited for seven years in a row. This kind of selective audit is just as insidious an abuse of power as the KGB intimidation of dissidents in the Soviet Union.

The institutionalization of life scares me. The American way is based on self-reliance and voluntarism. Our excesses in the past, such as frontier justice, were due to an absence of government. Today, we have government-funded programs to treat all of society's ills. We have day-care centers for the young, nursing homes for the old, psychologists in schools who use mental health as an instrument of discipline, and mental hospitals for those whose behavior does not conform to the norm. We have drug-abuse programs, methadone-maintenance programs, alcohol programs, vocational programs, rehabilitation programs, learning-how-to-cope-with-death-for-the-terminally-ill programs, make-friends-with-your-neighborhood-policeman programs, helping-emotionally-disturbed-children programs, and how-to-accept-divorce programs. Unemployment benefits and welfare are programs designed to institutionalize a growing body of citizens whose purpose in life is the avoidance of work. They are dependent on the state for their livelihood. We are deluged with programs. We can't even let people die in peace. We put them in hospitals for the dying, so that they can be programmed into dying correctly. They don't need to be hospitalized, they would be better off with their families, dying with dignity instead of in these macabre halfway houses. All this is a displacement of confidence from the individual to the program. We can't rely on people to take care of themselves anymore so we have to funnel them into programs. This is a self-perpetuating thing, for the more programs we make available, the more people will become accustomed to seeking help from the government. We can't take care of ourselves, so Big Mama has to take care of us, as in the welfare states with their cradle-to-grave pacifiers. We have become a society of dependent people who have to go to a specialist to make basic human decisions. A substantial percentage of the population is in some way institutionalized.

Television scares me. "I would die if I didn't have television," my eight-year-old daughter told her mother. For those of us who grew up in the pre-kinescope era, it's hard to imagine how a child can grow so dependent on the nonsense that passes for entertainment. Television is dangerous because we don't really understand what it does to us. For many people, the last thing they see before they go to bed and the first they see upon rising is a television image. I once visited a welfare hotel on New York's West Side with a doctor from St. Luke's Hospital, and saw these people, barricaded behind their triple-locked doors, drugged on television, the screen showing them all the things they could not afford. It made their lives seem like a continuous hallucination.

Television is the most effective brainwashing medium ever invented by man. Advertisers know this to be true. Children are affected by television in ways we scarcely understand. In the fall of 1973, I was assigned a story involving a young white woman living on the fringe of Boston's black ghetto. Her car had run out of gas. She had gone to a filling station with a can, and was returning to her car when she was trapped in an alley by a gang of black youths. The gang poured gasoline over her and set fire to her. She died of her burns. It was later established that some of the youths involved had, on the night before the killing, watched on television a rerun of an old movie in which a drifter is set on fire by an adolescent gang. There is some kind of strange reductive process at work here. To see something on television robs it of its reality, and then when the same thing is acted out it is like the reenactment of something unreal. In other words, when the gang set fire to the girl, they were imitating what they had seen on a screen, as if they themselves were on a screen, and in a story. I don't think we have even begun to realize how powerful a medium television is. It has already become abundantly clear that the candidate with the most television appeal wins the election.

Another thing that scares me is that the weapons industry is seen as just another business, both in terms of jobs at home and salesmanship abroad. The United States sells $8 billion worth of weapons abroad each year, and the Pentagon, instead of worrying about the proliferation of arms, acts as a business wholesaler, its main concern being that the greater the number of weapons produced, the cheaper each weapon becomes. Volume allows for lower prices. This is fine for automobiles, but when you are talking about missiles and fighter planes it is scary. The Pentagon behaves like a private corporation. It is sound business practice for it to order a weapon from an American manufacturer, sell it to a foreign buyer, and pass on part of the cost of research and development. The Pentagon pats itself on the back, because foreign purchases of the F-14 fighter plane saved $20.6 million in research and development. They are turning the world into an arsenal in the name of the business ethic.

What scares me most of all, and this is my *cri du coeur,* is that we have no more to say about how our tax dollar is spent than the Ugandans under Idi Amin. Why am I subsidizing weapons systems, welfare cheats, the voluntary jobless, the building of nuclear plants, and Colonel Theodore Wilson Guy (USAF ret.), who is receiving $1785 a month in pensions because he was a captive of the North Vietnamese for five years? He survived the experience without permanent damage, and now can stay home and make model planes. Power today is the power to spend, and I wonder whether we can really call ourselves a democracy when the individual turns in up to half of his earned income and then loses sight of it completely. The transaction seems a bit lopsided. Is this the consent of the governed?

A lot of other things scare me, that I would like to complain to the manager about, such as the estimated ten lobbyists for every member of Congress ("We hear you've got a tough campaign coming up, senator"), and the banks destroying cities through redlining, aggravating the problem of urban decay rather than contributing to its solution, but why go on? Our elected officials presumably are aware of the problems, and the necessary measures presumably will be taken. We must take it on faith that among them there are men of good will who are trying to do the right thing. What makes America the most interesting country in the world is precisely that its problems are on the same scale as its size.

Moving On

It is nearly four years since I came back to America, and I am taking stock. I have a vested interest in making the American idea work. I see my own progress and the progress of this country as somehow intertwined. I have become committed to all the things that make up an American identity. The idea of living in Europe has become unthinkable. I asked Nancy: "What would you think today about living in Paris?" "It wouldn't be possible," she said. After a dozen years in Europe, Nancy has rediscovered her own country. My son Gabriel isn't completely in the frame of reference yet. The other day he asked me, "Ted, what's a southpaw?" On the other hand he has turned into a pretty good basketball player and knows Woody Allen routines by heart. My daughter, Amber, having arrived here at the earliest age, had the smallest European past to shed. She grew up American from the age of four. As she already displays unusual independence of mind, and a deep suspicion of the institution of marriage, she may be one of the youngest women's libbers around. I have not encouraged my children to study a second language. Being monolingual is difficult enough.

In July 1977, we continued our migration westward, and settled in Northern California, a land of greater majesty than man has yet been able to spoil. Why live in an anthill when there is a continent to explore? California is to the rest of the country what the United States was to Europe, a new land, free from the constraints of the past, where people can invent themselves. I wanted to turn my back on Europe. I wanted the sense of space that America is about, the strong assertion of space . . . when you can see your neighbor's chimney, it's time to move on. I wanted to learn how to become an inhabitant of North America, to get more involved in public affairs, to put my shoulder to the wheel of the continent, and I had a hunch that I could do this in California.

We moved to a house on a 1000-acre ranch in the mountains above Palo Alto that belongs to a friend of mine. He makes it pay for itself by operating a pick-and-cut Christmas tree nursery. Here I get the feeling of what America should be — deep ravines, trout ponds, deer in the woods, horses grazing, hills covered with oats golden in the evening light, a feeling of abundance and untouched pastoral beauty. The ranch house is set on the lip of a canyon overlooking a vast wilderness. To the south lies the Santa Cruz range, to the east the San Francisco bay, and to the west, a state park planted with redwoods, and the Pacific. The ranch is at an altitude of 2000 feet, and the air is so clean you could export it.

The bumper sticker on my car says: HELP STAMP OUT FLATLAND-ERS. The only problem here is that there is a real estate boom. As a woman who was looking for a house said, "Pretty soon, only doctors, lawyers, and cocaine dealers will be able to afford to live here." On the other hand, across Skyline Boulevard, there is a 700-acre tract known as The Land, where an indeterminate number of the golden-tressed grandchildren of pioneers (denim-to-denim in three generations) are squatting. The owner is trying to get them off so he can sell to the Forest Service, and the case is in the courts. It is said that he wanders across his property with a shotgun, and, when he happens on squatters, points it at them and says: "I'm duck-hunting. Are you ducks?"

"Perfect happiness I believe was never intended by the deity to be the lot of any one of his creatures in the world," Jefferson wrote, "but . . . he has very much put in our power the nearness of our approaches to it." Perhaps, but there is always a flaw, and at the ranch, the human problems, such as the soaring real estate prices and the dispute at The Land, have their geological analogue, for the San Andreas Fault runs right through it.

The fault serves to provide the necessary sense of dread that seems always to be a backdrop to the American dream. There are natural disasters, and there are disasters of the spirit. In one way or another, all Americans are living on the fault.

One night not long ago, Sylvan Emerson, the forty-six-year-old ranch manager, a six-foot-five-inch transplanted Oklahoman with mutton-chop sideburns and a handlebar mustache, took his sleeping bag down to the trout pond, waiting to catch poachers. "At dawn," he recalled, "I heard a rumbling sound like a ten-ton trailer on the highway and the ground started shaking. I felt like I was in a king-size waterbed." I asked Sylvan whether the experience had given him second thoughts. "Let 'er rip," he said. "I'm not leaving. Is there any place that doesn't have some catastrophe? Sometimes I think about the quake. They say the horses get nervous — I'm going to start watching the horses very carefully."